Political and Economic Analysis of State-Owned Enterprise Reform

In revisiting the forty-year history of reforms to China's state-owned enterprises (SOE), the book assesses the experiences of this process of reform and scrutinizes how this has helped advance the country's economy overall.

The author finds that China's SOE reform not only commits to institutional innovation within the corporation in terms of operating mechanisms, management structure, legal organization and the economic system of the enterprise, but that it is also underpinned by a series of policies that highlight an increasing market orientation. The measures have given rise to a benign interaction between enterprise reform and market development while switching the SOE's role from appendages of government organs under a planned economic system to more autonomous entities that integrate public ownership and the market economy. In this regard, SOE reform's success in constructing a modern enterprise system serves as the micro-foundation and core of an improved socialist market economic system.

The book will appeal to academics and students interested in political economy and the Chinese economy, with particular reference to SOE reform and the recent economic transition in China.

Huiming Zhang is Professor of Economics in the Department of Economics at Fudan University. He specializes in political economy and Chinese economy.

China Perspectives

The *China Perspectives* series focuses on translating and publishing works by leading Chinese scholars, writing about both global topics and China-related themes. It covers Humanities & Social Sciences, Education, Media and Psychology, as well as many interdisciplinary themes.

This is the first time any of these books have been published in English for international readers. The series aims to put forward a Chinese perspective, give insights into cutting-edge academic thinking in China, and inspire researchers globally.

To submit proposals, please contact the Taylor & Francis Publisher for China Publishing Programme, Lian Sun (Lian.Sun@informa.com)

Titles in economics partly include:

Economics of the Pandemic
Weathering the Storm and Restoring Growth
Edited by Cai Fang

The Economics of Government Regulation
Fundamentals and Application in China
Wang Junhao

Macroeconomic Policy and Steady Growth in China
2020 Dancing with Black Swan
Edited by Zhang Xiaojing

Political and Economic Analysis of State-Owned Enterprise Reform
Huiming Zhang

Political Economy in the Evolution of China's Urban-Rural Economic Relations
Fan Gao

For more information, please visit https://www.routledge.com/China-Perspectives/book-series/CPH

Political and Economic Analysis of State-Owned Enterprise Reform

Huiming Zhang

Routledge
Taylor & Francis Group

LONDON AND NEW YORK

First published 2022
by Routledge
2 Park Square, Milton Park, Abingdon, Oxon OX14 4RN

and by Routledge
605 Third Avenue, New York, NY 10158

Routledge is an imprint of the Taylor & Francis Group, an informa business

English Version by permission of Fudan University Press.

British Library Cataloguing-in-Publication Data
A catalogue record for this book is available from the British Library

Library of Congress Cataloging-in-Publication Data
Names: Zhang, Huiming, 1956- author.
Title: Political and economic analysis of state-owned enterprise reform / Huiming Zhang.
Description: Abingdon, Oxon ; New York, NY : Routledge, 2021. | Series: China perspectives | Includes bibliographical references and index. |
Identifiers: LCCN 2021001408 (print) | LCCN 2021001409 (ebook) | ISBN 9781032028385 (hbk) | ISBN 9781003185444 (ebk)
Subjects: LCSH: Government corporations--China. | Government business enterprises--China. | Mixed economy--China. | China--Economic policy--1976-2000. | China--Economic policy--2000-
Classification: LCC HD4318 .Z443 2021 (print) | LCC HD4318 (ebook) | DDC 338.6/20951--dc23
LC record available at https://lccn.loc.gov/2021001408
LC ebook record available at https://lccn.loc.gov/2021001409

ISBN: 978-1-032-02838-5 (hbk)
ISBN: 978-1-032-02839-2 (pbk)
ISBN: 978-1-003-18544-4 (ebk)

Typeset in Times New Roman
by MPS Limited, Dehradun

Contents

Figures

Tables

Foreword

Starting with the Third Plenary Session of the 11th Central Committee of the Communist Party of China (CPC) convened in December 1978, China put its economic and social development on track through the process of reform and opening up. Over the past 40 years, Chinese people have made all-out endeavors to make the country prosperous and strong and pressed ahead with reform and opening up ever more vigorously. The reform of state-owned enterprises (SOEs) is no doubt an essential part of this trend. Regarding the content of "SOE reform", it is mainly about how to improve the public sector which is the cornerstone of the socialist economy, how to allocate public capital in economic structure and adopt appropriate means and tools for realizing this allocation, how can this allocation activate real economic operation and sustain the vigor of the public sector of the economy, how to organically integrate public ownership with the market economy while transforming the traditional planned economy into the socialist market economy, how to manage and operate state-owned capital scientifically and effectively to make it accord with the characteristics of the market economy running. Besides, state-owned capital controls and influences the entire national economy, and the joint development of state-owned capital and other types of capital constantly enhances China's economic competitiveness. Given this, how can we properly assign tasks to the two types of capital and facilitate their collaboration in particular allocation scenarios?

The 40 years' reform, based on a profound review of the drawbacks of the traditional planned economy, focuses on the fundamental proposition of how to vitalize economic operation. Enterprises are a micro-carrier of economic performance, and building up "enterprise vitality" is, therefore, the "central link" of economic restructuring. By revolving around this central link, the reform of economic structure has been unfolded step by step in the past four decades, and the "market-oriented" economic governance means have been employed for carrying out the "incremental reform", which is part of the efforts in replacing the traditional planned economy with the socialist market economy. During this period, the CPC held meetings of far-reaching significance one after another and made a slew of major policy decisions at these meetings with an aim to keep shackling off ideological straitjackets, regularly summarize the reform experiences and achievements and deploy new tasks for the next stage of development. All of these efforts prove that the Party always stands firm in the forefront of the times to lead the Chinese people to forge ahead with reform and opening up despite difficulties and risks.

In the initial stage of the reform launched at the end of 1978, the Chinese government, for the purpose of solving the outstanding problems in the national economic structure, focused on adjusting up the prices of agricultural and sideline products and stabilizing agricultural production which is the foundation of the national economy; at the same time, a group of enterprises was selected to carry out the pilot program of "decentralization of power and transfer of profits", so as to accumulate experiences for its all-round implementation. The Third Plenary Session of the 12th CPC Central Committee held in 1984 elevated China's reform to an urban-centered stage. The *Decision on Reform of the Economic Structure* adopted at the session comprehensively deployed economic restructuring tasks and decided to introduce commodity-money relationship and market mechanism to activate the "subject rationality" of enterprises, which injected vitality into the national economic operation. In the spring of 1992, Deng Xiaoping – the chief architect of reform and opening up – made an inspection tour of south China, visiting Wuchang, Shenzhen, Zhuhai and Shanghai. Deng gave some important talks that were collectively known as the "South Tour Talks", which set the tone for the 14th National Congress of the CPC held in that October to put forward the two propositions that "the market should be the basic means of allocating resources" and "the realization forms of public ownership should be diversified". On this basis, the Third Plenary Session of the 14th CPC Central Committee, held in November 1993, adopted the *Decision on Some Issues Concerning the Establishment of the Socialist Market Economy* which specified the establishment of the socialist market economy as the objective of China's economic restructuring. China had been stepping up efforts in the transition of economic structure in the 30 years after 1978. The Third Plenary Session of the 16th CPC Central Committee held in October 2003 adopted the *Decision on Some Issues Concerning the Improvement of the Socialist Market Economy*, which concluded that "the main framework of the socialist market economy has been established", and the focus of reform would shift to the in-depth improvement of economic structure. In November 2013, the Third Plenary Session of the 18th CPC Central Committee was convened and adopted the *Decision on Some Major Issues Concerning Comprehensively Deepening the Reform*, which defined the general objective of the reform as "modernization of the national governance system and capacity", and specified the new stage for comprehensively deepening the reform is to pursue the "five-in-one" overall layout (integrating economy, politics, society, culture and ecology).

"Facts have proved that reform and opening up is a critical choice that has determined the destiny of contemporary China, and also an important instrument for the undertakings of the CPC and the Chinese people to catch up with the times in great strides". Reform and opening up is the main driving force for the rapid, healthy and sustainable development of Chinese economy. Over the past 40 years, China has seen its economy maintain an average annual growth rate of 9.5% and quickly come out of a "shortage economy". The gross national economy (GDP) moved up one step after another to rank second in the world in 2009. The per capita output also rose sharply. According to the World Bank statistics, China's per capita GDP was only 156 US dollars in 1978, but it expanded to around 9,000 US dollars 40 years later. With greatly improved living standards, Chinese people have embarked on a new journey toward building a "moderately prosperous" society in all respects and opened up a path of socialist development with Chinese characteristics.

Today, we commemorate the fortieth anniversary of reform and opening up is to build consensus in a better way, "shatter fetters of outdated ideological concepts with greater determination, overcome the barriers of solidified interests, and promote the self-improvement and development of the system of socialism with Chinese characteristics".[1] In contrast to the previous reform that focused on the relatively low-level problems concerning the operation of economic system and mechanism, the current task of comprehensively deepening reform "has entered a period of overcoming major difficulties and a deep-water zone". With a strong sense of historic mission, we must "give full play to the leading role of economic system reform, balance the relations of production with the productive forces as well as the superstructure with the economic base, and promote sound, sustainable economic and social development", and "dare to face tough choices, ford dangerous rapids", for the purpose of fully demonstrating our confidence and determination to "carry the reform through to the end".

Note

1 *Tutoring reader of decision of the CCCPC on some major issues concerning comprehensively deepening the reform* (p. 7). (2013). Beijing: People's Publishing House.

1 Introduction

Let innovation of theories and change of concepts take the first step, which is known as the characteristic of China's economic structural reform. Guided by the Marxist thinking of "emancipating the mind and seeking truth from facts", the Chinese Communist Party (CPC) broke free from the rigid theoretical constraints to review the national socialist movement and probe into the fundamental defects of the traditional highly-concentrated planned economy. After confirming how economic structural arrangement decides and influences resource allocation and the importance of vital and efficient enterprise operation, the CPC endorses the economic structural reform. By affirming the "position" of the reform of state-owned enterprises (SOEs) in the overall economic structural reform, the CPC endeavors to enhance enterprise vitality and makes it the "core" of the reform to put in motion other changes that concern the economic structural construction, which underscores the structural characteristics of the Chinese economy with enterprises as micro-foundation.

1.1 "Emancipating the mind" opens the way for economic restructuring and "affirms the place" of enterprise reform

The Third Plenary Session of the 11th CPC Central Committee, which was convened in Beijing from December 18 to 22, 1978, marked a major turning point in the transition from "traditional socialism" to "socialism with Chinese characteristics", and an end to the long dominance of leftist dogmatism. The CPC established a correct guiding framework and reaffirmed its commitment to Marxist ideological, political and organizational guidelines. A new chapter in the history of the CPC and the state was opened since then.

At that time, China just came out of the ten-year-long disastrous Cultural Revolution. To fully prepare for this plenary session, the earlier Central Work Conference had lasted for 36 days. Guided by the new thinking of "emancipating the mind", the participants aired their opinions fully and freely at the conference. They looked back at the country's socialist construction in the past 30 years to accumulate experiences and draw lessons therefrom. The inter-Party democracy and the fine work style of seeking truth from facts, following the mass line, and criticism and self-criticism were revived and carried forward. The discussions in the session "centered on the issue of shifting the Party's focus to socialist modernization". And the Communiqué of this session states that "in line with existing realities and new practices, we should adopt a host of new and major economic measures to reform the economic governance system and means of operation. And on the basis of self-reliance, we should actively develop economic cooperation featuring equality and mutual benefits with other countries in the world and strive to adopt world-class technologies and advanced equipment. More efforts are ought to be made to improve the work in science and education for realizing modernization",[1] which is boiled down to the guideline of "reform and opening up". By sticking to this guideline since 40 years ago, China has gradually become a focus of world attention for its robust economic and social development.

In the *Communiqué of the Third Plenary Session of the 11th CPC Central Committee*, the part about economic restructuring tasks points out that "Now a serious shortcoming of our economic governance system is that powers are too concentrated. Leaders should boldly delegate powers so that localities and industrial and agricultural enterprises will have more autonomy in operation and management under the guidance of the national unified plan. Efforts should be made to downsize economic administrative agencies at all levels and transfer most of their powers and functions to specialized companies or joint companies. We should resolutely follow the law of economy, attach importance to the law of value, and combine ideological and political work with economic means, and fully mobilize the production enthusiasm of cadres and laborers. Under the unitary leadership of the Party, we should carefully resolve the phenomena such as indiscrimination between party and government or between government and enterprise, having party replacing government or having government replacing enterprise; implement a responsible person system by post grades and division of labor; solidify the authority and responsibility of the governance institution and personnel; reduce official documents and meetings, improve the work efficiency, and implement the systems of assessment, reward and punishment, as well as promotion and demotion. Only by taking these measures can we give full play to the initiative, proactivity and creativity of the Central Government, local governments, enterprises and individual laborers, so that all sectors of the socialist economy can develop vigorously and vibrantly".[2]

The Communiqué revolves around the centralization and decentralization (between central and local governments, and also between government and enterprises) of structural arrangement in economic operation; how to consciously follow the law of economy; how to properly deal with the party-government relationship and the government-enterprise relationship; how to define the work responsibilities and implement the systems of assessment, reward and punishment while making full use of the autonomy of the subjects of enterprise operation, for the purpose of fully mobilizing the enthusiasm of management personnel. In a word, the reform measures should fully release the vitality of economic operation and development.

After 40 years of reform, now when we review the afore-said Communiqué, we still feel grateful to its far-sightedness that it not only incisively points out the drawbacks in China's economic structure but also comes up with ideas and methods to solve the problems. Apparently, this is the result of "emancipating the mind". After shackling off the ideological straitjackets, the whole Party started an all-round and in-depth reflection on the socialist construction practices and articulately set out the tasks to reform the traditional system. It is precisely because of "emancipating the mind" that Chinese people gained new insights into the reality of the outside world and broke free from the imprisonment of old thoughts and rigid mindsets. They started thinking and comprehending problems proactively and probing into the difficulties in the course of development in a down-to-earth manner, with an aim to revive our socialist cause and carry on the socialist principles and requirements in an even better fashion. It can be seen how important it is to break away from the ideological constraints and old thoughts. It is no exaggeration to say that "emancipating the mind" is the source of the driving force for reform and opening up.

The *Decision on Some Major Issues Concerning Comprehensively Deepening the Reform*, which was adopted by the Third Plenary Session of the 18th CPC Central Committee, notes that "There will never be an end to practice, to emancipation of the mind, and to reform and opening up".[3] "There will never be an end" reminds us not to be contented with the status quo. Practice keeps moving forward in the process of constantly discovering and solving problems. In an ever-changing environment, existing knowledge and experiences will encounter challenges, and we shall be courageous enough to conquer these challenges through reform. The 40 years of reform is a process where existing theories are updated or replaced to expand the space for action; consequently, we are able to keep making progress, solving problems, and addressing economic and social contradictions. The special significance of ideological and theoretical innovation for the progress of social practice could be no more evident. This enlightens us that existing economic theories must be constantly tested and updated in the reform practice.

By emphasizing the role of "emancipating the mind" in advancing the reform and opening up, we intend to motivate people to understand its philosophical implications in methodology, that is, to proceed from reality when doing everything, rather than from available theoretical propositions; and to be "problem-oriented", rather than sticking to existing theoretical conclusions. In the process of reform, ideological emancipation has led to continuous changes in the economic governance system, which has greatly liberated productive forces. The prosperity of factor markets and the refinement of division of labor have diversified the development of production organizations and modes of transaction. The opening up measures have introduced the market economy into China, and at the same time, promoted the Chinese economy to be closely integrated with the tide of globalization. That's why China has seen its economical operation increasingly influenced by the international environment.

After solving the existing difficulties, we have to go on tackling new problems and challenges. How can we keep a sober mind to meet and cope with the challenges? The answer is to take root in the soil of practice, let ideological emancipation open the way for practice, keep shackling off the constraints of traditional ideas and theories, and work hard on theoretical innovation. It is right here that we are fully aware of the special importance of economic theory research and innovation in guiding practice.

Let's return to SOE reform – the theme of this book. After reviewing a portfolio of measures for economic restructuring at different stages of the reform and opening up, we can find that enterprise reform has always been a "dazzling scenery" in this process and has been valued as the central link of the entire economic structural reform.

The reform has been pushed forward by stages. Given the ingrained drawbacks of the highly centralized planned economy, the Chinese government started the reform by focusing on vitalizing enterprise operation and taking it as a breakthrough point. By following an "incremental reform" strategy, the government launched pilot reform programs from time to time to explore the ways of reform. Based on the experiences drawn from these pilot programs, the reform has been advanced steadily and progressively.

Such an important feature of the reform is defined and especially elucidated in the *Decision on Reform of the Economic Structure*, which was adopted at the Third Plenary Session of the 12th CPC Central Committee in October 1984. In this Decision which consists of ten chapters, the third chapter (Enhancing Enterprise Vitality is the Central Link of the Economic Structural Reform) stresses that "Enhancing the vitality of enterprises, especially the large and medium-sized enterprises owned by the whole people, is the central link of the entire economic structural reform that is mainly carried out in cities".[4] More than that, this Decision points out that the key to enterprise reform lies in handling the relationships between government and enterprises and between enterprises and employees. Enterprise reform is a central goal and task of the entire economic structural reform. Such a statement echoes the economic structure's basic function: to allocate production factors scientifically and rationally for developing productive forces. And enterprises happen to be the "organizational platform" or "organizational carrier" for resource allocation and productive forces by consolidating all kinds of production factors.

Regarding the complex economic relationships formed on the basis of the economic structure, they involve several pairs of economic categories such as government and enterprises, planned economy and market economy, macroeconomics and microeconomics, central government and local governments, citizens and society, as well as their functional coupling in economic operation. Among them, how to deal with the government-enterprise relationship directly determines whether the enterprises engaged in reproduction activities are dynamic. In turn, it determines the efficiency of reproduction input and output. Of course, other economic categories are also able to restrict enterprise behaviors. But we have identified the key to properly dealing with multiple economic relationships: take enterprise vitality as the "center link" of the reform to get rid of the drawbacks in the old economic structure. In the process of constantly deepening the reform, we have learned to make the socialist market economic structure the target and content of the reform and come up with a more straightforward proposition that "modern enterprises are the micro-foundation of the socialist market economic structure".

In this sense, the *Decision on Reform of the Economic Structure* makes a scientific positioning of enterprise reform in the reform blueprint by holding onto the "center link" of the economic structural construction and function, which is vital for the reform to keep going deeper in the future and worth being especially emphasized here. Comrade Deng Xiaoping once commented on this Decision. He described it as "a first draft of political economy and a political economy that combines the basic principles of Marxism with Chinese socialist practice".[5] Here, we still like to reiterate the special role of "emancipating the mind" in refreshing the theoretical concepts, activate and enhance people's ability to discover problems, analyze problems, and resolve problems. It also impresses us that the proposition of "emancipating the mind never ends up" accords with the Marxist methodology of "seeking truth from facts".

1.2 Overview of the SOE reform process from multiple perspectives

Over the past 40 years, China's economic structural reform has been unfolded by revolving around enterprise reform. We can summarize the 40 years' reform practice from different perspectives, and one of the most intuitive perspectives is to summarize and extract the characteristics of the reform in consecutive stages in chronological order. The 40-year enterprise reform process can be split into three major stages: The first stage (1978–1992) is characterized by "decentralization of power and transfer of profits" and adjustment of interest settlement relationship and settlement method between government and enterprises. At the second stage (1992–2012), the efforts were mainly made for exploring the innovation of enterprise system, implementing corporation system reform of SOEs, establishing and improving the corporate governance mechanism. In the third stage (from 2013 to date), usually known as the new stage, the government has been "actively developing mixed ownership" and comprehensively innovating the ways for realizing public ownership.

Today, the continuously advancing and deepening enterprise reform remains at this new stage. By splitting the enterprise reform process into three major stages, we can make it clear how China's economic structural reform keeps going deeper, how enterprise reform cooperates with other aspects of economic structural reform, and how the reform benefits are released to improve economic operation and expedite economic growth? Through an all-around analysis, we will have a more profound understanding of the entire economic structure and the proposition that the enterprise system is the micro-foundation of the economic structure.

1.2.1 Start the reform by taking adjustment of interest relationships as the key to stimulate enterprises vitality

After "reform and opening up" was specified as China's development policy at the Third Plenary Session of the 11th CPC Central Committee at the end of 1978, the government placed focus on resolving the outstanding problems in the national economic structure at that time and intensified efforts in adjusting the unreasonable arrangements. For example, since the extremely low prices of farm produce had dampened the production enthusiasm of farmers, the pricing system of agricultural and sideline products was reformed to stabilize the agricultural production expectations and consolidate the foundation of the national economy, as well as pave the way for the economic restructuring in urban areas.

At the same time, given that enterprises lacked vitality under the centralized planned economy, the government attempted to loosen control of enterprises by introducing such pilot programs as allowing enterprises to retain a certain percentage of the profits that they have created and use them discretionarily, including rewarding their employees. This has changed the existing centralized governance model of "unified collection and allocation of funds by the state", and mobilized the enthusiasm of enterprises to act as a microeconomic unit. In this way, several malpractices are likely to be eradicated, such as the government mandatory plan for enterprises, "unified collection and allocation of funds by the state", "getting an equal share regardless of the work done", "enterprises and government are messing together, and employers are obliged to provide for all of their employees".

By retaining certain profits, enterprises have become a rival to the government in the game, forcing the government to be fully capable of fiscal concentration. As early as 1980, a small number of enterprises began to implement the pilot program of "profit-to-tax". After accumulating some experiences in this regard, the "profit-to-tax" practice (co-existence of profits and taxes) was promoted in an all-round manner in 1983 and put into the second phase in 1984, for the purpose of bolstering up economic development and income growth based on improved enterprise vitality and bringing about higher returns to both government and enterprises. The original practice of "turning over profits to the state" was replaced by "paying tax according to regulations", making SOEs show up as tax-payers, which has highlighted the status of enterprises as independent legal persons. Consequently, some basic theories, such as the rules on the ownership of SOEs and the forms of ownership realization, shall be re-defined and reinterpreted, and some supporting changes in other areas of the economic structure, including pricing, employment, finance and banking, shall be initiated.

The reform itself cannot be advanced in a multi-targeted way. In order to stimulate enterprise vitality, certain "reform cost" has to be paid; that is, government transfers a certain percentage of profits to enterprises and tolerates insignificant growth in fiscal revenue. In this way, the adjustment of the government-enterprise interest relationship has yielded substantial results, and both the efficiency of the national economy and the scale of output have increased. More than that, in order to keep advancing the reform in other areas of the economic restructuring, the Central Government must have new means for fiscal concentration, which has presented additional difficulties and challenges in coordinating the interest distribution between government and enterprises.

It was against this background that the Third Plenary Session of the 12th CPC Central Committee held in October 1984 adopted the *Decision on Reform of the Economic Structure*. While shifting the focus of the economic structural reform to urban areas and specifying enterprise reform as the "central link" of the entire reform, this Decision put forward the argument that "ownership and management rights (of SOEs) may be properly separated", which was a theoretical innovation at that time. By defining SOEs as a type of enterprise and splitting the powers and functions of their ownership, this argument explains why SOEs can act as independent taxpayers from the standpoint of economic theory, showing that economic theory is in need to reform the economic structure.

In addition, although the enthusiasm of enterprises has been bolstered up, new changes in the external environment and information inconsistency arising from the double-track price system will interfere with their business objectives and decision-making philosophy and even disrupt their behaviors. More than that, the "profit-to-tax" system determines the tax rate based on the "vested interests" from enterprise profit sharing. On the basis of a unified profit income tax, a kind of flexible "regulation tax" is levied so that different enterprises are taxed by different rates, even those in the same industry bear inconsistent "tax burdens", which has resulted in an unfair outcome of "whipping fast horses". It will undoubtedly demoralize enterprises and obstruct the efforts to further mobilize their enthusiasm, which runs counter to the original intention of the reform to activate enterprises and their employees, and makes it hard to fully realize the objective of a concurrent increase in government revenue and enterprise income. This requires us to look for innovative institutional tools and means to deal with the interest relationship between government (state) and enterprises, not only relying on the existing practice of directly mobilizing the enthusiasm of enterprises and employees with "interest restraint".

As mentioned earlier, the ways of working such as "incremental reform", pilot going first, and continuous advancement have ensured the enterprise reform to be carried out in an orderly manner. In order to streamline administration and delegate powers and allow different enterprises to implement different economic responsibility systems, we began to select pilot enterprises to implement the "shareholding" (corporate) system – an option for keep deepening the reform – while comprehensively trying out the measures for reforming the enterprise management responsibility system.

On December 5, 1986, the State Council issued *Several Regulations on Deepening Enterprise Reform to Enhance Enterprise Vitality* which proposes that small-sized enterprises owned by the whole people can try out lease or contract operations, large and medium-sized enterprises owned by the whole people can implement different management responsibility systems. All localities can choose a small number of qualified large and medium-sized enterprises owned by the whole people to carry out the joint-stock pilot program. The promulgation of the Regulations was a major step in promoting the urban economic restructuring. It was of great significance for further streamlining administration and delegating powers, improving the external conditions of enterprises, expanding their autonomy, and motivating them to reform their internal mechanisms.

On February 27, 1988, the State Council released the *Interim Regulations on the Contract Management Responsibility System of Industrial Enterprises Owned by the Whole People*, effective March 1, 1988. According to these Interim Regulations, we could define the enterprise management responsibilities and rights in the form of a contract and deal with the interest distribution between government and enterprises through "contract restraint" instead of the existing "interest restraint".[6] While protecting the independent management consciousness and enthusiasm of enterprises activated by the existing "retained profit", we could introduce the means of "contract management",[7] that is, specify the management responsibilities, rights and interests of enterprises in a contract which is valid for 3 years, in an aim to guide enterprises to establish long-term business goals and work hard for continuous growth in economic output and in their own returns, as well as ensure the steady growth of the government fiscal revenue for covering the mounting spending in other aspects of the reform.

The reform has been going on along the train of thought for adjusting the "government-enterprise relationship" by expanding powers and transfer of profits to enterprises and implementing the enterprise management responsibility system. The content, method and realization mechanism of economic operation continue to deepen: from "surrendering profits" for activating enterprises' self-consciousness to "profit-for-tax" reform for developing enterprises as an independent legal entity in the market economy, and then to the "contract management responsibility system" for symmetrizing the powers, responsibilities and profits of enterprises as market subjects.

This series of adjustments to the production relations includes the institutional arrangements for implementing the socialist economy and the public ownership of means of production in real economic operations and the formation of a benign mechanism that facilitates mutual incentive of the rights and interests of different subjects (government – enterprises – employees[8]) under a certain institutional framework. This has further clarified our understanding of the real socialist practice in the basic economic system, economic governance system and concrete realization mechanism at three levels (economic system – economic structure – economic mechanism) and brought us with an on-site perception ability of scientific control. We have acquired a more comprehensive and complete understanding of the economic system structure and self-awareness of the forward-looking design for deepening the reform. It was also against this background that the State Council No. 103 Decree (*Regulations on Transformation of Management Mechanism of the Industrial Enterprises Owned by the Whole People*) was promulgated as of July 23, 1992, stressing to transform the enterprise management mechanism,[9] promote the enterprises owned by the whole people to enter the market, build up enterprise vitality and increase the economic benefits of enterprises. Starting from this, more efforts have been made to reform the enterprise management mechanism, promote them to better adapt to the external environment of market development, continuously improve the overall operating efficiency of the national economy, and coordinate the relationships between all aspects of economic restructuring.

Now when we look back the resource allocation mechanism and function of the traditional highly centralized planned economy, we can find that its understanding of the basic nature of "public ownership" is simplistic and abstract, believing that the public ownership of the means of production can "equalize" the rights of laborers in different scenarios. However, the specific production activities in real life have many restrictive factors, which make it impossible for indiscriminate resource allocation and function realization of the public ownership of the means of production, let alone the diversified allocation of the publicly owned means of production in both quantity (capital scale) and quality (industrial sectors of different divisions of labor, geographic location, the technical content of production equipment, and even the differences in laborers' educational background and technological level). Owing to diversified allocation in specific scenarios, it is particularly important for scientific and objective evaluation of the subjective effort of the enterprises of public ownership. But the approach of "unified collection and allocation of funds by the state", which is a feature of the traditional planned economy, disregards the individual rationality of laborers and the enterprise rationality based on joint services of laborers and excludes all commodity economic factors, which is sure to stifle the vitality of microeconomic units, lower the efficiency of the national economy and keep it in a long-term state of shortage and "tight operation".

To eliminate these system drawbacks, "decentralization of powers and transfer of profits" (calculate the input and output of the state-owned assets and funds used by enterprises, and then determine a certain proportion of profits to be retained and independently used by enterprises) was implemented to recover rationality of enterprises and foster their consciousness of being a legal entity. As a result of the reform that allows enterprises to retain certain profit as "disposable income", the "power" of using their own funds has given rise to an "unplanned" behavior in contrast to the traditional, highly centralized planned economy. On the basis of mobilized enterprise enthusiasm, further efforts were made to allow enterprises to "independently purchase" raw materials and arrange "unplanned production and sales", so there came independent pricing for the products based on unplanned production, thereby forming another price track and a gradually developed market price system. Such an "incremental reform" strategy has become a counterforce to the traditional system since it has fostered an unplanned market and promoted "dual-track" economic operation, and also developed the market forces based on efficiency evaluation. The "legal entity" status of enterprises as a microeconomic unit allocating resources for social reproduction has been gradually understood and recognized. Thanks to the efforts in mobilizing the business vitality of enterprises, the theoretical knowledge of economic mechanism, economic structure and economic system has been accumulating and enriching, which has, in the end, contributed to the formation of clear thinking and blueprints for the intact content and functions of the enterprise system and the target model design of the enterprise reform.

1.2.2 Protecting corporate vitality with system innovation, and shaping corporate governance mechanism with clear powers and responsibilities

The reform mainly for enhancing enterprise vitality has been carried out in an orderly way by first implementing pilot programs, which has injected strong impetus into the operation of the entire national economy. The achievements of enterprise reform have also spurred the reform of other aspects of the economic structure. In order to innovate the enterprise system, we have set out the requirements for investors under the condition that enterprises act as an independent market subject, especially established a system for managing the capital contribution function of state-owned assets, examined the compatibility of public ownership and market economy, and explored the market-oriented allocation ability and vitality of state-owned assets. Based on their legal status as a market subject, enterprises are restructured into corporate enterprises and transformed from traditional "state-owned enterprises" to "state-funded enterprises". Some typical problems have been addressed along with the enterprise restructuring, such as overextended state-owned capital allocation and scattered capital scale. According to the principle of both "advance and retreat" and "refraining from doing some things in order to accomplish other things" for the division of labor in a market economy, SOEs have been undergoing strategic reorganization. On the basis of enterprise system innovation and scale optimization, a modern enterprise governance mechanism has been introduced to establish and improve corporate governance structure, improve enterprise management quality, fully push enterprises to market, and shape an orderly market subject system.

1. **Enterprise reform triggers the supporting reform of the state-owned asset management system. The transformation of traditional state-owned enterprises into organizations of corporate legal system requires the reform of the state-owned asset management system and the establishment of a new management system**.

The gradually deepening "incremental reform" has opened up a new institutional space for "market regulation" and fostered a new regulatory mechanism for market-based resource allocation, which has been gradually understood and adopted by all types of economic and social subjects, and accumulated experiences and wisdom for defining the target model of economic restructuring. The coexistence of planned economy and market economy, which seems like a "double-track" economic restructure, has objectively resulted in double standards for evaluating resource allocation and operation efficiency, which requires us to have a correct understanding of basic theories. In his South Tour Talks in the spring of 1992, Deng Xiaoping commented that "The proportion of planning to market forces is not the essential difference between socialism and capitalism. A planned economy is not equivalent to socialism, because there is planning under capitalism too; a market economy is not capitalism, because there are markets under socialism too. Planning and market forces are both means of controlling economic activity".[10]

It was against this background that the 14th National Congress of the CPC convened in October 1992 established the "socialist market economy" as the target model of China's economic structural reform. In order to fulfill this objective, the *Decision on Some Issues Concerning the Establishment of the Socialist Market Economy*, adopted at the Third Plenary Session of the 18th CPC Central Committee in November 1993, gives a detailed description of the specific contents of various reform tasks, sets the direction of "establishing a modern corporate system", and points out that "the modern enterprise system with public ownership as the main body is the basis of the socialist market economy". The reform must be deepened to "let enterprises enter the market", the deep-seated contradictions must be resolved, "efforts must be intensified to innovate the enterprise system" for further liberating and developing productive forces. In this Decision, the legal organizational form of the "modern enterprise system" is the modern corporate system. The implementation of the new reform tasks centering on "corporate system transformation" marks that the enterprise reform has entered a stage of vigorously promoting innovation in system construction.

Regarding the traditional organizational form of SOEs, their means of production are owned by the whole people, and such nature determines that these enterprises adopt the legal organization form of "state ownership". The reform of decentralization of powers and transfer of profits has broken through the existing government-enterprise relationship and inspired the theoretical discovery of "separation of two powers"; the "profit-to-tax" endeavor has further highlighted the independent legal entity status of enterprises. In order to transform the management mechanism of enterprises into independent management and self-financing and facilitate enterprises to adapt to the changes in the market environment, the legal form of the enterprise organization must be adjusted, and the government-enterprise relationship must be properly handled at the system level. Therefore, the "modern enterprise system" is established as the "target model" of enterprise reform and the micro-foundation of the socialist market economy. An enterprise is an independent subject in market economic activities and is a legal entity funded by "contributors". The deepening of enterprise reform will inevitably propose to "clarify" the work content of contributors, which puts the reform of the state-owned asset management system on the stage. The deepening of reform calls for the establishment of an organizational system that specializes in the management of state-owned assets and exercises the function of "contributors". From the fresh standpoint of plutonomic theory, we need to answer "how can public ownership be combined with the market economy"? How to blend their operating mechanisms?

Reform practice has proved that the traditional system has deprived enterprises of vitality and reduced them to appendages of government. One of the most typical manifestations is the "mixed functions of the government and enterprises". On the one hand, government organs act as "owners" of SOEs, and on the other hand, they are managers of economic and social affairs. Government affairs and contributor affairs are all in one and the government-contributor relationship is entangled with the government-enterprise relationship, which has imposed too much control over the routine operational activities of enterprises and lowered their vitality. "Decentralization of powers and transfer of profits" to enterprises and other reforms for vitalizing enterprises require government organs to tease out and break down a variety of specific functions. The functions of contributors must be separated from the functions for managing economic and social affairs. For this purpose, an independent state-owned assets management system shall be established as a supporting measure for SOE reform.

As early as September 1988, the State Council decided to establish the state-owned assets administration bureau under the Ministry of Finance to exercise the right to represent state-owned assets owners, the right to supervision and administration of state-owned assets, as well as the rights to state investment, earnings and assets disposal. Local state-owned assets regulators were set up in succession. In addition, Shanghai and Shenzhen were designated as pilot cities to implement a new organizational system for state-owned assets management since 1993. A three-level state-owned assets management system thereby came into being, including the state-owned assets administration commission (with an executive office dealing with routine matters), state-owned assets holding companies authorized by this commission (exercising the right of management of state-owned assets contribution), and SOEs engaged in production and operation activities with state-owned assets contribution.

After 10 years' innovation of enterprise systems by establishing the modern enterprise system and exploring the compatibility of public ownership with a market economy, rich experiences had been accumulated to construct a complete state-owned assets management system.[11] The First Session of the Tenth National People's Congress, held in March 2003, decided to establish the State-owned Assets Supervision and Administration Commission (SASAC) to serve as a special agency under the State Council, which would separate government from contributors through organization structuring. Consequently, the SASAC would act as a contributor of SOEs on behalf of the State Council, the SOEs originally affiliated with the relevant ministries and commissions would be subject to the SASAC, thereby forming a group of enterprises under the administration of the central government and a group of enterprises under the administration of SASAC, which enables to rationalize the hierarchical system of social enterprise organizations with the capital contribution-utilization relationship according to the principles of the market economy. This has created external conditions for restructuring and registration of the enterprises transformed into corporate legal organizations.

2. **The Company Law standardizes and guides SOEs' restructuring and pushes enterprises to market**.

According to the requirements for building a socialist market economy, the modern enterprise system (the modern corporate system) is the microfoundation of the new system. This requires the reform of the corporate system of the enterprises owned by the whole people, that is, transform them into the modern corporate legal organizations that act as independent market subjects. In June 1992, five departments of the State Council issued the *Pilot Measures for Joint-stock Enterprises*. In order to better guide the reform of the corporate system for SOEs, the enactment of company law and other laws and regulations were put on the agenda, which also shows the promotion of the deepening of SOE reform on the improvement of the economic and legal systems. It was against this background that the Fifth Meeting of the Standing Committee of the 8th NPC held on December 29, 1993, passed the *Company Law of the People's Republic of China*, which came into force as of July 1, 1994, and provides legal support for innovation of enterprise system. Innovation provides legal support. Since then, the Company Law had undergone three amendments in December 1999, August 2004 and December 2013, reflecting that with the continuous deepening of enterprise reform, there have been extensive changes to the system and mechanisms related to the economic operation, and showing the special status and role of enterprise reform as the "central link" of economic system reform.

The enforcement of the Company Law and the establishment of the state-owned assets management system have created supporting conditions for the corporate system reform of SOEs and the establishment of a modern enterprise system and pushed the SOE reform to enter the stage of system innovation. The transformation of the legal organization form of the enterprise system has pushed enterprises to the market and changed the government-enterprise relationship into a kind of economic relationship between two different subjects of "capital contributor" and "capital user". The characteristics of the modern enterprise system ("explicit property rights, clear rights and responsibilities, separation of government and enterprise, and scientific management") have motivated enterprises to "improve themselves" to take part in market competition as an independent market subject, continue making efforts in fostering institutional functions, build up their competitive edge to harness the market through establishment and improvement of the corporate governance structure.

A series of supporting reforms were launched at this stage to create a level-playing field, such as the State Council's decisions made over December 1993 and January 1994 on the tax-sharing financial management system and on the reforms of financial system and foreign trade system, in an aim to form a combination of system innovations that are compatible with enterprise reform, and gradually form cooperative capability in the reform of economic structure.

According to the provisions of the Company Law, SOEs are about to be restructured into joint-stock companies or limited liability companies. Both the two corporate systems require a joint contribution by multiple (two or more) contributors for check and balance between them when making decisions so as to help make a market-oriented judgment for corporate governance. This kind of multi-subject cooperation and check and balance is said to be the core value and most basic traits of the corporate system. In addition, such a cooperative and check-and-balance relationship between multiple contributors involves positive negotiation like "voting by hand" and passive retreat like "voting by foot". The dropouts "punish" their partners in a disguised way, just like the Chinese saying goes, "I cannot afford to provoke them but surely I can avoid them". This fully guarantees the right to inject or withdraw the investment.

Through an overview of the history of world economic development and a review of the dynamic changes and evolution of the enterprise system, we can find that the shift from private enterprises (capitalist capitalism) to a modern corporate system (corporate capitalism) in the West broke the limitations of private capital behavior. It is a concrete manifestation of the deepened division of labor arising from the separation of "nominal" (monetary) capital ownership from "real" (actual) capital ownership, which was expounded and highly rated in K. Marx's masterpiece *Capital*.[12]

Through further discussion of the emergence of the modern corporate system, we can also find other changes in the system: the civil liability subject for enterprise operation has shifted from "natural person" (contributor) to "legal entity" (registered and established with a certain amount of capital jointly invested by multiple entities, and granted legal liability for civil liability), and from "unlimited liability" of natural persons to "limited liability" (contributors bear limited liability only within the limit of their capital contribution). Under the action of the productivity technology revolution and market competition, the flexibility of enterprise organization optimization and reorganization in the form of equity cooperation, business decision-making checks-and-balances, and capital investment equity are released releasing the market vitality of enterprise management. From the perspective of the dynamic economic development process, this flow of capital creates opportunities for mechanism optimization and forms the vitality of enterprise development that accommodates changes in economic structure and industrial-technological progress. The most classic academic works on the study of the vitality of this system are the ten-episode large-scale documentary *The Power of Corporations* created by CCTV and the works published under the same name.[13]

In the process of deepening the economic reform in China, the "entry" and practical application scenarios of introducing the modern corporate system are apparently different from those of the Western economy. We have to master its internal institutional mechanism through capital relations so as to foster the internal vitality for developing and utilizing the corporate system and promoting its service to the fundamental task of developing socialist productivity. It is because building a socialist market economy is the goal of economic restructuring that we shall begin with the requirements of the general principles of market economy and build enterprises into an independent market subject. It is extremely necessary to introduce such a mechanism and conform to the general rules of a market economy. However, the understanding of this mechanism and the deep understanding and practical application of the endogenous mechanism, of course, need to be explored and accumulated in follow-up practices.

In other words, for the corporate transformation of SOEs, there is objectively a transformation and innovation in the form of the existing corporate organizational system. Under this premise, we will continue to create corresponding conditional factors, including theoretical knowledge, legal norms, conceptual behaviors, and market environment factors, to promote the development of the internal mechanism of the modern corporate system to gradually mature. This is also the inevitability that the introduction of the corporate system in China's economic practice has its own special evolutionary trajectory, which requires a full understanding and psychological and practical preparation. Evidently, the practical application of this system has completely changed the traditional ownership arrangements of SOEs. Public-owned production relations (ownership rights) exercise capital contribution rights through state-owned asset management entities. This is manifested as a market-oriented contribution and investment behavior. The new ownership realization form organically integrates the operation of the market economy. As a new formal arrangement of ownership relations, it is an important breakthrough and innovation for the existing theory of socialist public ownership of the means of production. At the same time, it will definitely bring about a series of new economic phenomena that need to be answered by the systematic innovation of economic theory and provide academic support for the modern enterprise system.

Corporate organization has become the basic organizational form of enterprises in China's economic life since 1994. According to the statistics from Shanghai and Shenzhen stock exchanges, the number of joint-stock limited companies that have chosen public stock offerings had reached more than 3,500 as of June 2018. Enterprises choose to raise funds directly in the capital market through offerings of stocks and bonds, which have fostered the growth of China's capital market and promoted the development of the financial market and financial restructuring. The system reform of enterprises – micro-foundation of a market economy – has kept producing endogenously innovative forces that promote the overall economic restructuring to open up new prospects.

Here we still have to point out that after the restructuring of traditional SOEs into modern enterprises was carried out in full swing, the SOEs at the provincial and municipal levels on the whole actively adopted reform measures and took follow-up steps in reforming their governance mechanism after the restructuring. The publicly listed enterprises, in particular, were worthy of praise for doing a good job in setting up corporate governance bodies and standardizing the implementation of the listed company system. In contrast, the performance of the SOEs under the administration of the central government (central SOEs) in promoting the corporation system reform was unsatisfactory. Among the central SOEs, more than 90 group enterprises were affiliated to the SASAC, and 69 of them had not registered for corporation system reform. Similarly, among the approximate 50,000 central SOE subsidiaries, 3,200 had not registered for corporation system reform.

Given this, on July 18, 2017, the General Office of the State Council released a notice urging the central SOEs to complete the corporation system reform and re-register in accordance with the modern company system by the end of 2017. The notice pointed out that the corporate system is an effective organizational form of the modern enterprise system and a necessary condition for the establishment of a modern SOE system with Chinese characteristics.

After years of reforms, more than 90% of China's SOEs have completed corporation system reform, which has effectively promoted the separation of government functions from enterprises. The corporate governance structure of enterprises has been improved day by day, and the level of business management has gradually improved. However, there are still some SOEs, especially those central SOEs, that have not yet completed the corporation system reform. Subsequently, the SASAC formulated a work plan for the implementation of relevant measures and completed the registration of the relevant reforms before November 2017. This shows from one aspect, that the top-level reform of central SOEs have remained relatively slow. SOE reform has obvious problems of "unevenness" and "out-of-synchronization" across the society in the reform of organizational forms, which will naturally affect the follow-up of work measures for the reform of the internal governance mechanism based on the reform of organizational forms. Faced with the work requirements of comprehensively deepening reforms and starting again, this kind of problem needs to be paid enough attention.

3. **Upon restructuring SOEs to look like modern companies in appearance, more efforts shall be made to build them into genuine modern companies by strengthening the construction of corporate governance mechanism and consolidating the functions of the modern corporate system**.

In this tide of restructuring various types of enterprises into modern companies, some qualified enterprises chose to be reorganized into joint-stock listed companies through public offerings. As a result, the follow-up efforts for deepening the reform are bound to have the following content:

How to build a scientific governance structure based on the corporate system so as to get rid of the "path dependence" of SOEs and make enterprise operation and governance endogenously adaptable to market economy?

How to set up the corporate governance structure in accordance with the requirements of modern corporate governance? The relationship between "three new boards" (board of shareholders, board of directors and board of supervisors) and "three old meetings" in traditional SOEs (congress of workers and staff, party committee and manager administrative council) shall be carefully dealt with.

There is a new scientific explanation for the meaning of "employee master" under the condition of clear "contributor" in the arrangement of public ownership production relations. How to better organize and mobilize employees' labor enthusiasm and handle the relationship between capital and labor?

Obviously, a joint-stock company's corporate governance level and governance capabilities are due to the disclosure of financial reports and related business information, becoming an important observation "window" for evaluating corporate governance capabilities and governance performance levels.

Related to the aforementioned second question: Formulation of corporate governance rules and specific power and responsibility arrangements for governance content; the selection, appointment, assessment, rewards and punishments of specific parties of the corporate governance organization (including directors who enter the board of directors as shareholder representatives, supervisors of the board of supervisors, and general managers and other senior management personnel in charge of daily operation and management affairs) are a symmetrical arrangement of the incentive and restraint mechanism we often say, which has become the internal mechanism that the company system needs to strive to build after the legal form is changed.

Theoretically speaking, there are clear textual definitions for the specific division of labor and coordination functions of the actual operation of corporate governance and the decision-making mechanism and the symmetry of specific rights and responsibilities. All these reflect the specific requirements as the basic characteristics of the modern enterprise system "clear property rights, clear rights and responsibilities". According to the World Bank's definition and interpretation of corporate governance, "corporate governance in a broad sense" is actually business management. Returning to specific practical occasions, as a theoretical regulation of the division of labor and coordination of corporate governance, how to connect with the corporate management regulations and behaviors that have been formed in the past few decades requires us to constantly explore and work hard in follow-up work practices. Practice has proved that this work cannot be achieved overnight.

While traditional SOEs are reorganized into company system enterprises, the internal corporate governance structure has been adjusted accordingly, thus giving rise to the board of shareholders (contributors), board of directors and board of supervisors. Properly dock with the original enterprise management organization (that is, workers' congress, party committee, and the general manager work team) through the "cross-service, two-way entry"[14] personnel arrangement. The specific work for establishing a perfect modern enterprise system and a corporate governance structure that facilitates the system operation and plays a check-balance role has always been the focus of SOE reform. According to the *Decision on Some Issues*

Concerning the Establishment of the Socialist Market Economy, which was adopted at the Third Plenary Session of the 14th CPC Central Committee, the goal and task of the reform of state-owned enterprises is to "further transform the operating mechanism of SOEs and establish a modern enterprise system that meets the requirements of the market economy, has clear property rights, clear rights and responsibilities, separation of government and enterprises, and scientific management".[15] Since then, the reform promotion practice has always placed an important position in the reform of SOEs on how to improve the governance mechanism of modern enterprises (companies).

As required by the corporate governance guidelines, corresponding adjustments are made to the division of labor in business decision-makers, shareholders' meetings, board of directors and board of supervisors. In order to strengthen supervision of central SOEs which are fully state-funded, a supervisory system is established in the leadership, that is, the SASAC or the government department to which the enterprises are affiliated dispatch full-time supervisors to the decision-making body of these enterprises, so as to constitute external supervision over these enterprises' business decisions.

Regarding the personnel composition of the board of directors of corporate enterprises, an "independent director" system is being established to draw professionals with legal, financial, economic or banking backgrounds to work on the board. This system was initially introduced to establish norms for joint-stock listed companies. The China Securities Regulatory Commission (CSRS) specially issued guiding opinions[16] to define the role of the independent director system and set out the requirements for the professional qualifications of independent directors. The principles and concrete measures specified in the guiding opinions also provide reference and basis for other enterprises in the whole society. A large number of professionals have devoted themselves to corporate governance and played an active role in promoting modern corporate governance. This system has gradually evolved from its infancy into maturity through continuous explorations.

It is also in this process where we continue deepening our understanding of the establishment and functions of corporate governance mechanism and become fully aware that the development of modern corporate governance mechanism requires a market-oriented development environment; in other words, the market shall play a decisive role in the allocation of resources, so as to make enterprises accept the actual test of market competition, and highlight the objective importance of corporate governance capability. Meanwhile, the entire society better understands the mutual relationship between enterprise reform and other supporting reforms for economic restructuring and the significance of comprehensively deepening the reforms.

Fundamentally speaking, the modern corporate governance mechanism is a mechanism of mutual checks and balances among the enterprise's different shareholders. This kind of checks and balances originate from the different judgments of different shareholders on the content of the decision-making affairs so that the business decision-making of the enterprise can improve the rigor and effectiveness of the decision based on multiple judgments, in order to promote enterprises to "standardize business decision-making" and "adapt to the new situation of marketization and internationalization". In this regard, the *Decision on Some Major Issues Concerning Comprehensively Deepening the Reform*, adopted at the Third Plenary Session of the 18th CPC Central Committee, contains a systematic and complete explanation.

In recent years, in order to implement the reform tasks set forth in this Decision, "actively developing a mixed ownership economy" is taken as a new "breakthrough" for accelerating the SOE reform. That is to say, on the basis of the corporate system of SOEs, the reform of mixed ownership in the electric power, oil, natural gas, railway, civil aviation, telecommunications, military industry and other fields should be gradually promoted. Conditions should be created to implement "mixed-ownership" reform in the upstream fields of the industrial system. What we are trying to solve here is to introduce non-state-owned capital investors to make joint contributions based on the principle of "classification reform" of SOEs and to create a multi-subject check-and-balance mechanism.

In addition, for the enterprises that have been reorganized and have initially formed a diversified mixed co-investment, however, due to the "dominance" of state-owned capital in the equity structure, the corporate governance process cannot form checks and balances among shareholders. Therefore, it is necessary to further open up the equity arrangements, to transfer the original absolute control of state-owned capital (above 51%), and to reduce the proportion of state-owned capital holdings to relative control by absorbing private capital through the expansion of shares, in order to release private capital's discourse power in making business decisions. The most representative case of reform in this regard is China United Network Communications Limited (China Unicom) in 2017, through its own listed joint-stock company platform, in accordance with the Relevant Measures for the Private Issuance of Stocks, introduces emerging private companies with Internet technology applications such as Baidu, Alibaba, Tencent and JD.com as strategic investors, relatively reduced the proportion of state-owned capital's shareholding structure, while maintaining the relative controlling position of state-owned equity, it also improved the checks and balances of other social shareholders, including non-state-owned shareholders.

More than that, it organically integrated its own communication network and data resources with the service capabilities and data resources of Internet application companies, improved business vitality and market expansion competitiveness. It achieved a fundamental transformation of corporate governance mechanism. According to reports, the "Unicom's mixed-ownership reform" took half a year to quickly solve the problems of institutional overlap, overwhelming personnel, and wasted cost and strength that are always difficult to resolve. One of the most prominent internal reform actions is the rapid realization of the "slim down" of internal management institutions and staffing. The management organization of the group headquarters has been reduced from the original 27 departments to 18; the number of offices has been reduced from 238 to 127, a decrease of 46.64%, of which 56 are a net decrease and 55 are separated in production; the staffing was reduced from 1787 to 891, a decrease of 50.14%, of which 347 were net reduced and 549 were separated from production. It is particularly worth mentioning that Unicom's mixed-ownership reform plan also incorporates the introduction of employee stock ownership. More than 7,000 key management team members have been granted equity and invested in the purchase of shares to create a "community of destiny" for the development of employees and the enterprise. It can be seen that China Unicom's case has the distinctive characteristics of "three in one" (equity structure optimization, governance process reengineering, and introduction of employee stock ownership). By deepening the "mixed-ownership reform", the company's governance process and work content standards have been completely reshaped.[17] In terms of optimizing modern corporate governance mechanisms, it has set a new benchmark for the entire society.

Regarding the efforts in optimizing corporate governance structure and working mechanism, the more straightforward way is to reorganize the wholly state-owned enterprises into those of diversified or mixed ownership, then the contributors' meeting (or shareholders' meeting) attended by multiple contribution subjects will recommend property rights representatives to enter the board of directors, so as to form a check-and-balance mechanism for diversified contributors or contributors of different ownerships.

Special attention shall be paid to the central SOEs where the SASAC acts as a contributor. Their governance mechanism must be changed and optimized to prevent the state-owned assets-related decision-making behaviors from out of control or from "insider control". To this end, the 26th Executive Meeting of the State Council was convened on February 1, 2000, and adopted the *Interim Regulations on the Boards of Supervisors in State-owned Enterprises*,[18] which make it clear to set up the boards of supervisors in key large SOEs, and the State Council will directly dispatch the supervisors to supervise the maintenance and appreciation of the values of state-owned assets in these enterprises on behalf of the State. These Regulations specify that the boards of supervisors, by putting financial supervision at the first place, shall supervise the financial activities of the enterprises and the operation and management behavior of the responsible persons in light of relevant laws and administrative regulations, as well as pertinent provisions of the MOF, for the purpose of protecting the state-owned assets and their rights and interests from infringement. The board of supervisors and the enterprise are in a relationship between supervisor and being supervised. The board of supervisors does not participate in or interfere with the business decision-making and management activities of the enterprise. Practices have proved that the introduction of the board of supervisors in the key large central SOEs has accumulated relatively rich experiences in improving and strengthening the supervision mechanism of SOEs. In view of the adjustment and optimization of China's capital allocation pattern during the reform process, state-owned capital is concentrated in key fields and strategic industries that concern the national economy. It is of great reference significance for constructing a more scientific and effective corporate governance mechanism in the subsequent mixed-ownership reform of central SOEs.

As mentioned earlier, there have been many shortcomings in the construction of modern corporate governance mechanisms. On the one hand, there has been the "path dependence" of traditional concepts and behavioral inertia. On the other hand, the development of marketization in the external environment of enterprise operation needs to be further deepened, and in particular, definite norms are yet formed in dealing with the government-market relationship and the government-enterprise relationship. The *Guiding Opinions on Strengthening the Asset-Liability Constraint of State-owned Enterprises* have revealed the unhealthy phenomenon of excessively high debt ratios in SOEs, showing the problems in the governance mechanism of state-owned enterprises.[19] The Guiding Opinions, on the one hand, emphasize comprehensive coverage and incorporates all SOEs into the asset-liability constraint management system; and on the other hand, take into account the differences, emphasizing the classification and implementation of policies based on different enterprises, achieve precise constraints on the enterprises with high asset-liability ratios and high debt risks as far as possible. A clear work goal is put forward, that is, to promote the average asset-liability ratio of SOEs by the end of 2020 to reduce by about 2 percentage points from the end of 2017. Comparing with the above-mentioned structural goals of the enterprise reform that we are striving to build, we also realize that there are two aspects of the system information that are worth reviewing: First, the independence of the legal person property rights of SOEs, the enterprises themselves have not yet truly formed a market economy entity with "self-financing" and clear responsibilities, and the hard budget constraint mechanism for "self-management" of enterprises has not been fully formed. Second, the specific manifestation of the high debt ratio of SOEs reflects the administrative dependence on the government. Objectively, local governments are seeking rapid economic development to raise funds by forming "enterprises" as a "financing platform". The government's own debts are disguised as having "enterprises" come forward to bear. So that it is directly manifested in the economic phenomenon of excessively high corporate debt ratio. Such corporate management decisions must be accompanied by government intervention. It objectively reflects that the reform measures of "separation of government and capital" and "separation of government and enterprise" that have been promoted have not been in place. This also enlightens us that on the basis of earnestly summarizing the practical experience of reform and opening up, we need to further establish the determination to "carry the reform to the end".

4. **While implementing the corporate system reform and governance mechanism, the scale of enterprise organization and allocation fields shall be adjusted and optimized to improve the adaptability of the division of labor system between state-owned capital and other social capital.**

Along with the practical process of promoting SOE reform with the establishment of a modern corporate system, there is still an important issue that that must be discussed, this is the adjustment of the distribution and allocation scale of SOEs and the transformation and improvement of the quality of capital allocation directly affected by the characteristics of the distribution fields and the scale of allocation. After implementing the economic responsibility system and "delegating powers and transferring profits", SOEs have expanded their autonomy and stimulated the continuous enhancement of their endogenous business vitality. At the same time, attracting foreign capital and opening up private capital and forming a stimulus to competition in the external markets for business operations have greatly enhanced the vitality of economic operations. In the dynamic economic development, people will also find that under the traditional system, the ownership relationship is the one-sided pursuit of "large in size and collective in nature". The pattern of economic activities being taken over by SOEs has changed. The existing state-owned capital quantity and operating capacity allocation were overextended and too scattered, and the efficiency was low, which inspired us to change the organization of SOEs. It is necessary to scientifically deal with the issue of the efficiency of state-owned capital allocation in connection with the structure of the national economy and the technical characteristics of enterprise economic activities. To deepen the reform of enterprises while focusing on adjusting the relationship between the government and enterprises at the level of production relations, it is necessary to integrate the technical characteristics of productivity and reorganize the organizational structure of enterprises. The strength of the measures in this regard, especially when the Fourteenth National Congress clearly stated that the socialist market economy should be the target model of China's economic system reform, and the Third Plenary Session of the 14th CPC Central Committee made clear the specific work content of building a socialist market economy: to focus on the reform of SOEs, establish a modern corporate system reform, and combine enterprise restructuring with reorganization and transformation.

From the 15th National Congress of the CPC in September 1997 to its 19th National Congress in November 2017, the topic of how to continuously improve the modern corporate governance mechanism has taken up paragraphs in the reports delivered at these conferences, and how to allocate the property rights of the public sector of the economy and improve its operating efficiency based on the size of the organization and capital allocation of enterprises is particularly expounded. In his report delivered at the 15th CPC National Congress (1997), the then General Secretary Jiang Zemin pointed out to "explore enterprise leadership system and organization management system that conform to the laws of market economy and China's national conditions, establish a decision-making, execution and supervision system, form an effective incentive and restriction mechanism. We should build a good enterprise leadership team, give full play to the political core role of corporate party organizations, and adhere to the policy of relying wholeheartedly on the working class". Regarding the requirements for the reform of modern enterprise governance mechanism, the report delivered at the 16th CPC National Congress (2002) stated that "Large and medium state-owned enterprises must continue their reform to convert themselves into standard companies in compliance with the requirements of the modern enterprise system and improve their corporate governance". In the report delivered at the 17th CPC National Congress (2007), the then General Secretary Hu Jintao pointed out that "We will deepen the reform to introduce the corporate and shareholding systems in state-owned enterprises, improve the modern corporate structure and optimize the distribution and structure of the state sector of the economy to enhance its dynamism, dominance and influence". In the report delivered at the 18th CPC National Congress (2012), "We should unwaveringly consolidate and develop the public sector of the economy; allow public ownership to take diverse forms; deepen reform of state-owned enterprises; improve the mechanisms for managing all types of state assets; and invest more of state capital in major industries and key fields that comprise the lifeline of the economy and are vital to national security. Thus, we should steadily enhance the vitality of the state-owned sector of the economy and its capacity to leverage and influence the economy. At the same time, we must unswervingly encourage, support and guide the development of the non-public sector, and ensure that economic entities under all forms of ownership have equal access to factors of production in accordance with the law, compete on a level playing field and are protected by the law as equals". The *Decision on Some Major Issues Concerning Comprehensively Deepening the Reform*, adopted at the Third Plenary Session of the 18th CPC Central Committee, specified that "State-owned capital investment operations must serve the strategic goals of the state, invest more in key industries and areas that are vital to national security and are the lifeblood of the economy, focusing on offering public services, developing important and forward-looking strategic industries, protecting the ecological environment, supporting scientific and technological progress, and guaranteeing national security". "We will accurately define the functions of different SOEs. We will ensure state-owned capital increases its input into public-welfare enterprises and make greater contributions in the provision of public services".[20] In the report delivered at the 19th CPC National Congress (2017), General Secretary Xi Jinping pointed out that "In the state-owned sector, we will step up improved distribution, structural adjustment, and strategic reorganization. We will work to see that state assets maintain and increase their value; we will support state capital in becoming stronger, doing better, and growing bigger, and take effective measures to prevent the loss of state assets". "We will further reform of state-owned enterprises, develop mixed-ownership economic entities, and turn Chinese enterprises into world-class, globally competitive firms".

It can be seen that the systematic advancement of economic restructuring centering on SOE reform as the "central link", linkage promotion and supporting requirements require the optimization of various aspects such as the allocation of state-owned capital, the scale of enterprise organization and the adjustment of economic structure, the construction of the function of the economic system and the operating quality of the economy has been continuously improved.

In connection with the institutional environment of enterprise reform, the organizational structure adjustment of SOEs is mainly composed of the actions in the following stages:

In September 1999, the Fourth Plenary Session of the 15th CPC Central Committee adopted the *Decision on Some Major Issues Concerning the Reform and Development of State-owned Enterprises*, which explicitly proposed to strategically adjust the layout of the state-owned sector of the economy, combine the SOE reform with the optimization and upgrading of industrial structure and the adjustment and improvement of the ownership structure. We should concentrate on strengthening the control of state sector by adhering to the principle of both advance and retreat or refraining from doing some things in order to accomplish other things.

Through the reorganization of enterprise organizational structure, the state-owned capital distributed at the end of the industrial chain was going through "paid withdrawal" and diverted to key industries, and the front in the allocation of state-owned assets was thus shrunk. At the same time, the layers of hierarchy for state-owned capital investment were excised, and the problem of inefficient management was addressed. In actual economic work, it is expressed as "invigorating large enterprises while relaxing control over small ones". On the one hand, intensified efforts are made to foster large-sized enterprises and business groups both powerful and competitive, so as to develop them into large groups with cross-regional, cross-industry, cross-ownership and cross-border operations. On the other hand, small and medium-sized enterprises (SMEs) are liberalized and invigorated. Active efforts are made to support SMEs, especially the high-tech ones, to develop in the direction of "specialization, precision, uniqueness and newness", establish close cooperative relations with large enterprises, and improve the level of socialization of production. In light of the specific conditions and environment for the survival of SMEs, alliance, merger, leasing, contracted operation, joint-stock partnership, sales and other means may be adopted to liberalize and revitalize these enterprises.

Statistics show that during the 6 years from 1998 to 2003, the number of state-owned and state-controlled enterprises in China was 238,000 in 1998 and 150,000 in 2003, declining by 40%. The number of their employees dropped from 78.04 million in 1998 to 43.11 million in 2003, also down by 40%. Their realized profits were 21.4 billion yuan in 1998, increasing 22 times to 495.1 billion yuan in 2003. The total assets registered an increase of 35% from 14.9 trillion yuan in 1998 to 19.7 trillion yuan in 2003. The net SOE assets stood at 5.2 trillion yuan in 1998, surging 60% to 8.4 trillion yuan in 2003. The rate of return on state-owned assets in 2003 reached 5.9%.[21] These figures show that the reform measures for the strategic reorganization of SOEs have greatly improved the operating efficiency of the state-owned sector of the economy.

Invigorating large enterprises while relaxing control over small ones and carrying out the strategic reorganization of the state sector can also stimulate the growth of the market economy. Objectively speaking, the withdrawal of state-owned capital from certain areas of social reproduction and industrial sectors makes room for the expansion of the non-public sectors, which will form a competitive relationship between different capital owners and cultivate market functions. Moreover, the continuously developing market and maturing division of labor will promote the progress of productive forces. All of these endeavors tally with the principle of labor division to improve productivity and inspire the deepening of reforms in the future.[22]

Through large-scale layout adjustment of the state sector by "invigorating large enterprises while relaxing control over small ones" and through optimization of corporate organizational structure, the quality of China's economic performance has also improved. Amid the redistribution of state-owned capital and the reorganization of existing enterprises, SOEs have withdrawn from certain areas to make room for the development of other types of capital, which has increased the explorations into the ways for realizing the orderly division of labor and cooperation between SOEs and other enterprises (including foreign-funded and private ones) in social reproduction and at the same time fostered market mechanisms.

The division of labor and the competitive environment of different market players have undergone changes along with the optimization of corporate organizational structure. A landmark event was the establishment of the SASAC by the State Council in March 2003. While performing the functions as "investor" of state-owned capital, the SASAC has also taken continuous optimization of the corporate organizational structure as an important mission in the past 15 years. In line with the constant changes in the economic environment and the corporate operation mechanisms, and in institutions and market conditions, central SOEs have gone through mergers and reorganization for structural optimization, with their number dropping from 198 in 2003 to 93 in June 2018. Such downsizing has stimulated these enterprises to improve their scale competitiveness with main businesses at the core, cut their organizational costs, and raise the efficiency of capital management by reducing duplicated capital allocation.

Facts have proved that reorganization and downsizing are crucial means for deepening the reform of SOEs. In this process, the government-enterprise relationship has been constantly improved, and the understanding and designing of resource allocation, economical operation and institutional functions have been continuously refined.

1.2.3 Carrying out enterprise reform for consolidating the micro-foundation of the socialist market economy, as well as the supporting reforms in other aspects. Let economic restructuring take the lead in the comprehensive deepening of reform

We can confirm that enterprise reform is the "central link" of China's entire economic system reform through a longitudinal analysis of the enterprise reform process. In this process, we have reshaped the government-enterprise relationship through "appropriate separation of ownership from management", promoted the theoretical innovation for the ways to realize public ownership, and finally put forward the notion of "vigorously developing a mixed economy", which "is an important way to materialize the basic economic system of China" and to ensure the compatibility of public ownership with a market economy. We should push enterprises to participate in market competition. To this end, we should increase their vitality and competitiveness, reform their organizational structure for consolidating their status as micro-foundation of the market economy, and acknowledge that they are corporate legal persons enjoying property rights independently. Given this, it is necessary to transform them into modern "enterprise investors" and continue the reform of the state-owned assets management system. We should implement the modern enterprise system, encourage the co-investment of diversified sectors, and transform the corporate governance mechanisms through institutional innovation and the establishment of new ones so as to create an institutional foundation for the "scientific management" of enterprises and achieve the ultimate goal of improving their business operations. We should strengthen the scientific management of enterprises, and enact market rules that are fair, open and transparent, thereby stimulating the development of various factor markets and advancing the supporting reforms of financial, taxation, banking, credit and investment systems, and other aspects. More efforts must be made to create an environment of rule by law and an "inclusive" business environment for enterprises in all economic sectors to compete on an equal footing.

As stated in the *Decision on Several Major Issues in Comprehensively Deepening Reform*, "The state protects the property rights and legitimate interests of all economic sectors, ensures that they have equal access to the factors of production according to the law, participate in market competition on an open, fair and just footing, and are accorded with equal protection and oversight according to the law".[23] It indicates that in order to comprehensively deepen the economic restructuring, which centers on the enterprise reform, the reforms in other aspects ought to be carried out to stimulate one another and integrate institutional reform with mechanism transformation. In this way, the structure and functions of the economic system will be continuously improved.

Since the structure and functions of the economic system, the supporting reforms in other aspects and their interaction and progress have a bearing on the realization of the reform plans and objectives, a systematic summary and a thorough understanding of these matters are required so as to enlighten the follow-up actions for comprehensively deepening the reform.

At the Third Plenary Session of the 12th CPC Central Committee held in 1984, the *Decision on Reform of the Economic Structure* was adopted to define enterprise reform as the "central link" in the entire reform, which not only made it clear that enterprises are the micro-foundation of the economic structure but also affirmed the vital roles of the government and enterprises in the economic society; thus the adjustment of their relationship is of great importance to economic restructuring. This Decision stressed that "increasing the vitality of enterprises, especially the large and medium-sized ones owned by the whole people, is the key of the entire economic structural reform focusing on cities".[24] By centering on the transformation of the government-enterprises relationship, we can put the logical relationship between the focus of economic restructuring and other tasks in order. By pushing enterprises to the market, we can conform to the trend of the reform to define enterprises as independent market players and shape them into independent economic entities enjoying "legal person's property rights" in economic activities.

In such a context, the operating results of enterprises need to be evaluated scientifically and objectively. So we have to introduce economic accounting tools such as commodity currency and let enterprises perform their operating capability in a competitive market environment, thereby giving play to the role of the "market" in regulating resource allocation. This is a kind of "incremental reform" for the gradual transition from the "planned economy" where the government directly controls enterprise operation to the "socialist market economy". Such reform is also known as the "market-oriented" reform, which is often heard in the theoretical circle when they discuss economic restructuring.

In the process of adjusting the "government-enterprises" relationship, we must keep developing the "market" and make the best use of the "market" mechanisms, which has made us realize that a good "government-market" relationship is the "key" to the economic restructuring. Based on the conviction that the main characteristic of the economic system is to deal with resource allocation, the 14th National Congress of the CPC held in 1992 definitely proposed that the goal of China's economic structural reform is to establish a socialist market economy.

As a result of the "incremental reform", the application scope of the market mechanisms has been gradually expanded, and the "transition" of the economic system has in the main accomplished. In the process of improving the socialist market economy, we have become increasingly convinced that the "government-market" relationship is "at the core" of the economic restructuring. The *Decision on Some Major Issues Concerning Comprehensively Deepening the Reform*, which was adopted at the Third Plenary Session of the 18th CPC Central Committee in November 2013, pointed that "Economic system reform is the focus of deepening the reform comprehensively. The underlying issue is how to strike a balance between the role of the government and that of the market, and let the market play the decisive role in allocating resources and let the government play its functions better. It is a general rule of the market economy that the market decides the allocation of resources. We have to follow this rule when we improve the socialist market economy. We should work hard to address the problems of market imperfection, too much government interference and poor oversight".[25] This statement was further elaborated in the report delivered at the 19th CPC National Congress in 2017, "There must be no irresolution about working to consolidate and develop the public sector; and there must be no irresolution about working to encourage, support, and guide the development of the non-public sector. We must see that the market plays the decisive role in resource allocation, the government plays its role better".[26]

According to the above analysis, the major task of enterprise reform and the programs and means for resource allocation is the most important content of economic structuring. Properly resolving these issues will help to straighten out the relationships between the central and local governments, finance and banking, market structure and competition order, position these relationships in the economic structure, and improve the socialist market economy. While allowing the market to play a "decisive" role, the government performance also needs to be improved, which has become an arduous task after the economic structural reform enters a deep-water zone.

The role of the government seems like "a coin with two sides", since the government is an important component in both the economic system and political system. We must acquire a correct understanding of the role of the "government" in the process of comprehensively deepening the reform and let the economic restructuring lead the great reform to open up new prospects.

The reform of the enterprise system – an innovation of the micro-foundation of the socialist market economy – has been carried out in a continuously improved market environment which is attributed to the adjustment of layout and organizational structure of enterprises and also to the economic transition. As a result, the Chinese economy is able to maintain rapid and stable growth and reach new heights year after year. In 2009, China became the world's second-largest economy in terms of economic aggregate, and it has never stopped moving forward. Chinese companies, which have become more vitalized and competitive, have won themselves a place in the global market. In the "Fortune Global 500 List" released by *Fortune Magazine* in July 2018, there were 120 Chinese companies, an increase of 5 from the previous year.[27] China's economic success has fully proved that the CPC is right in upholding the Marxist thought and methodology of "seeking truth from facts" and "keeping pace with the times" and in its conviction that reform and opening up are ways to make China powerful. The Party will remain confident and determined to lead the Chinese people of all ethnic groups to "carry out the reform to the end".

The above analysis depicts the trajectory of deepening the economic structural reform in the past 40 years. All the clues of this trajectory are contained in the landmark documents adopted at the CPC's congresses over the years. Our Party always stands firm in the forefront of the reform, constantly brings forth theoretical innovation, and plays a leading role in establishing the principles and goals of reform and opening up at each stage, designing reform tasks and organizing the implementation of the reform. The practices in reform and opening up and in successful economic transition have deepened our understanding of the relationship between the basic economic system, economic structure and operating mechanisms from the political-economic perspective, provided new subjects to the research on economic system theory, and opened up a new realm in the socialist political economy theory with Chinese characteristics.

1.3 Explaining the results of SOE reform from the political-economic perspective and emancipating the mind continuously for making theoretical innovation and new breakthroughs

China's SOE reform has kept advancing in the past four decades, and every step forward is inseparable from the efforts in theoretical innovation. The breakthroughs of economic theory open the way for practice, and the results of practice verify the scientificity and objectivity of the theory. On the one hand, Chinese enterprises have become increasingly competitive thanks to the enterprise system reform, large-scale adjustment and optimization of the enterprise organizational structure. On the other hand, SOEs and other types of economic organizations have maintained orderly cooperation and division of labor. These two conditions have consolidated the micro-foundation of China's economy and supported it to score great achievements.

1.3.1 Innovation in theory of political economy for SOE reform: enterprise theory with Chinese characteristics

Thanks to the implementation of the policy of "reform and opening up", the application of the methodology of "emancipating the mind and seeking truth from facts", and an in-depth review of the main drawbacks of the traditional planned economy, the SOE reform is accurately positioned as the "central link"[28] of the entire economic system reform, so the "state-owned enterprises" which were merely appendants of government organs under the traditional economic system (based on the theory of "ownership by the whole people") have acquired more autonomy in management and gradually become "self-managing" enterprises (based on the theory of "separation of ownership from management").

After setting the goal of building a socialist market economy, the CPC confirmed that the enterprise reform is to establish a "modern enterprise system", that is, to reorganize the traditional SOEs registered as enterprises owned by the whole people into "state-funded" "modern companies", and transform them into an independent corporate legal person and qualified micro-foundation of the socialist market economy. Then an enterprise platform based on the corporate system has come into being, drawing investment from multiple sources and in various ownership, and becoming a corporate component of "a mixed sector of the economy" and "an important way to materialize the basic economic system of China", which is conducive to the organic integration of public ownership and market economy. While restructuring the organizational form of enterprises, their operating mechanisms are also reformed. From the above-mentioned reforms carried out in succession, we have accumulated rich experiences and theoretical elements to innovate the enterprise theory with Chinese characteristics. An interpretation of this theory from the political-economic perspective is summarized in the following aspects:

1. **Uphold and improve the basic economic system theory.** Based on the practices for gradually deepening the reform and opening up, the 14th National Congress of the CPC held in 1992 set the goal of economic restructuring is to build a socialist market economy, and then the 15th National Congress held in 1997 made it clear that "we must uphold and improve the basic economic system, with public ownership playing a dominant role and diverse forms of ownership developing side by side". In 2002, the 16th National Congress put forward the principle of "two unswervingly", that is, "it is necessary to consolidate and develop unswervingly the public sector of the economy" and "it is necessary to encourage, support and guide unswervingly the development of the non-public sectors of the economy". The *Decision on Some Major Issues Concerning Comprehensively Deepening the Reform*, adopted at the Third Plenary Session of the 18th CPC Central Committee held in

2013, reiterated the importance to adhere to the "basic economic system" and the principle of "two unswervingly", and elaborated on the ways to materialize the basic economic system as "vigorously developing a mixed economy"; and "the state protects the property rights and legitimate interests of all economic sectors, ensures that they have equal access to the factors of production according to the law, participate in market competition on an open, fair and just footing, and are accorded with equal protection and oversight according to the law".[29] In short, this Decision fully expounded the equal, cooperative relationship between the main bodies of different ownership by integrating with the economic operating mechanism.

Based on the established principles and framework of the basic socialist economic system with Chinese characteristics, we should give play to the "leading" role of the public sector that occupies a "dominant position" of the economy in the actual economic operation, and at the same time enable capital with all kinds of ownership to "draw on one another's strong points to offset weaknesses, stimulate one another and develop together", and let "a mixed economy" "materialize the basic economic system of China", so as to open up a new situation in which diverse forms of ownership "develop side by side" in the primary stage of socialism.

2. **The theory that "a mixed economy" is an important way to materialize the basic economic system.** Over the past 40 years of reform and opening up, we have been encouraging, supporting and guiding the development of the non-public sector, which has scored great achievements in terms of capital scale and number of enterprises. Thus, it is necessary to confirm that both the public and non-public sectors are important parts of the socialist market economy. We should give full play to the leading role of the state-owned sector, and continuously increase its vitality, controlling force and influence. And we should develop "mixed enterprises" and have the capital of diverse sources centralized through market means to create a situation where the capital of various ownership competes and cooperates with each other. It is easy to understand that a mixed sector – made up of the corporate bodies (based on legal person's property ownership) with investors of various ownership – has become an important way to implement an ownership system (based on investor ownership) and to materialize the basic economic system. It can be seen that mixed ownership is "derived" from capital contributions made by different investors. Investor (ultimate) ownership or ownership by investor and mixed ownership represent productive relations at two different levels. Keeping the public sector as the dominant player can go hand in hand with the vigorous development of the mixed sector.

3. **The theory of establishing a new state-owned assets management system to identify "investors" of state-owned capital.** For the purpose of increasing the vitality of enterprises and appropriately separating

"ownership" from "management" in SOEs, we must transform these enterprises from the ones "owned by the whole people" to modern companies through the "reform of the corporate system", and then push them to the market to take part in competition. To this end, we need to establish a new state-owned assets management system to identify the "investor" of state-owned capital. The ownership by the whole people should take the form of state ownership. In a pilot program for testing the functions in managing state-owned assets, the local governments of Shanghai and Shenzhen respectively set up a state-owned assets administration commission. Based on these experiences, the SASAC – a special regulator of SOEs under the State Council – was established in 2003 to act as an "investor" of state-owned capital. In this way, we can concretize the abstract concept of "ownership by the whole people". Then we established a state-owned assets management system made up of the administration commissions under the governments at all levels and continued carrying out the supporting reforms for advancing the corporate transformation of SOEs. In line with the market conditions of the market economy, we have to "divide the labor" between investors and the corporate legal persons that use invested capital to materialize the capital ownership and work out better ways to integrate public ownership with a market economy, which is conducive to strengthening the cooperation between state-owned and other sources of capital.

4. **The theory of handling governmental functions-investment and government-enterprise relationships based on "state-owned assets management".** According to the general laws of the market economy, we clarified the relationship between "investment" and "capital use" and, on this basis, defined the relationship between the government (investor) and enterprises (corporate legal person). The "government-enterprise relationship" refers to the relationship between the realization mechanism of public ownership, business activities of enterprises and governmental functions in administering economic and social affairs. After specifying the investment behavior of SOEs' "investors" and the governance mechanism of modern companies, we can find that the operating activities of mixed enterprises mainly include investment management, industry access, product quality control, financial accounting, cost and price management, energy and resource acquisition, payment and social security of employees. These activities are bound to be associated with the governmental functions in administering economic activities and regulating market order. Therefore, on the one hand, we must make certain the content and mechanism of "state-owned assets management" according to the Company Law so as to handle the "relationship between governmental functions and investment" in a scientific manner. On the other hand, regarding the "government-enterprise relationship", that is, the operating activities of SOEs are entangled with the economic

and social affairs in the external environment, we must give play the "decisive" role of the market and reduce the government's approval and direct administrative intervention in business activities. Since the 18th National Congress of the CPC, we have continued the reform of the governmental administrative functions by "streamlining administration, delegating more powers to lower-level governments and society, improving regulation and optimizing services", in an aim to improve the "government-enterprise relationship" and we are so optimistic that our persistent efforts in this regard will yield better results.

5. **The theory of modern corporate legal person's property rights and the theory of the relationship between shareholders (investors) and companies (capital users)**. According to the relevant provisions of the Company Law, an enterprise is an economic entity and corporate legal person that enjoys independent property rights in market economic activities, but all of its assets belong to capital owners (investors or shareholders). That's why it is often said that "enterprises have no assets of their own". It is investors (shareholders) that bear the responsibility for the profits or losses of enterprises. Once the investment is made and an enterprise is established and put into operation, it will have a certain degree of "sustainability" as a corporate legal person unless continued losses force the meeting of stockholders to pass a resolution to shut it down (or file for bankruptcy) for liquidation. This shows the characteristic relationship between "investor" and "capital user" in the modern corporate system. When investors (shareholders) intend to "withdraw shares" and redeem their invested capital, they have to go through a set of legal procedures. In a joint-stock company, shareholders may have their shares transferred to other (new) shareholders at the secondary capital market. In a limited liability company, their share transfer must be based on the consent of more than half of the shareholders. It can be seen that shareholders in modern companies enjoy full flexibility in "entry" and "exit". The practices in China's enterprise reform have proved that the restructuring of traditional SOEs into modern companies has greatly increased the flexibility in capital flow and reorganization of enterprises and standardized the conditions for adjusting and optimizing the distribution of state-owned capital, which in the end gives expression to more efficient capital allocation and even more dazzling economic success.

6. **The theory of corporate governance mechanism in which investors of mixed enterprises cooperate with and check and balance each other**. In a joint venture with investors of different ownership, their cooperative relationship is manifested in the "democratic" decision-making mechanism related to the corporate operation. The meeting of investors (shareholders) will develop a set of hierarchical empowering norms for deciding the business activities of the company. Labor is divided among the meeting of shareholders, the board of directors and

the board of supervisors, as well as the professional managers in charge of day-to-day operations. The rights and responsibilities of all investors will remain symmetric so that they can check and balance each other in corporate governance, which is conducive to improving the quality of the democratic decision-making mechanism. More than that, different investors can either take a "positive" or "negative" attitude toward their cooperation; that is, they are free to choose to participate in or withdraw from corporate governance. Thanks to the corporate system reform of traditional SOEs and the introduction of modern corporate governance mechanisms, Chinese companies have acquired a democratic decision-making mechanism and more efficient management. During the reform of traditional SOEs, we have to properly deal with the relationship between "stakeholders" of mixed enterprises, in addition to handling the relationship between investors, highlight the combination of capital contribution and labor contribution, let Party organization play a crucial role in corporate governance, and make an effort to develop a modern corporate governance theory with Chinese characteristics.

7. **The theory of "classified approach" to deepen SOE reform.** The essence and content of SOE reform are to vitalize the state-owned capital allocation and operation, that is, to preserve and increase the value of state property. The businesses undertaken by enterprises are realized in specific industrial fields and controlled by their technical features and functions in the national economy and the entire industrial system. How to reasonably divide the labor between state-owned and other sources of capital for improving the efficiency of capital allocation? It requires us to implement "classified" measures for advancing the SOE reform. We have to press ahead with the reform in combination with the capital allocation characteristics, technical features and division of labor in the state sector and adopt targeted approaches, which should be taken as a concrete manifestation of refined capital management and deepened reform of SOEs.

8. **The theory of "equal" competition among enterprises of different ownership.** After confirming that the property rights of different ownership are respected and protected, we should guarantee that capitals and enterprises of different ownership are entitled to equal and fair competition in specific scenarios of market economic activities, thereby creating an inclusive market environment where market access, acquisition of various production factors and taxation are non-discriminatory. This kind of market is bound to stimulate enterprises to improve labor productivity by pursuing technological progress and organizational optimization and enhancing their competitiveness and operating efficiency by innovating the business model. It will help China to create a new situation with aggressive corporate behaviors and robust

economic development and lay a solid micro-foundation for high-quality economic growth.

9. **The theory of pushing forward the reform in the key area of "factor market" as required by "supply-side structural reform".** In reference to the afore-mentioned "equal" competition theory, we must pay great attention to the development of market mechanisms which are beset by "bottlenecks" and defects in different industrial fields, different links of the industrial system, and different levels of product market and production factors market due to the inconsistent measures for restructuring China's economic system. The only exception is the relatively mature market pricing mechanism because the product market in economic life has become fully liberalized through the 40 years of reform. But there are still difficulties and constraints for the market of production factors (including labor, land, technology and capital) to be open for competition. This situation could be interpreted in two aspects: On the one hand, economic activity entities with different property rights have unequal access to production factors due to different regulatory means. On the other hand, the lack of objectivity caused by the inadequate competition in pricing for production factors has led to inaccurate assessment of corporate operating performance. Based on the above analysis, we can better understand the relationship between the deepening of enterprise reform and market development and the tough tasks in the reform.

10. **The theory that entrepreneurs play a unique role in corporate governance as special resources.** With some knowledge about the characteristics of the corporate system arrangement and governance mechanism, we can understand that it is the duty of entrepreneurs – the personification of enterprises – to implement and safeguard the corporate system and governance mechanism. It can be said that the modern enterprise system is an "organizational platform" for entrepreneurs to display their business talents. And the corporate governance mechanism also contains the requirements for the symmetrical arrangements for motivating and restraining entrepreneurial behaviors. The professional quality and special role of entrepreneurs directly affect the progress and outcome of the reform in specific micro-occasions. In other words, the quality and ability of entrepreneurs seem like a kind of subjective effort for remedying the unmatched reform measures and a kind of pioneering spirit for accomplishing the reform tasks through self-motivation. A large number of cases in the reform process have fully proved that entrepreneurs play a special role in promoting the healthy development of enterprises, especially amid the increasingly fierce market competition, sizing up the situation, making resolute decisions and winning business opportunities. For this reason, the Central Committee of the CPC and the State Council jointly released the *Opinions on Creating an Environment for the Healthy Growth of Entrepreneurs, Promoting*

Outstanding Entrepreneurship and Giving Better Play to the Role of Entrepreneurs in September 2017, identifying the status and value of entrepreneurship in an official document for the first time. This document also called upon people to carry forward "three entrepreneurial spirits", that is, "the spirit of being patriotic, dedicated, observing disciplines and obeying laws, and working hard to fight their way", "the spirit of innovating development model and pursuing quality and excellence", and "the spirit of fulfilling their responsibilities and daring to serve the society", which have demonstrated the attributes of entrepreneurs as "special resources" in modern economic life, and expressed the appeal that the whole society should attach great importance to the special role and function of entrepreneurs. Admittedly, we have kept working hard in optimizing the mechanisms for discovering, selecting, appointing, assessing, motivating and restraining entrepreneurs.

1.3.2 Building a modern economic system with public ownership as the mainstay and state sector playing a leading role, and a pivotal stage of the reform calls for continuous ideological emancipation and theoretical innovation

A summary of the past 40 years' reform enlightens us to further advance the reform in the future and it also presents new tasks after the reform has entered a pivotal stage. According to the economic and social development plan adopted at the 19th National Congress of the CPC, we must continue reforms to develop the socialist market economy, and "we should endeavor to develop an economy with more effective market mechanisms, dynamic micro-entities, and sound macro-regulation. This will steadily strengthen the innovation capacity and competitiveness of China's economy". In order to build a modern national governance system, we must continue improving the economic system, promoting the transformation of the economic growth model, optimizing economic structure, fostering new drivers of growth, and achieving high-quality economic development. The decades of the reform experiences and achievements have proved that the vitality of enterprises in the operation of the national economy directly determines and affects the efficiency of resource allocation. It must be noted that the deepening of SOE reform, which is inseparable from the market environment, still faces difficulties and bottlenecks. After spending years studying China's SOE reform, the author has found that some tough problems remain in existence and need to be further discussed. For example, some basic principles related to enterprise reform are already established, but they are explained and interpreted in different ways; some principles and implementation opinions are definite enough, but they cannot be carried out due to the constraints of specific environmental conditions.

1. We must uphold and improve the basic economic system, "with public ownership playing a dominant role and diverse forms of ownership

developing side by side," resulting in changes in the proportion of the non-public sectors in China's GDP. How can we explain this situation? During the reform and opening up process, the non-public sectors have made considerable progress; thus, the proportion of the state sector in GDP has dropped relatively, which has made some people worried about if it is a sign that the public sector no longer holds a dominant position. Besides, it is often asked that if there is any contradiction between "vigorously developing a mixed economy" and "keeping the public sector as the dominant player".

2. To focus on "management of capital" means that capital value should be made as to the main object under management. To this end, the government must transform the ways to administer enterprises and further adjust the government-enterprises relationship. What are the specific contents of this transformation? How about the relationship between the "investor" of state-owned capital (the government) and the "capital user" (enterprises)? Is it an administrative relationship or a market-oriented relationship? What is the difference between "state-owned enterprises" and "state-funded enterprises"? Why should we distinguish them from each other?

3. How can state-owned capital cooperate with and compete against other sources of capital on an equal footing? Is it possible to make sure that economic entities of different ownership have equal access to production factors and business opportunities either through competition or cooperation under the market economy? In dynamic national economic activities, how to reasonably divide the labor between the public and non-public sectors of the economy?

4. We need to understand that the vitality of SOEs is essentially the vitality of the allocation and operation of state-owned capital. On this basis, we must pay attention to the relationship between the market-oriented allocation of state-owned capital and industrial fields and industrial division of labor. In practice, due to the constraints of inertial operating behaviors arising from "path dependence" and "historical burden", classified measures are hard to be fully implemented. It is for this reason that this book, by combining the analysis of the extended relationships of property rights in corporate investment behaviors, further discusses the necessity to break down the property rights into different levels, and then identifies the "ultimate investor" by analyzing the investment behavior, which helps readers to understand the specific map of the ownership realization mechanism and discover the "stratified" existence of new "ultimate owners". We should explore new paths for deepening the enterprise reform by combining "classification" and "stratification", which is conducive to dealing with the interest relationship between various investors in a better way.

5. What is the relationship between "ownership" and "property rights"? After the traditional SOEs are reorganized into the enterprises of the

corporate system with "diversified investment", how to help them foster a mature and modern corporate governance mechanism? In real economic life, which factors are restricting the development of the corporate governance mechanism? The investors of different ownership in "mixed" enterprises check and balance each other. Is it important for corporate governance? What is the relationship between "diversified investment" and "mixed ownership"?

6. In combination with the characteristics of modern economic operation, especially under the conditions of the market economy, the corporate governance based on the separation of "currency ownership" (or "nominal ownership") and "real ownership" usually adopts a principal-agent approach that is, hiring professional managers to take charge of company's management and allowing these front-line managers to play a crucial role in business operation. We must properly handle this principal-agent relationship, give full play to the role of professional managers, foster "entrepreneurship" and cultivate the managers acting as an "agent" to be emerging entrepreneurs. To this end, we have to create more favorable conditions in terms of systems and mechanisms.

Based on the above-mentioned theories and practices about China's enterprise reform, the following chapters will further discuss how to continue and deepen the reforms in the future by absorbing the reform experiences in the past four decades.

Notes

1 *Communiqué of the Third Plenary Session of the 11th CPC Central Committee.* Retrieved December 22, 1978, from http://cpc.people.com.cn/GB/64162/64168/64563/65371/4441902.html

2 *Communiqué of the Third Plenary Session of the 11th CPC Central Committee.* Retrieved December 22, 1978, from http://cpc.people.com.cn/GB/64162/64168/64563/65371/4441902.html

3 *Tutoring reader of decision of the CCCPC on some major issues concerning comprehensively deepening the reform* (p. 2). (2013). Beijing: People's Publishing House.

4 *Decision the CPC Central Committee on reform of the economic structure.* Retrieved October, 1984, from http://www.gov.cn/test/2008-06/26/content_1028140.htm

5 Deng, X. P. (1993). Speech at the Third Plenary Meeting of the Central Advisory Commission. *Selected works of Deng Xiaoping* (Vol. 3, p. 83). Beijing: People's Publishing House.

6 Zhang, H. M. (1998). *The logic of China's state-owned enterprise reform.* Taiyuan: Shanxi Economic Publishing House.

7 With the deepening of the reform and the development of the market, the Fourth Session of the 5th National People's Congress adopted the *Economic Contract Law of the People's Republic of China* on December 13, 1981, with an aim to establish market behavior awareness and behavior norms with symmetrical rights

and responsibilities for various cooperation subjects in economic activities. The author of this book believes that it was against this background that the "contract restraint" was introduced into the reform for dealing with the interest distribution between government and enterprises.

8 The three subjects represent "fiscal revenue", "profit and loss ability of business accounting entities" and "labor income".

9 In addition to some general rules, these Regulations have clearly defined enterprises' management rights, responsibility for their own profit and loss, changes and termination, relationship with government, and legal liabilities. It is an important guideline document for China to advance enterprise reform.

10 Deng, X. P. (1993). Excerpts from talks given in Wuchang, Shenzhen, Zhuhai and Shanghai. *Selected works of Deng Xiaoping* (Vol. 3, p. 373). Beijing: People's Publishing House.

11 Xi, J. P. (October 18, 2017). *Secure a decisive victory in building a moderately prosperous society in all respects and strive for the great success of socialism with Chinese characteristics for a new era – delivered at the 19th National Congress of the Communist Party of China.* http://www.xinhuanet.com/politics/19cpcnc/201 7-10/27/c_1121867529.htm

12 Marx. (2014). *Capital* (Vols. 1–3). Beijing: People's Publishing House.

13 CCTV. (2010). *The power of corporations.* Taiyuan: Shanxi Education Press.

14 Translator's note: The secretary and chairman of the party committee (party group) shall be served by one person, Party committee members enter the board of directors, the board of supervisors and the management team through legal procedures, Party members from the board of directors, the board of supervisors, and the management team enter the party committee in accordance with relevant regulations.

15 *Decision on some issues concerning the establishment of the socialist market economy.* Retrieved November 14, 1993, from http://www.people.com.cn/item/2 0years/newfiles/b1080.html

16 *Guiding opinions on establishing the independent director system in listed companies.* Retrieved August, 2001, from http://www.csrc.gov.cn/pub/shenzhen/ztzl/ ssgsjgxx/jgfg/sszl/201506/t20150612_278984.htm.

17 *China Unicom's mixed-ownership reform for 180 days: The headquarters establishment is halved, and the profit distribution pattern is rewritten.* http:// finance.ce.cn/rolling/201802/10/t20180210_28144159.shtml

18 *Interim regulations on the boards of supervisors in state-owned enterprises – Decree No. 283 of the State Council of the People's Republic of China.* Retrieved May 15, 2000, from http://www.gov.cn/gongbao/content/2000/content_60091.htm

19 The *Guiding Opinions on Strengthening the Asset-Liability Constraint of State-owned Enterprises* were adopted at the second meeting of the Commission for Comprehensive Reform under the CPC Central Committee held on May 11, 2018, and made public by the General Office of the CPC Central Committee and the General Office of the State Council on September 13, 2018.

20 *Decision of the CPC Central Committee on some major issues concerning comprehensively deepening the reform.* Retrieved November 15, 2013, from http:// www.scio.gov.cn/zxbd/nd/2013/document/1374228/1374228_1.htm

21 Li, R. J. *Why should we invigorate large enterprises while relaxing control over small ones during SOE reform?* https://zhidao.baidu.com/question/2350843 98.html?fr=iks&word=%C0%EE%C8%F0%BD%A8%3A%A1%B6%B9% FA%C6%F3%B8%C4%B8%EF%2C+%CE%AA%CA%B2%C3%B4%D2 %AA%D7%A5%B4%F3%B7%C5%D0%A1%3F%A1%B7&ie=gbk

22 In his work *The logic of China's state-owned enterprise reform*, published by Shanxi Economic Press in 1998 for commemorating the 20th anniversary of

China's reform and opening up, the author of this book Zhang H. M. analyzes the theories and internal logic of SOE reform and argues that we should "divert more state-owned capital to strong enterprises and outstanding entrepreneurs" to press ahead with the reform in the future.

23 *Tutoring reader of decision of the CCCPC on some major issues concerning comprehensively deepening the reform.* (2013). Beijing: People's Publishing House.

24 *Decision the CPC Central Committee on reform of the economic structure.* Retrieved October, 1984, from http://www.gov.cn/test/2008-06/26/content_102 8140.htm

25 *Tutoring reader of decision of the CCCPC on some major issues concerning comprehensively deepening the reform* (pp. 5–6). (2013). Beijing: People's Publishing House.

26 Xi, J. P. (October 18, 2017). *Secure a decisive victory in building a moderately prosperous society in all respects and strive for the great success of socialism with Chinese characteristics for a new era – delivered at the 19th National Congress of the Communist Party of China.* http://www.xinhuanet.com/politics/19cpcnc/201 7-10/27/c_1121867529.htm

27 FORTUNEchina.com. *2018 fortune global 500.* http://www.fortunechina.com/ fortune500/c/2018-07/19/content_311046.htm

28 *Decision the CPC Central Committee on reform of the economic structure.* Retrieved October, 1984, from http://www.gov.cn/test/2008-06/26/content_102 8140.htm

29 *Tutoring reader of decision of the CCCPC on some major issues concerning comprehensively deepening the reform* (pp. 5–7). (2013). Beijing: People's Publishing House.

2 SOE reform in the process of economic transition and market development

Chinese SOEs are known for their unique growth path. At the preliminary stage, new China established its enterprise system by largely imitating the "Soviet model". The enterprises under the centralized planned economic system were production units directly at the government mandates, and they seemed like the materialized national economy and "administrative units" affiliated to government organs. In the following almost 30 years, "unified collection and allocation of funds" and "unified purchase and sale", which are intrinsic characteristics of a planned economy, had suppressed the production enthusiasm of laborers, strangled the vigor of enterprises and lowered the efficiency of the entire national economy. Through a profound review of the drawbacks of the centralized planned economy, and after a nationwide debate on bringing order out of chaos, "emancipating the mind" and "seeking truth from facts", the CPC decided to uphold the guidance of the "reform and opening up" policy advocated by Deng Xiaoping and launched the economic structural reform to transform the traditional planned economy into a socialist market economy. As the "central link" of the entire economic reform, SOE reform plays a vital and prominent role.

2.1 Formation of state-owned sector and traditional enterprise system

The SOE system of China has a special growth path and development background. Based on Chairman Mao Zedong's viewpoints in his works *On New Democracy*, the Seventh National Congress of the CPC held in 1945 established the guiding principle that the Chinese revolution was a two-step process, that is, after the seizure of power, the first step was to build a new democratic society and complete the transition from an agricultural country to an industrial country, and the second step was to transform a new democratic society into a socialist society. Regarding the timing of the transition to socialism, Deputy Chairman Liu Shaoqi noted that the socialist policies should not be adopted prematurely after the victory of the democratic revolution; the Communist Party should first focus on building a new democratic economy by cooperating with the bourgeoisie for "at least 10 to

15 years". "When will we start an all-out attack? Maybe 15 years after we win the countrywide victory",[1] Mao Zedong added. During the new democratic period, the policy of "taking both public and private interests into account, benefiting both labor and capital" was implemented to deal with the capitalist sector of the economy. But in 1953, Mao Zedong set out the general line for this transitional period and asked to basically complete the transition to socialism in 10–15 years. In order to make the state sector the only basis for the national economy, which was under the influence of the Soviet Union's "state ownership", a movement of socialist transformation was in full swing across the country after the general line in the transitional period was established. Thus, the tasks which were planned to be completed in more than 10 years were finished in less than 3 years. In 1956 when the "three major transformations" (the socialist transformation of agriculture, handicrafts and capitalist industry and commerce) came to an end, the capitalist economy was no longer in existence. The private sector almost disappeared from the scene, marking that China would officially enter the stage of socialism. Hence, the State began to establish an SOE system on a national scale by imitating the Soviet model.

In the early days of the People's Republic of China, the SOEs under direct administration of the State were mainly divided into three types: (1) All sorts of factories located in the liberated areas. (2) The enterprises were funded with the confiscated properties of the bureaucrat-comprador bourgeoisie. (3) The enterprises, which used to be owned by the national bourgeoisie, were nationalized through transformation and redemption.

At that time, Chinese enterprises were bounded to be owned and operated by the State because of the historical reasons and objective conditions: First, when New China was just founded, the social productivity was seriously destructed, and the economic situation couldn't be any worse off. The top priority of the country was to restore the economy and develop production as soon as possible. Concentrating our forces on a major task was no doubt the most effective shortcut. Second, the wartime enterprises within the liberated areas had been operated completely by observing the "supply system", and their production and management at the government directive were mainly for yielding physical output. Third, no applicable theory told us how to build a socialist country. We were still confined to the expositions of traditional Marxist writers on the socialist economic system, believing that socialism was mainly characterized by the planned economy, public ownership and distribution according to work, and ownership by the whole people (state ownership) was more advanced than collective ownership. Fourth, there were scarce socialist construction models for us to take reference after the founding of New China. The Soviet Union's centralized planned economy was the only example for us to follow. Fifth, the international environment had remained unfavorable to New China for a long time after its founding. But there was a crying need for the country to establish its own industrial system. Through highly centralized planning and management of enterprises, the Chinese government was able to allocate resources to the most important economic sectors.[2]

The traditional state-run economy was established with reference to the "State Syndicate" pattern set forth by Lenin. He elevated the role of the state to a very high level and took state ownership as the only economic foundation of socialism.[3] According to Lenin, in a socialist society, all citizens have become employees of the State (armed workers). All citizens have become the staff and workers of the "Syndicate" of the whole people and the State. And the entire society will become an administrative office and a factory with equal labor and equal pay.[4]

Looking at the specific operation of enterprises, the planned administration of input, output and sales (three major links in business operation), which was supplemented by the planned regulation of product pricing, labor employment, income distribution, fiscal and taxation and foreign trade, had guaranteed the country's integrated administration of both microeconomic and macroeconomic operations. Through the development of the state sector, New China initially established its industrial system and laid the foundation for the continuous advancement of industrialization.

However, with the development of the domestic economy, the shortcomings of the traditional SOE system have become more noticeable. First, the state-owned and state-run enterprises lack the incentive mechanism. The grading factor, grading and promotion system determined according to the principle of lifetime employment is linked to one's rank and seniority regardless of his performance, which has suppressed the work enthusiasm of employees. Moreover, these enterprises are engaged in production by following the state plan and implementing the system whereby the State sets product prices and takes charge of their profits and losses. Enterprises usually conceal their real productive capacity when carrying out the production plan and apply for more input from the competent authority at a higher level.[5] Second, state-run enterprises have multiple roles and multiple goals. They are not only producers but also perform a wide range of social and political functions. Being taken as a tool to achieve the political goals of the State, state-run enterprises are under an administration like Party and government organs. Third, the property relationship of state-run enterprises is ambiguous. Governments administer these enterprises at all levels according to their affiliation, but the power to operate these enterprises is then divided between governmental departments, which has given rise to the phenomenon of "overlapping management", that is, the unified state ownership is split, and each department can exercise partial ownership without taking responsibility for its actions. Fourth, soft budget constraints. The primary goal of state-run enterprises is to complete the state production plan. To this end, they have to maintain negotiation with the administrative organs to obtain more favorable production arrangements. Soft budget constraints are counted as an important feature of the government-enterprises relationship.

It should be pointed out that there were theoretical discussions and debates on how to design and choose an appropriate economic system during this period. As early as 1956, when Mao Zedong bought forth "the policy of letting a hundred flowers blossom and a hundred schools of thought contend", the economists represented by Sun Yefang and Gu Zhun started criticizing the planned economy model. Considering the specific situation at that time, the main economic planner Chen Yun proposed to create a "three primary and three supplementary" economic pattern, that is, in terms of industrial and commercial operations, state-owned and collective-owned sectors will play a leading role, while a certain amount of private businesses are allowed to exist as a supplement; in terms of production, the production at the government mandates will keep holding the dominant position, but supplemented by the free production in line with market changes and within the scope of the production plan; in the unified socialist market, the state market is the main body, but a free market led by the state within a certain scope is a supplement to the state market.[6]

In 1956, in his works *On the Ten Major Relationships,* Mao Zedong summed up the main drawbacks of the current system as over-concentration of power at the Central Government and rigid and excessive government control.[7] Under the guidance of Mao Zedong's thoughts, the Eighth National Congress of the CPC held in 1957 developed a reform plan focusing on delegating power to local governments. However, the "decentralization" plan was interrupted by the economic campaign of "Great Leap Forward" in 1958. As a result of this campaign, the economic growth began to plunge, loss-making enterprises failed to alleviate product undersupply, and the national economy sank into depression. In 1960, the Central Government put forward the policy of "readjustment, consolidation, filling out and raising standards" to overcome the difficulties caused by the "Great Leap Forward" and the "People's Commune Movement". By the end of the "Cultural Revolution" in 1976, it was hard for the market-oriented reform to break through ideological barriers due to the deep-rooted influence of the Soviet Union; therefore, the delegation of power to local governments became the main pathway of reform. The reform of the economic structure, accompanied by a slogan of "decentralization is revolution; more decentralized is more revolutionary" was carried out in 1970. But it failed to get rid of the vicious circle of "decentralization leads to disorder and administration leads to rigidity".

2.2 Market-oriented reform and "appropriate separation of ownership from management"

Around the Third Plenary Session of the 11th CPC Central Committee in 1978, there were generally two different views on how to implement the economic structural reform. One mainly stressed to expand the autonomy of SOEs, arguing that the direction of reform is to give enterprises more autonomy so as to let them enjoy independence in accounting and operation under the unified leadership of the State. The other view was that the goal of reform is the establishment of a socialist commodity economy. In 1980, in the *Preliminary Opinions on the Reform of Economic Structure* drafted for the State Council's Structural Reform Office, economist Xue Muqiao noted that "the principle and direction of China's economic reform requires that, under the condition that the public ownership of the means of production holds a predominant position, we should accord with the requirements for developing the commodity economy and consciously use the law of value, no longer rely on the single planned regulation but turn to giving full play to the role of market regulation under the guidance of the plan".[8]

Since the first option was more acceptable at that time, China's SOE reform set out to expand enterprise autonomy. In this regard, the *Communiqué of the Third Plenary Session of the 11th CPC Central Committee* sharply pointed out that a serious defect of China's economic system is excessive concentration of power, and the State should boldly decentralize its power to give local governments and enterprises more autonomy in operation and management. Before the reform, SOEs could not make operational decisions on their own. Their production and operation were completely subject to the administrative plan, with materials, production, personnel, wages and products uniformly arranged by the government. No personnel inside an SOE was allowed to make any operational decision, the production capacity of enterprises was insufficient, and commodities such as industrial and agricultural products were in a serious shortage. Deng Xiaoping once said that "our present economic management is marked by overstaffing, organizational overlapping, complicated procedures and extremely low efficiency".[9] "I assure you that, in any case, we should continue to give enterprises more decision-making power, because this helps us to expand production".[10]

In October 1978, with the approval of the State Council, six enterprises in Sichuan Province (Chongqing Iron and Steel Company, Chengdu Seamless Steel Tube Plant, Ningjiang Machine Tool Plant, Sichuan Chemical Plant, Xindu Nitrogen Fertilizer Plant, and Nanchong Steel Plant) began to experiment with enterprise autonomy. This pilot program stipulated that after the enterprises have completed their prescribed output and profit targets, they can withdraw a small amount of profits as corporate funds for reproduction or employee bonuses. Good results were achieved in the year the policy was introduced. Subsequently, Sichuan Province increased the number of pilot enterprises to 100. In April 1979, at a special meeting, the State Economic Commission discussed the pilot reform of enterprise management with the responsible persons of competent authorities and some enterprises and made public their consensus on the measures for expanding enterprise autonomy. On July 13, 1979, the State Council issued five documents, including the *Provisions on Expanding the Autonomy of Operation and Management of State-run Enterprises*, which stated to increase the pilot projects for enterprise autonomy nationwide, and stipulated that enterprises would enjoy autonomy in ten matters: production and operation decision-making, product sales, material procurement, fund retention, assets disposal, institutional setting, personnel management, product pricing, salary and bonus arrangements, and joint operations. As of the end of June 1980, there were more than 6,000 pilot enterprises nationwide, and the output value and profits of these enterprises in the first half of the year accounted for 60% and 70% of the entire year, respectively. On December 26, 1981, the Ministry of Finance and the State Economic Commission issued the *Provisions on the Measures for State-run Enterprises to Retain Some Profits and Implement the System Whereby the State is Responsible for Their Profits and Losses*. Enterprises welcomed the profit retention method in this document. However, due to the defective restraint mechanism, it was common to see that the State shared the profits with enterprises but turned a blind eye to their losses, which had to some extent hit the enthusiasm of enterprises. In May 1984, the State Council issued the *Interim Provisions on Further Expanding the Autonomy of State-run Industrial Enterprises* ("Ten Articles of Power Expansion"), which became a transitional document to start a new round of reform, and it also marked the end of the pilot work in the expansion of powers and transfer of profits.

The reform of delegation of powers and transfer of profits made a success, which was mainly because it focused on interest relation – the fundamental of economic relations, awakened enterprises to "find back their rationality" as subjects pursuing economic interests, and jumped out of the vicious circle of "decentralization leads to disorder and administration leads to rigidity". Interest relation is the core of productive relations. As the main body of economic operation, enterprises have their own independent interests. By delegating powers and transferring profits, enterprises acquired certain financial power, which has mobilized the initiative of the enterprises themselves and the work enthusiasm of their employees, and initially abolished the practice of "everyone eating from the same big pot".[11]

At that time, when the seller's market played a dominant role and necessities were in shortage, it was easier for enterprises to make a profit from the production with surplus materials. So they started developing production through various means and achieved the effect of delivering more profits to the State, retaining more for themselves and sharing more with employees, thus alleviating the shortage of necessities at that time.

According to the incomplete statistics about Beijing's state-run industrial enterprises, from 1979 to 1981, the city's total industrial output value increased by 7.5% year-on-year, realizing a profit increase of 5.9%; the profit delivery rose by 4.8% year-on-year, and the city's accumulated industrial profit was retained at 890 million yuan, accounting for 10.9% of the realized profit.[12]

In the meantime, since enterprises have the right to dispose of their retained profit, the exercise of this property right has triggered a game for defining rights between the State (owner of corporate assets) and enterprises (specific business operator), which gave rise to the issue of "separation of ownership from management". But at the same time, during the reform, due to information asymmetry, some interest-driven enterprises deliberately brought down the planned targets and failed to complete production tasks in an attempt to expand their self-sales, thus causing so many problems like rising fiscal deficit, inflation, and chaotic economic order.

"Delegation of powers and transfer profits" is, in essence, a contract between the government and enterprise. According to Western economic theories, due to the incompleteness of contracts, managers and owners will compete for the residual claim of the enterprise, and ownership is of key significance in this regard. Two or three years after the implementation of the delegation of powers and transfer profits, corporate profits continued to increase, but the national fiscal revenue failed to rise significantly. With more retained profits, enterprises kept raising their employees' wages, thus forcing the State to resume negotiations with enterprises and stimulating the promulgation of profit-to-tax policy. Delegation of powers and transfer profits has not altered the relationship between the State and enterprises, and the government remains powerful enough to intervene in corporate operations.

According to Wu Jinglian (2004), in the process of separating ownership from management which was boosted by the delegation of powers and transfer profits and profit-to-tax reform, the ownership of the State (investor) and the expropriation power of the government (administrator) were confused, and the ownership was split between the State and enterprises, which has further led to the chaos of property rights and the problem of "inside control".[13] Faced with these problems, some leaders argued that the delegation of powers and transfer profits were not done enough, and more powers should be given to enterprises.[14] Among the various reform plans, the market-oriented reform had large uncertainties and ideological obstacles, but the economic responsibility system was more acceptable since the earlier contract managerial system implemented in rural areas had achieved satisfying results. Therefore, China began to implement the economic responsibility system in 1981 and initiated the enterprise reform under contractual constraints, that is, to define the rights, responsibilities and interests between the State and enterprises in the legal form of a contract, which would halt the decline of state revenue, and thereby stabilizing the national economic growth and the reform progress.

As early as 1978, in the report delivered to the Third Plenary Session of the 11th CPC Central Committee, Deng Xiaoping pointed out that "in terms of the management system, we must pay special attention to strengthening the responsibility system".[15]

On October 28, 1981, the State Economic Commission and the State Council's Structural Reform Office issued the *Opinions on Several Issues Concerning the Implementation of the Economic Responsibility System for Industrial Production*. In November 1981, the State Council approved and forwarded the document *Several Issues Concerning the Current Improvement of the Economic Responsibility System in the Industrial Sector*, which stated that "the economic responsibility system, under the guidance of the national plan, is a system for managing production and operation in order to increase social and economic benefits. The implementation of an economic responsibility system has changed the long-standing problems of over-concentrated powers and rigid control in the economic management system, and enterprises have acquired a certain degree of autonomy in operation and management. By following the principle of material interests, this system has adjusted the interest relationship among the State, enterprises and employees, and to a certain extent overcome the shortcomings of 'eating from the same big pot' and egalitarianism, mobilized the activity of enterprises, and helped employees act with a high sense of responsibility as masters of the house".[16]

On the basis of the preliminary profit-to-tax pilot reform, in 1983 and 1984, the State Council forwarded the reports of the Ministry of Finance on the profit-to-tax reform, specifying that large and medium-sized SOEs should pay income tax at a duty rate of 55% after deducting loans from their realized profits, while small and medium-sized SOEs should exercise an eight-grade excess progressive of the tax rate.

In August 1987, the State Economic Commission and the State Council's Structural Reform Office issued the *Opinions on Deepening Enterprise Reform and Improving the Contract Managerial Responsibility System*, which stressed the basic characteristics of this system, that is, "fix the contracted base number, guarantee the delivery, retain more in case of more revenue, and make up for inadequate delivery on their own". After going through profit retention and profit-to-tax reform, large and medium-sized industrial SOEs began to adopt a variety of managerial responsibility systems since 1987, including contract operation and lease management, as well as the shareholding system. In practice, the contract managerial responsibility system is mainly realized in five forms: (1) "Two Guarantees and One Link": guarantee the delivery of national profits and taxes and guarantee the completion of the capital construction and technological transformation tasks within the contract period.[17] (2) Increase the delivered profits year by year according to a certain percentage. (3) Hand over the profit base in a lump sum and share excess revenue. (4) Low-profit enterprises hand over profit quota and loss-making enterprises are subsided by the amount of losses. (5) Other contract forms for special industries.[18]

There are two layers in the industrial economic responsibility system: one is the economic responsibility system that correctly handles the relationship between the State and enterprises, and the other is the internal economic responsibility system that deals with the relationship between enterprises and employees. At the time, Shougang Group (a major iron and steel company in China) was one of the role models that successfully implemented the internal economic responsibility system. This company handed over profits and profit-increase indicators and took a leading role in performing economic responsibilities by combining responsibilities and powers with interests. Ding Jiatiao (1982) pointed out that the economic responsibility of Shougang Group was divided into three parts: (1) Deliver profits, increase profits, and set personnel quota. (2) Guarantee output, quality, variety, cost, contract performance, consumption, working capital, safe production, environmental protection, new product trial production, and scientific research. (3) Guarantee cooperation.[19] Through the methods of contracting, guaranteeing and verification, all tasks could be traced back to each link and each person, which was described as "vertical to the end, horizontal to the edge". This kind of economic responsibility system was later taken as a model and promoted nationwide.

The contract system has clearly defined the rights and obligations of the government and enterprises in the form of a contract, ensured the revenue of the State, and achieved satisfying economic results. From January to October 1987, the output value of industrial enterprises within the national budget increased by 11.7%, and their profits and labor productivity went up by 9% and 7.9%, respectively. The corresponding figures for the previous year were only 4.8%, –10.4%, and 0.9%. The contract system has guaranteed the state fiscal revenue and empowered enterprises to manage their profits, which has motivated both business operators and employees to improve management and production so as to obtain more income after completing the state production plans. At the same time, after the implementation of the contract system, the State no longer provides free funds to enterprises, which has to some certain extent tightened the financial constraints of enterprises.

But the contract system is not flawless. First, the contract system transfers the residual control right and part of the residual income claim during the contract period to the contractor, which makes the definition of corporate property rights more ambiguous. Moreover, since the contractual relationship (as the content of the contract) has a certain time limit, many contractors prefer short-term behaviors to long-term investments. Second, in specific practices, whether the contract system can be implemented and whether an enterprise can have operational autonomy depends on the conditions provided by its competent authority, and whether subsequent contracts can be renewed also depends on the decision of the competent authority which still intervenes in corporate decision-making at will. The government functions as capital owner and macroeconomic regulator are confused, which is not conducive to guaranteeing corporate autonomy. Third, the contract system is an inheritance of the policy of expanding powers and transferring profits, meaning that it is only a reform of control power without altering the ownership system, so it is unable to break the administrative subordination of enterprises or change the basic institutional framework of SOEs.

In the process of "separating ownership from management" triggered by the market-oriented reform, the State began to reform the corporate leadership system, trying to straighten out the relationship between the State and the corporate property rights.

In 1980, Deng Xiaoping pointed out that we should "get prepared and gradually reform the factory director responsibility system and the manager responsibility system under the leadership of the Party Committee. After implementing pilot programs and through gradual promotion, we can implement the factory director responsibility system and the manager responsibility system under the leadership and supervision of the factory management committee, corporate board of directors, and joint committee of economic complex".[20] In 1981, relevant departments formulated three documents, including the *Interim Regulations on the Work of Factory Directors of State-run Industrial Enterprises*, and then the factory director responsibility system was fully implemented since 1987. These documents have further standardized the relationship between the State and enterprises and laid the foundation for China to enact its first enterprise law. In April 1988, the First Session of the 7th National People's Congress adopted the *Law of the People's Republic of China of Industrial Enterprises Owned by the Whole People*, in which Article 2 provides that "the property of an enterprise is owned by the whole people, and the State empowers the enterprise to operate and manage its businesses by following the principle of separating ownership from management. The enterprise has the right to possess, use and dispose of the property granted to it by the State for operation and management. The enterprise shall obtain the status of a legal person in accordance with the law, and bear civil liability for the property granted to it by the State for operation and management". Following the idea of "separation of ownership from management", Article 7 of this Law stipulates that "enterprises shall implement the factory director (manager) responsibility system. The factory director shall exercise his powers in accordance with the law and shall be protected by law".[21]

Thanks to this "enterprise law", the legal person status of the enterprises owned by the whole people and their rights to the property granted by the State for the operation were stipulated by law for the first time, and the principle of separation of ownership from management was made clear and definite. However, the term "grant" contained in the enterprise law is interpreted as an administrative authorization in practice, meaning that the administrative status of enterprises is not changed at all. Moreover, although the enterprise law has established the legal person status of an enterprise, it fails to specify whether the enterprise shall bear limited liability or unlimited liability. And the rights of the enterprise to the assets granted by the State exclude the right of disposition (with the exception of disposition of earnings according to law), thus resulting in incomplete property rights of the corporate legal person.[22]

At the same time, in the absence of a corporate governance mechanism like the board of directors, the granting of the autonomy of business operation to the legal agents of an enterprise has in fact given them incomplete ownership rights, which will finally stimulate many legal representatives of enterprises to try to convert this right into full ownership. Such motive can be seen in lots of corruption cases involving the legal representative of SOEs.

In July 1992, the State Council issued the *Regulations on the Transformation of Operating Mechanisms for Industrial Enterprises Owned by the Whole People*, which concretized the provisions of the above enterprise law and laid the foundation for the introduction of company law so as to end the reform of contractual relationship and embark on the reform of property rights relationships.

2.3 Establishing the goal of socialist market economy and innovating the realization form of public ownership

After undergoing the previous control power reform of SOEs and the incremental reform of the non-public sectors, the market-oriented reform has made some progress in China, and the shortage of necessities has been gradually resolved. By 1992, the GDP for the whole year was 2,719.45 billion yuan, and the per capita GDP reached 2,334 yuan. In the 1990s, affected by the previous political turmoil and severe inflation in 1988, coupled with the impact of the disintegration of the Soviet Union on the socialist system, more and more Chinese people began to suspect the path of market-oriented reform, which triggered a nationwide debate revolving around the following questions: Is market economy "capitalist" or "socialist"? How can we define the relationship between a planned economy and a market economy?

Amid the controversies about marketization, Deng Xiaoping specially made remarks during his inspection tour of south China in 1992, which finally settled the disputes about the planned economy and market economy, defined their relationship, and set the tone for the Fourteenth National Congress of the CPC to decide to establish a socialist market economy as the goal of reform and innovate the ways to materialize the public ownership. In his remarks, Deng pointed out that "the proportion of planning to market forces is not the essential difference between socialism and capitalism. A planned economy is not equivalent to socialism, because there is planning under capitalism too; a market economy is not capitalism, because there are markets under socialism too. Planning and market forces are both means of controlling economic activity. The essence of socialism is liberation and development of the productive forces, elimination of exploitation and polarization, and the ultimate achievement of prosperity for all".[23] Deng put forward the "three favorables" criteria for judging the nature ("capitalist" or "socialist") of ownership system and resolved people's suspicion about the market-oriented reform.

In October 1992, the Fourteenth National Congress decided to establish a socialist market economy as the goal of reform. In May 1993, the Political Bureau of the CPC Central Committee decided to discuss the topic of building a socialist market economy at the Third Plenary Session of the 14th CPC Central Committee.

In the process of transition to a market economy, apart from price adjustment, resource allocation, and the establishment of a fair and legal market platform, the cultivation of independent market players is also of crucial significance. Despite the previous reforms, the ultimate ownership and management of SOEs were yet separated, and enterprises remained as administrative units to a great extent. Moreover, the property rights relationship inside enterprises became even more ambiguous. The integration of SOEs with the market economy thus became an important issue.

When drafting the decision of the Third Plenary Session of the 14th CPC Central Committee, the then General Secretary of the CPC Central Committee Jiang Zemin presented an important question to the draftsmen: Whether public ownership, state-owned sector and market economy can be integrated? If so, how can we do that? If the relationship among public ownership, SOEs and market economy cannot be resolved, then in order to adhere to the public ownership and state-owned sector, we have to return to the planned economy or exchange public ownership for the market economy. Apparently, neither of them is an acceptable outcome.[24]

Before the Third Plenary Session of the 14th CPC Central Committee decided to establish a modern corporate system, some economists had organized discussions on SOE reform and realization of public ownership based on the previous price reform. In the debate on reform strategy in 1986, some economists argued that the reform of the operating mechanism of the socialist economy must be based on the premise of the reform of the ownership system. Li Yining (1987) pointed out that under the traditional planned economy, direct government involvement in the operation of enterprises owned by the whole people had all along been taken as the only correct way. For traditional SOEs, based on state ownership, everyone has a share in state-owned properties but bears no responsibility for the profits and losses of their operations; as the owner of enterprises, the State possesses their properties and provides assistance to them for various reasons, which has made enterprises suffer from the chronic disease of soft budget constraints, and it is hard for them to operate independently and assume sole responsibility for their own profits and losses.[25] According to Dong Fureng (1987), the reform of state ownership is to build enterprises into market players that operate independently and takes responsibility for their own profits and losses. He suggested that large and medium-sized SOEs should introduce the shareholding system to realize the state ownership reform, and the standardized shareholding system should be combined with the non-standardized contracting system. By adopting the approach of "contracting before shareholding, shareholding before contracting, contracting but shareholding or shareholding but contracting", SOEs may bring in non-state-owned entities (including employees) into their shareholders and let the State only act as a capital owner in the board of directors. Due to the restraint of other stakeholders, the State can no longer directly issue orders to enterprises as in the past, thereby promoting the separation of government functions from enterprise management and developing enterprises into an independent business entity.[26]

Based on plentiful researches and investigations, the Third Plenary Session of the 14th CPC Central Committee held in November 1993 adopted the *Decision on Some Issues Concerning the Establishment of the Socialist Market Economy*, proposing the target model of building a socialist market economy, and the combination of public ownership, state-owned sector and market economy by establishing a modern enterprise system. The Decision pointed out that "the establishment of a socialist market economy is to let the market play an essential role in the allocation of resources under the state macro-control. In order to achieve this goal, we must adhere to the principle of maintaining the public sector playing a dominant role and diverse sectors of the economy developing side by side, and further transform the operating mechanism of state-owned enterprises, establish a modern enterprise system that meets the requirements of the market economy and has clearly established ownership, well-defined rights and responsibilities, separation of ownership from management, and scientific management". "The establishment of a modern enterprise system is an inevitable requirement for developing socialized production and market economy, and is the direction of China's state-owned enterprise reform. Its basic characteristics are as follows: First, it has a clarified property rights relationship. All state-owned properties of an enterprise belong to the State, while the enterprise has all the legal person's property rights based on all the investments including those from the State, and serves as a legal entity enjoying civil rights and bearing civil liabilities. Second, with all of its corporate properties, an enterprise operates independently according to the law, assumes sole responsibility for its own profits and losses, pays taxes as required, and undertakes the due obligations for preserving and increasing the value of investors' properties. Third, investors enjoy the owner's equity based on the amount of their investment into the enterprise, that is, they enjoy the rights to benefit from assets, make major decisions, and choose managers, etc., when the enterprise goes bankrupt, investors shall bear limited liability for the debts of the enterprise only in the amount of capital invested in the enterprise. Fourth, enterprises organize production and operation according to market demand with the goal of improving labor productivity and economic benefits. The government does not directly intervene in the production and business activities of enterprises. In the market competition, enterprises shall follow the law of survival of the fittest, those with long-term losses and insolvency shall go bankrupt in accordance with the law. Fifth, a scientific enterprise leadership system and organizational management system shall be established for regulating the relationships among owners, operators and employees, and forming an operating mechanism that combines incentives and constraints".[27]

On the basis of the previous reform of corporate control power, China has, for the first time, promoted the SOE reform through the transformation of property rights relationships of enterprises and proposed to establish a modern enterprise system to innovate the realization form of public ownership. Through the establishment of a modern enterprise system which separates the ownership of investors from the property rights of corporate legal persons and also separates government functions from enterprise management, Chinese SOEs will get rid of dependence on administrative organs, and at the same time, the State will assume limited liability for enterprises, which is conducive to avoiding risks.

Based on the Decision made at the Third Plenary Session of the 14th CPC Central Committee, the *Company Law of the People's Republic of China* was adopted at the National People's Congress in 1993, specifying the establishment of the property rights system of corporate legal persons, defining and regulating the power boundary between enterprises and investors in legal form. Article 4 of the Company Law provides that "a company enjoys all legal person property rights constituted by the shareholders' investment, enjoys civil rights and assumes civil liabilities in accordance with law".[28] The legal person's property rights under the company system and the management rights under the ownership of the whole people have different meanings: First, unlike the property rights of corporate legal persons, the management rights do not include the right to earnings. Second, the property rights of corporate legal persons are independent, and they are routine powers relative to other civil rights. As far as ownership is concerned, management rights are derived from ownership and they are relative rights. An enterprise founded under the legal person property rights system will become a legal person enjoying civil rights and assuming civil obligations, and it is no longer an appendage of the government. And its independent operation is protected by law.

The modern enterprise system, which is mainly in the form of a company system, serves as the carrier of the combination of public ownership and market economy. The legal person governance mechanism based on the modern company system has clarified the separation of power and responsibility and the mutual checks and balances in the process of ownership realization. With the modern enterprise system as the carrier, the state-owned assets are placed under value-based management, equity allocation, privatization, and market-oriented flow, and public ownership is combined with the market economy in an organic manner, which has laid the micro-foundation for the socialist market economy. While maintaining the dominant position of the public sector, we should encourage and allow different economic sectors to develop side by side according to the "three favorables" criteria. Through the value-based allocation, state-owned assets may be contained in the mixed sectors of the economy. Moreover, such approaches as becoming shareholders or controlling shareholders have made it possible to expand the influence and control of public ownership.[29]

Through the capital game between different investors under the modern enterprise system, we have promoted the transformation of government functions, distinguished investment from capital use and separated government functions from enterprise management and then separated state-owned assets from particular SOEs. As the investor and owner, the government exercises shareholder's power by voting with hand and realizes the market-oriented allocation and value-based management of state-owned assets through voting with feet. Thus, enterprises have become market-oriented entities that operate independently and assume responsibility for their own profits and losses. The report delivered at the Fifteenth National Congress also pointed out that the ways to realize public ownership can be and should be diversified. All business practices and organizational forms that reflect the laws of socialized production can be used boldly. Efforts should be made to find a form of public ownership that can greatly promote the development of productive forces. A shareholding system is a form of capital organization of modern enterprises, which is conducive to separating ownership from management and improving the operational efficiency of enterprises and capital. It is applicable to both capitalist and socialist economies. In general, we cannot say whether the shareholding system is public or private since it is decided by the one who has a controlling stake. The state and collective holdings, which of course belong to the public sector, will help expand the scope of control of public capital and consolidate the dominant role of public ownership.[30]

To innovate the ways for realizing public ownership through the modern enterprise system and the constraints of property rights, on the one hand, it will gradually cultivate enterprises to be independent market entities and stimulate them to have more economic rationality as market entities while maintaining the influence and control of the public ownership; on the other hand, it will make the liquidity allocation of state-owned assets possible, provide theoretical support for the later strategic adjustment of state-owned assets, and promote the establishment and improvement of the state-owned assets management system. While promoting the establishment of a modern enterprise system, we have come to realize the need to set up a sound state-owned assets system for their management, operation, and supervision, which will help speed up the SOE reform and establish a modern enterprise system.[31] In 1999, the Fourth Plenary Session of the 15th CPC Central Committee explicitly stated that we should, by following the principles of state ownership, hierarchical management, authorized operation, division of labor, and supervision, gradually establish a state-owned assets management, supervision and operation mechanism. It also brought forth the concept of state-owned investors, clarified that state-owned assets management is different from specific SOE operations, and called upon the Chinese people to keep pressing ahead with establishing a modern enterprise system and improving the construction of market entities under the socialist market economy.

2.4 Development of non-public sectors and SOE reform

In the process of reform and opening up, under the influence of the traditional planned economy and the Soviet Union's "state ownership" theory, the development of the non-public economy in China still had ideological constraints. Under the background that the SOE reform was facing great difficulties, and reform measures such as "delegation of powers and transfer of profits" failed to score significant results, leaders such as Deng Xiaoping shifted their focus to the development of the non-public sectors and brought forth a "non-argument" strategy for doing so. They suggested implementing a dual-track system to end the monopoly of the state-owned sector and foster the non-public sectors, which has expanded the space for implementing more reform policies.

In the late 1970s, more than 15 million educated youths who were sent to rural areas to take part in manual labor returned to cities. How to help such a huge population find a job became an urgent problem in front of the government. In this case, the Central Government issued a document stating that "laborers can engage in individual industrial and commercial production and business". In February 1979, the State Administration for Industry and Commerce (SAIC) pointed out in a meeting that local governments should approve the idle laborers with a registered permanent residence to engage in repairs, services and handicrafts, but do not allow them to hire workers. At the end of the year, the number of self-employed individuals nationwide had increased to 310,000.

With the development of the market, when a single business owner finds it hard to expand production by himself, he desires to hire workers. In actual production, the number of individual businesses employing more than eight people had gradually increased, giving rise to many disputes. In January 1983, Deng Xiaoping commented that "some individual employees have violated the regulations of the State Council to hire employees, but it will not undermine socialism. As long as we stick to the right direction and keep a clear mind, this problem can never beat us".[32] The individual economy kept developing but in a low profile since it was not openly encouraged or explicitly prohibited. In Wuhu City, Anhui Province, a man running a store, "Fool's Sunflower Seeds", hired more than 100 employees at that time, which caused great controversies. Deng Xiaoping made a comment about this event in October 1983, "How can it affect our overall situation? If you take some action, the masses may say the policies are not reliable and feel uneasy. If you put the man who makes 'Fool's Sunflower Seeds' out of business, it will make many people anxious, and that won't do anybody any good".[33]

At the Sixth Plenary Session of the 12th CPC Central Committee held in 1986, a statement was made that "our country is still in the primary stage of socialism. We should not only implement distribution according to work, develop a socialist commodity economy and competition, but also develop diverse sectors of the economy over a long historical period under the premise of maintaining the dominant position of the public sector".[34] In this way, the private economy was able to continue developing, although not prescribed by law. By the end of 1986, there had been 12.11 million individual industrial and commercial households nationwide with 18.46 million employees.

In rural areas, the biggest reform was to lift the ban on "work contracted to households" and "fixing output quotas on the household basis". In 1980, the CPC Central Committee issued a document stating that "in those remote mountainous areas and impoverished areas, for quite a long time the production teams are 'buying grain for food after grain rendering, sustaining production based on loans, and making a living on relief', the masses have already lost confidence in the collectives. Therefore, if any household wants contracted work or fixed output quotas, we should give them support, and maintain this contract system unchanged for a long time to come".[35]

With the implementation of "fixing output quotas on the household basis", the rural economy took on a new look, and township and village enterprises dominated by collective ownership were also in a boom. The State began to focus on the reform of non-state-owned sectors by establishing market-oriented enterprises and implementing the "incremental reform" strategy (see Table 2.1).

In terms of absorbing foreign capital, after the reform and opening-up policy was established at the Third Plenary Session of the 11th CPC Central Committee in 1978, the *Law of the People's Republic of China on Chinese-Foreign Joint Ventures* was issued in 1979 to confirm the adoption of preferential policies for encouraging foreign direct investment. From 1979 to 1988, China established five special economic zones and opened 14 coastal cities. The introduction of foreign capital, on the one hand, brought in

Table 2.1 Total industrial output value of diverse economic sectors and their proportions (unit: billion yuan)

Year	Total industrial output value	State-owned industry	Collective industry	Urban and rural individual industry	Other economic types[*]
1978	423.7	328.9 (77.63%[**])	94.8 (22.37%)	0 (0%)	0 (0%)
1980	515.4	391.6 (75.98%)	121.3 (23.54%)	0.1 (0.02%)	2.4 (0.48%)
1985	971.6	630.2 (64.86%)	311.7 (32.08%)	18 (1.85%)	11.7 (1.20%)
1990	2,392.4	1,306.4 (54.61%)	852.3 (35.63%)	129 (5.39%)	104.7 (4.38%)

Source: *China Statistical Yearbook 1998.*

Notes
*Other economic types refer to public-private partnerships and private industries, the same below.
**Datum in brackets means relative value.

foreign advanced technologies, and on the other hand, improved the management capabilities of Chinese SOEs by learning from their foreign counterparts in corporate organization, management, and market operation.

At this stage, in order to solve the problems of urban employment and shortage of necessities, the non-public sectors had kept developing in the absence of government recognition. Since the non-public businesses were small-sized and mainly concentrated in light industry and operated by individuals, they did not cause any direct impact on the state-owned sector. The growth of the non-public sectors had stimulated the development of the market under the dual-track system, then the formation of an external market environment began to influence the management decisions of SOEs. At the time when the reform of non-state-owned sectors had scored some achievements and provided support for urban reform, Deng Xiaoping, initiator of "incremental reform", pointed out in June 1984 that we should "shift the focus of reform from the countryside to the cities. The urban reform will include not only industry and commerce but science and technology, education and all other fields of endeavor as well".[36] In October 1984, the Third Plenary Session of the 12th CPC Central Committee adopted the *Decision on Reform of the Economic Structure*, proposing to "speed up the reform of the entire economic structure with cities as the focus" and "develop a socialist commodity economy"; and confirmed that "the full development of commodity economy is an insurmountable stage of social and economic development and a necessary condition for realizing China's economic modernization. Only by fully developing the commodity economy can the economy be truly invigorated, and enterprises can be encouraged to improve efficiency, operate flexibly, and adapt nimbly to the complex and changing social demands".[37]

While the private sector was playing an increasingly important role and occupying a higher status, the market incremental reform had achieved results gradually, and its legal status was about to be officially recognized. In 1987, the Thirteenth National Congress proposed for the first time that "private economy is a necessary and beneficial supplement to the public economy". According to Article 11 of the *Amendments to the Constitution*, adopted at the First Session of the 7th National People's Congress in April 1988, "the State permits the private sector of the economy to exist and develop within the limits prescribed by law. The private economy is a supplement to the socialist economy under the public ownership. The State protects the lawful rights and interests of the private sector of the economy, and exercises guidance, supervision and control over the private sector of the economy".[38]

After Deng Xiaoping made the important remarks during his inspection tour of south China in 1992, the Fourteenth National Congress decided to establish the basic economic system "with public ownership playing a dominant role and different economic sectors developing side by side", which had boosted the enthusiasm for private investors. In addition to a large number of self-employed businessmen, some employees with SOEs quit their jobs to start their own businesses, thus forming a new upsurge in the development of the non-public sectors. In this process, the quality of entrepreneurs in the non-public sectors was greatly improved. Being motivated by Deng's talks, so many Party and government cadres and undergraduates joined this trend to become self-employed. Their expertise in technologies, customer resources and team management were unmatched by their predecessors in the early stage of reform and opening up. In January 1993, the SAIC made an announcement that "in principle, the production and operation of all industries except those concerning national security and people's health are allowed to have individual and private businesses". By the end of 1993, the number of individual industrial and commercial households nationwide had reached about 17.67 million, with 29.40 million employees; and the number of private enterprises rose 71.2% year-on-year to 238,000, showing that the non-public sectors were able to develop side by side with the public sector.

With the gradual formation of the socialist market economy, the non-public sectors began to directly compete with the public sector in the market. On the one hand, the operations of the non-public sectors are more flexible, and they have no burden of creating job opportunities or subsidizing their employees in their medical insurance, housing and children's education. On the other hand, with the development of the market and implementation of more preferential policies, the non-public businesses began to enter the fields dominated by the public ownership, a seller's market was gradually transforming into a buyer's market, and the phenomenon of making profits only by selling products in the early stage no longer existed.[39] Amid the competition from their non-public rivals, SOEs found it hard to adapt to the market-oriented reform due to their operation mechanism and began to suffer large-scale losses since 1993 (see Figure 2.1). From 1992 to 1997, the number of individual industrial and commercial households increased from

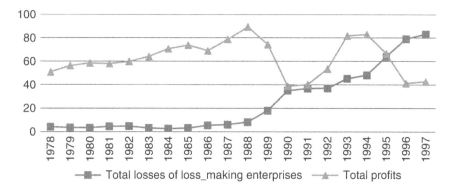

Figure 2.1 Losses of enterprises.
Note: This chart was drawn on the basis of the key financial indicators of the state-owned independent accounting industrial enterprises in *China Statistical Yearbook 1998* (Unit: billion yuan).

15.34 million to 28.5 million, with the number of employees rising from 24.68 million to 54.42 million. During the same period, both the state-owned and collective economies experienced negative growth (Table 2.2). With the opening of the market, the competition between the public and non-public sectors further forced SOEs to advance their reform and triggered the strategic adjustment of the state-owned sector.

By 1995, China had altogether 87,900 independent accounting industrial enterprises, of which 72,200 were small and medium-sized ones, and there were more than 500,000 township and village enterprises. With the deepening of reforms, the government realized that it was too hard to invigorate hundreds of thousands of small and medium-sized SOEs; it was both impossible and unnecessary. Given this, the reform policies changed from "developing all state-owned enterprises" to "invigorating the overall state-owned sector", "classified guidance", and "invigorating large enterprises while relaxing control over small ones". In 1995, in his speech delivered at the Fifth Plenary Session of the 14th CPC Central Committee, Jiang Zemin said that we should "study and formulate the development strategy and layout of the state-owned sector, actively promote the reform of state-owned enterprises in line with the goal of establishing a modern enterprise system, concentrate on rejuvenating large state-owned enterprises and give a freer rein to the small and medium-sized ones to invigorate themselves".[40] Since 1993, the SOEs located in Zhucheng of Shandong and Shunde of Guangdong began to implement the policy of "relaxing control over small enterprises", and carried out the property rights reform centering on the transformation of the subjects of ownership structure. However, due to ideological constraints, this policy was only implemented in a few areas instead of being promoted throughout the country. Fortunately, the State, for the first time, proposed a strategic adjustment of the layout of the state-owned sector, shifting focus from the efficiency of individual SOEs to that of state-owned capital allocation, which played a transitional role for the next-stage reform.

Table 2.2 Total industrial output value of various economic types (unit: billion yuan).

	1993	1994	1995	1996	1997
State-owned industry	2,272.5	2,620.1	3,122	2,836.1	2,902.7
Collective industry	1,646.4	2,647.2	3,362.3	3,923.2	4,334.7
Township industry	537.4	810.2	1,193.2	1,173	
Village industry	516.3	965.8	1,184.7	1,590	1,794
Cooperative joint ventures	132.2	261.1	213.4	338.7	466.9
Urban and rural individual industry	386.1	708.2	1,182.1	1,542	2,037.6
Other economic types	535.2	1,042.1	1,523.1	1,658.2	2,098.2
Total industrial output value	4,840.2	7,017.6	9,189.4	9,959.5	1,173.3

Note: All the data are excerpted from the years' China Statistical Yearbook.

In 1997, the Fifteenth National Congress made it clear that the non-public sectors are an important part of China's socialist market economy. Such a statement was added into the constitutional amendment in 1999, marking that the status of the non-public sectors in China's economic system was established in the Constitution. During the same period, SOEs incurred large-scale losses around 1997. Among the 16,874 large and medium-sized SOEs nationwide, 6,599 were mired in losses. There were many reasons for the dilemma of SOEs, which could be summarized as follows: First, during the Ninth Five-Year Plan period (1996–2000), the State was implementing tight fiscal and monetary policies. In addition to plunging effective domestic demand, the Asian financial crisis in the same year slashed China's foreign trade demand, severely restricting its production capacity. Second, with the development of the market economy, the preferential treatment to SOEs based on their public ownership system gradually disappeared, and the State began to "replace appropriation by loans" for funding these enterprises, which had increased their financial burden. Coupled with the impact of the Asian financial crisis, banks became more cautious about corporate lending. Third, the continuously developing non-public sectors had become a direct rival of SOEs. With the reform and opening up, a large number of foreign-funded enterprises entered China with investments, technologies and advanced management methods and gained a competitive edge in many industries. Local non-public enterprises also made significant progress by taking advantage of lower labor costs. At the same time, in order to get ready to enter the WTO, China began to drastically cut tariffs and open its market even wider. Fourth, SOEs had been accustomed to low-level and repeated construction for years, and their industrial structure between regions tended to be increasingly similar, thus leading to overcapacity. As the buyer's market (at the time of shortage economy) gradually transformed into a seller's market, it was difficult for SOEs to adapt to the new market requirements. Fifth, undertaking too many social functions had made SOEs overburdened. Sixth, the operating mechanism of SOEs had not undergone fundamental transformation.[41]

Facing such a difficult situation, during his inspection tour in July 1997, the then Vice Premier Zhu Rongji proposed to take 3 years to get most large and medium-sized SOEs out of the predicament. In September of the same year, the Fifteenth National Congress pointed out that "the ways of realizing public ownership could be and should be diversified". "We must lay stress on invigorating the entire state-owned sector by properly managing large enterprises and adopting a flexible policy towards small ones. We must implement a strategic reorganization of the state-owned sector, adopt the policy of both advancing and retreating, and keep aware that there are things must be done and things must not be done",[42] which negates the direct connection between the proportion of the state-owned economy and the nature of socialism. With the textile industry as a breakthrough point,

China launched a three-year strategic reform to save the state-owned sector economy out of difficulties. The reform measures included the separation of powers, bankruptcy, reorganization, and decentralization of powers. In the process of reorganization, the biggest problem was to solve the reemployment and social security of laid-off workers. Apart from the government assistance, the rapidly developing non-public sectors provided a buffer for the strategic reorganization of SOEs; their job opportunities for laid-off workers had reduced the resistance to the strategic reorganization of SOEs. In June 1998, the State Council issued the *Notice on Doing a Good Job in Guaranteeing the Basic Living and Reemployment of Laid-off Workers from State-owned Enterprises*, proposing that we should solve the reemployment problem of laid-off workers by developing private and small and medium-sized enterprises, implement preferential financial and taxation policies, and in the meantime eliminate the ideological obstacles to the development of the private sector. In this way, the state-owned and non-state-owned sectors will integrate and develop together in the process of "reorganization".[43] By 2000, state-owned and state-holding enterprises had realized a total profit of 239.2 billion yuan, turning losses into profits. After 2004, with the improvement of the external environment, the profitability of SOEs began to turn for the better, the SOE reform was no longer as vigorous as before, and the phenomena known as "renationalization" or "new nationalization" were sometimes reported by the media.

At the Third Plenary Session of the 18th CPC Central Committee in 2013, the Party Central Committee proposed to further promote the reform of mixed ownership and strengthen the cooperation between state-owned capital and private capital, making mixed-ownership an important way to realize the basic economic system.

Li Yining (2014) pointed out that mixed ownership can bring together the strong capital advantage of the state-owned sector and the flexible mechanism of the private sector, which is conducive to mixed enterprises' going global without the restriction of other countries and also to their success despite a small size. The mixed-ownership reform is an opportunity for cooperation between state-owned capital and private capital. After the reform, it will be possible for SOEs to obtain a double-sided win, and private enterprises can compete and cooperate with their state-owned counterparts on an equal footing.[44]

Taking the mixed ownership as a breakthrough in the new round of SOE reform will benefit the development of the public and non-public economies and their integration. But mixed ownership is not "a panacea". The commercialization of corporate governance in modern enterprises is not as simple as the transformation of the ownership structure, these must be a credible legal system for protecting the legitimate rights and interests of each shareholder, then it will be possible to sustain corporate governance and enable enterprises to develop on the right track.

2.5 The "Catfish Effect" of non-public enterprises and the vitality of SOEs

Huang Qunhui et al. (2017) pointed out that the vitality of SOEs must come from the result of fair competition. As enterprises under the socialist market economy, SOEs cannot become truly vigorous unless they establish firm footing in the market, only in this way can the superiority of the basic socialist economic system be demonstrated in a better way; no SOE can maintain its vitality if it departs from the market.[45] The competition and demonstration brought by the emerging non-public sectors have not only provided a buffer for the SOE reform but also injected vitality into the state-owned sector and stimulated the rational return and market vitality of SOEs as market players. The impact of the non-public sectors on the vitality of SOEs is reflected in the following five aspects:

First, the market-oriented development driven by the non-public sectors of the economy requires SOEs to transform their operating mechanisms. SOEs that have grown up under the traditional economic system are highly administrative, while the non-public sectors that emerged through incremental reforms have kept developing along with the progress of marketization, so their property rights structure, governance structure, business management, marketing, and organizational structure can better adapt to the market (Chen Xian, 1999).[46] The changes in the market environment caused by the development of non-public enterprises have stimulated the transformation of SOEs' operating mechanisms. On the one hand, such transformation is an adjustment to continuously adapt to changes in the external environment, and on the other hand, an active or passive adjustment to cope with the competition from non-public enterprises. For example, as the main means for companies to compete in the market, marketing is a key link in business operations. Traditional SOEs did not need marketing at all in the era of planned economy and shortage economy. However, with the development of the non-public sectors and increasingly fierce market competition, SOEs have begun to learn marketing strategies from non-public enterprises (including the foreign-funded ones) and pay attention to cultivating enterprise brands. Several SOEs did make a hit in marketing, like Shanghai Jahwa United Co., Ltd. Besides, the internal organizational structure of traditional SOEs is highly administrative, making them hard to adapt to the rapid changes in the market. By learning from the organizational structure of foreign enterprises and the operation of domestic non-public sectors, SOEs have established a more standardized governance structure, including (general) meeting of stockholders, board of directors, and board of supervisors. They are more and more integrated with the market and gradually able to accustomed to the constant changes in the market.

Second, the market development driven by the non-public sectors requires the removal of the historical burdens of SOEs. Lin Yifu et al. (2014) pointed out that Chinese SOEs have, for quite a long time, remained a vital means for creating job opportunities, which has brought them too many redundant employees. SOEs themselves seem like a society performing several governmental functions, including guaranteeing employment, medical care, living security and social insurance, which has increased their financial burdens and affected their market operation.[47] With the development of the non-public economy, the State started establishing a social security system so as to make SOEs concentrate on market operation. In addition, the non-public sectors have absorbed a large number of laid-off workers from SOEs, thus facilitating them to keep the reform of downsizing for efficiency.

Third, the development of the non-public sectors has a far-reaching impact on the operation of SOEs. As the main body for implementing the state production plans, traditional SOEs are engaged in production mainly for product output. Faced with the non-public enterprises that have cost advantages, SOEs have changed their focus of production from output to cost and carried out business operations to make profits. Thus, these enterprises have seen the status of their purchasing and sales departments become increasingly prominent. And in order to improve economic efficiency, they have to cut costs in production, management and sales (Zhang Huiming, 1998).[48] Since entering the 21st century, the emerging Internet economy has boosted the development of related industries, making the accumulation of human capital, innovation and R&D become increasingly important for enterprises. Under the pressure that foreign-funded and private enterprises have advantages in R&D, human capital investment, SOEs have stepped up efforts in technological research through various approaches such as independent R&D, technical cooperation and equity merger, forming a group of companies with independent intellectual property rights and international competitiveness, such as CRRC and CNNC.

Fourth, the development of the non-public sectors has also led to the property rights reform of SOEs. Under the traditional system, the nature of the property rights of the SOEs (as part of the sector owned by the whole people) was not clear. The ownership of enterprises was not separated from their management, and the allocation of state-owned capital was bound up with particular enterprises, making the property rights of SOEs lack mobility. With the development of the market, on the one hand, in order to expand enterprise autonomy and establish a modern enterprise system, the property rights relationship between an enterprise and its investors must be clarified; on the other hand, the non-public enterprises with clear property rights have demonstrated prominent advantages in market competition, which has triggered SOEs to redefine their property rights. Clear property rights between an enterprise and its investors are able to become a trading object. Based on the separation of ownership from management, the State, as an investor of SOEs, has shifted focus from assets management to capital management, which has created conditions for the market-oriented transactions of state-owned capital and the cross integration of non-public and state-owned capital.

Fifth, the non-public sectors have an integration effect on the reform of SOEs. In the process of establishing a modern enterprise system for SOEs, multiple investors have played an active role, which is of vital importance for expanding the influence and control of state-owned capital and forming a fair competition pattern. Diversified investors are one of the basic characteristics of the modern enterprise system. The development of the non-public sectors and the growth of their scale make it possible to integrate their property rights with those of the public sector. In the process of integrating state-owned and non-state-owned capital, the total social capital is increased and the fields with SOEs have subject to structural adjustment, which has, on the one hand, built up the overall economic strength of the state-owned sector, and on the other hand, stimulated state-owned and non-state-owned capital to play a role in their respective areas of strength. For a long time, the State has implemented different management systems and policies to SOEs and other enterprises, and the former usually enjoy more preferential policies than the latter. Since more and more mixed enterprises have emerged because of the integration of state-owned and non-state-owned capital, a continuously improving market environment for fair competition will drive the advancement of marketization and invigorate SOEs.

2.6 The deepening of enterprise reform requires fundamental changes in the state-owned capital management system

With the separation of ownership from management triggered by the modern enterprise system, the reform of the traditional state-owned assets management system has become an inevitable requirement for developing the modern enterprise system. As early as 1993, when the Third Plenary Session of the 14th CPC Central Committee decided to establish a modern enterprise system, it also brought forth the task of reforming the state-owned assets management system. However, the State must remain cautious when reforming this system since it concerns the national basic economic system. In 1997, the Fifteenth National Congress presented that the state-owned sector should be aware that "there are things must be done and things must not be done", and that "the state-owned assets management, operation, and supervision system needs to be improved". The Fourth Plenary Session of the 14th CPC Central Committee in 1999 proposed to establish a state-owned assets management system that is capable of "state ownership, hierarchical management, authorized operation, division of labor, and supervision". After the establishment of the SASAC in 2003, the management system for "administering assets, personnel and other affairs" was implemented for the SASAC-funded enterprises.

The traditional state-owned capital management system has so many drawbacks. It is in need of being transformed as the enterprise reform keeps deepening. The shortcomings of the traditional state-owned capital management system are mainly manifested in the following six aspects:

First, unclear property rights and responsibilities arising from state ownership, hierarchical management and overlapping management.[49] In an enterprise with capital owned by the whole people, it is the State that acts as its investor. After its establishment in 2003, the SASAC started uniformly exercising the powers of an investor on behalf of the State, but the boundaries of rights and responsibilities between the Central and local governments, between government organs, state-owned assets, investment institutions and enterprises remained unclarified, and complete incentive and restraint mechanisms were still absent. Different government organs could exercise part of the owner's power based on their administrative affiliation without assuming any responsibility for their actions. In fact, state-owned capital was caught in a situation of unclarified powers and responsibilities.

Second, investor and capital user or government functions and enterprise management are not separated; and SOEs, as the main body of administration, are incompatible with the market economic system. The government not only acts as an agent implementing the ownership of the state-owned asset but also performs functions in public administration. With the development of all economic sectors, the conflict between the government as a state-owned assets investor and administrator of public utilities has begun to emerge. Due to its de facto dual functions, the government is treating different companies unequally while exercising public power and implementing resource allocation. The government is both an athlete and a referee, thus making SOEs highly administrative and incompatible with equal market competition like other enterprises.

Third, in the process of specific state-owned assets management, the state-owned assets investor performs its duties for capital contribution; but in the process of "administering assets, personnel and other affairs", the state-owned assets investor is not operating state-owned capital as an investor, but taking over management of SOEs directly, thus confusing ownership and management. Inside large and medium-sized SOEs, when the state-owned capital investor performs its functions as an investor, it usually surpasses the corporate governance organs like the meeting of shareholders and board of directors and directly exercises the rights to ownership over the subsidiaries and sub-subsidiaries funded by its invested company. As a result, the independent legal person status of these subsidiaries and sub-subsidiaries is denied, and the incentive and restraint mechanism of property rights is weakened.

Fourth, in an environment with overlapping management of government organs, the internal owners of enterprises exist in name only, the corporate governance mechanism is incomplete, and insider control makes the loss of state-owned capital serious. The government exercises the powers of investors but not assumes responsibility for its actions, and the corporate internal governance mechanism is incomplete, which has made insider control ubiquitous. Although the government as an investor can implement supervision through external regulation and other means, the information asymmetry has given rise to the phenomena of haphazard investment, misreporting performance, borrowing heavily, and privately dividing state-owned assets inside enterprises. Some enterprises are, in fact, controlled by insiders, with state ownership having no substantive meaning.

Fifth, under the traditional state-owned assets management system, SOEs also perform social functions that should be undertaken by the government, which has lowered the operating efficiency of state-owned capital and made it difficult to accurately assess the performance of state-funded enterprises. According to Lin Yifu et al. (2014), SOEs are taken as a tool by the government to perform social and public functions in specific scenarios since they are owned by the whole people. In addition to organizing production, these enterprises have to take care of childbirth, old age and illness, and even children's schooling of their employees. Running social services has increased the financial burden of SOEs, resulting in the redundancy of employees and lower operating efficiency. Moreover, since SOEs perform social functions, it is difficult for the government to accurately assess the operating efficiency of state-owned assets of enterprises. And when the performance of an enterprise is not satisfying, administrators are prone to pass the buck, which makes the incentive and restraint mechanism invalid.[50]

Sixth, when the property rights of corporate legal persons are fully established, the State as an investor assumes unlimited responsibility for its funded enterprises. The Company Law has established the property rights of corporate legal persons at the legislative level and specified that the State, as an investor, shall only bear limited liability for the invested enterprise to the limit of the capital invested, however, under the influence of the traditional system, people tend to believe that corporate property is part of state property, and there is no distinction between state ownership and the property rights of corporate legal persons, thus blurring the boundary between government and corporate properties. Compared with other enterprises, SOEs have a higher debt ratio, and their operators even speculate in the housing or stock market with loans since they bear no responsibility for the performance of their enterprises, while the State has to assume unlimited responsibility for these enterprises.

With the deepening of the SOE reform and the establishment of the modern enterprise system, it has become necessary for us to innovate the traditional state-owned assets management system, distinguish the reform of SOEs from that of the state-owned assets management system, and define the property rights relationship between the State as an investor and the enterprise as an independent corporate legal person. After the Third Plenary Session of the 18th CPC Central Committee in 2013, the State started a new round of SOE reform and put forward new requirements for the state-owned assets management system. The policy requires the transformation of the functions of state-owned assets regulators by placing focus on capital management. State-owned capital operation or investment companies shall be established to facilitate the rational flow of state-owned capital and optimize its allocation with capital management at the core, keep aware that there are things that must be done and things that must not be done, and promote the unified management of operational state-owned assets.

The innovation of the state-owned assets management system from "assets management" to "capital management" has turned the State's management of state-owned assets into "value-based management". Under the premise of guaranteeing the State ownership, the focus of the reform is to preserve and increase the value of state-owned assets, gradually separate government functions from the specific business management, integrate the State as a state-owned capital investor and invested enterprises with the market economy, define the power boundary of the investor, and distinguish the reform of the state-owned assets management system from that of particular SOEs, which has laid the foundation for further deepening the reform of SOEs and developing the mixed sectors. We should innovate the state-owned assets management system by establishing state-owned assets operational or investment companies. Through authorized operation, we can change the non-separation of investor and capital user and the non-separation of government and enterprises caused by the traditional system that "administers assets, personnel and other affairs", realize the marketization of operational state-owned capital, change the phenomenon of power rent-seeking arising from ownership of the whole people manifested as the state ownership, state ownership as government ownership, and government ownership as department ownership under the traditional system, so as to help the government get rid of the burden of specific business operations and integrate the operation of state-owned capital with the market.

In summary, with the advancement of the SOE reform, the relationship between the enterprise system and the capital structure has been continuously deepened from interest relationship constraints to contract constraints and property rights constraints. The state-run factory system established at the preliminary stage has profound historical reasons. Under this system, the primary goal of the enterprise as an administrative appendage of the government is to implement the state production plan; the government takes over all the behaviors of the enterprise and has created a supporting external economic environment for this purpose. The State is both the owner and the operator of an enterprise, responsible for its profits and losses and assuming unlimited responsibilities for the enterprise. After the reform and opening up, with the gradual establishment of market mechanisms, it is necessary to build enterprises into microeconomic entities compatible with market mechanisms and able to take part in the market competition. Enterprises have larger autonomy and ever more important status as corporate legal persons. The promulgation of the *Law of Industrial Enterprises Owned by the Whole People* has transformed the operating mechanism of enterprises from state-owned or state-run to state-owned but independently managed by enterprises. However, since the enterprises wholly owned by the whole people are state-funded, the State still assumes unlimited liability to these enterprises, which have no independent legal person property rights. This enterprise system is unstable and transitional. Under this organizational system, state-owned capital lacks liquidity and cannot enter the market.

With the deepening of reforms, our understanding of SOEs has also deepened. The promulgation of the Company Law, for the first time, established the independent legal person status and legal person property rights of enterprises in law. Since then, the reform of SOEs was gradually replaced by the reform for invigorating the state-owned sector by implementing strategic adjustment to the state-owned economy and establishing a modern enterprise system. As a result of such strategic adjustment, state-owned assets began to enter the market and the concept of "state-owned investors" was thereby introduced. The capital game between different owners brought about by the diversification of the property rights inside enterprises is extremely important for establishing a modern enterprise system. SOEs have got a new definition as "state-funded enterprises". State-owned investors and other investors under the modern enterprise system can cooperate in the same enterprise on an equal basis, and the enterprises established by other investors have the same legal status in the market. By separating the ownership of state-owned investors from corporate property rights, enterprises have become independent legal entities. The organizational structure of diversified funding under the modern enterprise system is an innovation in the realization form of public ownership. State-owned assets can be distributed to different industrial fields through marketized allocation, realizing the mutual integration of diversified capital, and solving the deep-seated problem of integrating state-owned ownership with a market economy on a microscopic basis. We can illustrate the evolution of China's enterprise system and the deepening of capital relations in the process of SOE reform (see Figure 2.2).

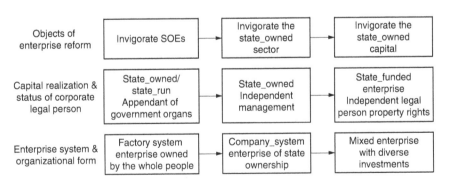

Figure 2.2 The evolution of the enterprise system and the deepening of capital relations brought forth by reform.

From the three levels summarized in Figure 2.2, we can see the trajectory of the continuously deepened enterprise reform and its impact on the transformation of the entire economic system. From the perspective of market development, we can learn that market orientation stimulates the improvement of the functioning of market mechanisms, which inevitably requires the transformation of the organizational and institutional forms adopted for the main body of market activities so as to promote the enterprise organizational system itself to accord with the characteristics of the market economy and make the enterprise organization a new type of carrier for solving the organic combination of public ownership and market economy. As the main body of social reproduction activities, enterprises have acquired independent legal person property rights and become a truly independent economic, legal person and dynamic main body of market operations.

Notes

1 Bo, Y. B. (1991). *Review of some major decisions and events* (Vol. 1, pp. 46–66). Beijing: CPC Central Party School Press.
2 Zhang, H. M. (1998). *The logic of China's state-owned enterprise reform* (pp. 100–103). Taiyuan: Shanxi Economic Publishing House.
3 Wu, J. L. (2016). *Tutorial of economic reform of contemporary China* (p. 180). Shanghai: Shanghai Far East Publishers.
4 Lenin. (1995). *Lenin Collected Works* (Vol. 3, p. 202). Beijing: People's Publishing House.
5 Zhang, H. M. (1998). *The logic of China's state-owned enterprise reform* (pp. 105–107). Taiyuan: Shanxi Economic Publishing House.
6 Chen, Y. (1986). New issues after the basic completion of socialist transformation. *Selected works of Chen Yun* (Vol. 3, pp. 1–13). Beijing: People's Publishing House.
7 Mao, Z. D. (1999). On the ten major relationships. *Selected works of Mao Zedong* (Vol. 7, pp. 23–49). Beijing: People's Publishing House.
8 Wu, J. L. (2016). *Tutorial of economic reform of contemporary China* (p. 57). Shanghai: Shanghai Far East Publishers.
9 Deng, X. P. (1994). Emancipate the mind, seek truth from facts and unite as one in looking to the future. *Selected works of Deng Xiaoping* (Vol. 2, p. 150). Beijing: People's Publishing House.
10 Deng, X. P. (1994). Several opinions on economic work. *Selected works of Deng Xiaoping* (Vol. 2, p. 200). Beijing: People's Publishing House.
11 Translator's note: "everyone eating from the same big pot" is to describe an equalitarian practice which should be interpreted from two aspects: (1) Enterprises are "fed" by the State regardless of their operating results. (2) All employees of an enterprise have their wages paid in full amount and on time despite their performance.
12 Chen, Q. T. (2008). Reshaping the enterprise system: 30 years' changes on China's enterprise system (p. 7). Beijing: China Development Press.
13 Wu, J. L. (2016). *Tutorial of economic reform of contemporary China* (p. 153). Shanghai: Shanghai Far East Publishers.
14 He, Y. M. (2003). Expanding powers and transferring profits: A breakthrough in state-owned enterprise reform – interview with Comrade Yuan Baohua. *Journal of Hundred Year Tide*, Issue 8.

15 Deng, X. P. (1994). Emancipate the mind, seek truth from facts and unite as one in looking to the future. *Selected works of Deng Xiaoping* (Vol. 2, p. 150). Beijing: People's Publishing House.

16 *Opinions on several issues concerning the implementation of the economic responsibility system for industrial production.* Retrieved November 11, 1971, from https://wenku.baidu.com/view/c5495c9fe97101f69e3143323968011ca300f7f4.html

17 Translator's note: "One Link" indicates that the total wages of employees are linked to the realization of taxes and profits.

18 Zhang, H. M. (1998). *The logic of China's state-owned enterprise reform* (pp. 100–103). Taiyuan: Shanxi Economic Publishing House.

19 Ding, J. T. (1982). How does Shougang Group implement the economic responsibility system? *Economic Management Journal*, Issue 3.

20 Deng, X. P. (1994). On the reform of the system of party and state leadership. *Selected works of Deng Xiaoping* (Vol. 2, p. 140). Beijing: People's Publishing House.

21 *Law of the People's Republic of China of industrial enterprises owned by the whole people* (p. 2). (1997). Beijing: China Legal Publishing House.

22 Kong, X. J. (1996). Study on the property rights of corporate legal persons – the inevitable trend from management rights, legal person's property rights to legal person's ownership. *Journal of Renmin University of China*, Issue 3.

23 Deng, X. P. (1993). Excerpts from talks given in Wuchang, Shenzhen, Zhuhai and Shanghai. *Selected works of Deng Xiaoping* (Vol. 3, p. 373). Beijing: People's Publishing House.

24 Chen, Q. T. (2008). Reshaping the enterprise system: 30 years' changes on China's enterprise system (p. 35). Beijing: China Development Press.

25 Li, Y. N. (1987). Explorations into the socialist ownership system. *Hebei Academic Journal*, Issue 1.

26 Dong, F. R. (1987). Ownership reform and economic operating mechanism reform. *Journal of Graduate School of Chinese Academy of Social Sciences*, Issue 1.

27 *Decision on some issues concerning the establishment of the socialist market economy.* Retrieved November 14, 1993, from http://www.people.com.cn/item/2 0years/newfiles/b1080.html

28 *Company law of the People's Republic of China* (p. 3). (2014). Beijing: China Legal Publishing House.

29 Zhang, H. M. (1998). *The logic of China's state-owned enterprise reform* (pp. 134–139). Taiyuan: Shanxi Economic Publishing House.

30 The report titled *Hold high the great banner of Deng Xiaoping Theory for an all-round advancement of the cause of building socialism with Chinese characteristics into the 21st century* delivered by Jiang Zemin at the 15th National Congress on September 12, 1997.

31 Jiang, Q. G. (1995). Construct a state-owned assets management, supervision and operation system with clarified powers and responsibilities. *China Economic & Trade Herald*, Issue 15.

32 Deng, X. P. (1994). In everything we do we must proceed from the realities of the primary stage of socialism, *Selected Works of Deng Xiaoping* (Vol. 3, p. 252). Beijing: People's Publishing House.

33 Deng, X. P. (1994). Speech at the Third Plenary Meeting of the Central Advisory Committee. *Selected works of Deng Xiaoping* (Vol. 3, p. 91). Beijing: People's Publishing House.

34 *Resolution on the guidelines for the construction of socialist spiritual civilization.* (1986). http://www.wenming.cn/ziliao/wenjian/jigou/zhonggongzhongyang/201 602/t20160215_3144911_1.shtml

35 *Notice of the CPC Central Committee on several issues concerning further strengthening and improving the agricultural production responsibility system.* (1980). http://www.ce.cn/xwzx/gnsz/szyw/200706/13/t20070613_11735658.shtml

36 Deng, X. P. (1994). Build socialism with Chinese characteristics. *Selected works of Deng Xiaoping* (Vol. 3, p. 65). Beijing: People's Publishing House.

37 Decision the CPC Central Committee on reform of the economic structure. (1984). *Journal of Reform of Economic System*, Issue 5.

38 *Constitution of the People's Republic of China.* (2018). Beijing: China Legal Publishing House.

39 Lin, Y. F., et al. (2014). *Sufficient information and state-owned enterprise reform* (pp. 68–75). Shanghai: Truth & Wisdom Press.

40 Jiang, Z. M. (2006). Correctly handling several important relations in the construction of socialist modernization. *Selected works of Jiang Zemin* (Vol. 1, p. 468). Beijing: People's Publishing House.

41 Chen, Q. T. (2008). Reshaping the enterprise system: 30 years' changes on China's enterprise system (p. 53–57). Beijing: China Development Press.

42 Jiang, Z. M. (September 12, 1997). *Hold high the great banner of Deng Xiaoping Theory for an all-round advancement of the cause of building socialism with Chinese characteristics into the 21st century.* http://www.people.com.cn/item/sj/sdldr/jzm/A106.html

43 Wu, J. L. (2016). *Tutorial of economic reform of contemporary China* (pp. 190–195). Shanghai: Shanghai Far East Publishers.

44 Li, Y. N. (2014). Four benefits of mixed ownership. *West China Development*, Issue 3.

45 Yu, J., & Huang, Q. H. (2017). Progress and problems of and suggestions for comprehensively deepening state-owned enterprise reform in the new era. *Journal of The Party School of The Central Committee of the C.T.C*, Issue 21.

46 Chen, X. (1999). Development of the non-public sectors and state-owned enterprise reform. *Capital Shanghai*, Issue 11.

47 Lin, Y. F., et al. (2014). *Sufficient information and state-owned enterprise reform* (pp. 121–126). Shanghai: Truth & Wisdom Press.

48 Zhang, H. M. (1998). *The logic of China's state-owned enterprise reform* (pp. 170–175). Taiyuan: Shanxi Economic Publishing House.

49 Chen, Q. T. (2005). Thoughts for reform of state-owned enterprises and reform of state-owned assets management system. *Review of Economic Research*, Issue 50.

50 Lin, Y. F., et al. (2014). *Sufficient information and state-owned enterprise reform* (pp. 121–126). Shanghai: Truth & Wisdom Press.

3 Transformation of enterprise system

From "wholly owned" and "state-owned" to "mixed ownership"

The advancement of reforms has clarified the status of enterprise reform and identified the starting point of the reform for invigorating enterprises, so the following reform measures will be unfolded gradually by following the law of economic operation itself. Through "delegation of powers and transfer of profits", we can confirm that ownership can be "appropriately separated" from management. Since enterprises have become more aware of their independent status as corporate legal persons, especially because of the development of the external market environment, it is necessary to further transform the enterprise organizational forms for creating a "fully independent" identity as market players for them. The enterprises of the "ownership by the whole people" are transformed into "corporate system enterprises", and they are pushed into the market to take part in competition. By building an organization platform for corporate system enterprises, they can absorb investment from both state-owned capital and other social capital so that the enterprises will show up as a part of the "mixed sector of the economy".

3.1 Corporate system reform of SOEs: diversified investment and "mixed" ownership

The process of a continuous deepening of reform is also a process of continuous ideological emancipation. In the early days of reform, owing to ideological constraints, we decided to turn from the "state-owned or state-run" enterprise management to separation of ownership from management, and started reforming the enterprise operating rights through delegation of powers and transfer of profits and implementation of the contract system, in an aim to stimulate the initiative of enterprises, improve operating efficiency, increase output, and solve the most pressing problem of product shortage at that time.

It is not difficult to understand that the reform with the separation of ownership from management as the main idea is essentially a contractual arrangement between the State and enterprises. Objectively, due to the incompleteness of the contract, ownership remains to play a great significant role therein. According to Zhang Wenkui (2015), under the traditional system, the state ownership managed enterprises through administrative systems, plans and instructions, the mechanisms for realizing their specific property rights were unclear. In terms of residual claims, most enterprise surpluses flowed into the enterprise itself, while the revenue of the State as enterprise owner has stagnated, and there was even the problem of insider control.[1]

With the development of the market, the autonomy of enterprises in operation has expanded correspondingly, and there have been market requirements for clarifying corporate property rights. Only on the basis of a well-defined relationship between the ownership of investors and property rights of enterprises can we separate ownership from management and help enterprises operate their businesses independently.

On the basis of the previous reforms, the Seventh National People's Congress held in April 1988 passed the *Law of Industrial Enterprises Owned by the Whole People*. Article 2 of this Law stipulates that "the properties of enterprises belong to the whole people, and the State grants them business management in accordance with the principle of separation of ownership from management. Enterprises have the right to possess, use and dispose of the properties granted to them by the State for operation and management. Enterprises shall obtain the status of a legal person in accordance with the law and bear civil liability with the properties granted to them for operation and management by the State".[2]

The establishment of the legal person status of an enterprise owned by the whole people marks the transition from the state-owned factory system to the state-owned enterprise system, and the legal person status of the enterprise has been established and consolidated in law. However, at this stage, enterprises owned by the whole people generally adopted the wholly state-owned enterprise system, state-owned assets had not entered the market, and the State as an investor still bore unlimited joint and several liabilities for enterprises. As a transitional corporate organization system connecting the state-owned factory system and the modern enterprise system, enterprise owned by the whole people was indeed an unstable form of business.

In 1992, the remarks made by Deng Xiaoping during his inspection tour of south China set off a new wave of ideological emancipation, breaking people's long-term ideological constraints. In October 1992, the Fourteenth National Congress set the goal of reform is to establish a socialist market economy. In May 1993, the Political Bureau of the Central Committee decided to include the development of a socialist market economy system on the agenda of the Third Plenary Session of the 14th CPC Central Committee before its convening. The primary problem facing the development of the socialist market economy is to handle the relationship between SOEs and the market economy.

When drafting the decision of the Third Plenary Session of the 14th CPC Central Committee, the then General Secretary of the CPC Central

Committee Jiang Zemin presented an important question to the draftsmen: Whether public ownership, state-owned sector and market economy can be integrated? If so, how can we do that?[3] To this end, the Central Committee conducted extensive researches, abandoned the thought of relying on policies to invigorate enterprises under the traditional system, and proposed that "a modern enterprise system with public ownership playing a dominant role is the foundation of a socialist market economy system".[4] We should reform the property rights system and innovate the enterprise organization system to construct independent market entities under the socialist market economic system and realize the compatibility between the state-owned sector and the market economy.

The Decision adopted at the Third Plenary Session of the 14th CPC Central Committee pointed out that the goal of the reform is to "establish a modern enterprise system that meets the requirements of the market economy, with explicit property rights, clear rights and responsibilities, separation of government and enterprise, and scientific management". In order to better guide and standardize enterprise reform and advance the corporate system reform of SOEs, China officially promulgated the Company Law in December 1993, clarifying the legal status of corporate legal person property rights and the relationship between corporate investor and corporate property legal person, and specifying that "a company enjoys all legal person property rights constituted by the shareholders' investment, enjoys civil rights and assumes civil liabilities in accordance with law".[5]

The decision to establish the modern enterprise system would make China's enterprise system evolve into a modern corporate system. By making enterprises – the main body of microeconomic operation – the organizational carrier of capital allocation, we can explore the concrete paths for realizing public ownership under the conditions of the market economy and solve the compatibility of public ownership, state-owned sector and market economy. At the same time, the modern corporate system has updated our understanding of SOEs as state-funded enterprises because the enterprises registered in accordance with the Company Law have specified the specific organizational objects of the "investors" who set up the enterprise, and the relationship between the investor and the invested enterprise, that is, the relationship between capital contribution and capital use. This will change the concept of "SOEs" that has been used in general terms.

According to Chen Qingtai (2008), former director of the Development Research Center of the State Council, we can integrate the state-owned sector and market economy through the corporate system reform of SOEs, the significance of this reform is reflected in the following six aspects: First, the establishment of the property rights of a corporate legal person enables the enterprise to become a legal person with independent legal status and clear property rights. Second, the owner only assumes limited liability to the enterprise with its invested capital, reducing investment risks and preventing the State from bearing unlimited liability. Third, under the modern enterprise system, representatives of the investor will enter the enterprise. The enterprise itself will establish a scientific and effective governance structure under the condition of ensuring the ultimate control of the owner to form a reasonable incentive and restraint mechanism. Fourth, the modern enterprise system makes it possible for the flow of state-owned assets. In addition to selecting shareholder representatives to enter the enterprise to participate in enterprise management, an owner can also "vote with their feet", that is, the owner may sell its equity in the market to convert the forms of assets, thus making the flow of state-owned assets possible. Fifth, the modern enterprise system provides conditions for enterprises to operate independently and assume responsibility for their own profits and losses. The State as an investor only bears limited liability with its investment; therefore, operators have to think about their own market conditions when making investment, financing or business decisions, and thereby assuming responsibility for their own decisions, profits and losses. Sixth, the liquidity of corporate property rights will realize the cross-integration of state-owned and other sources of capital, which makes it possible to develop the mixed sectors of the economy.[6]

According to the provisions of China's Company Law at that time, companies are divided into three types according to their corporate structure: a company limited by shares, a limited liability company and a wholly state-owned company. According to the Decision of the Third Plenary Session of the 14th CPC Central Committee, qualified large and medium-sized SOEs with a single investor could be reorganized into sole proprietorship companies, while those with multiple investors could be reorganized into limited liability companies or companies limited by shares.

Only a small number of companies limited by shares were allowed to go for public listing upon strict examination and approval. Regardless of the shareholding system reform advocated by scholars and the corporate organization for diversified property rights subjects under the traditional corporate system, the form of a wholly state-owned company was determined as a separate form. In the process of corporate system reform of SOEs, most enterprises chose the form of a wholly state-owned company. The reason is that, on the one hand, the cost of converting to a wholly state-owned company is low; they only need to change the company name, formulate new articles of association and modify the organizational structure without making other adjustments. On the other hand, most of the SOEs under the corporate system reform were in a state of loss, and the quality of their stock assets was not ideal at all, making other investors discouraged to get involved.

The wholly state-owned companies, after restructuring, are generally authorized by the government. Without the meeting of shareholders or investment intermediaries as property representatives, they are prone to be intervened by the government, thus affecting the separation of ownership and management and the marketization of state-owned assets. Even for some SOEs reorganized into limited liability companies or companies limited by shares, they were still facing lots of problems: First, the stagnation of state-owned shares within the company is not conducive to the overall strategic adjustment of the state-owned sector. Even there is a certain flow of state-owned shares, the transactions are mostly over-the-counter or based on negotiated prices. There is no reasonable criterion for evaluating the fairness of the prices. Second, the integration of the modern corporate governance structure with the original SOE management model is of great significance in reality. The functions of the "new three meetings" under the modern corporate system, including shareholders' meeting, board of directors and board of supervisors, are to a certain extent conflicting with the "old three meetings" in traditional SOEs, including Party Committee, general manager workshop and congress of workers and staff, thus impeding the modern corporate governance structure to play its role. Third, after the implementation of the corporate system reform, business operators are required to change their roles correspondingly. The SOE operators are no longer assessed like Party and government officials but for the market performance of their enterprises, which calls for operators to update their management style.[7] Fourth, the corporate system reform is mainly realized through the financial and assets restructuring of SOEs. In the case of limited liability companies or companies limited by shares, although they have diversified investment, most of their internal investors are of wholly state-owned ownership, thus weakening the effect of incentives and restraints between different owners.[8]

In the late 1990s, with the strategic adjustment of the layout of the state-owned sector, the State began to invigorate large enterprises while relaxing control over small ones and restructure SOEs. In some small SOEs and subsidiaries of SOEs, management began to hold shares or transfer state-owned stock shares to other stockholders, then these enterprises began to have shareholders of different ownership, and the SOEs with diversified investments have developed into mixed enterprises. In 1999, the Fourth Plenary Session of the 15th CPC Central Committee denied the direct connection between the proportion of state-owned sector and the nature of socialism and proposed to vigorously develop the shareholding system and expand the scope of reform to medium-sized SOEs. A statement made at this Session said that "if some large and medium-sized state-owned enterprises, especially powerful enterprises, are suitable to implement a shareholding system, they may be transformed into stock enterprises through the standardized listing, Sino-foreign joint venture and mutual equity participation. We should develop the mixed sectors of the economy and let the key enterprises be controlled by the State".[9]

Since then, some large SOEs have also started selling state-owned shares to certain private and foreign-funded enterprises through asset stock transfer and incremental share issuance. The Third Plenary Session of the 16th CPC Central Committee held in 2003 proposed to vigorously develop the mixed sector of the economy and make the shareholding system an important way to materialize public ownership. In the process of a new round of SOE reform, the Third Plenary Session of the 18th CPC Central Committee in 2013 decided to actively develop the mixed sector, stating that "a mixed economy with cross-holding by and mutual fusion between state-owned capital, collective capital and non-public capital is an important way to materialize the basic economic system of China. It is conducive to improving the amplification function of state-owned capital, ensuring the appreciation of its value and raising its competitiveness, and it is conducive to enabling capital with all kinds of ownership to draw on one another's strong points to offset weaknesses, stimulate one another and develop together".[10]

Making mixed ownership as an important form for materializing the basic economic system is another innovation of the corporate organization from the perspective of the ultimate investor and within the framework of the modern corporate system, and it is a new endeavor for achieving the mutual integration of public ownership and market economy. A mixed economy is essentially an economy organized and operated in line with market laws. Through the democratization of capital triggered in the process of "mixing", we can widely mobilize social capital and stimulate the development enthusiasm of different subjects in society, thereby driving checks and balances, scientific decision-making and improving the efficiency of state-owned capital allocation, so as to provide targeted solutions to state-owned capital management, and "no separation of investment from capital use" and "non-separation of government functions and enterprise management", and integrate state-owned capital management with the market economy.

As of the end of 2018, the proportion of central enterprises of mixed ownership had reached 76%, and the proportion of mixed enterprises under the regulation of provincial governments and their subsidiaries at all levels exceeded 60%. However, in developing mixed enterprises, some people hold that if an enterprise wholly invested by the State was restructured into the one with multiple investments, it should also be deemed a mixed enterprise. But in fact, they have confused the concept of diversified investments (shareholding system) with the concept of mixed ownership, thus leading to a situation where some SOEs tried every means to become mixed.

Huang Qunhui (2017) pointed out that this kind of view has confused diversification of funding with mixed ownership. In fact, the former only requires multiple legal persons to hold shares, regardless of the nature of the shareholders; while the latter refers to the ownership reform of the enterprises in which property rights belong to different owners, these enterprises may be joint ventures with state-owned (or collective) and foreign funds, combined enterprises made up of state-owned (or collective) and domestic private enterprises, or mixed enterprises composed of state-owned shares and individual properties.[11] Chang Xiuze (2017) defined the connotation of mixed ownership as "two levels, one pluralism": The "two levels" refer to the "mixed economy" at the level of important fields (such as monopoly fields) and the "mixed enterprises" at the micro-cellular level; this kind of "mixed enterprise" does not refer to "homogeneous property diversification" within state-owned capital, but "heterogeneous property diversification" through cross-holding and mutual fusion of state-owned capital, collective capital and non-public capital. This is the strict economic definition of mixed ownership.[12]

Compared with traditional diversified investments, mixed ownership has a "pro-market" nature which is conducive to further promoting the market to play a decisive role in resource allocation, valuating factors and resources and discovering fair value. The effects of mixed-ownership reform are reflected in the following four aspects: First, it is convenient to deal with the relationship between public ownership and the market economy. Making mixed-ownership an important way to materialize public ownership is conducive to the transformation and system construction of enterprises as the micro-foundation of the market economy. Mixed ownership will help create an equal relationship between sources of capital within an enterprise. Capitals of different ownerships can cooperate within the same organizational framework, complement each other's advantages, and have consistent resource allocation and evaluation rules.

Second, it is able to promote the legalization of corporate governance and economic operations. The implementation of mixed ownership through the establishment of state-owned capital operations or investment companies is conducive to standardizing the relationship between government and enterprises. Through value-based management and equity allocation of state-owned assets, the operation of enterprises will become more market-oriented. Their internal governance mechanism will become more standardized, from "rule by men" to "rule by law", so that entrepreneurs can devote themselves to enterprise management. The market can better play the decisive role in resource allocation. Third, it is conducive to reforming the administrative personnel system. Under the traditional management system, the evaluation of managers is highly administrative, that is, mainly based on their administrative level. The marketization effect driven by the mixed-ownership reform will enable the market to play a greater role in the process of managerial evaluation, stimulate the development of the entrepreneurial human capital market, and protect the enthusiasm and legitimate rights and interests of investors. Fourth, it is conducive to handling the relationship between capital and labor and mobilizing the enthusiasm of various subjects and owners of factors and resources. But at the same time, we must realize that mixed ownership is not a panacea, relevant laws, policies and measures need to be enacted, revised, promulgated or abolished, and we must have a correct understanding of relevant concepts, which are of important fundamental significance to the development of mixed ownership.

3.2 Establishing corporate property rights: from state-owned to state-funded enterprises with well-defined investors

The concept of "legal person property rights" was put forward in the process of SOEs' corporate system reform, which was considered to be a major breakthrough of this reform. As required by the Third Plenary Session of the 14th CPC Central Committee, "the implementation of a corporate system in state-owned enterprises is a useful exploration for establishing a modern enterprise system. A standardized company can effectively separate the ownership of investors from the property rights of corporate legal persons, which is conducive to the separation of government functions from enterprise management and the transformation of operating mechanisms. Enterprises can get rid of their dependence on administrative organs, and the State can no longer bear the unlimited liability to enterprises".[13]

Article 4 of the Company Law (1993) defined the corporate legal person property rights, that is, "the shareholders of a company, as capital contributors, have the right to enjoy the benefits of the assets of the company, make major decisions, choose managers, etc. in accordance with the amount of capital they have invested in the company. A company enjoys all legal person property rights constituted by the shareholders' investment, enjoys civil rights and assumes civil liabilities in accordance with law. Ownership of the State-owned assets in a company belongs to the state".[14]

Although the specific understanding of corporate legal person property rights remains in disputes,[15] this concept was of great significance for the de-administration of SOEs, clarifying state-owned investors, and making SOEs independent market entities. Hong Hu, then deputy director of the State Commission for Restructuring Economy, believed that the key to establishing a corporate legal person system is to establish the legal status of the corporate legal person, legal person properties and property rights.

The corporate legal person property rights denote that corporate legal person enjoys the rights to control the enterprise properties independently, the subject of rights is the corporate legal person, the object is the properties of the corporate legal person, and the content of rights is independent control of the legal person properties in accordance with the law. The legal system of corporate legal person properties mainly regulates the ownership relationship between corporate legal person, investor, creditor and corporate legal person properties, as well as the rights and obligations between the corporate legal person and corporate properties. Hong Hu believes that legal person property rights include both real right and creditor's right, and intellectual property right, reflecting that the controller of the legal person properties, through control over the properties of persons, enjoys the ownership of corporate legal person.[16]

Although the *Law of Industrial Enterprises Owned by the Whole People* has established the status of the corporate legal person and resolved the defect of confused ownership and management in traditional SOEs to a certain extent, enterprises do not have independent control over their corporate properties, while the State, as the investor, still exercises specific control of properties and substantively assumes unlimited liability to the enterprises. Besides, since the corporate property rights belong to the whole people, different administrative organs can exercise part of the owner's rights based on their administrative affiliation without being responsible for their actions, thus weakening the incentive and restraint mechanism for corporate property rights and making the enterprises unaware of the status of their investors.

In the process of corporate system reform of SOEs, the establishment of the corporate legal person property rights system has clarified that enterprises have the right to control corporate properties as independent legal persons. As a result of the separation of investor ownership from the property rights of corporate legal persons, enterprises have become independent legal persons in the market and assume responsibilities only with their assets. Once the owner has made an investment in the enterprise, the owner's disposal of his properties can only be achieved through the company's internal governance mechanisms such as shareholders' meeting, the appointment of investor's representatives, or transfer of equity on the market, which in turn requires to identify the investor of state-owned assets within the enterprise for exercising shareholders' rights.

As the Third Plenary Session of the 14th CPC Central Committee pointed out, the implementation of the management system of "uniform state ownership, hierarchical government supervision, and self-management of enterprises" for state-owned assets has fundamentally denied the proposition of partial ownership, local ownership and enterprise ownership. Let the State Council exercise the ownership of state-owned assets on behalf of the State and play a leading role in implementing hierarchical management of state-owned assets. Let the state-owned assets management institution under the State Council implement hierarchical administrative management of state-owned assets across the country in accordance with the law, which not only reflects the consistency in state-owned assets administrative management but also reflects the requirements of hierarchical responsibility. With the establishment of the corporate legal person property rights system, the State as an investor has transformed from a specific operator to a shareholder exercising shareholders' rights. As most SOEs have completed the corporate system reform in the form of wholly state ownership, the traditional concept of state-run enterprises was replaced by that of SOEs and written into the Constitution in 1993.

As the market develops, state-funded enterprises established in the form of limited liability companies and companies limited by shares have become the main organizational forms for the enterprises funded with state-owned capital. At the same time, with the development of the mixed economy, new changes have taken place in the internal property rights of enterprises and in the relationship between enterprises and investors, which has also brought new changes to the traditional definition of SOEs. For a long time, SOEs have a specific meaning in China; they refer to the enterprises established by the *Law of Industrial Enterprises Owned by the Whole People*, not those based on the *Company Law*. With the advancement of the corporate system reform, the definition of SOEs, in reality, started to blur. Some scholars consulted with some German doctrines that an enterprise with over 50% of "government" funds in its total investment should be deemed as a "public enterprise" or "state-run enterprise", and an enterprise with over 50% of state-owned funds is an SOE.[17]

In daily management of SOEs and our everyday life, enterprises owned by the whole people or wholly state-owned, state-owned capital holding or joint-stock companies, as well as their subsidiaries and sub-subsidiaries, are indiscriminately called SOEs, thereby giving rise to the situation where the ultimate ownership is directly exercised across the enterprise level. However, the above distinction and management methods have certain flaws: regarding the corporate internal property rights (ownership in the sense of configuration), for limited liability companies (except one-person limited liability companies) and companies limited by shares, with the diversification of the internal capital contributions of enterprises in the development of mixed ownership, we should not define SOEs indiscriminately or only based on its controlling stake. Article 7 of the Constitution reads, "the state-owned economy, that is, the socialist economy under ownership by the whole people, is the leading force in the national economy". Article 12 specifies that "socialist public property is sacred and inviolable". And Article 13 provides that "citizens' legal private property will not be infringed upon. The state protects by law the right of citizens to inherit private property".[18]

If an SOE is defined by having the State as the investor, then for non-state investors, their capital contribution and ownership are not confirmed in fact, but it is obvious that not the ultimate ownership of an enterprise as a whole is owned by the whole people. And if an SOE is defined solely based on whether the State has a controlling stake, then for the enterprises with state-owned capital not holding a controlling position, the status of their ultimate investor of state-owned capital is not protected. With a view to the ultimate ownership of the investor and the derivative ownership of the enterprise and its subsidiaries, an enterprise enjoys legal person property rights as an independent legal person. It has the rights to possess, use, benefit from, and dispose of the properties invested by the investor. In contrast, the investor can only realize ownership through the corporate internal governance mechanism or equity transfer.

Setting subsidiaries based on their needs is to exercise the property rights of an enterprise. Subsidiaries also enjoy independent legal person property rights, and their parent company should realize the rights and interests of their investors. If we do not distinguish the concepts of SOEs, or unify policy management and let state-owned investors directly exercise their share-holders' rights, it will break the independence of corporate legal person property rights and then confuses the ultimate ownership of investors and the derived property rights of enterprises, which is not conducive to clarifying the property rights relationship. In this regard, the *Guiding Opinions of the CPC Central Committee and the State Council on Deepening the Reform of State-owned Enterprises* released in 2015 stated that "the business matters that ought to be determined by the enterprises independently shall be given back to them, while the management of subsidiaries shall be at the hands of the first-level enterprises in principle".[19]

With the further advancement of corporate system reform and mixed-ownership reform, we will find that the traditional definition of SOEs is no longer applicable. In connection with the aforementioned concept of "state contribution", in specific business occasions with multiple investors, what investors care about is the effective operation and value-added capability of their invested capital. It is not difficult to discover that "capital" is more important; to be specific, the top concern of the investors of state-owned capital is how to preserve and increase the value of "state-owned capital". Therefore, in order to clarify the property rights relationship of enterprises, it is necessary to introduce and distinguish between state-owned and state-funded enterprises. In the future, the concept of SOEs can be divided into several levels. The first level is in the narrowest sense, both the enterprises owned by the whole people and wholly state-owned are the purest SOEs. Some limited liability companies that are funded by multiple state-owned investors also fall under this category because such companies are still owned by the State from the ultimate perspective of property rights.

For the enterprises with all types of non-state-owned investors, they may be classified as state-funded enterprises, and at the same time, according to the proportion of state-owned capital in their total investment, they can be divided into state-owned capital holding companies and state-owned capital equity participation companies for differentiated management. Through redefinition, it can be seen that the most important concept is state-owned capital, that is, the sum of owners' equity in China in the future, rather than the concept of SOEs. State-owned capital must maintain a certain scale and quantity, and the vitality of value preservation and appreciation for reflecting the proportion and status of the state-owned sector in the national economy. State-owned capital and its corresponding liabilities will constitute state-owned assets and then operate in the market. A correct understanding of this problem has significance for determining the nature of state-funded enterprises in the mixed economy, setting the statistical caliber of state-owned assets, and exploring how state-owned assets play their role in the national economy.[20]

3.3 Thoughts from the characteristics of the introduction of corporate system

The "mixed ownership" represented by the modern corporate system has been valued in China's economic life and actively introduced into practice as an endeavor to promote the innovation of forms of public ownership, a new measure to deepen the SOE reform, and a new theoretical breakthrough after the economic structural reform entered the deep water zone. The introduction of the modern corporate system is directly related to the transformation of resource allocation methods and forms of public ownership.

Looking at the history of human society, with the development of productivity, technological progress and the expansion of the scope of production exchange, the enterprise itself as a way of organizing production is also constantly developing. When the scale of an enterprise is beyond the amount of capital held by individual capitalists and their management capabilities, a new method for capital allocation and corporate governance that separates ownership from management will appear within the enterprise. Then there will be the transition from "private capitalism" based on the proprietorship enterprise to "manager capitalism" based on the corporate system.

With the development of economic activities, this organizational form of a joint investment by private capital must overcome the limitations of individual capital; therefore, in terms of civil liability, a "legal person" system was established so that investors no longer have to bear unlimited joint and several liabilities, but only assume limited liability. And this "mixed ownership" has finally obtained a relatively stable organizational form and the status of a legal entity, that is a modern corporate system.

Within the framework of the capitalist system, although the joint investment of private capital has contributed to the sublation of private capital in the social sphere under the capitalist system, it has not essentially changed the basic nature of private possession of the means of production. In contrast, in terms of mobilizing social capital and realizing the equity allocation of assets, and in terms of the relationship between nominal ownership of capital and actual ownership (the right to use capital), the modern corporate system boasts flexible entry and exit through the creation the nominal ownership on the secondary market, thereby enabling capital allocation to flow flexibly according to changes in productivity and technologies. Related to this form of capital allocation, the internal operation and governance mechanisms of companies under the modern corporate system have gradually formed a set of systematic governance rules, which become an important part of the corporate system which, as an organizational form of capital allocation, has been an important driving force in the process of promoting productivity and economic development. As K. Marx had commented, "Suppose we had to wait for an accumulation of a single capital to the point where we could build a railroad, I'm afraid that there are no railways in the world until today, but joint-stock companies have made it in an instant".[21]

In order to explore the corporate system based on the capitalist mode of production, the accompanying market economic and cultural value factors are worth digging deeper into. First, under the corporate system, a single investor can break the integration of ownership and management by investing its own capital so as to realize the separation of nominal capital from real capital, which has reflected the openness of capital relations. Second, different investors inside an enterprise of the corporate system enjoy equal status in capital cooperation, with shares of the same class having the same rights. In an enterprise of the corporate system, the capital allocation is based on the quantity of capital and decided in a democratic way of "the minority is subordinate to the majority". On this basis, capital owners may participate in corporate management in a positive way as "voting by hand", or in a passive way as "voting with their feet", and withdraw from the capital cooperation through secondary market transfers, thus forming a restraint mechanism of major shareholders. Third, the information openness of the power game in the process of capital cooperation. No matter it is the establishment of a capital cooperative relationship or the entry and exit of investor equity, it needs to be transparently carried out pursuant to law, which is a kind of legal protection of capital rights. All of them can mark the development level of the market.

The corporate system has already emerged and developed extensively under the previous socialized production. The practices have proved that the internal mechanism of the corporate system better explains the significance of the corporate system reform and the development of mixed economy for deepening the reform in a new stage. In the course of 40 years of reform and opening up, the reform of enterprises – the micro-foundation of the socialist market economy – occupies an important position in all fields of reforms.

After going through delegation of powers and transfer of profits, contractual reform, property rights reform, corporate system reform, and the recent mixed-ownership system, Chinese enterprises have been transformed into economic organizations with diverse investments or of mixed-ownership that multiple investors jointly fund. In addition to the mixed-ownership reform of the existing wholly state-funded companies, many mixed enterprises have come into being as driven by business opportunities. Despite this, mixed ownership is a product of practice rather than policy design, making the mixed economy only passively recognized by the existing theories that hold that public ownership includes state-owned and collective components in the mixed sectors and stockholding system an important way to materialize public ownership.

Zhang Wenkui (2015) pointed out that the government intentionally promoted China's mixed-ownership system. It originated from the "Economic and Technological Cooperation and Horizontal Economic Union" strongly supported by the government in the 1980s, which encourage enterprises to break departmental boundaries, regional boundaries, and even ownership boundaries, and collaborate and unite with each other, with the goal of allocating resources on a larger scale to complement each other's advantages.

Since there were few non-state-owned sectors at that time, Horizontal Economic Union was usually carried out between SOEs. However, once Horizontal Economic Union is carried out, it is difficult to be confined to SOEs. With the development of township and village enterprises, mixed enterprises were formed between collective ownership and state-owned ownership, and there were even joint operations and joint investments between private and state-owned (or collective) enterprises, which gave rise to mixed enterprises containing private, collective and state-owned shares. The private enterprises that combine their flexible operating mechanisms with the rich production factors of SOEs have realized mutual complementarity and radiated great vitality in practice. This is also an important reason why many mixed enterprises have come out.[22]

Since the reform practices have proved the vitality of mixed ownership, the Decision adopted at the Third Plenary Session of the 18th Central Committee pointed out that the mixed economy is an important way to materialize the basic economic system of China and established the status and role of mixed ownership in the construction of a socialist market economy. It suggested that we should vigorously develop the mixed economy with cross-holding and mutual fusion between state-owned capital, collective capital and non-public capital and achieve integrated operation. It will be a new breakthrough and new development in the theory of ownership by taking the development of the mixed economy as an important way to deepen the reform of state-owned assets and enterprises and then achieve the organic integration of public ownership and market economy.

Let's return our discussion to the practical level – actively developing a mixed economy in China can open up more room for reform. Through summarizing the reforms of SOE and the state-owned assets management system, we will find that the top priority is to properly handle the relationship between public ownership and the market economy and allocate public capital more flexibly and effectively to inject vitality into enterprise operation. The corporate system of China was established under the background when a planned economy was transiting to a market economy. In the reform process with SOEs at the core, we had been invigorating SOEs, allowing the non-public sectors to develop side by side with the public sector, working hard to build a socialist market economy, and finally absorbing the concept of "mixed ownership" into our economic development theory. This kind of "mixed ownership" (corporate system) differs greatly from the existing capitalist mixed ownership in terms of generation, development and content. In practice, the mixed economy has yielded some results, and the results of reforms must be affirmed in theory and incorporated into the theoretical system of the socialist market economy.[23]

3.4 Adherence to public ownership and vigorous development of mixed ownership can go hand in hand

In the process of the mixed-ownership reform, state-owned equity will be sold to non-state-owned parties, and if there are problems such as non-transparent information, unreasonable transaction pricing or unfair procedures, it is easy to cause the loss of state-owned assets. Therefore, some people regard the sale of state-owned equity in the mixed-ownership reform as the loss or even privatization of state-owned assets.[24] With the development of the mixed economy, China has made strategic adjustments to its economic layout, which would change the allocation and distribution of state-owned capital in the whole society, and the indicators such as the number of SOEs, total profits, and the proportion of employed people have declined. Thus, some scholars argued that the development of the mixed economy would have an impact on the dominant status of the public sector and even deny public ownership.[25] This is a problem that needs to be analyzed and discussed in depth in theory; otherwise, it may cause theoretical ambiguity and affect the actual measures of reform.

The mixed-ownership reform of SOEs does not necessarily lead to the loss of state-owned assets. When advancing the mixed-ownership reform and allowing multiple property rights owners to form a mixed enterprise, no matter it is a newly-built or a restructured one, the key issues are how to form the capital "consideration" of multiple investors, how to set the "appraisal value" of the existing capital stock of an existing enterprise, and at what "appraisal value" price the new capital can be introduced, the key solution here is to implement the pricing mechanism of state-owned assets and design a set of evaluating and trading systems with fair transactions, fair procedures and open information.

The view that selling state-owned equity to non-state shareholders is equivalent to privatization is to view mixed-ownership reform from a static perspective. In developing the market economy, property rights are a dynamic concept. The value of an enterprise needs to be measured dynamically, state-owned equity also needs to reflect its value in transactions. The concept that would rather statically degrade state-owned shares in an enterprise than optimize resource allocation through transactions to achieve greater benefits is a misconception since it will restrict the reforms of mixed ownership and SOEs.

During the process of mixed-ownership reform, the transfer of state-owned equity is not a free transfer but achieved through market pricing. In terms of capital allocation in the entire society, state-owned capital is transformed from corporate equity into state-owned assets in the form of non-corporate equity, and non-state-owned assets are transformed into a form of corporate equity; as a result, the proportion of public assets in the entire society has not changed. The whole process is the process of realizing the market-oriented allocation of resources, which cannot be equated with privatization. The realization of public ownership cannot only rely on the corporate system. The transformation of forms between different types of capital is the realization of ownership's own disposal function, which is not to deny public ownership.

From the perspective of mixed ownership properties, it is necessary to distinguish the ultimate ownership at the level of the ultimate investor from the derivative ownership formed by the relationship between investor and capital user (see Figure 3.1). "Mixed ownership" is "corporate ownership" based on different investors (ultimate owners), and it is legal person ownership based on the capital contribution made by the ultimate investor. The vigorous development of mixed ownership can go hand in hand with adherence to socialist public ownership.

When discussing the ownership of the means of production, Marxist political economy holds that there are two types of basic forms of ownership in social and economic life: private ownership and public ownership, which have completely different properties. Various specific forms of ownership in social-economic life are evolved and developed from these two basic ownerships (or "ultimate ownership"). "Mixed economy" is a new form of economy based on joint investments made by different types of owners. Therefore, it can be regarded as ownership in the "second level" (not in the sense of ultimate ownership).

At a macro level, a mixed economy means that the ownership structure of a country or region is not unitary. The ultimate owners of different ownerships can coexist, like state-owned, collective and the public sectors (including individual, private and foreign-funded businesses). From a micro level, a mixed economy refers to the enterprises jointly funded by the investors of different ownerships.

Inside mixed enterprises, capitals of different ownerships cooperate with each other to form a joint force to achieve a common goal. The conceptual

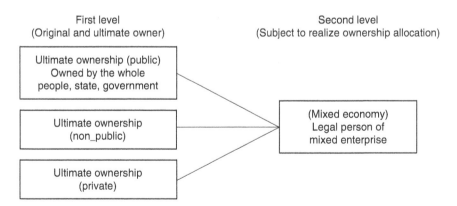

Figure 3.1 Mixed enterprises funded by investors to form the legal person property rights.

category of "mixed ownership" in this book refers to the mixed ownership of enterprises at the organizational level. In a capital-integrated enterprise, it is conducive to enabling cross-holding ultimate owners with all kinds of ownership to draw on one another's strong points to offset weaknesses, stimulate one another and develop together.

Adhering to the public ownership of the means of production and the development of a mixed economy can go hand in hand because the ownership of the means of production in the ultimate sense and the mixed ownership in the sense of specific allocation are at two different levels and have different positioning. The report delivered to the Fifteenth National Congress in 1997 stressed that we must uphold and improve the basic economic system, with public ownership playing a dominant role and diverse forms of ownership developing side by side. Being the foundation of China's socialist economic system, the public sector includes the state-owned economy and the collective economy and the state-owned and collective components in the mixed economy.

The nature of ownership in the sense of ultimate ownership depends on the nature of ownership of the ultimate investor. Mixed-ownership is not an independent form of ownership. It is a mixture of public and non-public economic components, with the "nominal" "monetary" ownership separated from "real" ownership by means of "investment", "joint capital contribution" from investors of diverse ownerships, and pursuing common goals objectively. This will dilute the opposition between the existing capitals of different natures and motivate investors to pay more attention to their common goals so that joint investors will have a legal person's status and a survival goal. The general qualitative questioning will obtain the qualitative basis from the attributes of the entities occupying an absolute number (controlling) in the mixed-ownership relationship.

The general qualitative questioning will obtain the qualitative basis from the attributes of the entities occupying a controlling position in mixed ownership. However, considering the effectiveness of the corporate governance mechanism and shaping the mutual checks and balances between different investors, large shareholders usually do not hold more than 50% of the total share. Therefore, the qualitative nature of a mixed enterprise funded by multiple investors should get rid of the traditional way of thinking and be given new prescriptions.

From the perspective of the operating characteristics of the corporate governance mechanism, we need to look at the economic attributes of the largest shareholder that plays a leading role, which enables the largest shareholder's ability to mobilize other minority shareholders and deal with their interest appeal, and ultimately affect the materialization of the mixed economy. However, if we look at the characteristics of modern corporate governance mechanisms, there will be frictions in capital cooperation, which will increase the cost of corporate governance, and even disintegrate the joint relationship.

In the final analysis, a mixed enterprise's social attributes depend on the power comparison between the public and non-public economic components and the harmonious realization of their common goals. It also depends on the specific economic and political environment, depend on specific policies and regulations, and most importantly, they depend on the nature of the basic economic system. The nature of a single mixed enterprise does not need to be determined, and the public ownership of the socialist system is determined in the social scope.

Through further inference, in a mixed enterprise jointly funded by state-owned and private capital, this joint investment has produced a new mechanism, that is, the openness of the realization of capital rights and the "sublation" of privateness by capital in the social scope, in other words, the "investment" of private capital has been used "socially" in the "corporate capital" (enterprise). This kind of social sublation will objectively transform the attributes of private capital.[26]

3.5 Develop the dominance and influence of mixed and public sectors

The Decision made by the Third Plenary Session of the 18th CPC Central Committee pointed out that "a mixed economy with cross-holding by and mutual fusion between state-owned capital, collective capital and non-public capital is an important way to materialize the basic economic system of China", and "it is an effective way and an inevitable choice for maintaining the dominant position of public ownership and enhance the dynamism, dominance and influence of the state sector of the economy under new circumstances".[27]

However, in the process of developing a mixed economy, two views have emerged to oppose mixed ownership, although they are mutually contradictory. One view is that the proportion of the state sector in the national economy is too low to be further decreased. A mixed economy is to dilute and weaken the state ownership, shake the national economic foundation, and deviate the Chinese economy to the road of privatization. The other view is that the mixed economy will annex the private sector. It is a new round of "entry of state-owned capital and exit of private capital", a "new public-private partnership movement", and an "attempt to restore the monopoly of state-owned sector".[28] These two views, to a certain extent, are misinterpretations of mixed ownership. The development of a mixed economy is neither going for privatization nor nationalization of the private sector. Instead, under the premise of adhering to the dominant position of public ownership, allowing capitals of various sources to cooperate and develop together is not only conducive to expanding the influence and control of the public sector but also conducive to developing the non-public sectors.

While developing the mixed economy, the dominant position of public ownership must be maintained. And we should correctly understand the leading role of public ownership from the perspectives of ultimate property rights and derivative property rights and examine the nature of property rights of mixed ownership objectively and dynamically. Public capital must dominate the total social capital, but the proportion of public property rights of individual enterprises shall be analyzed case by case. There are mainly two types of mixed enterprises according to the ratio of their public capital: the first type is the mixed enterprises mainly invested by public capital. In these enterprises, public capital occupies the dominant position, and the ultimate investor exercises investor's rights through legal procedures. By taking advantage of mixed ownership, the ultimate investor is able to control and divert a wider range of capital, extensively mobilize social capital, expand the scope of control of public capital, and enhance the influence and dominance of the public sector. Moreover, the democratization of capital contained in the mixed economy has mobilized the enthusiasm of different social subjects and promoted the development of the check-balance mechanism for corporate governance and the scientific decision-making, which is conducive to improving the operating efficiency of state-owned capital, preserving and increasing the value of state property. The introduction of non-public capital will facilitate SOEs to transform operating mechanisms, raise the allocation and operational efficiency of state-owned capital, amplify the functions of state-owned capital, and give full play to the role of the market. The other type is the mixed enterprises in which state-owned (or collectively owned) capital only accounts for a certain proportion instead of being a dominant force. These enterprises may be beyond the category of the public sector, but we cannot say that they have state-owned capital privatized. As mentioned earlier, the ultimate ownership of the public sector and the derived ownership of corporate properties are two different concepts. In this type of mixed enterprise, state-owned capital remains entitled to control a wider range of capital to a certain extent through correct guidance and mobilization. However, the exercise of this right should be realized according to legal procedures through the corporate internal governance mechanism; otherwise, "one investor may hoodwink all the others" and arouse people's suspicion of infringing on the property rights of the non-public sectors.

Therefore, under the premise of maintaining the dominant position of public ownership, the introduction of non-public capitals by developing a mixed economy at the level of derivative property rights will help to amplify the functions of state-owned capital, improve the management and operation of state-funded enterprises, and preserve and increase the value of state property. We cannot take the development of a mixed economy as shaking the foundation of our country directly, and this issue should be looked at from a dynamic and overall perspective.

3.6 The significance of developing a mixed economy to the innovation of ownership theory

The development of a mixed economy has refreshed people's understanding of the ways for realizing socialist public ownership. After 1949, under the influence of the Soviet Political Economy Schoolbook, people generally believed that socialist public ownership and commodity economy (market economy) were incompatible like water and fire. This Schoolbook argues that socialist productive relations are based on two types of public ownership of means of production, that is, state ownership (owned by the whole people) and collective ownership. State ownership is the most advanced form of socialist ownership since it embodies the most mature and thorough socialist productive relations and plays a leading and decisive role in the entire national economy. The development prospect of the two types of public ownership is to transit to comprehensive ownership by the whole people (state ownership). The State's comprehensive planning guidance of the national economy is regarded as the most important feature of the socialist economy,[29] but the reform and opening-up practice of China is a challenge to this theory. While implementing the reform and opening-up policy in the 1980s, China had kept adjusting the relationship between a planned economy and market economy: keeping planned economy as the mainstay with market regulation serving as a supplement (1980), planned commodity economy (1984), internal unification of planning and market (1987), a combination of planned economy and market regulation (1989). Until Deng Xiaoping made his famous remarks during his tour in south China in 1992, the Fourteenth National Congress decided to "establish the socialist market economy", which was seen as a major breakthrough in the socialist economic theory. Regarding the essence and core content of the socialist market economy, the Fourteenth National Congress provided an official statement as "make sure that the market forces play an essential role in the allocation of resources under the state's macroeconomic control". Later, the Decision of the Third Plenary Session of the 18th CPC Central Committee stressed that "let the market play the decisive role in allocating resources and let the government play its functions better". It shows that our understanding of the combination of the socialist system and the market economy has kept developing and deepening.

The ownership structure is closely related to socio-economic formation. The traditional socialist planned economy corresponds to the overall socialist public ownership of means of production, and the public sector dominates the national economy. After acquiring an in-depth understanding of ownership and market economy since the reform and opening up, we started allowing the existence and development of individual, private, and foreign-funded economies, and the Fifteenth National Congress proposed that "we will continue to follow the basic economic system to keep public ownership in a dominant position and have diverse forms of ownership develop side by side". Since the reform and opening up, with the development of the market economy, our understanding of the effective ways for realizing public ownership and the basic economic system has continued to innovate and deepen. In 1993, the Third Plenary Session of the 14th CPC Central Committee proposed that "with the flow and reorganization of property rights, there will be more and more economic units with mixed property ownership, which will give rise to a new property ownership structure".[30] IT was the first time that the concept of "mixed ownership" was contained in an official document. In 1997, the report of the Fifteenth National Congress clearly pointed out that "the ways for realizing public ownership can be and should be diversified". "Efforts should be made to find a way for realizing public ownership that can greatly promote the development of productive forces. The shareholding system is a form of capital organization of modern enterprises, which is conducive to separating ownership from management and[31] is conducive to improving the operational efficiency of enterprises and capital. It can be used both under capitalism and under socialism". In 2003, the Third Plenary Session of the 16th CPC Central Committee proposed that "in order to adapt to the continuous development of economic marketization, we must further increase the vitality of the public economy, vigorously develop a mixed economy involving state-owned capital, collective capital, and non-public capital, realize the diversification of investment entities and make the shareholding system the main form for realizing public ownership".[32] Since the Third Plenary Session of the 18th Central Committee in 2013, the Party Central Committee with General Secretary Xi Jinping at the core has put forward a series of new theories on ownership issues and developed the theory of socialist ownership. The Third Plenary Session of the 18th CPC Central Committee pointed out that both the public and non-public sectors are key components of the socialist market economy and are important bases for the economic and social development of China; the state protects the property rights and legitimate interests of all economic sectors, ensures that they have equal access to the factors of production according to the law, participate in market competition on an open, fair and just footing, and are accorded with equal protection and oversight according to the law; a mixed economy is an important way to materialize the basic economic system of China; and we will improve the state-owned assets management system, strengthen state-owned assets oversight with capital management at the core.[33]

According to Hu Jiayong (2016), taking a mixed economy as an important way for realizing the basic economic system represents our deepened understanding of the realization form of ownership, and also a further innovation to strengthen the compatibility of public ownership with the market economy. In order to develop a mixed economy, we must have a deep understanding of the dominant position of public ownership, the nature of socialism with Chinese characteristics, and the internal operating laws of a modern market economy. The dominant position of the public sector of the economy needs quantitative prescriptions, but more importantly, it is reflected in the quality. State-owned capital and state-owned sector can be mainly distributed in important industries and key fields related to national security, the lifeline of the national economy and people's livelihood. They can become the "universal light" that radiates the entire economy through the penetration and amplification of the market mechanism. A mixed economy with cross-holding by and mutual fusion between state-owned capital, collective capital and non-public capital will become an important way to materialize the basic economic system of China, and a mixed economy will mainly exist by implementing the stock-holding system. A scientific understanding of the nature of the shareholding system is of great significance for developing a mixed economy and making it an important way for materializing the basic economic system. When describing the shareholding system, Marx pointed out that "the capital, which is based on the social mode of production and presupposes the social concentration of the means of production and labor force, directly obtains the form of social capital (that is, the capital of individuals directly united) which is opposite to private capital, and its enterprises behave like social enterprises which are opposite to private enterprises. This is the transcendence of capital as private property within the capitalist mode of production itself". As Engels had commented, "the capitalist production operated by joint-stock companies is no longer private production, but production jointly managed by many people". Compared with the conditions of capitalism, in a socialist market economy with public ownership as the mainstay, share capital can reflect the nature of "social capital" and "joint production" to a greater extent and thus integrate with the dominant status of public ownership.[34]

From the transformation of the corporate organizational system, we can fully understand the significance of innovating the corporate system to increase corporate vitality and the entire economic system. In the process where "ownership by the whole people" is first transformed to "state ownership" and then to "mixed ownership", the changes in corporate organizational forms reflect the benign interaction and mutual promotion between the micro corporate organizations and the deepening of market-oriented reform. It is able to promote the supporting reforms of resource allocation and the system for economic management and operation, stimulate the changes in economic relations between various subjects participating in social reproduction, and boost the activity of various production factors. The changes in the quality of the economic system will eventually manifest themselves in the continuous improvement of economic performance, and thereby demonstrating the capacity of reform and opening up in "liberating productive forces" and "developing productive forces", and giving the socialist system the vitality and superiority of self-regulation, self-improvement, and advancement with the times.

Notes

1 Zhang, W. K. (2015). *Governance and performance of mixed enterprises* (pp. 41–43). Beijing: Tsinghua University Press.
2 *Law of the People's Republic of China of industrial enterprises owned by the whole people* (p. 2). (1997). Beijing: China Legal Publishing House.
3 Chen, Q. T. (2008). Reshaping the enterprise system: 30 years' changes on China's enterprise system (p. 35). Beijing: China Development Press.
4 *Decision on some issues concerning the establishment of the socialist market economy.* Retrieved November 14, 1993, from http://www.people.com.cn/item/2 0years/newfiles/b1080.html
5 *Company law of the People's Republic of China* (p. 3). (2014). Beijing: China Legal Publishing House.
6 Chen, Q. T. (2008). Reshaping the enterprise system: 30 years' changes on China's enterprise system (pp. 38–41). Beijing: China Development Press.
7 Zhang, H. M. (1998). *The logic of China's state-owned enterprise reform* (pp. 129–133). Taiyuan: Shanxi Economic Publishing House.
8 Zhang, W. K. (2015). *Governance and performance of mixed enterprises* (pp. 182–183). Beijing: Tsinghua University Press.
9 *Decision of the CPC Central Committee on several major issues concerning the reform and development of state-owned enterprises.* Retrieved September 22, 1999, from http://www.gcdr.gov.cn/content.html?id=16800
10 *Decision of the CPC Central Committee on some major issues concerning comprehensively deepening the reform.* Retrieved November 15, 2013, from http://www.scio.gov.cn/zxbd/nd/2013/document/1374228/1374228_1.htm
11 Huang, Q. H. (2017). Clarifying the eight misunderstandings of mixed-ownership reform. *Modern Enterprise*, Issue 9.
12 Chang, X. Z. (2017). An outline of China's mixed-ownership economy. *Academics*, Issue 10.
13 *Decision on some issues concerning the establishment of the socialist market economy.* Retrieved November 14, 1993, from http://www.people.com.cn/item/2 0years/newfiles/b1080.html
14 *Company law of the People's Republic of China* (p. 3). (2014). Beijing: China Legal Publishing House.
15 After the concept of corporate legal person property rights was put forward, there have been different views in academia on how to understand this concept, which can be summarized in three types: 1. "Dual ownership view". (1) Doctrine of possession. It holds that the State has ownership of the properties of the whole people, and SOEs' possession of corporate properties is a kind of relative ownership or jus in re aliena. (2) Doctrine of legal ownership and economic ownership. In reference to Marx's "mere ownership" and "economic ownership", this doctrine holds that in SOEs, the State only enjoys ownership in name, and the actual power of ownership is owned by these enterprises. Therefore, the State merely enjoys legal ownership, while the enterprises have economic ownership of their properties and can directly exercise all the powers contained in ownership. It not only retains the mere ownership of the State, safeguards the national interests, but also enables enterprises to have autonomy. (3) Doctrine of legal person ownership. This doctrine draws on the property rights structure of limited companies and joint-stock companies in European and American countries, arguing that when a property owner invests in the establishment of an enterprise, the owner's ownership is transformed into the enterprise's equity, then the enterprise obtains legal person ownership, while the investor retains the ultimate ownership of the enterprise properties. The properties can only be retrieved when the business is terminated, bankrupt and

liquidated. Therefore, legal person ownership is a relative ownership. 2. Managerial view. This view is closely associated with the reform SOEs by separating ownership from management in the process of reform and opening up. Article 82 of the *General Principles of the Civil Law* (1986) defines the nature of the property rights of enterprises owned by the whole people as managerial rights. The *Law Industrial Enterprises Owned by the Whole People* (1988) defines the managerial rights like this: "the enterprises have the rights to possess, use, and dispose of the properties granted by the State to operate and manage according to law", and the rights to earnings and the rights "not according to law" are still reserved by the State. This managerial view inherits the statements about SOE reform at the preliminary stage, and has been gradually accepted by the government. 3. Shareholder ownership view. It holds that the legal person property rights are fictitious, the corporate properties are still at the hands of shareholders, while the company has control over corporate properties on specific occasions (Shi Jichun, 2008).

16 Hong, H. (1997). Thoughts on the property rights of corporate legal persons. *China Industrial Economics*, Issue 1.
17 Shi, J. C. (2015). *Enterprise and company law* (4th ed., pp. 226–230). Beijing: China Renmin University Press.
18 *Constitution of the People's Republic of China* (pp. 6–7). (2018). Beijing: China Legal Publishing House.
19 *Guiding opinions of the CPC Central Committee and the State Council on deepening the reform of state-owned enterprises*. Retrieved August 24, 2015, from http://www.gov.cn/zhengce/2015-09/13/content_2930440.htm
20 Zhang, H. M. (1998). *The logic of China's state-owned enterprise reform* (pp. 100–103). Taiyuan: Shanxi Economic Publishing House.
21 Marx. (2014). *Capital* (Vols. 1–3, p. 688). Beijing: People's Publishing House.
22 Zhang, W. K. (2015). *Governance and performance of mixed enterprises* (p. 85). Beijing: Tsinghua University Press.
23 Zhang, H. M., & Lu, J. F. (2015). A new inquiry into the attributes and introduction features of mixed economy. *Research on the Theories of Mao Zedong and Deng Xiaoping*, Issue 2.
24 Huang, Q. H. (2017). Clarifying the eight misunderstandings of mixed-ownership reform. *Modern Enterprise*, Issue 9.
25 Zhou, X. C. (2017). Thoughts on the issue of keeping the public sector as the dominant player. *Contemporary Economic Research*, Issue 6.
26 Zhang, H. M., & Lu, J. F. (2015). A new inquiry into the attributes and introduction features of mixed economy. *Research on the Theories of Mao Zedong and Deng Xiaoping*, Issue 2.
27 *Decision of the CPC Central Committee on some major issues concerning comprehensively deepening the reform*. Retrieved November 15, 2013, from http://www.scio.gov.cn/zxbd/nd/2013/document/1374228/1374228_1.htm
28 Chang, X. Z. (2017). An outline of China's mixed-ownership economy. *Academics*, Issue 10.
29 Wu, J. L. (2016). *Tutorial of economic reform of contemporary China* (p. 180). Shanghai: Shanghai Far East Publishers.
30 *Decision on some issues concerning the establishment of the socialist market economy*. Retrieved November 14, 1993, from http://www.people.com.cn/item/2 0years/newfiles/b1080.html
31 Jiang, Z. M. (September 12, 1997). *Hold high the great banner of Deng Xiaoping Theory for an all-round advancement of the cause of building socialism with Chinese characteristics into the 21st century*. http://www.people.com.cn/item/sj/sdldr/jzm/A106.html

32 *Decision on some issues concerning the improvement of the socialist market economy*. Retrieved October 14, 2003, from http://jingji.cntv.cn/2012/11/05/ARTI1352087360703188.shtml
33 *Decision of the CPC Central Committee on some major issues concerning comprehensively deepening the reform*. Retrieved November 15, 2013, from http://www.scio.gov.cn/zxbd/nd/2013/document/1374228/1374228_1.htm
34 Hu, J. Y. (August 1, 2016). *The innovative development of ownership theory in the new era*. http://theory.people.com.cn/n1/2016/0801/c40531-28599328.html

4 A new state-owned assets management system is required

From "management of assets" to "management of capital"

China's enterprise reform, which has been advanced progressively and developing together with the market economy, is on the way to be deepened along their own logic. Now that the inherent limitations of the existing "administration of enterprises" have become more apparent, what is the right way to handle the "government-enterprises" relationship? Looking at the positive "entry" and negative "exit" of investors in corporate enterprises under the market economic condition, the vitality of SOEs lies in the vitality of state-owned capital, which boils down to the basic prescription of capital's own ability to preserve and increase value. It is precisely for this reason that the existing administration of SOEs shall be transformed to "management of capital".

4.1 Capital allocation under market economy

4.1.1 "Capital" and "assets"

The state-owned assets management system is an important institutional guarantee for the reform and development of SOEs to stick in the right direction. The *Decision on Some Major Issues Concerning Comprehensively Deepening the Reform* (hereinafter referred to as the "Decision") adopted by the Third Plenary Session of the 18th CPC Central Committee clearly stated that "we will improve the state-owned assets management system, strengthen state-owned assets oversight with capital management at the core, reform the authorized operation mechanism for state-owned capital, establish a number of state-owned capital operating companies, support qualified SOEs to reorganize themselves into state-owned capital investment companies".[1] "Management of assets" is only slightly different from "management of capital", but the connotations of the two concepts are worlds apart.

"Assets" and "capital" in the meaning of economics are two different concepts. We should first discuss the difference and connection between the two concepts.

In Marxist political economics, "capital" is defined as the value that can bring surplus value and realize value multiplication. According to Marx, "Capital, as a self-proliferating value, not only contains class relations but also contains a certain social nature based on the existence of labor as hired labor. It is a kind of movement, a cyclic process that is divided into various stages, and this process itself involves three different forms of the cyclic process. Therefore, it can only be understood as movement, rather than any stationary object".[2] He also said that "when he merges the living labor force with the dead matters like commodities, he is to turn value, and the past, materialized and dead labor into capital and self-proliferating value".[3]

From an abstract perspective, the analysis of Marks abstracted various concrete manifestations of capital and revealed the value-added and liquid attributes of capital. From a concrete perspective, the neoclassical comprehensive economics argues that capital is a kind of production factor, capital and other forms of production factors such as labor, technology and energy will form a certain production technical structure or relationship and jointly create products and services that meet people's needs; in this process, the natural attributes of capital such as value-added, liquidity, profit-seeking and flexibility will be demonstrated.

Assets are more of a concept in accounting. As prescribed by the *Accounting Standards for Enterprises of China*, assets refer to the resources formed by past transactions or events of an enterprise, possessed or controlled by the enterprise, and expected to bring economic benefits to the enterprise. In the sense of economics, assets are generally considered to be economic resources that can be measured in currency and possessed or controlled by enterprises, natural persons, countries or other organizations. Economic resources are made up of natural resources, human resources, financial resources, information resources, etc. These resources play an extremely important role in social and economic development. The level of resource allocation efficiency often determines the level of productivity and economic development of a country or region.

Regarding enterprises – micro-foundation of the market economy, the differences between their capital and assets are mainly reflected in the following aspects:

> First, assets are economic resources owned or controlled by enterprises, while capital reflects the owner's equity enjoyed by investors. According to the rules of modern corporate system, investors pour funds into enterprises to form capital, and enjoy the owner's equity according to the amount of their investment, that is, the right to claim residual, the right to make major decisions, and the right to choose the operator. In contrast, the connotations of assets are more related to the objects of enterprise organization, which is the result of fund using in specific business scenarios of the enterprise. In order to ensure that funds can play the role of maintaining and increasing value after flowing into an enterprise,

they shall be subject to unified and centralized planning, control and use, so that the existence of assets has diversified forms, such as plant, equipment, raw materials and intangible assets. As an independent legal person, an enterprise has the right to control its physical assets, that is, the legal person property rights. It conducts independent operations in accordance with the law, assumes responsibility for its own profits and losses, and for maintaining and increasing the value of properties. Therefore, capital is a concept associated with investors and corresponds to the ownership of investors, while assets is a concept related to corporate organizations and corresponds to legal person property rights.

Second, from the perspective of quantitative relation, capital is a part of assets. The corporate balance sheet clearly reflects the relationship between assets and capital (owner's equity). The funds entering an enterprise must meet the requirement of "fund utilization = sources of funds". The owner and creditor invest funds into an enterprise to form owner's equity and debts, respectively, while assets reflect the use of funds, and there must be "assets = debts + owner's equity", the quantity of assets must be greater than that of capital.

Third, compared to assets, capital is more flexible and liquid. Assets often exist in enterprises in the form of various means of production, and they are in physical form, while capital exists in enterprises in the form of equity, which is a form of value. What capital pursues is investment income, it flows in and out of enterprises, and its liquidity will release great vitality and efficiency. The asset allocation of an enterprise relies on a certain amount of labor. Therefore, the disposal of enterprise assets is subject to the task deployment for laborers, and this is a problem that must be properly resolved when mergers and acquisitions occur between enterprises. In this regard, the liquidity of assets is poor.

Fourth, assets have multiple accounting measurement attributes, and capital is directly expressed in a quantity of money. According to China's Accounting Standards for Enterprises, there are different evaluation and measurement standards for the accounting measurement of corporate assets. In addition to the value of "ledger assets" recorded for business accounting, there are also "cost replacement value" which is evaluated based on the use-value attributes and technical features of real assets and the "value of discount interest profit" calculated based on the assets' operating profitability as an evaluation standard; if the company's assets enter the market for reorganization or for mergers and acquisitions, there must be the "market transaction value" of the corporate assets negotiated between the buyer and seller based on their respective market positioning. It can be seen that the measurement results of "assets" have different valuations, and there are uncertainties or inconsistencies in the amount of value between them, while the concept of "capital" is relatively simple, it is directly expressed in the amount of money, and with the "owner's equity" as the purpose.

4.1.2 Physical management of state-owned assets under the planned economy

Before the reform and opening up (1949–1978), China's economic system had been a highly centralized and planned economic management system characterized by administrative management. The planned economy emphasized physical indicators and use-value while ignoring or rejecting value and the law of value. At that time, Chinese people dared not talk about "capital". That's why the means of production in SOEs must be called "assets", and the evaluation of assets was only based on physical integrity and quantity indicators. State-owned assets were more regarded as a concept of use-value, which was under physical management through administrative means. Enterprises, as micro-organizational carriers for the allocation of operating state-owned assets, had been set up by the State. That is, they were wholly state-owned, with reproduction activities directly operated by the government. The ways of operating enterprises had been highly administrative and deviating from their essential attribute as an economic organization.[4] The competent authority at a higher level had direct control over the people, finances, materials, supply, production and sales of enterprises. In the production plans issued to enterprises, there were detailed arrangements for the types and quantity of products to be produced, applicable technologies, sources of raw materials, sales of products, types of new products to be developed, amount of additional investment, and types of projects, and all of these arrangements had been prescribed in physical quantity.[5] SOEs were nominally in an "independent" accounting position, but in fact, they were not truly independent economic units. Since they rejected commodity currency relations, Chinese SOEs could not be counted as independent commodity producers. They were at best "workshops" in a large social factory. They were fully subordinate to the higher administrative department. Some foreign scholars even pointed out that "China has no enterprises". Without independent legal person property rights, enterprises lacked the inherent motivation to maximize profits. In this situation, the driving force for the economic operation of the entire society mainly came from the government, which used administrative means and political mobilization to ask the grassroots units to "respond to the call" and perform their responsibilities.[6]

The resource allocation through administrative means will lead to obstacles in terms of information and incentives when an enterprise makes or carries out decisions. With respect to information, the central planning agency cannot have all the information about all economic activities, including the status of materials and human resources, technical feasibility, and demand structure.

Therefore, it is difficult to ensure that the indicators specified in production plans are completely correct. With respect to incentive mechanism, the parties to economic activities, including plan makers and executors, have their own interests. In the process of providing information, preparing and implementing plans, they are sure to be affected by their own partial interests consciously or unconsciously and deviate from the overall interests of society. Owing to the above two aspects, the content of the administrative plan is often inconsistent with real economic life. Enterprises without any autonomy can only "make the best of a mistake" while implementing these plans, which will result in a rigid economic structure economy, imbalanced stock structure, and inefficient allocation of state-owned assets. Facts have proved that the highly centralized planned economy has played a vital role in consolidating the newborn socialist system and rapidly promoting large-scale industrialization. However, it has such shortcomings as non-separation of government functions from enterprise management, ignoring the role of commodity currency relations and market-based resource allocation, which severely restricts the development of productive forces. The operation of the traditional planned economy has remained in a state of "shortage economy", and the low efficiency of resource allocation may even threaten the sustainability of the economic system itself.

For the above reasons, under the leadership of Deng Xiaoping, the CPC reestablished the ideological guideline of "seeking truth from facts". After "emancipation their mind" and conducting a profound reflection on the experiences and lessons in developing the traditional planned economy, the Third Plenary Session of the 11th CPC Central Committee convened at the end of 1978 put forward the policy of "reform and opening up", thus making the transition from a planned economy to a socialist market economy a historical necessity.

4.1.3 *Value allocation of state-owned capital under market economy*

Since the reform and opening up, the "incremental reform" was adopted to develop "unplanned" economic activities, which gave rise to a transitional "dual-track" economy involving both planned and market economies. In 1992, the Fourteenth National Congress decided to establish "a socialist market economy" as the goal of reform.

The reform of economic structure has become a strong driving force for the rapid development of the Chinese economy. The reform has mobilized the enthusiasm of multiple subjects in society, enabling China to maintain an average annual growth rate of about 10% for the past 40 years and making it the second-largest economy in the world in terms of economic aggregate.

In order to summarize the historical experiences of China's development, understand the path of socialism with Chinese characteristics, and construct the political economy of socialism with Chinese characteristics, the most fundamental point is to establish a socialist market economic system and realize the organic combination of public ownership and market economy.

In neoliberal economics, socialism and the market economy are sharply opposed. In *Socialism: An Economic and Sociological Analysis*, Mises made a systematic demonstration of the incompatibility between socialism and market economy, arguing that it is impossible for public ownership to coexist with production factor markets, and it is impossible to form reasonable prices and economic accounting under public ownership, so it is impossible to separate the market and its price formation mechanism from the social functions based on private ownership of the means of production.[7] In terms of system choice, "either socialism or market economy".[8] Hayek agrees that socialism and market economy are incompatible and contends that market economy can only be built on the basis of private ownership. But such kind of viewpoint is actually dogmatic. The practices in China's economic restructuring reform have proved that the requirements of socialist principles and theories for system solve the problems about "basic economic system", while "market economy" solves the problem of resource allocation for economic operation.

With the advancement of reform, the socialist political economics with Chinese characteristics has accumulated an in-depth and more scientific understanding of socialism and the market economy. The changes in our understanding of the relationship between "plan" and "market" are recorded in the conference proceedings of the Party's landmark meetings over the years. The Third Plenary Session of the 11th CPC Central Committee stressed the role of the law of value, the Twelfth National Congress proposed to "ensure the leading role of planned economy and the supplementary role of a market economy", and the Third Plenary Session of the 12th CPC Central Committee decided to develop a "planned commodity economy". In 1992, in his inspection tour of south China, Deng Xiaoping sharply pointed out that "the proportion of planning to market forces is not the essential difference between socialism and capitalism. A planned economy is not equivalent to socialism because there is planning under capitalism too; a market economy is not capitalism because there are markets under socialism too. Planning and market forces are both means of controlling economic activity".[9] Supported by Deng Xiaoping's important remarks, the Fourteenth National Congress decided to establish a socialist market economy as the goal of reform, marking an innovation at the level of the national economic system, and a great leap forward in our understanding of socialism and market economy. From the perspective of resource allocation, "the socialist market economy we want to build is to make sure that the market forces play an essential role in the allocation of resources under the state's macroeconomic control".

Under the new historical conditions, the Decision adopted at the Third Plenary Session of the 18th CPC Central Committee presented that we should "let the market play the decisive role in allocating resources and let the government play its functions better". It is a new argument that replaces the term "basic" with "decisive" to describe the role of market-based resource allocation and combines the abstract and concrete understandings of the role of the market mechanism so as to strengthen the understanding and compliance with the objective laws of real economic operations. This argument has become a basic principle of socialist political economics with Chinese characteristics. The market decides the allocation of resources, which is a general law of the market economy, which means that most of the economic resources in society (including labor, capital, land, technology, energy, and information, etc.) should be allocated to the fields with better economic benefits through market mechanisms. With public ownership playing a dominant role and diverse forms of ownership developing side by side, the basic economic system is an important pillar of the socialist system with Chinese characteristics and the foundation of the socialist market economy. The Decision highlights the importance of maintaining the dominant position of public ownership. In recent years, the non-public sectors have developed rapidly. At present, the contribution rate of the non-public sectors to China's GDP, taxation and employment has exceeded 60%, 50% and 80%, respectively, thus playing an ever more important role in the national economy.[10] Some scholars doubt that the dominant position of public ownership has been broken and the foundation of socialism has been shaken. But in fact, this argument is one-sided. According to the Fifteenth National Congress report, the dominant position of public ownership is mainly decided by two conditions: public assets occupy a dominant share in total social assets; state-owned sector controls the lifeline of the national economy and plays a leading role in economic development. China's public assets include corporate state-owned assets, financial assets, land, natural resources, etc. From the perspective of their scale, public assets possess an absolute advantage in the total assets of the whole society, and the state-owned sector firmly controls the lifeline of the national economy and dominates economic development, so the dominant position of public ownership remains fairly stable and has not been shaken.

In his report to the Nineteenth National Congress, Xi Jinping further pointed out that "there must be no irresolution about working to consolidate and develop the public sector; and there must be no irresolution about working to encourage, support, and guide the development of the non-public sector. We must see that the market plays the decisive role in resource allocation, the government plays its role better".[11] We must adhere to the goal of reform to build a socialist market economy, which is a basic principle for deepening the reform of the state-owned assets management system and the reform of SOEs. Under the conditions of a socialist market economy, state-owned assets must be capitalized mainly for the following reasons:

> On the one hand, fair competition is the basic feature of market economy. Enterprises, starting from their own interests, compete for better production and marketing conditions and more economic resources. Competition will facilitate the survival of the fittest

enterprises, and then realize the optimal allocation of resources. The report to the Nineteenth National Congress stated that we will implement negative list management system, and significantly ease market access. All businesses registered in China will be treated equally.[12] It can be inferred from this that, as the main body of market competition, SOEs must compete with other economic entities on an "equal" footing and content for the market by investing capital to produce commodities, and then preserve and increase the value of their capital. Otherwise, SOEs will consume social resources for no reason, and drag down the efficiency of economic operation.

On the other hand, the important goal of deepening the reform is to develop a mixed economy with cross-holding by and mutual fusion between state-owned capital, collective capital and non-public capital. With the vigorous development of the mixed sectors, the investors of SOEs have become increasingly diversified. Whether state-owned capital is in a controlling position or not, these mixed enterprises jointly funded by investors of different ownership are no longer SOEs in the original sense, they should be called "state-funded enterprises". The measurement of state-owned assets in these state-funded enterprises will become increasingly complex, but the measurement of capital is relatively simple. Therefore, the measurement of operating state-owned assets should be mainly based on state-owned capital, and the key to maintaining and increasing the value of state-owned assets lies in the value of state-owned capital.

As mentioned above, capital is the value that is capable of multiplication, and the life of capital lies in multiplication. The more profit it makes, the more vitality it has. Moreover, capital is multiplying in constant movement, so liquidity is another basic characteristic of capital. Capital must be poured into reproduction activities to go through the circulation of various re-production stages to achieve value appreciation in the flow. From the per-spective of productivity, maximizing output with minimal input means the development of productivity. Whether it is state-owned capital, private ca-pital, foreign capital or social capital, they all have their general attributes as capital – multiplication and liquidity. As a scarce resource controlled by the State, state-owned capital should pursue return on investment (ROI) and investment efficiency, maintain its general attributes and operation methods of capital, and integrate with the market economic system.

Owing to different allocation structures and distribution fields, the state-owned capital in China has different functions in the overall social re-production structure. State-owned capital can be generally divided into two categories: One is commercial capital that serves as a financial investment, mainly pursuing ROI with the direct purpose of making a profit. The other is public beneficial capital mainly invested into social public services and public products, including infrastructure, education, medical care, health and other social undertakings; this type of capital has strong externalities for its public goals and functions. It is needless to say that commercial state-owned capital pursues the goal of maintaining and increasing its value, while public beneficial capital should also while fulfilling some special public objectives of the State, guarantee investment efficiency, and maintain and increase its value indirectly, so as to avoid inefficient resource allocation. In other words, although profitability is not the primary goal of state-owned public beneficial capital, we cannot simply draw a conclusion that the operation of such capital cannot be compatible with self-financing, profit-making and value appreciation. In fact, the state-owned capital invested in infrastructure projects is able to support the overall structure of the national economy. Based on appropriate infrastructure, the environment for the effective operation of social reproduction guarantees the capital operation performance in competitive fields. There are also contributions to the national fiscal revenue, which indirectly achieves the goal of maintaining and increasing the value of state-owned capital.

To sum up, the State is free to pour or withdraw investment according to the development needs of the national economy and following the rules of the modern corporate system, and flexibly allocate state-owned capital among industries and enterprises. Related to this, the management of state-owned capital must turn to value-based management, that is, to adjust the allocation structure of state-owned capital through the throughput of value, judge the efficiency of state-owned capital operation from the social average profit rate, and let the market, which seems like an "invisible hand", play a fundamental and decisive role in the allocation of state-owned capital. In other words, it is necessary to fully integrate state-owned capital into the environment of the market economy, place it under the evaluation of the market, discover the unreasonable, unscientific, and inefficient problems that may exist in the existing stock capital allocation, find a basis for adjusting stock capital and the points to be adjusted, so as to find the direction and goal for optimizing capital allocation, and then seek the alternative ways of optimization. This will enable the rational flow of state-owned capital across the entire society and improve macroeconomic benefits.

4.2 Significance of "capital management" for the path dependence of "two non-separations"

4.2.1 "Non-separation of government functions from enterprise management" has been a long-standing problem

Non-separation of government functions from enterprise management is a major characteristic of the economic operation under the centralized planning system. In a planned economy, the government manages enterprises in dual identities as social-economic administrators and owners of state-owned assets. Enterprises are appendages of government organs, rather than genuinely independent legal persons, and their business activities are subject to "soft budget constraints". At that time, SOEs were generally "state-run", meaning that the government directly operated them. As the investor of an SOE, the government should assume unlimited liability for all of its debts. With the expansion of economic scale, especially the capital came from the "price scissors" obtained from the procurement of agricultural products, more and more state-owned (run) enterprises funded by the government had emerged. The highly centralized state-owned assets management system began to expose serious problems, for example, non-separation of government functions from enterprise management, overlapping management, unclear rights and responsibilities, and barriers between the departments. As a result, SOEs had neither autonomy nor vitality to respond to market demands; low operating efficiency and large scale of losses had led to a serious waste of resources. Through 40 years of reform and after a socialist market economy is basically established, theoretically speaking, the nominal planned economy has died out. Still, we may be influenced by, consciously or unconsciously, the institutionalized actions and habits formed when dealing with the government-enterprises relationship, thus forming path dependence and hindering the realization of reform goals.

As mentioned earlier, the Third Plenary Session of the 11th CPC Central Committee held in December 1978 decided to implement the policy of "reform and opening up", then the Third Plenary Session of the 12th CPC Central Committee held in October 1984 made it clear to "increase the vitality of large and medium-sized state-owned enterprises and take it as the central link in the entire economic restructuring", marking that China's enterprise reform had kept deepening in stages.

Through "delegating powers and transferring profits", the enthusiasm of enterprises will be mobilized and the government-enterprises relationship will be continuously adjusted. Enterprises will be increasingly aware of their legal person status and independent rights and then require new breakthroughs in both institutions and legislation. To make enterprises vitalized and capable of independent operation, we must adjust their relationship with the government, including the redefinition of the government's administrative functions and assets management functions, while assets management is highly professional. Therefore, separating the state-owned assets management from the daily administration of the government was placed on the agenda. It was against this background that establishing a state-owned assets management system, which was about to be specialized in state-owned assets management, became an important task to support the enterprise reform. In 1988, the State Council established the National Administration of State-owned Assets (a deputy ministerial-level agency), which was specialized in performing the government functions of state-owned assets management, and affiliated to the Ministry of Finance. Local governments at all levels set up state-owned assets management bureaus accordingly.

However, due to the absence of supporting government institutional reforms, the National Administration of State-owned Assets failed to separate state-owned assets management from the government's administration of public and other economic affairs. Specifically, some functions of the National Administration of State-owned Assets and other government departments were overlapped and crossed, the state-owned asset management functions of various government departments were not truly transferred to this Administration. As a result, this Administration was unable to fully implement the supervisory functions of a state-owned assets investor, with the administration of assets, personnel and other affairs separated from each other. This Administration seemed to be dispensable amid the problems of overlapping management and insider control. The situation at that time could be described as "Five Dragons Controlling Water": administrative organs such as the Planning Committee were exercising the decision-making powers involving investment and production; Party organizations and government's personnel departments were responsible for the appointment, removal, assessment and supervision of major managers of enterprises; financial departments took charge of the income and spending of SOEs, and collected taxes, fees and profits; trade unions had been the authority to implement "democratic management".[13] In this case, the unified ownership was still divided into multiple government organs. The existing Party and government organs were exercising their assigned powers according to their own requirements, instead of assuming any direct responsibility for the operating results of enterprises, which was sure to impede the improvement of the operating efficiency of SOEs.

In the final analysis, the above situation was attributed to the inconsistencies and discoordination between reforms. That's why the National Administration of State-owned Assets was abolished in 1998 when the State Council started institutional restructuring.

However, during this period, the central link of economic system reform – enterprise reform – remained as the focus of attention of the whole society. In order to protect the enthusiasm of enterprises, the Fourteenth National Congress held in 1992 decided to establish a socialist market economy as the goal of reform. Focusing on this goal, the *Decision on Some Issues Concerning the Establishment of the Socialist Market Economy*, which was adopted at the Congress, further specified that we should take "a modern corporate system" as the micro-foundation of the socialist market economy, which finally clarified the position of corporate system in the entire economic structure.

The specific work for promoting enterprise reform mainly included "restructuring, reorganization, and transformation": the enterprises "owned by the whole people" would be restructured into "modern companies"; the original corporate structure would be reorganized and optimized; the production technologies would be transformed, and the traditional operation and management modes would be replaced by modern corporate governance mechanism.

According to the Company Law, the traditional SOEs registered in accordance with the *Law of Industrial Enterprises Owned by the Whole People* would be restructured into the enterprises of the corporate system. This put forward the reform task of "identifying investors", so the specific functions of the state-owned assets management system and the supervision and management system needed to be further improved.

In this context, Shanghai and Shenzhen, as the "bellwethers" of reform and opening up, have been actively exploring the ways for reforming state-owned assets management and operation based on their own characteristics since 1993, thus forming a unique "Shanghai model" and "Shenzhen Model",[14] and accumulating practicable and valuable experiences for reforming China's state-owned assets management system. Take Shanghai as an example. Shanghai established the State-owned Assets Management Commission and the State-owned Assets Management Office in July 1993, thus making the state-owned assets management departments that were originally attached to the fiscal system become independent institutions to keep deepening the pilot reform of the state-owned assets management system.

At the same time, in response to the calls for "liberating enterprises", the government departments that were administering enterprises, that is, the industrial business bureaus were being "restructured" into "state-owned capital operating companies" specialized in capital management; moreover, these companies attempted "authorization management" as required by the SASAC. The original administrative companies with industry management as their main function were abolished. A three-level organizational system for management and operation of state-owned assets was formed: the SASAC under the municipal government (the "State-owned Assets Supervision and Administration Office" or SASAO for handling routine matters) – state-owned assets operating companies – SOEs engaged in production activities. It should be noted that during the nationwide institutional reform in 1998, Shanghai's SASAC and SASAO were retained, which can be seen as the Central Government's affirmation of the successful exploration of Shanghai in state-owned assets reform.

The success of Shanghai lies in its realization of the reform goals for "three separations" and useful explorations into a reasonable state-owned assets management model.[15] The "three separations" refer to (1) the separation of government's social and economic administration from its ownership of state-owned assets; (2) regarding the functions of assets owner, the separation of administrative management of state-owned assets from their operating management; (3) in assets operations, the separation of the ownership of state-owned assets from the property rights of corporate legal persons.

In the three-tier organizational structure of state-owned assets management, the authorized operating companies at the core not only form a "separation zone" that guarantees the separation of government from enterprises, effectively promotes the formation of a mechanism for maintaining and increasing the value of state-owned assets and greatly enhances the control ability of state-owned capital.

Based on the pilot reform experiences in Shanghai and Shenzhen, efforts shall be made to construct and identify the main body of state-owned assets ownership, separate the government's general functions from the state-owned assets supervision and management, continue the integration of state-owned capital allocation and operation with the market economy, properly separate government's administration from capital management, and finally achieve the goals of separating ownership from management and separating from government functions from enterprise operation. It has become an objective requirement for further deepening the reform.

At this time, the conditions for building a society-wide state-owned assets management system and a government functional system had become relatively mature. The Tenth National People's Congress held in 2003 decided to establish the State-owned Assets Supervision and Administration Commission (SASAC) of the State Council, and stressed to combine "administration of assets, personnel and other affairs", in order to reshape the original multi-management pattern in state-owned assets management, eliminate the common phenomenon of "internal control" in the operation of enterprises, which would stimulate the enterprise vitality and promote the healthy development of social productivity.

According to the data released by the Ministry of Finance, at the end of 2004, the total owner's equity (state-owned equity) of state-owned and state-controlled enterprises nationwide was 14.8 trillion yuan. By the end of 2017, this figure had jumped to 52 trillion yuan. At the same time, more and more large SOEs have entered the ranks of the global top 500. In "Fortune Global 500", in 2004, there were 14 Chinese companies listed among the top 500 companies of the world. Stare Grid Corporation of China, ranking 46th place, was the only Chinese company that had entered the top 50. In 2017, among the 115 Chinese companies in the ranks of the global top 500, 48 were central enterprises (among them State Grid, Sinopec, and PetroChina ranked second, third and fourth, respectively) and 18 were local SOEs.

With the deepening of the reform of the state-owned assets management system, the system dividend has gradually been released. But this does not mean that the reform is finished. In reference to the requirements of "comprehensively deepening reform", there are still outstanding contradictions and problems that ought to be resolved as soon as possible in the current state-owned assets supervision model. The long-standing problems of "non-separation of government functions from enterprise management" and "non-separation of the government from the state-owned asset management" have not been fundamentally resolved.

Administrative management thinking and behavioral habits are everywhere in daily economic operations and management occasions. The SASAC is both the assets manager and administrative manager of enterprises. On the one hand, the SASAC, a special institution established by the State Council, undertakes the mission of "assets management", but it will find it had to stay out of the matters beyond the operation of corporate assets. On the other hand, it is difficult to clearly define the powers and responsibilities in the operation of the central enterprises, and there will inevitably be instructions and reports for either important or trivial affairs. These constraints make it difficult to form a standardized and complete corporate governance structure. In many cases, the boards of directors in SOEs exist in name only, which dampens the initiative and enthusiasm of SOEs and holds them back from becoming the main market players taking part in the equal competition.

According to a news report, before July 2017, among central SOEs, there were still 69 (accounting for almost 70% of the total 101 central SOEs at that time) that had not registered for restructuring in accordance with the Company Law,[16] and they were still of the ownership by the whole people. The content of the modern corporate system reform was specified in 1993, and then the Company Law was promulgated on December 29, 1993, and put into force as of July 1, 1994. In the following 23 years, the top-level corporate organization of central SOEs had remained the same as before. The underlying reason behind this phenomenon deserves in-depth discussion both theoretically and practically.

Perhaps it is precisely because reform is an overhaul that will change someone or some organs' position, powers or "vested interests", there are so many obstacles in front of reforms, no wonder the problem of non-separation of government functions from enterprise management is yet fully resolved.

First, there are no basic specifications for dealing with the rights and responsibilities in the relationship between capital contribution and capital use. Although the SASAC acts as the formal investor (shareholder) of central enterprises, it is not skilled at utilizing market economic rules to exercise its shareholder's rights. It seems that the relationship between the SASAC and the invested enterprises remains a kind of administrative relationship, and it is prone to address all problems in the ways to deal with administrative affairs.

Second, the leaders of SOEs are selected in a non-marketize manner. As of July 2018, among the 96 central enterprises directly supervised by the SASAC, 49 central enterprises were directly under the management of the Central Government (at deputy-ministerial level), their leadership team was managed by the No. 1 Entrepreneur Management Bureau of the SASAC (with principal leaders appointed by the Central Organization Department), the other 47 central enterprises were at the bureau level with their leadership team managed by the No. 2 Entrepreneur Management Bureau of the SASAC. In practice, leaders of SOEs usually see themselves more as government officials than as business operators. They lack the motivation to pursue long-term development and technological innovation. They are interested in short-term profits, which will benefit their promotion in their political career, so they tend to exchange long-term development of their enterprises for short-term profits. There is even a negative phenomenon that the selection of SOEs' leaders is based more on personal relationships and political allegiance than on entrepreneurial talent.

Third, the regulatory scope of the SASAC is too excessive, resulting in too much intervention in enterprises. When it was just established, the SASAC was given several duties according to the *Regulations on the Supervision and Administration of State-owned Assets of Enterprises* which the State Council promulgated in May 2003. For example, Article 13 of these Regulations stipulated that the SASAC shall "appoint, remove, and assess the heads of enterprises in accordance with legal procedures, and reward and punish them according to the assessment results", "perform other duties of the investor and undertake other tasks assigned by the government at the same level". Such provisions have some defects since the invested enterprises include wholly state-funded enterprises and state-controlled enterprises and shareholding enterprises. For state-owned holding and joint-stock enterprises, the appointment, dismissal, assessment, rewards and punishments of their responsible persons shall be determined by the shareholders collectively in accordance with the Company Law and the company's articles of association. The SASAC, which is a member of all shareholders, cannot make independent decisions. In actual life, the SASAC intervenes in the business decisions of the invested enterprises based on its rights and responsibilities as a shareholder and intervenes in public policy management and internal management and Party and mass affairs. The regulations and normative documents released by the SASAC, which are related to the shareholders' rights and responsibilities, and public policy management, contain a wide scope of content, including the determination of the company's main business, review of the company's strategy, approval of budget and final accounts, recommendation of the appointment and removal of senior executives, assessment and compensation, environmental protection, social responsibility, technological innovation, and informatization. These contents have far exceeded the scope of the company law in other countries. After the Decision adopted at the Third Plenary Session of the Eighteenth CPC Central Committee presented the reform requirement of "shifting from assets management to capital management", the SASAC made public a list of policy documents to be cleared up in 2016,[17] marking that relevant management methods were undergoing a positive transformation.

Fourth, the state-owned assets supervision and control methods have strong administrative overtones. When the SASAC performs its investor responsibilities for enterprises, many items must be examined, approved, verified, and filed. While implementing specific supervisory tasks, it relies too much on traditional methods such as documents, meetings, and inspections, which has to a certain extent increased the burden of enterprises' submission for approval, and lowered decision-making efficiency.[18]

4.2.2 Non-separation of government functions from enterprise management restricts the improvement of corporate efficiency

According to the Decision adopted at the Third Plenary Session of the 14th CPC Central Committee, the characteristics of the modern corporate system were described as "clearly established ownership, well-defined power and re-sponsibility, separation of enterprise from the administration, and scientific management". It can be seen that the existing enterprises are far from being genuine modern enterprises, especially in terms of their incomplete corporate governance structure. Undoubtedly, because of the non-separation of gov-ernment functions from enterprise management, it is difficult for SOEs to establish a sound corporate governance structure, and it is impossible to achieve fair competition between SOEs and private enterprises, thus re-stricting the improvement of corporate efficiency. The abilities and vitality of enterprises – micro-foundation of the national economy – cannot be given full play, which will inevitably restrict the continuous and healthy development of the national economy.

Corporate governance has two basic functions: one is to select people with entrepreneurial qualities to lead the enterprise; the other is to motivate and supervise enterprise leaders to create value in a better way.[19] For an en-terprise, the choice of its leaders is of great importance. Whether the en-terprise is led by people with entrepreneurial qualities directly determines its operating efficiency. Generally speaking, people with entrepreneurial talents are more imaginative than ordinary people and more sensitive to profit opportunities. They are more capable of making accurate judgments about the future, acting decisively in decision-making, encouraging innovation and daring to take risks. Let these people decide the type and quantity of pro-ducts and services the enterprise provides, as well as the means of doing so and their target customers, and it will significantly reduce transaction costs and improve corporate performance. As mentioned earlier, the appointment of heads of SOEs is based more on personal relationships and political al-legiance than on entrepreneurial talents. According to the requirements of the Company Law, the chairman and general manager of a company are appointed by the board of directors, but in fact, the chairman and general manager of an SOE are appointed by the Organization Department of the Party Committee, and the SASAC generally appoints the deputy positions of the company. In terms of remuneration, the board of directors' re-muneration committee can discuss remuneration issues, but it has no decision-making power. The upper limit of the salary of the chairman and general manager is generally set by the government, while some middle-level managers are recruited from the market, and their salary may be higher than that of the upper-level managers, resulting in a "salary upside down" situation. Such a corporate governance mechanism is not perfect.

One of the important characteristics of the market economy is fair com-petition which requires all enterprises to be equal before laws and policies.

There is neither government discrimination nor government granting privileges to enterprises. But in fact, even in general competitive fields, it is difficult for private enterprise properties to obtain the same legal protection as SOEs properties, and SOEs generally enjoy more concessions than their private counterparts in terms of taxation, credit and loan, land use, and permits. If SOEs suffer losses, they may receive government subsidies or credit support, resulting in a "SOEs never go bankrupt" situation. In contrast, if private enterprises are losing money, they are likely to face collapse. That's why their heads have stronger incentives to improve corporate governance, reduce costs, and increase efficiency. The inequality between SOEs and private enterprises actually restricts the improvement of the efficiency of SOEs.

4.2.3 Strengthening the management of state-owned assets by focusing on "capital management", which helps to separate government from enterprises

With the advancement of reforms, the drawbacks of non-separation of government and enterprises have become increasingly prominent. The prerequisite and key to the separation of government from enterprises lie in the separation of government from capital management, that is, the separation of the government's social and economic administrative functions from its functions as owner of the state-owned capital and the separation of supervision and management of state-owned capital from its operation. This inevitably calls for a new state-owned assets management system. The shift from "managing assets" to "managing capital" has become a historical necessity. Its essence is to reform the realization form of operational state-owned assets, from SOEs in physical form to state-owned capital in value form with good liquidity, and it can be clearly defined in financial language, available for market-oriented operation and the establishment of a principal-agent system with financial constraint as the main line.[20]

The establishment of state-owned capital investment and operation companies is an important means to strengthen the supervision of state-owned assets mainly based on capital management. Learning from the successful examples as Temasek Holdings in Singapore, China Investment Corporation and the "Shanghai Model" of state-owned assets management, we can conclude that an efficient state-owned capital management system should include three important subjects: government departments, state-owned capital investment and operation companies, and entity enterprises.

In the three-level framework of government departments – state-owned capital investment and operation companies – entity enterprises, state-owned capital investment and operation companies at the intermediate level are a key link in the state-owned capital principal-agent chain. They are marketized capital operation entities and established in accordance with the Company Law. They mainly exist in the form of wholly state-funded companies, representing state-owned capital contributors, enjoying the rights of investors and operating state-owned capital in accordance with the law. State-owned capital investment and operation companies obtain ROI by holding or participating in enterprises, preserving and increasing the value of state-owned capital. At the same time, they can optimize capital allocation and investment efficiency by continuously adjusting the shares held by state-owned capital among enterprises. As the link and isolation layer between the government and enterprises, the capital contribution relationship between state-owned capital investment and operation companies and invested enterprises is a market relationship in the full sense, rather than an administrative subordinate relationship. State-owned capital investment and operation companies should participate in the governance of invested enterprises as a shareholder in accordance with the provisions of the Company Law and shall not interfere with the daily operating activities of invested enterprises by administrative means. They are not allowed to directly control the corporate properties of invested enterprises or extract the invested capital by illegal means.

After the three-level framework is constructed, the administrative relationship and capital contribution relationship between government departments and enterprises will no longer be retained, which will prevent state-owned assets management institutions from directly dealing with enterprises and from excessive involvement in business activities, and truly realize the separation of the government from capital management and enterprise operation, thereby leaving more free space for corporate legal persons to improve the corporate governance structure, and separate investor ownership from corporate legal person property rights. This will also enable the investor to perform its responsibilities by exercising corresponding rights in the general meeting of shareholders or the board of directors in accordance with the identity of the shareholder, make more efforts to increase capital liquidity, and choose the entry and exit mechanism according to the characteristics of state-owned assets and market environment conditions. Under the system of managing capital regardless of enterprise, the government can exclusively perform its public administration functions and conduct public administration from the perspective of economic regulation and social management. State-funded enterprises have become the main body of market competition with independent operation, self-financing, risk-bearing, and self-development. These enterprises obtain legal person property rights, enjoy civil rights and assume civil obligations, conduct independent operation of legal person properties in accordance with the law, carry out daily business activities in line with market rules, and assume responsibility for value preservation and appreciation of all corporate properties.

4.3 Comparison of work content, work focus and work methods between "capital management" and "assets management"

The innovation of the state-owned capital management system from "managing assets" to "managing capital" objectively requires the management object to be transformed from organizational object to value object of state-owned capital. Changes in management objects and content inevitably require changes in management objectives and work methods.

The report to the Sixteenth National Congress stated that the state should make laws and regulations and establish a state property management system under which the Central Government and local governments perform the responsibilities of the investor on behalf of the state respectively, enjoying owner's equity, combining rights with obligations and duties and administering assets, personnel and other affairs. If the middle-level and top-level SOEs have not yet undergone overall restructuring, the SASAC, which performs the responsibilities of investors on behalf of the state, still deals with SOEs, with enterprises as the object of its management. The *Interim Regulations on the Supervision and Administration of State-owned Assets of Enterprises*, which the State Council promulgated, have been enriched and improved based on the experiences in reform practices.

In October 2008, the *Law of the People's Republic of China on State-owned Assets in Enterprises* was passed at the Fifth Meeting of the Standing Committee of the 11th National People's Congress and came into force on May 1, 2009. The state-owned assets management system that combines administration of assets, personnel and other affairs ("three administrations") was finally specified in legal provisions. The specific content of the "three administrations" is as follows:

In terms of administering personnel, the SASAC manages the heads of SOEs in accordance with the law through the establishment of an employment mechanism and an stimulation and restraint mechanism that meets the requirements of the modern corporate system, the appointment, removal or suggestion of the appointment and removal of the heads of funded enterprises, the establishment of a performance evaluation system for the heads of enterprises, and the determination of the salaries of the heads of wholly state-funded enterprises, and reward and penalizes the heads of enterprises based on their assessment results.

In terms of administering other affairs, the rights enjoyed by the SASAC include: (1) Guide state-owned and state-controlled enterprises to establish a modern corporate system, review the plans for reorganization of wholly state-funded enterprises, shareholding system reform and company articles; (2) Decide on major matters such as the division, merger, bankruptcy, dissolution, increase or decrease of capital, and issuance of corporate bonds of wholly state-funded enterprises; (3) Decide on the transfer of state-owned equity of the enterprises invested by it; (4) Organize and coordinate the merger and bankruptcy of wholly state-funded enterprises, and cooperate with relevant departments in the resettlement of laid-off employees; (5) Formulate guidelines for the reform of the income distribution system of the invested enterprises, and regulate the overall level of wage distribution of these enterprises; and (6) Allow the qualified wholly state-funded enterprises among the invested enterprises to conduct authorized operation.

In terms of administering assets, the main contents of supervision and management of state-owned assets of enterprises include: (1) Administering property rights of state-owned assets, including property rights definition, property rights registration, assets evaluation and supervision, assets clearance and capital verification, assets statistics, comprehensive evaluation, property rights dispute coordination, property rights transaction supervision, etc.; (2) Performing the responsibilities of the investor in the income from state-owned assets, major investments and financing plans, development strategies and plans of the invested enterprises; (3) Supervise the finances of the invested enterprises in accordance with the law, establish and improve the indicator system for preserving and increasing the value of state-owned assets, and safeguard the rights and interests of state-owned assets investors.

"Capital management", which features "value-based management", focuses on preserving and increasing the value of state-owned capital and improving the vitality of capital, which will benefit the mutual fusion between state-owned capital and the market economy.

In November 2015, the State Council issued the *Several Opinions on Reforming and Improving the State-owned Assets Management System* (hereinafter referred to as the "Opinions"), which became a programmatic document guiding the reform of the state-owned assets management system. The Opinions comprehensively demonstrate the innovations of the state-owned assets management system in work contents, priorities, and methods.

In terms of work contents, the state-owned assets regulator, as an ad hoc governmental agency, specializes in the supervision and management of state-owned assets instead of performing the government function in social administration and public services. It is dedicated to capital management and free from interference with the independent operation of enterprises. In order to fulfill the goal of improving the allocation and operational efficiency of state-owned capital, the state-owned assets regulator should, as required by macro-policies and relevant regulations, build a sound advancing and retreating mechanism for state-owned capital and work out negative lists for state-owned capital investment. At the same time, a market-based exit mechanism shall be built to facilitate the survival of the fittest, promote the reform of natural monopoly industries controlled by state-owned capital, and liberalize competitive businesses in light of the characteristics of different industries. In addition, the state-owned assets regulator shall establish a state-owned capital operating budget management system covering all SOEs and implementing hierarchical management in collaboration with the financial department. In the process of forming state-owned capital investment and operating companies and reorganizing SOEs, the State will transfer part of the state-owned equity to social security funds management agency. In this way, the equity dividends and transfer income can make up for the financing gap in social security funds such as pensions.

In terms of work priorities, state-owned assets regulators should concentrate on capital management by optimizing state-owned capital, standardizing capital operations, increasing capital returns, safeguarding capital security, preserving and increasing the value of capital, which will help to achieve the national strategic goals. To satisfy the requirements for adjusting the layout of state-owned capital, efforts must be made to promote state-owned capital to be concentrated in important trades, key fields, infrastructure, forward-looking strategic industries, key links in industrial chain and high-end areas of the value chain, as well as advantage enterprises with core competitiveness. The report to the Nineteenth National Congress contained an important statement: "we will support state capital in becoming stronger, doing better, and growing bigger", marking a great leap in our cognition that strong SOEs must be in a big size. This statement requires enterprises to step up efforts in the disposal of inefficient assets, shake off "zombie companies", lower the financial leverage level, pay attention to the indicators such as value-added and return on capital, and attach importance to intensive development and optimization of the capital allocation structure.

In terms of work methods, it is necessary to change the current administrative management methods, further reduce administrative procedures for examination and approval, and slash the administrative allocation of resources via SOEs. More legal means and market-based regulation shall be employed, and the operation of the board of directors shall be standardized to effectively reflect the will of state-owned capital investors in the corporate governance structure. The establishment of state-owned capital investment and operation companies is an important way to reform the state-owned capital authorized operation system and give priority to capital management. The so-called "authorized operation" is to authorize state-owned capital investment and operation companies to perform the functions of investors on behalf of the State. In the process of advancing the reform, both "indirect authorization" and "direct authorization" models can be tried for accumulating experiences and exploring replicable models which may be implemented across the nation. By implementing the indirect authorization model, the state-owned assets regulator performs the responsibilities of the investor for state-owned capital investment and operating companies in accordance with the law and authorizes these companies to perform the responsibilities of the investor for the authorized state-owned capital. By implementing the direct authorization model, the State Council directly authorizes state-owned capital investment and operating companies to perform the responsibilities of the investor. As a professional platform for the value management and market operation of state-owned capital, state-owned capital investment and operating companies carry out state-owned capital operations independently, exercise shareholder's rights and responsibilities over the invested enterprises, and assume the responsibility for preserving and increasing the value of state-owned capital.

4.4 Temasek model sets an example for China's state-owned capital management system

4.4.1 Main characteristics of Temasek model

Temasek Holdings (Private) Limited, an investment company headquartered in Singapore, was founded in 1974 in accordance with *Singapore Companies Act*. Although Temasek sounds like a "private" company, it is a veritable state-owned company fully controlled by the Singapore Ministry of Finance. It was founded to exercise state-owned capital management and operation functions on behalf of the Singapore Government, act as a shareholder of multiple subordinate companies, and create and maximize long-term returns after risk adjustment.

Temasek is an unlisted company exempt from disclosing any financial information to the public, but it still follows the "Santiago Principles"[21] that apply to the Sovereign Wealth Funds (SWF) and keeps releasing annual reports since 2004 to make public its financial status and portfolio results. According to Temasek's Annual Report 2017,[22] as of March 31, 2017, the company's net investment portfolio had reached 275 billion Singapore dollars, with a total shareholder return (TSR) arriving at 15% since its inception. And its TSR for 1-year, 3-year, 10-year, and 20-year periods calculated in Singapore dollars was 13.37%, 7.13%, 4%, and 6%, respectively. Temasek not only succeeded in helping Singapore to preserve and increase the value of state-owned capital but also won itself an overall credit rating of AAA by Moody's Investors Service (Moody's) and S&P Global Ratings (S&P), respectively, which is a remarkable achievement hardly won by Asian companies.

Temasek is a highly internationalized investment company and SWF, with investments distributed in Asia, Europe, America, Africa and Australia. Among them, the investments in Asia account for the highest proportion, and the assets in Singapore and China account for 29% and 25%, respectively, of its portfolio. In China, Temasek invests both state-owned and non-state-owned enterprises. Being highly interested in investing in Chinese SOEs, Temasek is now holding a large number of shares in the Industrial and Commercial Bank of China, Bank of China, China Construction Bank, and Kunlun Energy. More than that, it is also investors of China Ping An Insurance Group, China Pacific Insurance Group, Alibaba, Didi Taxi, Huiyuan Juice, and Yashili International. The investment scope of Temasek mainly includes telecommunications, media and technology, transportation and industry, life sciences and agriculture, financial services, real estate, and energy. It controls almost all of Singapore's largest and most important companies, like Singapore Telecom, Singapore Airlines, SMRT Trains, DBS Bank, PSA International, Neptune Orient Lines, and Singapore Power. With the market value of shares accounting for 47% of the entire Singapore stock market, Temasek almost controls the economic lifeline of Singapore.

As a government-controlled company, Temasek mainly has the following operational characteristics:

First, it effectively isolates the property rights relationship between the government and enterprises, and realizes the separation of government functions from enterprise management. From the perspective of whether the government directly exercises the ownership of state-owned capital as an investor, there are basically two models in the world[23]: The first model is that the state sets up a special competent authority to exercise the ownership of the investor, with Germany and France as typical examples. The German Ministry of Finance exercises the ownership of investors in SOEs on behalf of the state, enjoys decision-making powers in approving the establishment of SOEs and capital supply, and controls the development of enterprises via the board of supervisors. The second model is to found national holding companies to exercise the investor's ownership, with Italy and Singapore as typical examples. Singapore has built a three-level framework of government departments – statutory bodies and government-controlled companies – Temasek's subsidiaries. As an independent legal person at the intermediate level, Temasek exercises the ownership of the investor and acts as a bridge between the government and Temasek's subsidiaries, which effectively cuts the direct property rights relationship between the government and enterprises, thereby avoiding direct government interference in enterprise operation, and realizing the separation of government functions from enterprise operation. The government plays a regulatory role in major issues such as changing capital of SOEs, appointing or dismissing key members of the board of directors. Although the government investigates Temasek's subsidiaries from time to time, it is free from interfering with their daily activities such as business management and performance evaluation. Temasek takes part in market competition by holding or controlling shares in its subsidiaries, concentrates on capital operation and equity management, and carries on its businesses free from any government intervention, thus realizing the value management of state-owned capital.

Second, it observes the principle of market-oriented operation. (1) Marketization is reflected in Temasek's exercise of investor ownership independently of administrative power. In the aforementioned three-level framework, the Ministry of Finance of Singapore, as a statutory body, acts on behalf of the government to manage state-owned capital, but after the ministry grants the investor's rights to Temasek, the responsibilities of the two parties are clearly divided. The Ministry of Finance specializes in policy formulation and market supervision, while Temasek focuses on equity operations and commercial investment to pursue long-term returns. The company has become a commercial investment institution independent of government departments. Temasek's subsidiaries are real market entities with daily operating activities free from excessive interference from the government and Temasek. (2) The market-oriented characteristics of Temasek are also reflected in the fact that the company was founded in accordance with the *Companies Act of Singapore*. While participating in economic activities, Temasek enjoys the same rights and performs the same duties as other companies. Regarding the funding sources of Temasek, except for the 354 million Singapore dollars of state-owned capital injected by the Singapore government at its inception, the subsequent funds mainly come from the company's productivity-induced economic growth. The company relies on the board of directors as the core of governance, operates independently in accordance with the principles of market-ization, seeks profit in daily operations, and takes real economic performance as the evaluation indicator. Generally, the Singapore Government does not interfere with the normal business activities of Temasek, and in accordance with the past practice, the Temasek Board of Directors has the right to reject unreasonable government orders.

Third, it has formed a corporate governance structure that, centered on the Temasek Charter and the board of directors, fully empowers the board of directors. Temasek's board of directors has the right to approve the company's overall strategic plan, annual budget and final accounts, a major investment and financing projects, appointment and removal of senior managers, and remodeling of the board of directors. The board of directors runs the company's business in accordance with market stan-dards. Temasek's board of directors is composed of 8–12 board members. Except for shareholder directors and executive directors, most of the members are independent directors. The board of directors has an executive committee, an audit committee and a leadership development and compensation committee. The executive committee is responsible for reviewing and approving investment and financing projects and assets transfer projects, formulating dividend policies, major purchase and sales contracts, and annual investment budgets. The audit committee, an important watchdog composed of independent directors, is mainly responsible for reviewing the internal control system, financial reporting process, auditing process, and monitoring process for compliance with laws and regulations. The leadership development and compensation committee recommends director candidates to the board of directors and formulates the leadership development plans for the management (including succession plans for directors and chief executives), as well as provides guidelines and policies related to performance measurement and compensation. In order to achieve checks and balances of powers, the powers of Temasek's chairman and CEO are clearly divided. After obtaining the consent of the President of Singapore, Temasek's board of directors has the right to appoint and remove the CEO. The management of the company makes independent decisions under the guidance of the board of directors and free from being affected by the government, and each subsidiary of Temasek conducts business independently in light of its own situation.

Fourth, it has established a diversified check-and-balance mechanism and a supervisory mechanism. These two mechanisms are an institutional guarantee for Temasek to effectively operate the principal-agent system and realize efficient capital allocation. With a view to the check-and-balance mechanism, the company's board of directors comprises government officials, corporate managers, and non-governmental persons (including private entrepreneurs, scholars, or other professionals). The directors with different backgrounds can check and balance the game of interests, mitigate the possibility for any director to become autocrats, and separate the interests of the company from those of government departments, business groups or specific organizations, thereby making the company's decision-making process more equitable and impartial. Moreover, in order to ensure fairness and neutrality, official directors of Temasek do not receive material remuneration from the company, and their incentive is job promotion based on the company's operating conditions. According to the *Constitution of the Republic of Singapore (Amendment)*, the elected President of Singapore has an independent veto over the appointment and removal of Temasek's directors or CEO. This means that the elected president under the constitutional system can restrict the behavior of official directors to a certain extent and restrain the impulses of government officials for "personal gains". With a view to the supervisory mechanism, the government, holding companies, the general public, and the news media jointly participate in the supervision of SOEs. The Singapore Government implements supervision of SOEs by regularly reviewing the financial statements of holding companies such as Temasek or conducting temporary inspections in accordance with the law. The holding company supervises Temasek's subsidiaries in line with market rules. The general public can conduct public supervision of state-owned capital and related enterprises through public information means, and any institution or individual can access the information of any enterprise in the registry at a low cost. In addition, the supervision of news media is ubiquitous and it has become another powerful means of public supervision. This diversified check-and-balance mechanism and supervisory mechanism ensure that Temasek can compete fiercely with other capitals in an independent and "private" capacity in the market and maximize the value preservation and appreciation of state-owned capital.

4.4.2 The enlightenment of Temasek model to China's state-owned capital management system reform

Since its establishment 44 years ago, Temasek has created huge wealth for its shareholders and set an example in the successful management and operation of state-owned capital for other countries. Although the national conditions of China are different from those of Singapore, that is, the two countries have differences in terms of land area, development of the capital market, the scale of state-owned capital, residents' price affordability, the maturity of the market system, and the boundary between public and administrative goals, the model of Temasek can still provide experience and inspiration for China to transform its state-owned capital management system and further advance the SOE reform.

The success of the Temasek model is attributed to several factors, the most critical of which is that state-owned capital allocated in the commercial sector, on the premise of balancing public and economic goals, follows the market rules independent of administrative goals and administrative powers.[24] The SOEs in Singapore undertake two major functions: economic functions and social functions. On the one hand, they provide public products and services to society and citizens, and on the other hand, they pursue the value preservation and appreciation of state-owned capital. It can be seen in the classification of Temasek's subsidiaries. According to the nature and functions of their businesses, the subsidiaries of Temasek are divided into two types: one is the SOEs that participate in market competition for profit; the other is the enterprises that concern national strategy and public policy goals. The enterprises of the second type, which are not directly profit-driven and governed by the "public law" system, are mainly distributed in energy, water resources, airports, ports, education, medical, and residential industries. When dealing with two different types of SOEs, Temasek is skilled at preserving and increasing the value of their capital through equity operations. For the first type of companies involved in market competition, Temasek allocates their state-owned capital in a variety of ways such as acquisition, sale, increase and decrease of shares, so as to promote the effective operation of these companies; for the second type of SOEs that undertake the mission to fulfill some policy objectives, Temasek will hold all or a majority of their shares.

The smart capital operation model created by Temasek is an important reference for the equity allocation of state-owned capital in China. The basic logic of enterprise operation is that "mission determines strategic positioning, strategic positioning determines strategy content, strategy content determines the organizational structure, organizational structure determines enterprise operating efficiency, while enterprise operating efficiency determines the realization of corporate mission".[25] In general market economy countries, the mission of SOEs is fairly simple, that is, they shall fulfill some social and public goals that are beyond the capacity of the market, but the mission of Chinese SOEs includes not only making up for market failures but also consolidating the basic socialist economic system, ensuring national economic security, and maintaining and increasing the value of state-owned capital. While pursuing economic benefits, Chinese SOEs also bear policy burdens, including strategic policy burdens and social policy burdens. In the case of information asymmetry and incompatible incentives, the soft budget constraints, which arise from policy burdens, will seriously affect the operating efficiency and incentive mechanisms of SOEs.[26] There have been appeals from the theoretical circle for implementing classified management and classified governance of SOEs in view of the conflict between the SOEs' missions of "making profit" and "carrying out public policies".

According to the *Guiding Opinions of the CPC Central Committee and the State Council on Deepening the Reform of State-owned Enterprises*, which were released in August 2015, we should carry out classified reform of SOEs by dividing them into commercial and public welfare categories. The commercial SOEs are subdivided into competitive and functional enterprises according to their industrial function characteristics and market competition characteristics, thus opening a new chapter in deepening the reform of SOEs. On the basis of classified reform, two types of state-owned capital investment and operating companies can be established: policy-oriented companies and commercial companies. Both of them implement the Temasek model for capital operation or equity allocation. The function of policy-oriented state-owned capital investment and operating companies is to maximize the value preservation and appreciation of state-owned capital on the premise of achieving policy objectives. Their scope of investment covers public services, strategic and forward-looking industries, ecological environment protection, science and technology, and national security. They can hold all or the majority of the shares of public welfare SOEs. Commercial state-owned capital investment and operating companies have a relatively simple goal of maximizing returns. They engage in equity investment and capital operation, adjust investment portfolios in accordance with market rules, dynamically withdraw from low-return fields, and look for high-return investment opportunities.

Another important revelation of the Temasek model is to properly handle the cooperative and competitive relationships between state-owned capital and private capital. In the domestic competitive fields, the contradiction between state-owned capital and private capital has become increasingly intensified. This antagonism is not only due to market competition but also to a large extent due to the unequal status of SOEs and private enterprises in competition, since the former is as advantageous as "the eldest son of the Republic". Such inequality has caused differences in competitiveness and quantity of gains and leads to the loss of competition efficiency and social total welfare. The successful experience of Temasek shows that when dealing with the relationship between state-owned capital and private capital, we must find the right position of state-owned capital in market competition. If there are industries that are completely suitable to private capital, then state-owned capital should gradually exit. Throughout its entire development process, Temasek Holdings first gets its subsidiaries listed and then has them marketized step by step based on market developments.

For industries suitable for the implementation of mixed ownership, private capital shall have enough discourse power; otherwise, it will be difficult to attract private capital. Even if private capital is injected, it is unlikely for the investors to play a check-and-balance role in the shareholding structure but eventually become passive shareholders who vote with their feet.

Theoretically speaking, the goal of China in reforming its state-owned capital management system is to set up a number of state-owned capital investment and operating companies, build a three-level framework similar to the Temasek model, form a corporate governance structure relying on the board of directors and make the board fully empowered, build diversified check-and-balance and oversight mechanisms, and adhere to the principle of market-oriented operation. In the course of practice, due to the large differences in the national conditions, China cannot simply replicate Singapore's Temasek model but make a concrete analysis of concrete problems and advance the reform of its state capital management system step by step.

The unique legal environment of Singapore is the institutional guarantee for Temasek's excellent corporate governance. American scholar Margaret Blair argues that corporate governance is a set of legal, cultural and institutional arrangements concerning the distribution of corporate control rights and residual claim rights. Singapore is a typical common law country. Since its founding, it has enacted more than 500 laws and has quite complete laws and regulations in all aspects of the national system, social governance, economic activities, culture and education, race and religion, and urban management.[27] Singapore is known for its severe penalties and insistence on using heavy punishments (including brutal corporal punishment) to curb uncivilized and criminal behaviors. It has so far retained caning, hanging and the death penalty. Owing to a complete legal system and strict law enforcement, Singapore has seldom seen a loss of state-owned assets, so that the governance structure formed by Temasek with the board of directors as the core and full empowerment to the board can be maintained for a long time. In China, in order to deepen the reform of the state-owned assets management system, the board of directors of SOEs shall be fully empowered and taken as the core for enterprise operation; at the same time, we must pay great attention to the rule-of-law construction, use legal means to restrain the behavior of SOEs' stakeholders, and prevent insider control and the loss of state-owned assets.

In addition, the Lee Kuan Yew family's strong control of Temasek has, to some extent, alleviated the problem of the nominal owner of state-owned capital, which is another factor in Temasek's success. The so-called nominal owner means that everyone is an owner, but everyone is unable to achieve true ownership of state-owned capital. Temasek was co-founded by Lee Kuan Yew and Goh Keng Swee. At its inception, the company was engaged in supervising the SOEs that were transferred to it. The Lee family has for years firmly controlled Temasek. Lee Hsien Loong, the eldest son of Lee Kuan Yew, is Singapore Prime Minister, and Lee Hsien Loong's wife Ho Ching is CEO of Temasek. Thanks to this kind of family control, the problem of the nominal owner of state-owned capital is not serious in Singapore. In contrast, China's state-owned capital is owned by the whole people, while the government is representative of the capital owner. Departments perform the government functions, and the department functions are undertaken by individuals holding certain positions, while these individuals act as the parties to truly perform the duties of state capital investors. But they are incapable of doing so, thus causing the problem of the nominal owner of state-owned capital. Unlike Singapore, which is a city-state, China has a vast territory and a huge amount of state-owned capital. According to the *Economic Operation of State-owned and State-controlled Enterprises in China from January to June 2018* issued by the Ministry of Finance, by the end of June 2018, the total amount of state-owned equity had reached 59.98 trillion yuan, and the investment chain within enterprise groups was relatively long and the investment relationships were fairly complicated. According to the actual situation, dozens of state-owned capital investment and operating companies may be established, and it is impossible for these companies to be subject to family-controlled corporate governance.

It is worth noting that most of Singapore's companies invested and managed by Temasek have grown up in the market environment. In the early days of Singapore's founding, the government established a number of SOEs to complete the investments in transportation, shipbuilding and other industries and built the Singapore Economic Development Board (EDB) to be their administrator. When the EDB was reorganized in 1968, these investments were taken over by the Ministry of Finance. Later, the above-mentioned SOEs, together with those managed by the statutory agencies such as the electric power bureau and the port authority, were incorporated into Temasek. In 1985, the company came up with a plan for adjusting the layout of SOEs, requiring government-funded companies to withdraw from all the non-strategic industries that did not need government leadership. The investment philosophy of Temasek is that SOEs should withdraw from the industries when they are mature enough for the entry of private enterprises. Therefore, the environment in which the companies invested and managed by Temasek must be market-oriented, while Chinese SOEs still shoulder policy-oriented missions and undertake social functions. The social functions of Chinese SOEs mainly refer to "water supply, power supply, gas supply and property service". In addition, some resource-based old SOEs are obliged to take care of their retirees.[28] In order to establish state-owned capital investment and operating companies like Temasek to manage SOEs, more efforts must be made to help them get rid of social functions and other historical burdens.

4.5 The relationship between state-owned assets management and reform of government finance system (with a goal of "big finance")

According to the previous analyses, in order to build a new state-owned assets management system centered on capital management, we must improve capital liquidity, further sort out the state-owned capital account system, adapt to the operating characteristics of the market economy, properly handle the relationship between the "stock" and "flow" of state-owned capital, and build up the government's ability in financial management. It is understandable that the stock of state-owned capital is regarded as the accumulated government fiscal capacity in the past, and the profit from the operation of state-owned capital is part of government fiscal revenue (manifested in the form of taxes and dividends from state-owned assets), it is in this sense that we can see the connectivity between state-owned capital management and government fiscal account management.

4.5.1 State-owned assets classification, accounts and management

1.   State-owned assets classification

Literally, state-owned assets refer to the sum of all properties and property rights owned by the state. In real economic life, state-owned assets can be divided into broad and narrow senses. In a broad sense, state-owned assets refer to the state-owned properties or property rights acquired by the government through various forms of investment and its returns, acceptance of donations and grants, and acquisitions according to state laws or by exercising administrative powers, including operating assets, non-operating assets and resource assets. In a narrow sense, state-owned assets refer to operating state-owned assets, which are capital and equity legally owned by the government through investment, including the state-owned assets of enterprises, the state-owned assets occupied and used by administrative institutions for business purposes only to obtain profit, and the state-owned resource assets that have been put into production and operation.[29]

According to the *Opinions of the CPC Central Committee on Establishing a System for the State Council to Report State-owned Assets Management to the*

Standing Committee of the National People's Congress, state-owned assets include the state-owned assets of enterprises (excluding financial enterprises), the state-owned assets of financial enterprises, the state-owned assets of administrative institutions, and state-owned natural resources; in general, there are three types of state-owned assets: operating, administrative, and resource. The state-owned assets discussed in this book are of three types.

Operating state-owned assets, which have the same meaning as state-owned capital, refer to the owner's equity in state-funded enterprises (including industrial and commercial enterprises and financial enterprises) that belong to the state or the government. Administrative and institutional state-owned assets refer to the sum of various assets that are occupied and used by administrative organs and institutions, legally owned by the state, and available to be measured in currency; their sources include budget appropriations, acceptance of donations and grants according to policies and regulations, and the use of state-owned assets to organize income. State-owned assets of administrative units are generally non-operating assets, while those of public institutions can be divided into operating assets and non-operating assets based on the condition of whether they are used for production and business activities. Although some public institutions do not do economic accounting like enterprises, they have strong market operation capabilities. This part of state-owned assets for operation shall be subject to supervision to prevent the loss of assets. State-owned resource assets refer to the state-owned resources that can bring economic value through development based on the current knowledge and technologies, including state-owned land, mineral deposits, forests, oceans, lakes, etc.

2.   State-owned assets accounts

By drawing on the compiling technique for making enterprise balance sheets, the national balance sheet classifies the assets and liabilities of all economic sectors (governments, non-financial enterprises, financial institutions, residents, etc.) of a country and then sums them up to form a statement. It comprehensively reflects the total assets and liabilities of a country and its structure at a certain point in time and belongs to stock accounting. It is an important tool to find out about the national conditions, and also an important content of national economic accounting.[30] In 1936, American scholars Dickingson and Earkin took the lead in proposing the idea of applying the enterprise balance sheet compiling technique to the national economy. In the 1960s, the United States compiled comprehensive and sectoral balance sheets for several years from the early 20th century to 1980. Britain compiled a national balance sheet from 1957 to 1961. At present, the United States, Britain, Canada, Australia, Japan and other countries are able to regularly compile and publish their national balance sheets, and most OECD member countries have published their financial balance sheets that do not contain physical assets.[31]

China is a latecomer in the research and compilation of national balance sheets. Although the NBS had published the *Methods for Compiling China's State-owned Assets Balance Sheet* in 1997 and 2007, the compilation of an official balance remains in trial up to now. By 2012, three teams led by Ma Jun, former chief economist of Deutsche Bank (Greater China), Cao Yuanzheng, chief economist of Bank of China, and Li Yang, vice president of the Chinese Academy of Social Sciences, had made an attempt in this regard and respectively compiled a national balance sheet of China, including a government balance sheet. The sovereign balance sheet compiled by Li Yang's team is the totaling and merging of the assets and liabilities of the government or related sovereign departments, involving the government, state-owned and state-controlled financial institutions, and non-financial SOEs. It is actually a broadly defined government balance sheet. This sheet describes the government-level assets and liabilities relatively completely. It clearly shows the stock characteristics of state-owned operating, administrative and resource assets, as well as sovereign debt (Table 4.1).

3.   State-owned assets management

The Report to the Nineteenth National Congress stated that "we will improve the systems for managing different types of state assets, and reform the system of authorized operation of the state capital. In the state-owned

Table 4.1 Simple list of China's sovereign balance sheet (compiled by Li's team)[32]

Assets	Government debt and net assets value
Government deposits in the central bank	Central financial domestic debt
Reserve assets	Sovereign debt
Land and resource assets	Non-financing platform local government debt
State-owned assets of administrative and public institutions	Local financing platform debt
State-owned assets of non-financial enterprises	Non-financial SOE debt (deducted from the financing platform local government debt)
State-owned assets of financial enterprises	Financial bonds of policy banks
	Non-performing loans of banks
	Contingent liability arising from the disposal of non-performing bank assets
State-owned assets in the national social security fund	Implicit pension debt
Total assets	Total debts
	Net fiscal assets value

sector, we will step up improved distribution, structural adjustment, and strategic reorganization. We will work to see that state assets maintain and increase their value; we will support state capital in becoming stronger, doing better, and growing bigger, and take effective measures to prevent the loss of state assets". Regarding the three types of state-owned assets (operating, administrative and institutional, and resource state-owned assets), their management has different priorities, and different methods of management shall be employed.

In terms of operating state-owned assets (state-owned capital), it is subject to value management, equity allocation, privatized operation, and market-based flow. As mentioned above, under the conditions of the socialist market economy, state-owned capital should be subject to value-based management. Enterprises of the modern corporate system shall serve as a carrier to realize the advancement and retreat of state-owned capital in different industries and regions through equity allocation. State-owned capital is allocated to an enterprise in the form of equity, and then the enterprise becomes a state-funded enterprise. It should stick to the "state-funded and independent management" operating model and operate in a privatized manner free from any form of administrative interference. State-owned capital in a competitive field should dynamically adjust its allocation structure according to the rate of return on assets so that the market can play a decisive role in the flow of equity.

In terms of administrative state-owned assets, budget management constraints shall be strengthened. We should combine assets management with a financial budget, use statistical reports and assets calculations to analyze stock assets, evaluate assets use efficiency, match assets allocation with the responsibilities of the administrative organs or public institutions, and form a complete state-owned assets budget for these units according to their plans for assets disposal income and capital needs.

In terms of state-owned resource assets, a scientific resource pricing system should be established. In China, a major obstacle in the management of state-owned resource assets is incomplete information of national resources, which is mainly due to the absence of a scientific resource valuation system. At present, we should invite experts in various fields to join in the research in this regard, learn from foreign experiences and technical means, improve resource price calculation, and form a systematic pricing system for the development, use and sale of resource products determined by market supply and demand, so as to ensure the efficiency of resource allocation and maximize its social benefits.

4.5.2 Government fiscal account

China implements a tax sharing system, that is, on the basis of rationally dividing the scope of powers of governments at all levels, the budget revenues of governments at all levels are divided mainly by taxation. Budgets at all levels are relatively independent and have clear responsibilities for balancing. The differences between levels and regions are adjusted through the transfer payment system.

The core of the tax-sharing system is that the State shall establish a budget at each level of the government, namely, at the five levels: the Central Government; the provinces, autonomous regions and municipalities directly under the Central Government; the cities divided into districts and autonomous prefectures; the counties, autonomous counties, cities not divided into districts, and municipal districts; the townships, nationality townships and towns.

The government fiscal account is a system to conduct accounting for the current value distribution with the government as the main body. In China, the MOF takes charge of the government fiscal account system. In contrast, local government departments at all levels compile the fiscal statements of local governments at the same level, and the statistical scope includes administrative units, some public institutions, and some SOEs. China's fiscal account system is based on budget and final accounts with the flow of fiscal funds at the core and materialized through the combination of financial accounting and statistical accounting. The statistics are mainly about cash transactions. In terms of accounting basis, it is generally based on a cash basis instead of an accrual basis, which is mainly applicable to business accounting. China's government fiscal account system consists of four statements: budget and final accounts statement for revenue and expenditure of general public budget, budget and final accounts statement for revenue and expenditure of government funds, budget and final accounts statement for operating income and expenditure of state-owned capital, and budget and final accounts statement for income and expenditure of social insurance funds.

At present, the international standard System of Government Finance Statistics (GFS) is made up of four statements: balance sheet, government operation statement, source and application of funds statement, and other economic flow statements, which can reflect both flow and stock of assets. In contrast, China's government fiscal account system only includes the budget and final accounts statement reflecting sources and application (flow) of cash. Since there is no balance sheet reflecting the stock, it is impossible to establish a correlation between stock and flow. The fiscal status can only be summarized in terms of deficit or surplus, thus precluding an in-depth analysis of the structure of assets and liabilities.

4.5.3   The goal of achieving "big finance" that integrates operation of stock and flow

In recent years, the establishment of a "national (government) balance sheet" and a complete "state-owned assets account system" for the whole society has received great attention from the Chinese economic theory community. Special research groups were set up and related research results were published. These efforts will guide the government to strengthen financial awareness and financial management capability. Studies have shown that the national balance sheet and the government's financial budget and final accounts "is like a company's accounts. There is a cash flow statement showing the amount of revenue and expenditure and a balance sheet showing the ratio of assets to liabilities. Similarly, the fiscal deficit of a country could be taken as a cash flow statement showing the difference between fiscal revenue and spending. As far as the country is concerned, we must pay great attention to big accounts (national balance sheet), rather than constrained by cash flow and small accounts.

The resources of the whole society are owned by the public sector (government) and private sector (enterprises and natural persons). The public resources owned by the State (government) include stock resources and flow resources. The scale of state-owned stock resources is huge, but many of them are hard to be priced. The acquisition of flow resources is closely related to the overall economic operation of the society, such as tax revenue and interest revenue. Fiscal budget revenue and expenditure represent flow resources, while national assets and debts represent stock resources, both of them incorporate past resources and operating results into the current accounting scope, based on which the government can make expectations and judgments about future economic development.

On December 31, 2014, the State Council approved and forwarded the MOF's *Reform Program for Government Comprehensive Financial Reporting System on Accrual Basis*,[33] which pointed out that it is necessary to "establish a government comprehensive financial reporting system on accrual basis that fully reflects the financial information of government, including assets and liabilities, revenue and expenses, operating costs, and cash flow". In the future, China should incorporate the state-owned assets balance sheet (stock sheet) into the government fiscal account system to realize the integrated operation of stock and flow.

To build a "big finance" model for integrated operation of stock and flow will incorporate state-owned assets management into a higher platform of "government financial management", and strengthen the government's ability to manage the macroeconomy. After the reform of the tax-sharing system, the division of fiscal resources in China mainly relies on taxation. In contrast, state-owned capital, administrative and resource state-owned assets, which are important parts of the government's disposable financial resources, are rarely considered. If these parts of earnings could be included in the government fiscal revenue, they can enable rapid accumulation of government revenue in case of a sound macroeconomic situation, and the resulting fiscal surplus will vigorously support the modernization of China's national defense, science and technology, and health care. When the economic situation deteriorates, a part of the fiscal stock funds will be used to subsidize the companies with good benefits but suffering from financial stress as a substitute to bank loans, which will help avoid the rise in corporate financial leverage and violent macroeconomic fluctuations.

In addition, if different forms of state-owned assets are transformed and thus causing capital flows, they will be reflected in the flow statement as income, but in the state-owned assets balance sheet, it is only an adjustment between different forms of assets, and the net assets may be free from any change. For example, the transfer of the land lease to the book is not the appreciation of state-owned resource assets but a way of value utilization of the land assets themselves. In this case, it cannot be counted as the government's performance because it cannot truly reflect the government's financial management ability. This is the significance of connecting the flow statement with the stock statement.

Notes

1 *Decision of the CPC Central Committee on some major issues concerning comprehensively deepening the reform.* Retrieved November 15, 2013, from http://www.scio.gov.cn/zxbd/nd/2013/document/1374228/1374228_1.htm
2 *Karl Marx and Frederick Engels* (Vol. 24, p. 122). (1973). Beijing: People's Publishing House.
3 *Karl Marx and Frederick Engels* (Vol. 23, p. 221). (1973). Beijing: People's Publishing House.
4 Zhang, H. M., & Deng, T. (1999). *Study on the structural adjustment of state-owned stock capital.* Shanghai: Fudan University Press.
5 Wu, J. L. (1991). On planning and market as a method for resource allocation. *Social Sciences in China*, Issue 6.
6 Zhang, H. M. (1998). *The logic of China's state-owned enterprise reform.* Taiyuan: Shanxi Economic Publishing House.
7 Ludwig, V. M. (2008). *Socialism: An economic and sociological analysis* (p. 103). Beijing: China Social Sciences Press.
8 Ludwig, V. M. (2008). *Socialism: An economic and sociological analysis* (p. 107). Beijing: China Social Sciences Press.
9 Deng, X. P. (1993). Excerpts from talks given in Wuchang, Shenzhen, Zhuhai and Shanghai. *Selected works of Deng Xiaoping* (Vol. 3, p. 371). Beijing: People's Publishing House.
10 Commentator article *Everyone should be a qualified constructor to build the China dream*, People's Daily, November 26, 2014, Edition 01. Commentator. (November 26, 2014). *Everyone should be a qualified constructor to build the China dream.* Retrieved November 26, 2014, from http://opinion.people.com.cn/n/2014/1202/c49217–26132992.html
11 Xi, J. P. (October 18, 2017). *Secure a decisive victory in building a moderately prosperous society in all respects and strive for the great success of socialism with Chinese characteristics for a new era – delivered at the 19th National Congress of the Communist Party of China.* http://www.xinhuanet.com/politics/19cpcnc/2017-10/27/c_1121867529.htm
12 Xi, J. P. (October 18, 2017). *Secure a decisive victory in building a moderately prosperous society in all respects and strive for the great success of socialism with Chinese characteristics for a new era – delivered at the 19th National Congress of the Communist Party of China.* http://www.xinhuanet.com/politics/19cpcnc/2017-10/27/c_1121867529.htm
13 Wu, J. L. (2016). *Tutorial of economic reform of contemporary China.* Shanghai: Shanghai Far East Publishers.

14 SASAC Research Office. (2007). *Exploration and research: research report on state-owned assets supervision & management and state-owned enterprise reform (2006)*. Beijing: Economic Press China.

15 Chen, B. L., Zhang, H. M., & Li, Y. J. (2004). *The process and thinking of taking the lead in exploring: Review and outlook of Shanghai's state-owned assets management system reform*. Shanghai: Shanghai People's Publishing House.

16 Xinhua News Agency. (July 26, 2017). *The General Office of the State Council issued the implementation plan for the corporate system reform of central enterprises*, which required that all central enterprises supervised by the SASAC to complete the corporate system reform before the end of the year. Of the subsidiaries of central enterprises at all levels, 92% have implemented this reform, but the top-level corporate organization has not been restructured. http://www.xinhuanet.com/politics/2017-07/26/c_1121381768.htm

17 SASAC. http://www.sasac.gov.cn/n2588030/n2588964/c4405592/content.html

18 Lou, J. W. (2016). Reform and improve the state-owned assets management system focusing on "capital management". *Current Affairs Report (Party Committee Central Group of Study)*, Issue 1.

19 Zhang, W. Y. (2013). *Understanding companies: Property rights, incentives and governance*. Shanghai: Shanghai People's Publishing House.

20 Chen, Q. T. (2016). Capitalization is a breakthrough in state-owned enterprise reform. *China Finance*, Issue 4.

21 The "Santiago Principles" refer to a consensus on SWF reached by the members to the International Forum of Sovereign Wealth Funds held in Santiago, with information disclosure as a core requirement.

22 Unless otherwise specified, most of the operating data of Temasek in this chapter come from open documents such as Temasek's Annual Report 2017.

23 Geng, M. Z., & Li, Y. (2003). *Survival boundary and management model of state-owned capital*. Beijing: Economic Press China.

24 Zhang, H. M., & Zhang, L. L. (2010). Reconsideration of the functions and positioning of state-owned capital – starting from the name of Temasek Holdings Private Limited. *Dongyue Tribune*, Issue 4.

25 Huang, Q. H., & Yu, J. (2013). New ideas in the new era: Classified reform and governance of state-owned enterprises. *China Industrial Economics*, Issue 11.

26 Lin, Y. F., & Li, Z. Y. (2004). Policy burden, moral hazard and soft budget constraints. *Economic Research Journal*, Issue 2.

27 Zhong, X. (June 19, 2015). *Government promotion, public participation, and legal protection – enlightenment from the building of common values in Singapore*. http://china.chinadaily.com.cn/2015-06/19/content_21051741.htm

28 Ma, J., & Zhang, W. K. (2015). *Research on the reform of state-owned capital management system* (p. 93). Beijing: China Development Press.

29 Li, S. S. (2004). *Management of state-owned assets* (1st ed.). Beijing: China Financial & Economic Publishing House.

30 Li, J. H. (2015). Pedigree of China's national balance sheet and methodology for compilation. *Management World*, Issue 9.

31 Li Y., Zhang, X. J., et al. (2012). China's sovereign balance sheet and its risk assessment (part 1). *Economic Research Journal*, Issue 6.

32 Li, Y., et al. (2012). China's sovereign balance sheet and its risk assessment (part 1). *Economic Research Journal*, Issue 6, 7.

33 On December 31, 2014, the State Council approved and forwarded the MOF's *Reform Program for Government Comprehensive Financial Reporting System on Accrual Basis*, which was made public to the whole society in document Guofa [2014] No. 63.

5 Relationship between "classified reform" and industrial fields and market structure

China's SOE reform has gone through several stages: "delegation of powers and transfer of profits" for vitalizing enterprises (to transform the government-dominated enterprise operation), invigorating large enterprises while relaxing control over small ones (to solve the problems in the layout and size of SOEs), and cultivating enterprises to be independent market entities through the corporate system reform (to identify the legal organizational forms of enterprises and improve their compatibility with the market economy). In particular, we are increasingly aware that enterprise vitality lies in capital vitality. That's why we stress the central role of "capital management" in improving the government-enterprises relationship and increasing the flexibility of state-owned capital allocation. On this basis, we need to think about the relationship between the allocation of state-owned capital and industrial fields (technical features) and market structure characteristics. In the end, we came up with the guideline of the "classified" reform of SOEs.

5.1 Bringing forth "classified reform": influence of market development on SOE reform

5.1.1 "Classified reform" marks a new breakthrough

With the deepening of reform, the Chinese economy has sustained rapid and healthy growth with economic structure and development quality going through dramatic changes. In the past four decades, enterprises as the main body of social reproduction have also undergone a multi-layer transformation and remolded themselves thoroughly. Enterprise reform is always a "central link" of the entire economic structural reform. This "positioning" was made clear in the *Decision on Reform of the Economic Structure* adopted by the Third Plenary Session of the 12th CPC Central Committee in October 1984.

From 1978 to 2012, reforms were carried out in various aspects such as enterprise independent operation, enterprise size, administrative affiliation, responsibilities, and governance mechanism. There have been stages of "delegation of powers and transfer of profits", expansion of enterprise autonomy, separation of tax from profit, and definition of enterprises as independent legal persons; implementing the "contract system", strengthening enterprise managerial responsibility, invigorating large enterprises while relaxing control over small ones, separating government functions from enterprise management, and activating enterprise managerial mechanism; corporate system transformation, the establishment of a modern corporate system, and optimization of the corporate governance structure.

The enterprise reform has continued to deepen and moved forward on the track of integrating public ownership with the market economy. SOEs' overall operating quality and efficiency have been significantly improved, thereby forming dynamic integration with the market economy on the whole.

The above-mentioned reforms in various stages have achieved remarkable results: (1) The development quality and operational efficiency of SOEs are greatly improved; they have become more competitive and made more contributions to national economic and social development. With regard to enterprise competitiveness, the number of Chinese SOEs on the "Fortune Global 500 list" rose from 6 in 2003 to 54 in 2012 and then further went up to 120 in 2017. (2) The operating mechanism of SOEs has undergone major changes. The vast majority of them have implemented the corporate system and shareholding reforms initially established a modern corporate system and gradually improved their corporate governance. More than 90% of Chinese SOEs have completed the corporate system and shareholding reforms. Among the centrally-controlled SOEs, only 30.4% of them carried out the corporate system reform in 2003, and such proportion rose to 72% in 2011. By the end of 2017, all SOEs had completed business registration in accordance with the provisions of the Company Law. (3) Small and medium-sized enterprises have gradually withdrawn from the state-owned sector, which greatly downsized the coverage of SOEs and optimized their layout. Among the 39 industrial sectors, the total output value of SOEs in 18 sectors accounted for less than 10% because state-owned capital is more and more concentrated in the industries and fields concerning the lifeline of the national economy and national security. (4) The relationship between the government and enterprises has changed. The fiscal budget is no longer arranged to supplement SOEs' capital expenditure, nor is it arranged to make up for the operating losses of enterprises. SOEs assume external responsibilities with all legal person properties and become independent legal entities.[1]

At the same time, we must also realize that the SOE reform has not achieved complete success since there are still lots of problems that need to be addressed.

First, the overall output size and capacity of SOEs remain strong, but their relative performance indicators are not satisfactory. Since the reform of the external operating environment, especially the factor market, remains somewhat backward, SOEs still enjoy certain privileges from policies and management styles. Such a situation also has something to do with people's long-held beliefs. Compared with their private counterparts, the relative indicators of SOEs remain unsatisfactory.

Second, as mentioned in the previous chapter, Chinese SOEs are on the whole undertaking dual missions of "providing public services" and "making profits". But how can an SOE attend to everything at once? On the one hand, SOEs must pursue economic benefits to continuously develop themselves and preserve and increase the value of state-owned capital. To this end, they are motivated to use their status (owner of state-owned assets) to seek all profit-making opportunities, such as using administrative resources to obtain a monopoly and restrict market access of other enterprises. On the other hand, SOEs have to make up for market failures, serve national strategies, and provide public products and services, which will sacrifice economic interests to a certain extent. As a result, SOEs are caught in an embarrassing dilemma: they must be profit-driven to preserve and increase the value of state-owned capital, but their profit-seeking behaviors may undermine market fairness and their performance of social responsibilities. The conflicts between the two missions have created so many underlying problems for SOEs and restricted the vigorous development of the state-owned sector.

Third, the government treats enterprises of different ownership differently, and SOEs are in a powerful position. Since the progressive reform was carried out in the early days, enterprises of various ownership have been receiving differentiated treatment from the government. This practice was then strengthened while the government-led economic growth kept playing a dominant role. Consequently, enterprises of different ownership have "various grades and ranks". Being "part of the public sector", SOEs have administrative attributes and occupy supreme social status and discourse power. They have obvious advantages in acquiring land, minerals and other natural resources, government projects, and bank loans, franchise rights, capital market financing and market access. For example, the output of SOEs was only one-third of the output of all enterprises, but their bank loans account for about 70%. By forming an oligopoly in some upstream industries and basic service industries, SOEs can obtain supernormal profit. Even competitive fields have two thresholds for administrative approval and market access. Administrative approval is affected by the relationship between enterprises and the government; while the access conditions in some major industries are often "tailor-made" for SOEs, no wonder lots of private enterprises are blocked from this "glass door". With leading technologies, foreign-funded enterprises advanced management experiences and competitive strength and favored by the central and local governments, while domestic private enterprises are in the most disadvantaged position. For the sake of cultivating large SOEs, some local governments even force profitable private enterprises to be merged by loss-making SOEs. It is a common occurrence in coal and civil aviation industries that private enterprises are squeezed out by SOEs.[2]

Fourth, the layout of the state-owned economy needs to be further optimized. The layout of the state-owned sector is too broad at the macro-level. There are many SOEs, especially in general competitive fields, but not many of them are truly competitive; the problem of "big and complete, small and complete" is quite prominent. In forward-looking and strategic industries, the guiding role of the state-owned sector is not good enough, and SOEs fail to generate any demonstration effect. Moreover, the state-owned sector is supposed to play a greater role in public welfare, but in fact, what they have done in this regard is not good enough. At the micro-level, among the companies that have achieved equity diversification, state-owned capital usually occupies a dominant position, thus making non-state-owned investors have no enough discourse power, small and medium shareholders find their interests hard to be protected, which is not conducive to the mutual checks and balances and positive interaction between state-owned and non-state-owned capitals.

The problems listed above are only the prominent ones. In fact, the underlying problem in SOE reform is the mutual fusion between public ownership, state-owned sector and market economy.

In November 2013, the Third Plenary Session of the 18th CPC Central Committee adopted the *Decision on Some Major Issues Concerning Comprehensively Deepening the Reform*, which tightened the connection between enterprise reform with the development and improvement of the basic socialist economic system. It presented that "a mixed economy with cross-holding by and mutual fusion between state-owned capital, collective capital and non-public capital is an important way to materialize the basic economic system of China", and stressed the importance of "vigorously developing a mixed economy", for the purpose of promoting the integration of public ownership and market economy. From then on, the SOE reform entered a new stage with mixed-ownership reform as a key starting point. In order to better implement this Decision, the CPC Central Committee and the State Council jointly issued the *Guiding Opinions on Deepening the Reform of State-owned Enterprises* on September 13, 2015. This document clarified the implementation of the "classified reform" of SOEs. There are three types of SOEs: the SOEs dedicated to public services, the commercial SOEs with main business in fully competitive industries, and the commercial SOEs with main business in important industries and key fields. This kind of "classification", which determines the "position" and "nature" of SOEs based on the industries to which they belong, and the content of their business activities and historical burdens, as well as their economic and social objectives, has opened up new prospects for deepening SOE reform.

On the one hand, "classification" benefits the compatibility of public ownership with a market economy. With special economic attributes and social functions, public-owned capital serves as the material basis of the socialist system. It plays a crucial role in the economic and social development in the primary stage of socialism in China. Under the conditions of a market economy, the mechanisms of the public-owned sector shall be transformed, and the relationships between government and assets management and between government and enterprises shall be reformed, so that public-owned capital can adapt to and actively use the laws and operating rules of the market economy. "Classification" is of positive significance for deepening the reform since it helps to define the functions of capital allocation, refine the contents of reform, establish goals and paths of development, carry out scientific regulation, clarify business responsibilities, and form a dynamic and optimized assessment method, to achieve more targeted reform, more effective regulation and more scientific assessment.

On the other hand, the "classification" has ushered SOE reform into a new realm. In the past, the management of SOEs seemed like a "one size fits all" style, which has resulted in many contradictions. For example, the "one size fits all" assessment of economic indicators may encourage enterprises to concentrate on profitable businesses and ignore public services, while enterprises with poor performance may take public services as an excuse to flee from responsibility. The classified reform of the SOEs in different industries, contrary to the "one size fits all" approach, is more precise and targeted, thereby improving the effectiveness of solving problems. The "commercial" and "public services" SOEs specified in the above Guiding Opinions are classified based on the characteristics of their capital allocation domains and the characteristics of their business objectives. "Commercial" SOEs pay more attention to satisfying the market requirements. They allocate capital flexibly and build appropriate governance structures by following market rules, and they make an effort to fulfill business objectives and assessment indicators, preserve and increase the value of state-owned capital, and enhance the competitiveness of state-owned capital. This kind of enterprise is a mainstay for the state-owned sector to integrate into the market economy. "Public services" SOEs care more about social undertakings. They focus on strengthening the cost management of enterprise operation, quality of products or services, efficiency of operation, and the ability to guarantee social functions. Such classification has created a new pattern for managing the state-owned capital allocation and for the operation of SOEs. On this basis, we can develop specific reform schemes for SOEs "in accordance with the time, the place and the enterprise", so as to make the reform measures more scientific and more targeted and achieve a better reform outcome in the end. This is bound to create a new situation in the reform of SOEs – micro-foundation of the entire economic structure.

5.1.2 The boundary of classification depends on the level of market development

It is true that "classified" reform has opened up new horizons for us. What we should do next is to make an objective and scientific classification. After that, we can carry out a series of work, including the choice of measures for enterprise reform and development, properly handle the relationship between investors and invested enterprises, specify the operating responsibilities of invested enterprises, reasonably design the contents, methods and intensity of supervision, and then conscientiously implement the assessment and incentive mechanisms.

Theoretically speaking, it is easy to "classify" existing SOEs based on the attributes of their respective main businesses. But for specific enterprises, as a result of economic and social evolution and certain historical reasons, an SOE is likely to deal with business activities and public services simultaneously, and different enterprises may have interwoven functions and business activities, which will affect the content of the classified assessment and the result of performance evaluation. For example, Shanghai divides municipal enterprises into three categories: competitive, functional, and public services. SAIC Motor is an SOE of the competitive category. The overall listing of this automobile group has promoted the transformation of the assessment of its entire organizational system and business system. But things are not that simple. As the most powerful SOE in Shanghai, SAIC has undertaken some special tasks assigned by the government in the past. Some of its investments did not aim at returns but to solve the financial difficulties of another municipal company at that time. It shows that for an SOE with rich capital and strong profitability like SAIC, it also performs a special function in the macroeconomic operation. SAIC is classified as a competitive SOE, meaning that the top indicator to be assessed is its profit. Under such assessment constraints, whether the government-required investments could fall into its scope of capital management became a separate issue. How to look at the quantity of capital contribution assigned by the government? To have it listed out separately or deleted from the assessment indicators? Shanghai SASAC brought forth a creative solution, that is, to list some businesses separately for assessment under the condition of definite classification of all businesses.

This case is an inspiration for us. SOEs under the traditional system are engaged in both main business and sideline business. Especially in a certain economic cycle, they will be assigned by the government to help certain enterprises out of financial difficulties or fund certain social undertakings; of course, these tasks will cost them a percentage of assets (funds). Therefore, in the case of classification of SOEs, it is sometimes difficult to resolve these complicated "historical burdens" on their business structure, then it inevitably enables enterprises to "bargain" with the government. Thus it is difficult to use objective and strict indicators to assess these enterprises. For this reason, it may affect the expected effect and deepening of the "classified" reform.

From the above analysis, we can conclude that "classification" is relative and conditional. How can we carry out the supporting reforms? For the SOEs that may undertake "public services", although classified as "commercial" enterprises, we have to separate the "public services" from their business activities through non-governmental acquisition, but it is quite an arduous task. In the final analysis, from the perspective of the whole society, the boundaries of SOE "classification" depend on the development of the market economy. The level of market development determines the discovery of these boundaries. Looking at market development from a dynamic perspective, the boundaries of "classification" are moving and changing because the continuous deepening of market reforms will trigger the movement of these boundaries. It is in this sense that the continuous deepening of reforms and advancement of market development go hand in hand with the classified reform of SOEs.

5.2 Competition and cooperation between state-owned capital and other social capital upon classification of SOEs

5.2.1 Developing mixed ownership based on "classified" reform

Through 40 years of reform and opening up and as a result of rapid economic growth, China has seen its state-owned capital, collective capital, and non-public capital have increased by tens or even hundreds of times. According to the data released by the MOF, by the end of 2017, the total assets of Chinese SOEs nationwide had reached 151.71 trillion yuan, and their total owner's equity was 52 trillion yuan. Reform practice shows that allowing the development of non-public sectors in addition to the SOE reform is a successful incremental reform. Such reform refers to the vigorous development of private enterprises while maintaining the state-owned sector temporarily unchanged. Driven by the incremental reform, state-owned capital has increased exponentially, and various types of social capital and private investment in fixed assets have also increased substantially. As of September 2017, the number of Chinese private enterprises was about 26.07 million, accounting for 89.7% of the total number of enterprises; their combined registered capital was 165.38 trillion yuan, accounting for 60.3% of the total registered capital of all enterprises.[3] The NBS data show that the private investment in fixed assets reached 38.15 trillion yuan in 2017, accounting for 60.4% of the national total fixed-asset investment. A large amount of social capital requires further broadened investment channels, the same legal protection and social trust as state-owned capital, thus creating preconditions for the development of a mixed economy.

In fact, a major theme throughout the reform and opening-up process is that we have been working hard to explore effective forms of public ownership and the basic economic system. In 1993, the Third Plenary Session of the 14th CPC Central Committee adopted the *Decision on Some Issues Concerning the Establishment of the Socialist Market Economy*, stating that "with the flow and reorganization of property rights, there will be more and more economic units of mixed ownership, and a new property ownership structure will be formed". This was the first time that the concept of "mixed ownership" appeared in an official document.[4] But this concept was not uplifted to an institutional level at that time. In 1997, the report to the Fifteenth National Congress put forward that "publicly-owned economy includes not only both state-owned enterprises and collectively-owned enterprise but also either state-owned elements or collectively-owned elements in its mixed sector of the economy". "Efforts should be made to find a form of public ownership that can greatly promote the development of productive forces. The joint-stock system is a form of capital organization of modern enterprises. It can be used both under capitalism and under socialism".[5] It can be seen that the Central Government had already taken mixed ownership as a "system". In 1999, the Fourth Plenary Session of the 15th CPC Central Committee decided that "large and medium-sized state-owned enterprises, especially advantageous enterprises, that are suitable for implementing a shareholding system should be transformed into joint-stock enterprises through standardized listing, Sino-foreign joint ventures, and mutual equity participation by enterprises, and develop a mixed sector of the economy". In 2002, the Sixteenth National Congress clearly pointed out that "Except for a tiny number of enterprises that must be funded solely by the state, all the others should introduce the joint-stock system to develop a mixed sector of the economy".[6] In 2003, the Third Plenary Session of the 16th CPC Central Committee further proposed that "it is necessary to adapt to the continuous development of economic marketization, further enhance the vitality of the public sector, vigorously develop a mixed economy involving state-owned capital, collective capital and non-public capital, realize the diversification of investment entities, and make shareholding the main form of public ownership".[7] The Decision made by the Third Plenary Session of the 18th CPC Central Committee, which contained the important thesis of "vigorously developing a mixed economy", directly expressed that we should "embrace" the mixed economy, which was the inheritance and development of the previous explorations into the mixed-ownership theory and practice, marking the deepening of China's reform practices and achievements.

There are multiple reasons for the formation of mixed ownership with Chinese characteristics. Zhang Wenkui, a Chinese chief expert in the study of SOE reform, made an authoritative summary of these reasons: (1) In the early days, the government vigorously encouraged "economic and technological collaboration and horizontal economic union". The state-owned sector, which possesses vast production factors, started complementing private enterprises which boast flexible operating mechanisms, thereby giving birth to mixed ownership. (2) The combination of radical control rights reform and progressive ownership reform is prone to cause partial transfers of state ownership rather than complete transfer, thus giving birth to a large number of mixed enterprises. (3) Incremental economic reforms laid the foundation for mixed ownership. (4) Since the government is in-experienced in managing purely private enterprises, it is willing to retain some state-owned shares by developing mixed enterprises. (5) SOEs are more likely to gain the trust of customers, the public, banks and other parties, thus making private enterprises actively choose mixed ownership. (6) "State ownership is a strong pillar", which stimulates private enterprises to be incorporated into mixed enterprises. (7) SOEs have easier access to various resources and government support, leading private enterprises to actively choose mixed ownership.[8]

At present, there are a large number of mixed enterprises distributed in China's all economic sectors. According to the statistics from the Development Research Center (DRC) of the State Council, as of the end of 2014, there had been 171,400 mixed enterprises nationwide, accounting for 46.11% of the total number of state-invested enterprises and 0.94% of all enterprises. Looking at the whole society, the number of mixed enterprises is small, but they have a large scale. The registered capital of mixed enterprises accounted for 18.69% of that of all enterprises. In terms of both quantity and registered capital, almost half of the state-invested enterprises are of mixed ownership. Regarding the distribution of mixed enterprises, in the industries with low-density state investment, such as agriculture, for-estry, animal husbandry and fishery, wholesale and retail, real estate, hotel and catering, residential services, repair and other services, manufacturing, scientific research and technical services, culture, sports and entertainment, the registered capital of mixed enterprises accounted for more than 50% of that of state-invested enterprises. In contrast, in the industries with high-density state investment, such as electricity, heat, gas, water production and supply, transportation, warehousing and postal services, banking, water conservancy, environment and public facilities management, leasing and business services, information transmission, software and information technology, the proportion of registered capital of mixed enterprises in state-invested enterprises was less than 50%.[9]

"Classification" has far-reaching significance for deepening the reform of SOEs. In order to conscientiously implement the major reform measures such as the establishment of state-owned capital investment and operating companies, development of the mixed sectors, and improvement of the modern corporate system, the first thing to do is to clearly define the functions and categories of SOEs. After SOEs are classified, we can decide how to carry out the property rights reform of different types of enterprises, whether state-owned capital should have a controlling interest, and what shall we do to make the classified SOE reform more reasonable and more scientific. The mixed-ownership of state-owned capital and other social capital in concrete industrial fields has become an important way to materialize the basic economic system "with public ownership playing a dominant role and diverse forms of ownership developing side by side". The development of a mixed economy based on "classification" has become a key direction for deepening the SOE reform in the new era.

The competitive fields should become the main battlefield for advancing the mixed-ownership reform. For the commercial SOEs whose main business is in fully competitive industries and fields, their mixed-ownership reform must comply with the requirements of marketization and internationalization, mainly pursuing the goals of vitalizing the state-owned economy, amplifying the functions of state-owned capital, preserving and increasing the value of state-owned capital. Various sources of capital can be introduced to diversify equities, state-owned capital can be absolutely holding, relative holding, or of equity participation, efforts shall be intensified for listing reorganized SOEs and for promoting overall listing. At the same time, we must improve the governance structure and management styles of mixed enterprises by taking capital as the link. All capital contributors, state-owned and non-state-owned, shall perform their rights and duties as shareholders and constitute a relationship of equal cooperation and competition. The governance of mixed enterprises goes through the decision-making procedures of the shareholders' meeting and the board of directors. The government also needs to transform its functions and learn to influence mixed-enterprises through an indirect marketization approach rather than directly issues instructions to these enterprises. By introducing social capital, the check and balance between private equity and state-owned equity will, to a certain extent, alleviate the efficiency loss caused by the "dominance" of SOEs. The case of "Fighting for Control Power of Wuhan Department Store Group" shows that private shareholders in mixed enterprises will play an increasingly important role in enterprise development, and the check-and-balance effect on state-owned controlling shareholders are closely related to the ownership property, cash flow rights, and shareholding ratio of the second-largest shareholder. By introducing interested shareholders, fighting for the board seats or utilizing legal means, the second-largest shareholder is able to check and balance the controlling shareholder. More than that, the market-oriented behaviors of control power will correct the strategic actions of major shareholders and form a reasonably balanced shareholding structure.[10]

It is worth noting that when SOEs in a competitive field carry out mixed-ownership reform, their optimal shareholding structure should be determined by the market. If state-owned capital seeks industrial "control" in a competitive field, it will have a huge impact on the market. In this sense, lots of theorists have proposed that "state-owned capital should be withdrawn from competitive fields", which is not unreasonable. However, the scale of state-owned capital is too enormous to be fully withdrawn. Not only that, if state-owned capital completely withdraws from competitive fields, there would be no basis for making use of the control, influence, and anti-risk ability of the state-owned sector, nor is it possible to form a new pattern of equal competition and mutual promotion of various sectors of the economy. So, what is the optimal shareholding ratio of state-owned capital within a mixed enterprise? Many scholars at home and abroad have conducted a comparative analysis on the efficiency of mixed enterprises in the transitional period. Researches of Liu Xiaoxuan and Li Shouxi show that the performance of mixed enterprises is significantly higher than that of pure-equity ones. Whether they are state-owned mixed, private mixed or foreign-funded mixed enterprises, their efficiency is higher than that of similar enterprises with single equity to varying degrees. For state-owned mixed enterprises, when their state-owned equity is roughly 10–50% or around 30%, they will have relatively optimal efficiency.[11] In their studies, Ma Lianfu and Wang Lili have found that simple equity mixing cannot improve enterprise performance. The advantages of diversified investors will not show up unless there is a relatively perfect external institutional environment. For example, when the proportion of non-state-owned shares reaches 30–40%, the enterprise will have optimal performance.[12] According to Zhang Wenkui, for an SOE going through mixed-ownership reform, the proportion of non-state-owned shares shall reach at least 33.4% to be of substantial significance, because such proportion will enable the exercise of the veto in the general meeting of shareholders on matters such as changing the company's articles of association and capital restructuring. In this way, non-state shareholders will have sufficient conditions to become active shareholders.[13] The above research are of positive significance in building an optimal proportional relationship between state-owned and non-state-owned capitals and then improving enterprise performance. However, the author holds that in the process of promoting mixed-ownership reform, the optimal equity structure should be determined by the market since various industries differ greatly in market structure, enterprise scale and competitiveness. The key is not to fix the proportion of state-owned equity but to transform state-owned capital functions in competitive fields with the times and shift focus from "control" of industries and enterprises to the returns on state-owned investment. That is, we should implement value-based capital management.

In the commercial SOEs whose main businesses are in major industries and key fields that concern national security and the lifeline of the national economy or major special tasks, state-owned capital may hold a controlling stake, with equity participation of non-state-owned capital. For natural monopoly industries, we should "separate market entities from the infrastructure characterized with natural monopoly" and liberalize competitive businesses according to the characteristics of different industries, follow the principle of "separating government functions from enterprise management and separating the government from state-owned assets management", implement reforms with franchising and government regulation as the main content, promote the market-oriented resource allocation, and at the same time strengthen legal supervision by classification and standardize profit models.

In the industries and fields that provide public products and services such as water, electricity, heat, public transportation, communal facilities, it is necessary to strengthen classified guidance according to different business characteristics and promote qualified enterprises to diversify their investment entities. We can encourage the participation of non-state-owned enterprises through the purchase of services, franchising, and entrustment of agents. The government should strengthen the regulation of their price level, cost control, operational efficiency, service quality, safety standards, information disclosure and guarantee capability, and assess their operating performance and state-owned capital value maintenance and appreciation according to the different characteristics of enterprises. A social evaluation mechanism can be introduced in this regard.[14] When assessing the performance of public services SOEs, we should not take capital appreciation as the main assessment index but focus on their cost control and service quality.

5.2.2 *Correctly understand the dominant role of the public sector of the economy*

Some people worry that the new round of mixed-ownership reform is mainly beneficial to non-state-owned capital, and it will create a situation where mixed ownership is the mainstay and shake the dominant position of public ownership. Such worry is completely unnecessary. When the Fifteenth National Congress established the basic economic system, it clearly explained the connotation of the dominant position of public ownership. According to the report to the Congress, "the dominant position of the public sector is mainly reflected that public assets occupy a greater share in total social assets; the state-owned sector controls the lifeline of the national economy and plays a leading role in economic development".[15]

From the perspective of the quantity of public assets, the status of public ownership as the mainstay remains stable. In a research report produced by the Institute of Economics of Chinese Academy of Social Sciences, the amount and proportion of China's public assets by 2012 were estimated as follows: the total operating assets of three industries were about 487.53 trillion yuan, of which the public assets stood at 258.39 trillion yuan, accounting for 53%.[16] If we reckon in the non-operating state-owned assets such as urban land, rural collectively-owned land and natural resources, the proportion of public assets will be greatly higher. In this sense, the dominant position of public ownership remains stable and has not been shaken. Furthermore, the dominance of public ownership needs a quantitative prescription, and more importantly, it needs a qualitative prescription. This is to scientifically view the dominant position of public ownership from the nature of socialism with Chinese characteristics and the inherent operating laws of a modern market economy. The state-owned capital should be concentrated in major industries, key fields and important links related to national security, the lifeline of the national economy, and the people's basic livelihood, so as to form the framework of economic and social development, and then become a "light" shining on the entire economy and society through the penetration and amplification of the market mechanism.[17] At this stage, the vigorous development of a mixed economy may lead to a decrease in the proportion of state-owned capital in certain fields, but if we look at the whole society and from both "quantitative" and "qualitative" perspectives, the dominant position of public ownership will remain as firm as a rock.

Besides, giving play to the leading role of the state-owned economy does not mean that there should be more and more SOEs or an increasingly higher proportion of state-owned sector in the national economy; instead, we should increase the vitality of the state-owned sector, build up its control, influence and anti-risk ability.

In his speech delivered at the Central Economic Work Conference held in 2014, General Secretary Xi Jinping emphasized that "we must unswervingly support state-owned enterprises in becoming stronger, doing better, and growing bigger, and steadily enhance the vitality of the state-owned sector of the economy and its capacity to leverage and influence the economy, as well as to withstand risks".[18]

According to a research report produced by the Macroeconomic Research Institute of the National Development and Reform Commission, at this stage, the state-owned economy firmly occupies a dominant position in industries that concern national security and the lifeline of the national economy, key mineral resources, and industries that provide important public products and services. As of 2012, state-owned capital accounted for more than 50% of the combined capital of 21 basic and pillar industries. It occupies an absolute dominant position in major industries and key fields such as defense, banking, post and telecommunications, aerospace, railways, and energy. In the fields of military industry, telecommunications, civil aviation, oil and natural gas exploitation, as well as power and heat supply, the state-owned capital accounted for more than 90%, and its proportion in key industries such as aerospace and railways even exceeded 95%. In the industries of oil and natural gas extraction, power and heat production and supply, and water production and supply, the main business income of state-owned and state-controlled enterprises accounted for 89.4%, 93.5% and 69.2%, respectively. In the petroleum refining industry and coal mining and processing industry, the main business income of state-owned and state-controlled enterprises accounted for 69.7% and 59.2%, respectively. In the industries of transportation equipment, metallurgy, and non-ferrous metal, the state-owned and state-holding industries occupied a share of 33.7–44% in the total capital.[19] According to the *Comprehensive Report on the Management of State-owned Assets in 2017* submitted by the State Council to the Sixth Session of the 13th National People's Congress for deliberation, by the end of 2017, the total assets of SOEs nationwide were 183.5 trillion yuan (RMB, the same below), and their total debts were 118.5 trillion yuan; the total state-owned capital and equity reached 50.3 trillion yuan. The total overseas assets of SOEs nationwide were 16.7 trillion yuan.[20]

After the release of the *Opinions of the CPC Central Committee on Establishing a System for the State Council to Report State-owned Assets Management to the Standing Committee of the National People's Congress*, it was the first time for the State Council to report the management of state-owned assets to the Standing Committee of the NPC, and also the first time for the state-owned financial assets to be exposed to the people all over the country. This also reflected the requirements to "improve the mechanisms for managing all types of state assets"[21] as presented by the report to the Nineteenth National Congress. We must make statistics of state-owned assets in the whole society, especially the valuation of land and resource assets, stick to the basic principles of public ownership of land and state ownership of mineral resources, and unswervingly uphold the dominant position of the public sector of the economy.

Promoting the mixed-ownership reform based on SOE classification will more effectively demonstrate the "four powers" (vitality, control, influence, and risk resistance) of state-owned capital. By rationally introducing social capital, it is possible to optimize the financial structure of enterprises, reduce their debt ratio and financial cost, and greatly improve their profitability, thereby activating the state-owned stock capital and increasing the capital value.

The successful mixed-ownership reform of China National Building Materials Group Corporation (CNBM) set a good example for other Chinese SOEs. This company is in a fully competitive industry. In 2002, it was insolvent with an operating income of above 2 billion yuan but overdue loans of more than 3 billion yuan. By following the guideline of "restructuring central SOEs", CNBM "mixed" with thousands of private enterprises. After more than a decade of effort, the company has become the world's largest building material manufacturer and the world's leading integrated service provider. It had remained as a Fortune 500 company for 8 consecutive years and ranked 243 in 2018. CNBM has total assets of nearly 600 billion yuan, an annual operating income of more than 302.1 billion yuan, a total profit of 15.1 billion yuan, and a tax paid of 19.68 billion yuan. The number of its employees is as many as 250,000. The company has undergone earth-shaking changes in business vitality, control and influence. It first controlled 156-billion-yuan net assets with 21-billion-yuan state-owned capital and then controlled 591.5-billion-yuan total assets with 156.4-billion-yuan net assets. As a result, the allocation scope of state-owned capital has been greatly expanded, and the dominant position of the state-owned economy has been further consolidated.

5.3 The relationship between SOE reform and the opening of industrial fields

After the *Guiding Opinions of the CPC Central Committee and the State Council on Deepening the Reform of State-owned Enterprises* was released, the supporting policies were promulgated one after another. After more than 3 years of exploration, a "1 + N" policy framework was formed, with "1" representing the Guiding Opinions and "N" representing the supporting documents (see Table 5.1). An institutional framework for comprehensively deepening SOE reform in the new era initially took shape.

At present, the mixed-ownership reform is proceeding in an orderly manner. As of the end of 2016, the proportion of mixed central enterprises and their subsidiaries (including those through equity participation) under the supervision of the SASAC had reached 68.9%. The total assets, operating income and profits of listed companies respectively accounted for 61.3%, 62.8% and 76.2% of those of central enterprises. Among the SOEs and their subsidiaries at all levels invested by the provincial-level SASAC, the proportion of mixed enterprises had reached 47%.[22]

In the process of advancing the mixed-ownership reform, it is necessary to diversify equity, improve the corporate governance structure, break industry monopolies, realize the fundamental reform of SOEs, and avoid the phenomenon of "mixing for the sake of mixing". However, the pilot reform of several enterprises has shown that such an adverse phenomenon indeed exists.

Take Sinopec Sales Company as an example. In February 2014, Sinopec announced the introduction of social and private capitals to achieve mixed operations of its oil product sales business. Later in September, the "Agreement on Capital Increase of Sinopec Sales Company" was signed with 25 domestic and foreign investors, and all of them would subscribe for 29.99% of the equity of Sinopec Sales Company with cash of 107.094 billion yuan[23] (see Table 5.2). Among these 25 investors, there were only 9 industrial investors and those that form groups with industrial investors; their funds of 32.69 billion yuan accounted for 30.5% of the total investment. The remaining investors were fund and insurance firms such as China Asset Management, Harvest Fund, ICBC Credit Suisse and China Life. These institutions were probably "stakeholders" of Sinopec Sales Company. In addition, 25 investors held a total of about 30% of Sinopec Sales Company's shares. The highest shareholding ratio of a single shareholder was less than 3%, and the lowest was only 0.1%. There were also 11 private investors with shares "small and scattered", which was hard for them to effectively check and balance against major shareholders. State-owned investors still had the final say, and the corporate governance mechanism had not changed much from that of an SOE. The so-called mixed-ownership reform was just "old wine in a new bottle".

Table 5.1 The "1 + N" policy framework for deepening SOE reform

Document type	Title	Release date
"1"	Guiding Opinions of the CPC Central Committee and the State Council on Deepening the Reform of State-owned Enterprises	September 2015
"N"	Opinions on Reasonably Determining and Strictly Regulating the Responsibilities and Business Expenses of the Heads of Central Enterprises	September 2014
	Opinions on Deepening the Reform of the Remuneration System for the Heads of Central Enterprises	November 2014
	Opinions on Strengthening and Improving the Supervision of State-owned Assets of Enterprises to Prevent the Loss of State-owned Assets (adopted at the 13th Meeting of the Central Leading Group for Comprehensively Deepening Reform)	June 2015
	Notice on the Guiding Opinions on the Separation and Transfer of "Water, Power and Heat Supplies and Property Management" in the Family Areas of State-owned Enterprise Employees	June 2015
	Several Opinions on Upholding Party Leadership and Strengthening Party Building in Deepening the Reform of State-owned Enterprises	June 2015
	Opinions of the State Council on the Development of Mixed Economy by State-owned Enterprises	September 2015
	Several Opinions on Reforming and Improving the State-owned Assets Management System	October 2015
	Guiding Opinions on Encouraging and Regulating the Introduction of Non-State-owned Capital into the Projects Invested by State-owned Enterprises	October 2015
	Opinions on Strengthening and Improving the Supervision of State-owned Assets of Enterprises to Prevent the Loss of State-owned Assets (issued by the State Council)	October 2015
	Notice on Issuance of Supporting Documents for Power System Reform	November 2015
	Opinions on Comprehensively Promoting the Construction of the Rule of Law in Central Enterprises	December 2015
	Guiding Opinions on the Definition and Classification of State-owned Enterprises' Functions	December 2015
	Guiding Opinions on Further Standardizing and Strengthening the Management of State-owned Assets of Administrative Institutions	December 2015
	Interim Measures for Equity and Dividend Incentives of State-owned Technology Enterprises	February 2016

(*Continued*)

Table 5.1 (Continued)

Document type	Title	Release date
	Measures for Supervision and Administration of Enterprise State-owned Assets Transactions	June 2016
	Guiding Opinions on Promoting the Structural Adjustment and Reorganization of Central Enterprises	July 2016
	Opinions on Establishing a System of Investigating the Responsibility of State-owned Enterprises' Illegal Operation and Investment	August 2016
	Opinions on the Pilot Program for Implementing Employee Stock Ownership in State-controlled Mixed Enterprises	August 2016
	Implementation Plan for Improving the Classified Assessment of the Functions of Central Enterprises	August 2016
	Notice on Issuing the Work Plan for Speeding up the Stripping of State-owned Enterprises' Social Functions and Solving Issues Left over from History	September 2016
	Notice on Doing a Good Job in Equity and Dividend Incentives of Central Technology Enterprises	October 2016
	Guiding Opinions on Further Improving the Corporate Governance Structure of State-owned Enterprises	May 2017
	Plan for Promoting Functional Transformation of SASAC of the State Council with Capital Management at the Core	May 2017

Source: Documents made public by the State Council.

It should be noted that China has yet fully liberalized oil price to date, so we still have to carefully decide oil sales price and settle accounts among production, processing and sales companies. China's petroleum industry has remained under special control for a long time. PetroChina, Sinopec and CNOOC, known as "three barrels of oil", have almost monopolized domestic markets of crude oil refining and wholesale of refined oil, so the entry threshold is too high for both foreign and private capital. At present, a marketized pricing mechanism for refined oil products remains absent in the domestic market. The current refined oil pricing mechanism is operated in a way that the NDRC first assesses the international oil prices in Singapore, New York and Rotterdam in a 22-workday cycle and then adjusts the price of domestic refined oil.

In this context, the mixed-ownership reform of Sinopec Sales Company is bound to make people worry about whether there is "benefit transfer" or loss of state-owned assets. Objectively speaking, as a pilot to implement

Table 5.2 List of 25 investors of Sinopec Sales Company (unit: billion yuan)

No.	Investor	Place of registration	Actual controller/investor	Subscription price	Shareholding ratio
1	Harvest Capital Management Co., Ltd.	Beijing	Harvest Fund Management Co., Ltd.	10	2.80%
2	China Life Insurance Company Limited	Beijing	China Life Insurance (Group) Company	10	2.80%
3	Shenzhen PICC, Tencent & Munsun Energy Investment Fund Company	Shenzhen	PICC, Tencent Technology (Shenzhen) Co., Ltd. Munsun Asset Management Co., Ltd.	10	2.80%
4	Qianhai Golden Bridge Fund ILP	Cayman Islands	CICC-Qianhai (Shenzhen) Fund	10	2.80%
5	HuaXia SSF1 Investors Limited	British Virgin Islands	China Asset Management Co., Ltd.	7.75	2.17%
6	Changjiang Pension Insurance Co., Ltd.	Shanghai	CPIC	6.15	1.72%
7	BHR Equity Investment Fund Management Co., Ltd.	Shanghai	Bank of China Limited	6	1.68%
8	Sino Life Insurance Co., Ltd.	Shenzhen	Sino Life Insurance Co., Ltd.	5.5	1.54%
9	CICC Evergreen Fund, L.P.	Cayman Islands	CICC	5	1.40%
10	Harvest Fund Management Co., Ltd.	Beijing	Harvest Fund Management Co., Ltd.	5	1.40%
11	ENN Energy China Investment Limited	Hongkong	ENN Energy Holdings Limited	4	1.12%
12	Kingsbridge Asset Holding Ltd.	British Virgin Islands	RRJ Capital	3.6	1.01%
13	New Promise Enterprise Limited	British Virgin Islands	Haixia Huifu Industry Investment Fund Management Co., Ltd., Haier Group	3.402	0.95%
14	China Deyuan Capital (Hong Kong) Limited	Hongkong	Huiyuan International Holdings Limited	3	0.84%

(*Continued*)

Table 5.2 (Continued)

No.	Investor	Place of registration	Actual controller/investor	Subscription price	Shareholding ratio
15	CindaSino-Rock International Energy Company Limited	British Virgin Islands	China Cinda Asset Management Co., Ltd.	2.575	0.72%
16	Tianjin Jiaxing Commercial Investment Center	Tianjin	CICC Jiacheng Investment Management Co., Ltd.	2.425	0.68%
17	Pingtao (Hong Kong) Limited	Hongkong	Fosun International Limited	2.153	0.60%
18	ICBC Credit Suisse Asset Management Co., Ltd.	Shanghai	Industrial and Commercial Bank of China Limited	2	0.56%
19	Beijing Longhui Investment Management Co. Ltd.	Beijing	Sanzhou Longhui Industrial Limited Company	1.5	0.42%
20	Qingdao GoldStone Zhixin Investment Center (LP)	Qingdao	Qingdao GoldStone Runhui Investment Management Co., Ltd.	1.5	0.42%
21	China Post Insurance	Beijing	China Post Group Corporation	1.5	0.42%
22	Concerto Company Ltd.	Cayman Islands	HOPU Investment Management Co., Ltd., RT-Mart	1.421	0.40%
23	Foreland Agents Limited	British Virgin Islands	Haier Electronics Group Co., Ltd.	1.218	0.34%
24	China Shuangwei Investment Corporation	Beijing	China National Tobacco Corporation	1	0.28%
25	Huaxia Solar Development Limited	British Virgin Islands	China Asset Management Co., Ltd.	0.4	0.11%
Total				107.094	29.99%

Source: Announcement of Sinopec.

the mixed-ownership reform, Sinopec Sales Company worked hard to satisfy the basic requirements of information disclosure in the process of raising social capital and comply with the norms of openness and fairness, which is of groundbreaking significance. Therefore, it is particularly urgent to create supporting conditions and cultivate a fair and open market environment for the purpose of advancing the mixed-ownership reform. While looking at the current reforms, we must prevent "pseudo-mixing" and "mixing for the sake of mixing". The genuine "mixing" means the cooperation between different types of ownership, while the deep-level reform requires "openness in industrial fields". This is a long-term reform task; its fulfillment requires our efforts to create more standardized external conditions.

The current mixed-ownership reform in China is a unique one. The book *The Power of Corporations*[24] depicts the emergence of the corporate system in western countries. In this stage, they introduced social capital, how did they do that, how important is social capital to protect and expand their social productive forces, which is significantly different from the circumstance in China: we are promoting the cooperation and integration of state-owned and social capitals on the premise of adhering to public ownership. Behind the "mixing" is the opening of industries, the opening of property rights and the opening of market access. The opening of industries must be done cautiously since it concerns national economic security. It seems that we are "crossing the river by feeling the stones". In this sense, the mixed-ownership reform is a long-term endeavor. We must have a full understanding of it and maintain peace of mind. "To change for the sake of change" is hollow and formalistic.

In conclusion, from the Decision adopted at the Third Plenary Session of the 18th CPC Central Committee to the Guiding Opinions and a series of supporting policies and then to their implementation, the theoretical framework for the mixed-ownership reform is fairly complete, but the practice is not always satisfactory. This reform can neither be procrastinated nor advanced recklessly. We have to think about all sorts of factors such as the industrial fields and institutional environment where mixed enterprises are located and the market structure. For SOEs in competitive fields, their reform may be accelerated; but for those in major industries and key fields that concern national security, the lifeline of the national economy, and industries providing public products and services, their reform must be carried out cautiously. With respect to the fields of natural monopoly, they should not carry out the mixed-ownership reform, according to Chen Lin, but improve the existing government regulatory system, which is mainly because, in the urban public sectors of natural monopoly, mixed-ownership reform cannot significantly increase the efficiency of enterprise production.[25]

5.4 Influence of state-owned capital allocation on the market structure

For the purpose of increasing the vitality of enterprises, China's SOE reform has gone through the three stages of "invigorating enterprises", "invigorating the state-owned economy", and "invigorating state-owned capital", which reflects that our theoretical knowledge of the reform has kept deepening. The idea of "invigorating enterprises" focuses on the specific corporate organizational form at the micro-level. In a competitive market environment, some enterprises are vibrant and efficient, while others are uncompetitive and inefficient and even on the verge of bankruptcy. Such difference is attributed to their varied organizational scale, technical strength and operating capability. In the mid-1990s, the Party and the government realized that reforms should not only address the problems of SOEs. The underlying problems are ownership and property rights. So they started strengthening the compatibility between the forms of economic components and the market, and thereby coming up with the idea of "invigorating the state-owned economy". However, as a basic category, the state-owned economy is a matter of ownership relations and economic component relations. There is no way to invigorate the state-owned economy by solely relying on state ownership. In the practice of reforms, the non-public sectors have expanded substantially and become a rival of the state-owned sector. In order to properly handle this competitive relationship and realize the integration of public ownership and market economy, the notion of "invigorating state-owned capital" came into being.

How can we "invigorate state-owned capital"? To solve this problem, we must proceed from the allocation structure of state-owned capital and correctly handle the competitive and cooperative relationship between state-owned and non-state-owned capitals. The allocation structure of state-owned capital determines the cooperative relationship and degree of cooperation between capital contributors of different ownership and determines the industrial organization, industrial openness, market competition pattern and market opportunities in specific industrial fields. Moreover, as a result of changes in stage and level of economic development and in technical features, the distribution of state-owned capital will be in need of dynamic adjustment.

After the establishment of the SASAC in 2003, the optimization of state-owned capital allocation has entered a new stage. By following the principle of "advancing and retreating, refraining from doing something in order to accomplish other things", the SASAC established the direction and priorities of the strategic adjustment of state-owned capital: On the one hand, through the introduction of private capital and policy-mandated bankruptcy, state-owned capital is withdrawn from small and medium-sized enterprises and some enterprises in financial difficulties. On the other hand, encourage the cross-regional unification and reorganization of central SOEs, and promote state-owned capital to be concentrated in major industries and key fields, in advantageous enterprises, and in leading entrepreneurs.[26]

According to the *Guiding Opinions on Promoting State-owned Capital Adjustment and State-owned Enterprise Restructuring* released in 2006, we should "promote the concentration of state-owned capital in major industries and key fields that concern national security and the lifeline of the national economy", and specify that "major industries and key fields mainly include the industries related to national security, key infrastructure and important mineral resources, the industries that provide necessary public products and services, as well as the backbone enterprises in pillar industries and high-tech industries".

After a series of adjustments in the energy industries such as oil and natural gas extraction and coal mining and processing, national monopoly industries such as tobacco, and public utility industries such as production and supply of electricity, heat and water, the net assets of state-owned enterprises accounted for more than 70% of the total net assets of industry-wide enterprises.[27]

The Decision adopted at the Third Plenary Session of the 18th CPC Central Committee clearly put forward the key directions for optimizing the distribution of state-owned capital: "state-owned capital investment operations must serve the strategic goals of the state, invest more in key industries and areas that are vital to national security and are the lifeblood of the economy, focusing on offering public services, developing important and forward-looking strategic industries, protecting the ecological environment, supporting scientific and technological progress, and guaranteeing national security".

At present, the industrial layout of state-owned capital presents the following characteristics:

First, the proportion of state-owned capital in general competitive fields is too high. According to statistics from the MOF, in 2014, state-owned capital allocated to competitive industries accounted for 56.29% of total state-owned capital, followed by monopolistic industries, accounting for 30.08%; the proportion of state-owned capital in public services industries was only 13.63%.[28] A large amount of state-owned capital is distributed in general competitive fields, which has affected the market structure of some industries to a certain extent, closed the market access of these industries, and squeezed out the investment opportunities of social capital. As a result, it restricts the overall development of these competitive fields, since state-owned capital is usually uncompetitive in fields.

Second, the distribution of state-owned capital in public services industries is far from insufficient. From 2003 to 2007, state-owned capital in public services industries had been increasing rapidly, but after 2008, it had kept the same growth pace with the industry-wide state-owned capital, with a proportion remaining stable at around 13%,[29] which was the lowest proportion among the three industries. This shows that the function of state-owned capital in providing public services has not been effectively performed. Given this, it is necessary to invest more state-owned capital into public services industries so that it will make greater contributions in providing public services.

Third, state-owned capital maintains extremely high control in traditional monopoly industries. In industrial fields such as coal mining, oil and gas extraction, oil processing, power and water supply, and tobacco, and service industries such as telecommunications, civil aviation, railways, and ports, state-owned capital has all along held a dominant position. For example, in the oil and gas extraction industry, SOEs accounted for 87.3% of the industry revenue in 2014, which is mainly attributed to administrative monopoly. The over-high proportion of state-owned capital in some traditional monopoly industries and its barbaric growth have caused serious overcapacity in these industries. As of the end of 2014, state-owned capital accounted for 90%[30] of the listed companies in industries with severe overcapacity, as affirmed by the NDRC.

Fourth, state-owned capital has not fully played the role of leading the development of strategic emerging industries. Among listed companies in strategic emerging industries, private enterprises accounted for more than 60%, while SOEs accounted for only 26.8%. Strategic emerging industries need to be cultivated, while there must be an incubation period for cultivating industry and also a preparation period for financial investment. The cost of investment in this preparation stage needs to be led by the government and must be borne by state-owned capital. In order to centralize capital power and make it play a leading role, the existing state-owned capital in competitive fields can be withdrawn to be diverted into emerging industries.

In fact, the strategic adjustment of the layout of state-owned capital through classified reform will trigger corresponding changes in the market structure. For example, if we gradually liberalize some competitive fields in traditional monopoly industries and then divert their state-owned capital into strategic emerging industries, it will cause two aspects of consequences. On the one hand, it will increase the proportion of social capital in traditional monopoly industries, break the monopoly status of SOEs, help create a level playing field, and improve the industrial economic benefits on the whole through more intensive competition. On the other hand, it increases the proportion of state-owned capital in strategic emerging industries so that state-owned capital can better perform its supporting and leading functions like a "beacon", and ultimately enable China to vigorously cultivate strategic emerging industries and raise the overall level of scientific and technological innovation to seize the commanding heights of future competition.

5.5 Supporting conditions for further developing "mixed economy" through "classified" reform

Undoubtedly, the policies and measures for promoting mixed-ownership reform by classification have drawn a beautiful blueprint for the SOE reform. Still, we should remain sober that there are bound to be various resistances in the reform process. More social capital flowing into SOEs may meet with obstruction by SOE interest groups. In highly monopolistic industries, existing interest groups do not welcome the entry of private capital because anyone who obtains monopoly profits is desperate for a peaceful life, just like the Nobel Economics Prize winner John Hicks has commented. Once social capital enters a monopoly industry, then the SOEs that are accustomed to monopoly profits will find their "peaceful life" interrupted. They have to make excess earnings through competition rather than their monopoly position. In addition, the existing monopolists usually think that the entry of social capital will "share the same cake" with them. Even though the cake may be made bigger, they still have to make the extra effort and no longer enjoy the "peaceful life" as monopolists.[31] Under policy pressure, existing interest groups may open some insignificant fields to social capital and carry out mixed-ownership reform, but their mixing is only for the sake of mixing. Therefore, after SOEs bring in social capital through mixed-ownership reform, it is possible to see that private investors conspire with existing interest groups to create new industry monopolies. Therefore, we should reasonably liberalize market access, allow social capital to enter traditional monopoly industries, and enable private enterprises to directly compete with SOEs so as to truly break the monopoly of interest groups.

In 2005, the State Council issued *Several Opinions on Encouraging, Supporting and Guiding the Development of Individual and Private Enterprises and Other Non-public Sectors of the Economy*, which are known as "36 Items on Non-public Economy". However, part of these items failed to be effectively implemented due to various reasons. Statistics show that private investment accounted for 13.6% in electricity and heat production and supply industries, 12.3% in education, 11.8% in health, social security and social welfare, 7.8% in information transmission, computer services and software, 7.5% in transportation, warehousing and postal industries, 6.6% in water conservancy, environment and public utilities management industries, and 5.9% in public administration and social organizations.[32]

In 2010, the State Council issued *Several Opinions on Encouraging and Guiding the Healthy Development of Private Investment*,[33] which are known as the "New 36 Items on Non-public Economy", explicitly proposing to "standardize the establishment of investment access thresholds and create a market environment of fair competition and equal access", and "create a broader market space for private capital in general competitive fields". Furthermore, these items also required that we should encourage and guide private capital to enter basic industries and infrastructure, municipal public utilities and policy-based housing construction, social undertakings, financial services, commercial circulation, and science and technology industry of national defense; encourage and guide private capital to reorganize and take part in SOE reform, and actively participate in international competitions; and promote private enterprises to strengthen independent innovation, transformation and upgrading. But in practice, some private enterprises say that there are still "glass doors" in the public sector, they can have a clear vision of the inside, but they are turned away at the door. Today, in order to open industry access in the public sector, we must provide private enterprises with legal protection and transform the government regulatory thinking and even people's thinking orientation of the whole society. A common thinking orientation is that private enterprises tend to break their word, have bad debts or make and sell fake products; such "stale opinion" needs to be discarded. We cannot always have a bias against private enterprises but rediscover their social responsibilities at the enterprise level.

After opening market access in several fields, another major problem or critical problem to be solved is the driving force for the entry of social capital. If social capital owners cannot truly participate in corporate governance and become active shareholders, they will be less motivated to invest in the public sector. In order to solve this problem, we must help mixed enterprises build a perfect corporate governance mechanism by protecting their shareholder rights, strengthening their governance through the board of directors, and cultivating and selecting entrepreneurial talents.

First, we must intensify the protection of shareholder rights. (1) Legislation should be strengthened since we need to prescribe in law that shareholders of state-owned capital enjoy the same rights and fulfill the same obligations as other social capital owners in mixed enterprises, and capitals of different ownership must be equally protected by law. A withdrawal mechanism for social capital also needs to be specified. (2) Let the market play a decisive role in the arrangement of corporate equity structure. In competitive fields, mixed enterprises shall form a reasonable and effective equity structure based on the market and avoid the occurrence of "dominance by a single shareholder". In competitive fields, it is not necessary for state-owned capital to maintain a dominant position. Even if it is to hold a controlling stake, it can try the means of comparative control. Moreover, the gap between the shareholding ratios of state-owned shareholders and other social capital shareholders should not be too large. Otherwise, state-owned shareholders may become the single dominant shareholder that excessively intervenes in corporate governance. On a level playing field, in mixed enterprises controlled by state-owned shareholders and joined by private shareholders or vice versa, all investors are equally entitled to participating in corporate decision-making and receiving dividends, so that state-owned and private capitals can compete with each other, check and balance each other, and realize mutual fusion and common development. (3) The government should abolish special policy support and protection of state-owned capital. The purpose of developing a mixed economy is to preserve and increase the value of capital and maximize national welfare. The government should treat the capitals of different ownership equally. Otherwise, it may lead to the unreasonable arrangement of equity structure and prevent different shareholders from participating in corporate governance on an equal basis.

Second, we must improve the board of directors' governance mechanism. A mixed enterprise is a company with more than two shareholders, and it shall set up a board of directors or an executive board as required by the Company Law. Just like M. Jensen (1993) has pointed out, the board of directors has the right to select and supervise the management and determine the corresponding incentive methods, while directors have fiduciary responsibilities to shareholders, so the board of directors should be at the core of corporate governance.[34] A soundboard of directors' governance mechanism is the guarantee for advancing mixed-ownership reform. After establishing the board of directors, lots of important decisions must be made: the number of directors to represent different shareholders, the person to serve as the chairman of the board, and the persons to be CEO, CFO and other key management personnel. Board seats should be distributed reasonably according to the equity ratio of shareholders. Despite this, it is still possible to see different capital contributors compete for the chairman's seat and important management positions, and their shareholding ratio does not decide the outcome of this power grab. In addition, the independence of the board of directors of mixed enterprises should be guaranteed. The government and state-owned assets regulator shall not interfere with the board of directors, and the assignment of responsibilities between the Party Committee and the board of directors should be clarified. The board of directors should clarify its fiduciary responsibilities to all shareholders and perform the functions of strategy formulation and supervision of management.

Third, it is necessary to establish a market-based entrepreneur selection mechanism and ability evaluation system. In the context of a highly concentrated shareholding structure, most senior executives of SOEs are government officials with certain administrative ranks rather than genuine entrepreneurs. Running enterprises is, to a large extent, for their political promotion. In fact, the executives of SOEs are hardly constrained by the product market and capital market. It is difficult for small and medium shareholders to restrict the behaviors of these executives either by "voting with hand" or "voting with feet", and thus becoming passive shareholders. Generally, the entrepreneurs selected through administrative appointments do not have a professional background or management experience, and they are far from being qualified entrepreneurial talents. In view of this, it is necessary to establish a market-based entrepreneur selection mechanism and ability evaluation system for mixed enterprises. The ideal way is to select entrepreneurs from the professional manager market and evaluate their performance based on their contribution. Under normal circumstances, entrepreneurs can influence corporate culture, business thinking and the internal environment. From a long-term perspective, selecting entrepreneurs within SOEs will bring their inherent thinking and workstyle to mixed enterprises, which will then inhibit these enterprises from gaining new vitality and holding back their innovation. Appointing entrepreneurs with different backgrounds, especially successful private entrepreneurs, and establishing a diversified business model will cause conflicts between different ideas, yet these conflicts may be a blessing for enterprises. It is the full competition between state-owned and private capitals that prevent mixed enterprises from becoming complacent and conservative. Correspondingly, the executives of mixed enterprises shall be free from any administrative rank. Their remuneration should be determined completely in accordance with market rules without an upper limit to motivate them to maximize shareholder wealth under market economic conditions.

Fourth, we must improve the systems respectively for financial supervision and information disclosure. Mixed enterprises should strive to realize the scientific and standardized financial rights allocation and the institutionalized and normalized financial supervision. Financial management and control should be strengthened to guard against major financial risks. In terms of information disclosure, major decision-making matters such as the dividend distribution scheme should be disclosed in detail; information transparency should be maintained to prevent information concealment and fraud; listed companies should regularly disclose their financial reports and ensure the authenticity and reliability of financial data. In terms of supervision, the important role of the board of supervisors should be brought into play to prevent major shareholders from "emptying" the enterprise.

In order to promote the mixed-ownership reform more efficiently, government departments should get rid of their traditional thinking of only pursuing political achievements, do not rush to achieve success or emphasize "quantity" over "quality". Otherwise, there will be consequences like departmentalization of government functions and short-term behaviors, which is not conducive to the entire economic work and the development of the entire society. Competent government departments should take the lead in the process of reform. They should no longer overemphasize political achievements and post-maintenance; instead, they should put an end to the tendency of "department-oriented government functions, post-oriented department functions, individual-oriented post functions, and interest-oriented individual behavior", and further promote the marketized flow of SOE property rights. For the whole society, the vitality and creativity of various sources of capital should be stimulated in the ways as follows: (1) Equally protect the capital property rights of various ownership. The property rights of both state-owned and non-state-owned capitals are inviolable. (2) Give capitals of diverse ownership the right to use all kinds of production factors equally. (3) Create an open, fair and just market environment for competition.

5.6 Interaction between enterprise reform and market development

As mentioned earlier, the boundary of "classification" depends on the level of market development. In fact, the reform of SOEs and market development are going hand in hand. The continuously deepening SOE reform has awakened the sense of independence of enterprises and their awareness of corporate property rights, which has transformed SOEs from appendants to administrative organs into market entities, and propelled them to "establish a modern enterprise system that meets the requirements of the market economy, with explicit property rights, clear rights and responsibilities, separation of government and enterprise, and scientific management". This has broadened and deepened market exchanges, and the continuously improved pricing, competition and anti-risk mechanisms have promoted the in-depth development of marketization. Conversely, the continuous market development has made the pricing system of products, factors and financial markets increasingly perfect, which has, in turn, promoted the deepening of SOE reform.

This section analyzes the evolution of the relationship between enterprise reform and market development and demonstrates that they are in a symbiotic relationship. That is, enterprise reform and market development supplement each other and support each other.

5.6.1 Enterprise reform advances market development

The measures for "delegating powers and transferring profits" adopted at the beginning of SOE reform were, in essence, to allow independent or "market-oriented" enterprise operation beyond the direct production directives. The resulting "unplanned" production, procurement, sales and pricing began to replace the planned economic activities step by step and keep moving towards the state where the market freely decides enterprise behaviors.

In the process of industrialization driven by the introduction of foreign technologies, surplus rural laborers have become a vital force in China's labor resources – a key production factor. It broke the long-standing fetters on rural residents to work in cities, and a labor force for modern industries quickly took shape. To date, there are about 250 million rural migrant workers in urban areas nationwide, together with their families or fellow countrymen. It has promoted the transformation of China's population distribution, labor employment structure, income level and lifestyle of residents, social services, education, medical care and social security.

After multiple stages of progressive reforms such as the expansion of enterprise autonomy, replacement of profit delivery by taxes, the establishment of the contract system and the modern corporate system, the product market has become well developed with product prices gradually liberalized and the law of value playing a vital role. The factor market has been further opened up. Although the prices of some important materials have not been fully liberalized, the financial market and capital market have developed to a certain extent. After implementing the "appropriation-to-loan" policy, enterprises started paying more attention to fund accounting in business activities. At the same time, capital marketization was speeding up, which has increased the financing business between financial institutions and stimulated the formation of financial markets. A financial system was required to boost the development of enterprises. In 1990, the Shanghai Stock Exchange and the Shenzhen Stock Exchange were established in succession. By the end of 1991, a relatively complete financial system had been formed with banks, stock exchanges, trust companies, finance companies, financial leasing companies and insurance companies as its mainstay.

The reform of enterprise ownership drives the development of the capital market. After Deng Xiaoping affirmed the shareholding system during his inspection tour of south China in 1992, breakthroughs were made in the shareholding reform of SOEs, and stock exchanges sprung up and developed rapidly. With respect to the capital market, in the wake of the establishment of the Shanghai Stock Exchange, there had been heated discussions on the issues such as what is "socialist" and what is "capitalist", the position of state holding, and transactions of state-owned assets. At that time, the prevailing argument was that state ownership may lose control if SOEs implement the shareholding system. In order to circumvent the above-mentioned conflicts, in a public opinion environment of "having a try", Chinese people creatively designed a "split-share structure",[35] on this basis, there have come out two types of shares (tradable and non-tradable) in listed companies. Tradable shares refer to the stocks that are issued by listed companies to the public and traded on the Shanghai and Shenzhen Stock Exchanges; while non-tradable stocks refer to the stocks issued by listed companies but not listed for trading for the time being. At that time, a majority of tradable shares were public shares, while non-tradable shares were mainly state-owned shares and legal person shares, accounting for a large proportion of listed company stocks. The cost of holding tradable shares was much higher than that of holding non-tradable shares, thus resulting in uncoordinated interests between the two types of shareholders. Institutional defects such as different prices, different rights and different benefits for the same stock have distorted the pricing mechanism of the securities market, resulting in the lack of a common interest basis for corporate governance. This has seriously affected the development of the capital market and the reform of the state-owned assets management system. In order to solve this problem, in April 2005, with the approval of the State Council, the China Securities Regulatory Commission (CSRC) issued the *Notice on Issues Concerning the Pilot Reform of the Split-share Structure of Listed Companies*, marking an official start of the pilot work in the split-share structure reform. In August of the same year, five ministries and commissions, including the CSRC, the People's Bank of China, the SASAC, the MOF, and the Ministry of Commerce (MOC), jointly issued the *Guiding Opinions on the Split-share Structure Reform of Listed Companies*, which improved the institutional arrangements for the pilot reform. Later, the CSRC, the Shanghai and Shenzhen Stock Exchanges and other institutions came up with relevant supporting rules to guarantee this reform to move forward steadily. By the end of 2006, there were 1,301 listed companies in Shanghai and Shenzhen that had completed or started the split-share structure reform, accounting for 97% of the local companies that should join in this reform; and their combined market value accounted for 98% of the local total; only 40 listed companies had not implemented this reform. After the split-share structure reform in these two places had in the main completed, the problems that had plagued China's capital market for more than 10 years were finally resolved.[36]

In the labor market, the SOE reform has expedited the marketization of the employment system. In the planned economy era, and even throughout the 1980s, SOEs had been strictly implementing the traditional personnel management system, which was characterized by "lifelong job, fixed wage, and permanent official position". SOEs had to apply for employment quotas from the labor management department when recruiting employees, and all recruited personnel would obtain a lifelong job. Although employees earned a low wage which was not marketized, they were granted all sorts of benefits, including housing allocation and medical reimbursement. For some enterprises with good benefits, they also took charge of the heating fees and children's kindergarten admission of their employees. Enterprise managers were subject to the performance evaluation available for government cadres. That is, their promotion must go through the investigation and approval of the Party and government departments. And in fact, enterprise managers were bound to be promoted, hardly any of them were demoted.[37]

In the middle and later periods of the 1990s, under the adverse impact of the macroeconomic recession and the Southeast Asian financial crisis, Chinese SOEs were in a state of widespread loss, so they were forced to implement the reform of "invigorating large enterprises while relaxing control over small ones", and downsize staff for improving efficiency, thus resulting in tens of millions of laid-off workers and a rising unemployment rate in urban areas. From 1996 to 2000, China's urban surveyed unemployment rate was 3.9%, 4.5%, 6.3%, 5.9%, and 7.6% respectively.[38] The vast majority of these jobless urban workers entered the labor market and got reemployed. In addition, in the process of SOE restructuring, part of the employees received compensation for "identity

Table 5.3 Replacement of employee identity in SOE reform

Type	Restructured SOEs whose largest shareholder is non-state-owned	Restructured SOEs whose largest shareholder is state-owned
Compensation was paid for replacing employee identity	70.20%	13.60%
No compensation was paid for replacing employee identity but guaranteed to secure their jobs	13.20%	41.00%
Others	16.60%	45.40%

Source: Zhang Wenkui (2015). *Governance and performance of mixed enterprises*. Beijing: Tsinghua University Press.

replacement", meaning that they would no longer have a lifelong job but sign an employment contract with a time limit with their employers; enterprises would no longer perform any welfare functions and transfer employees' pension and medical care into the social security system; jobless persons could register with the social security department to apply for unemployment benefits. The transformation of employee status has accelerated the marketization of SOEs' employment system (Table 5.3).

In the context of incremental reforms, the rapid development of individual, private and other non-public sectors of the economy has caused changes in the market competition landscape. From 1992 to 2001, China's private economy had maintained an annual growth rate of above 15%. And the number of operating households increased by more than 50% for three consecutive years in 1993, 1994, and 1995. In the process of "invigorating large enterprises while relaxing control over small ones" and optimizing the layout of state-owned assets, state-owned capital was gradually withdrawing from the competitive fields such as the consumer goods market. The continuously expanding private sector has become an important component of the market economy. According to statistics from the SAIC, in 2002, there were around 2.64 million private enterprises and 23.77 million self-employed households. These two figures in 2013 rose to 12.54 million and 44.36 million, respectively. In 2002, the registered capital of private enterprises in China was 2.48 trillion yuan, accounting for 12.61% of the total registered capital of all enterprises; by 2013, the registered capital of private enterprises had reached 39.31 trillion yuan, accounting for 40.58% of the total. The rise of the individual and private sectors has broken the dominance of SOEs and enabled the competition mechanism to play an increasingly important role. Economic resources are allocated to efficient sectors and enterprises through market means, and the overall economic efficiency of the society has been greatly improved.

5.6.2 Market development promotes the deepening of enterprise reform

Without independent interests, there will be no rational corporate behavior. Through the expansion of enterprise autonomy, SOEs obtained the right of disposal of a small proportion of their products, which was the beginning of the formation of independent interests of enterprises. In addition to fulfilling the government production plan, SOEs could obtain raw and auxiliary materials through a "two-way approach" (buying raw materials from and selling products to overseas markets), selling part of their products independently, and retaining the resulting profits for their own discretionary spending. In this way, enterprises have acquired more economic rationality. Enterprises have learned market transactions and cost accounting and realized the importance of product sales, marketing channels, and sales network construction. After implementing the "tax-for-profits" reform, the different "adjustment tax" rates have led to unfair tax burdens among enterprises and induced their negative behaviors. The contract system has awakened the main body consciousness of enterprises and motivated them to actively join up the market mechanism and complete the profit and tax targets turned over to the State through a market operation. In this process, enterprises have learned to bargain with the government, try to resist government restraint and intervention, and at the same time strive to retain more profit for their own disposal. In addition, enterprises have learned to make profits through the price difference created by a double-track pricing system.

The product market and the factor market are developing in-depth according to their own laws, more and more enterprises get involved, and the scope of national plans has constantly been shrinking, forcing the government to gradually abandon administrative intervention and turn to the market to raise production factor resources. In addition to applying for bank loans which had been the only way for financing in the past, the government opened the stock issuance market for direct financing, which has provided enterprises with new financing channels and facilitated SOEs to advance their shareholding system reform. In the end, the whole society has realized the importance of cultivating property rights trading market, currency market and capital market, and embarked on the road of enterprise reorganization and transformation, which has vigorously promoted SOE restructuring and listing and laid a solid foundation for establishing the modern corporate system.[39]

By the mid to late 1990s, China had in the main completed the marketization of the prices of physical goods and services in industry and agriculture. In terms of the total retail sales of social goods, the total sales of industrial production materials, and the total purchases of agricultural and sideline products, the proportion of market-adjusted prices all exceeded 80% in 1997, marking that the market price system had been initially established. After the Third Plenary Session of the 18th CPC Central Committee, the price reform of resource products was gradually advanced. In October 2015, the CPC Central Committee and the State Council jointly issued the *Several Opinions on Promoting the Reform of the Price Mechanism*, which set out six major tasks for future reforms: improve the pricing mechanism for agricultural products, accelerate the marketization of energy price, refine policies for environmental service price, rationalize medical service price, improve the transportation price mechanism, and innovate price management for public utilities and public welfare services.

At present, competitive fields have basically liberalized their market access, but public services and functional fields have not done so. With the further development of the market, all fields may be liberalized in the future, but it depends on the level of market development, such as whether certain services are competitive and whether price discovery is available on the market. In mature market economies, private enterprises can manufacture munitions and build prisons with the government acting as a buyer. But China is yet capable of doing this at present, so it still implements classified management of state-owned capital. It can be seen that the breakthroughs in price reform directly affect the progress of classified SOE reform. As a result of deepening market-oriented reform, there have been intensified requirements for a fairer "business environment" with "competitive" factor prices, the equal opening of business opportunities and industrial fields, and equal access to production factors, and continuous breakthroughs in this reform. Only in this way can we truly improve the market competition efficiency. To this end, we have to satisfy the new and higher requirements for continuing and deepening the enterprise reform, and motivate enterprises to increase their vitality through technological progress, optimization of organizational structure, governance mechanism and governance capability, which will lay a solid micro-foundation for high-quality development.

Notes

1 Wang, Y. (2012). *Report of the State Council on the work in the reform and development of state-owned enterprises – at the 29th Meeting of the Standing Committee of the Eleventh National People's Congress.* http://www.npc.gov.cn/wxzl/gongbao/2013-02/25/content_1790879.htm

2 Chen, Q. T. (2012). Transformation of state-owned enterprises reform to state-owned assets reform. *Capital Shanghai*, Issue 6.

3 SAIC. (2017). *Analysis of national enterprise development since the 18th CPC National Congress.* Retrieved October 27, 2017, from http://www.gov.cn/zhuanti/2017-10/27/content_5234848.htm

4 *Decision on some issues concerning the establishment of the socialist market economy.* Retrieved November 14, 1993, from http://www.people.com.cn/item/20years/newfiles/b1080.html

5 Jiang, Z. M. (September 12, 1997). *Hold high the great banner of Deng Xiaoping Theory for an all-round advancement of the cause of building socialism with Chinese characteristics into the 21st century.* http://www.people.com.cn/item/sj/sdldr/jzm/A106.html

6 Jiang, Z. M. (November 17, 2002). *Build a well-off society in an all-round way and create a new situation in building socialism with Chinese characteristics.* http://www.china.com.cn/zhuanti2005/txt/2002-11/17/content_5233867.htm

7 *Decision on some issues concerning the improvement of the socialist market economy.* Retrieved October 14, 2003, from http://jingji.cntv.cn/2012/11/05/ARTI1352087360703188.shtml

8 Zhang, W. K. (2015). *Governance and performance of mixed enterprises.* Beijing: Tsinghua University Press.

9 Xiao, Q. W. *Quantity, type and industry distribution of mixed enterprises.* https://cdrf.org.cn/xqw/3973.jhtml

10 Hao, Y. H., & Wang, Q. (2015). Research on the equity check-and-balance mechanism of mixed enterprises – based on the case of "fighting for control power of Wuhan Department Store Group". *China Industrial Economics.*

11 Liu, X. X., & Li, S. X. (2007). The relative efficiency of mixed enterprise in the transitional period: an analysis of the empirical data of China's electronic and electrical manufacturing industry from 2000 to 2004. *World Economic Papers,* Issue 1.

12 Ma, L. F., et al. (2015). The priority choice of mixed ownership: The logic of the market. *China Industrial Economics,* Issue 7.

13 Zhang, W. K. (2015). *Governance and performance of mixed enterprises* (p. 173). Beijing: Tsinghua University Press.

14 *Opinions of the State Council on the development of mixed economy by state-owned enterprises.* Retrieved September 24, 2015, from http://www.gov.cn/zhengce/content/2015-09/24/content_10177.htm

15 Jiang, Z. M. (September 12, 1997). *Hold high the great banner of Deng Xiaoping Theory for an all-round advancement of the cause of building socialism with Chinese characteristics into the 21st century.* http://www.people.com.cn/item/sj/sdldr/jzm/A106.html

16 Pei, C. H. (2014). Quantitative estimation of the dominating position of public ownership in China and its development trend. *Social Sciences in China,* Issue 4.

17 Hu, J. Y. (August 1, 2016). *The innovative development of ownership theory in the new era.* http://theory.people.com.cn/n1/2016/0801/c40531-28599328.html

18 See the speech delivered by Xi Jinping at the Central Economic Work Conference. (December 9, 2014).

19 *Social responsibility report (2017) of China national building materials group corporation.*

20 The State Council's first "public financial disclosure": the total assets of SOEs nationwide reached 183.5 trillion yuan in 2017. Retrieved October 24, 2018, from https://www.guancha.cn/economy/2018_10_24_476683.shtml

21 Xi, J. P. (October 18, 2017). *Secure a decisive victory in building a moderately prosperous society in all respects and strive for the great success of socialism with Chinese characteristics for a new era – delivered at the 19th National Congress of the Communist Party of China.* http://www.xinhuanet.com/politics/19cpcnc/2017-10/27/c_1121867529.htm

22 SASAC of the State Council. (2017). *State-owned enterprise reform has achieved important phased results.* Retrieved June 2, 2017, from http://finance.sina.com.cn/wm/2017-06-02/doc-ifyfuzym7756726.shtml

23 *Completing mixed-ownership reform and settlement, Sinopec Sales saw 105 billion yuan on its account.* Retrieved March 7, 2015, from https://www.guancha.cn/economy/2015_03_07_311392.shtml

24 CCTV. (2010). *The power of corporations.* Taiyuan: Shanxi Education Press.

25 Chen, L. (2018). Natural monopoly and mixed-ownership reform – based on natural experiments and cost function analysis. *Economic Research Journal,* Issue 1.

26 Joint Research Group of the Institute of Industrial Economics of CASS and the State-owned Investment Company Professional Committee of IAC. (2017). *Optimizing the layout of state-owned economy and industrial integration of state-owned investment companies.* Beijing: Economic Management Press.
27 Joint Research Group of the Institute of Industrial Economics of CASS and the State-owned Investment Company Professional Committee of IAC. (2017). *Optimizing the layout of state-owned economy and industrial integration of state-owned investment companies.* Beijing: Economic Management Press.
28 The DRC's Research Group on the "prominent challenges and countermeasures in deepening SOE reform", suggestions for promoting the adjustment of China's state-owned capital distribution. (2016). *Development Research*, Issue 10.
29 The DRC's Research Group on the "prominent challenges and countermeasures in deepening SOE reform", suggestions for promoting the adjustment of China's state-owned capital distribution. (2016). *Development Research*, Issue 10.
30 Yuan, D. M. (2006). A new probe into the adjustment of state-owned assets distribution. *China Policy Review*, Issue 9.
31 Gao, M. H., Du W., et al. (2014). Several issues regarding the development of a mixed economy. *China Review of Political Economy*, Issue 4.
32 *State Council's new 36 opinions on promoting the healthy development of non-public economy.* (2008). http://www.gov.cn/zhengce/content/2008-03/28/content_1 647.htm
33 *State Council's new 36 opinions on promoting the healthy development of non-public economy.* (2008). http://www.gov.cn/zhengce/content/2008-03/28/content_1 647.htm
34 Jensen, M. (1993). The modern industrial revolution, exit, and the failure of internal control system. *Journal of Finance*, 48(3), 831–880.
35 Two years' anniversary of China's shareholding reform: origin and direction of the robust bull market. (June 18, 2017). *China Economic Weekly*, Issue 23.
36 School of Economics and Resource Management of Beijing Normal University. (2008). *Report on China's market economy development in 2008* (p. 80). Beijing: Beijing Normal University Publishing Group.
37 Zhang, Z. Y., Fang, H. T., et al. (2017). *Historical breakthroughs decided by the market: 40 years of China's market development and modern market system construction.* Guangzhou: Guangdong Economy Publishing House.
38 Cai, F. (2010). *Economic essays of Cai Fang* (p. 116). Beijing: China Times Economic Publishing House.
39 Zhang, H. M. (1998). *The logic of China's state-owned enterprise reform.* Taiyuan: Shanxi Economic Publishing House.

6 Reform setting out again

From "classification" to "stratification"

The *Decision on Some Major Issues Concerning Comprehensively Deepening the Reform* (hereinafter referred to as the "Deepening Reform Decision" or "Decision"), which was adopted at the Third Plenary Session of the 18th CPC Central Committee in November 2013, linked enterprise reform with the development of the basic socialist economic system, required for "vigorously developing a mixed economy" and took it as an important way to materialize the basic economic system, so as to scientifically and effectively achieve the organic integration of public ownership with a market economy. It can be seen that this Decision presented daunting tasks for the reform of enterprises, especially that of SOEs.

In order to implement the Deepening Reform Decision in a better way, the CPC Central Committee and the State Council jointly issued the *Guiding Opinions on Deepening the Reform of State-owned Enterprises* (hereinafter referred to as the "Guiding Opinions" or "Opinions") in August 2015, reiterating to shift the focus from "assets management" to "capital management" when handling the relationship between the government and the state-owned assets management. They specified the "classified reform" of the state-funded enterprises in different industrial sectors in light of their technical features and characteristics of market activities to open up a new space for deepening enterprise reform.

6.1 Significance of the Guiding Opinions for expanding and deepening the enterprise system innovation

The biggest highlight of the Guiding Opinions is the explicit requirement for "classifying" existing SOEs and adopting different reform measures based on classification. For the purpose of developing a "mixed economy" – new "breakthrough" of enterprise reform, the Guiding Opinions divide SOEs in real economic life into "commercial enterprises" and "public services enterprises". Commercial SOEs are subdivided into Class A enterprises and Class B enterprises according to the functions and market competitiveness of the industries to which state-owned capital is allocated. Relative shareholding (or "equity participation" not seeking to be the largest shareholder) and absolute holding (wholly-owned) are separately available for Class A enterprises and Class B enterprises for the sake of creating a diversified equity structure and a corresponding governance structure.

6.1.1 Essentials for the design of "classified reform"

"Classified" reform denotes that reform measures are determined by combining the state-owned capital allocation with the technical and market characteristics of the industrial fields to which the capital is allocated. It takes into account the economic implications of both "state-owned capital" and "industrial fields". On the one hand, "classified" reform represents a deepened understanding that is closer to the characteristics of the actual economic operation. On the other hand, it is a set of new reform actions based on the summary of previous reform experience. On the basis of enterprise classification, we should employ different measures for reforming the SOEs in different industries, rather than adopting a "one-size-fits-all approach", which of course makes these reform measures more precise and targeted, thereby improving their effectiveness in solving problems. Therefore, we must fully affirm the positive significance of "classification" in advancing and deepening the reform. This will help determine the scale and proportion of non-public capital to be introduced into the public sector in the process of advancing the mixed-ownership reform to ensure that the reform will lead to a relatively reasonable equity structure and lay a basis for establishing a reasonable corporate organizational structure and a benign corporate governance mechanism.

The Guiding Opinions, which have made it clear for state-owned assets regulator to perform its responsibilities as an investor in accordance with the law, will direct the shift of focus from management of enterprises to the management of capital. The main aim of managing capital is to realize "value-based management" of capital movement, which will help to further straighten out the relationship between the government and SOEs, clarify the regulatory boundary of state-owned assets investors in accordance with the law, and gradually eliminate the problems caused by non-separation of government from enterprises and assets management.

The state-owned assets management system with capital management at the core helps classify the SOEs in different economic development stages or different industries, pursue different goals or perform different functions, and determine corresponding reform measures. We must take into full consideration of the real characteristics of market economy operations such as the layout of SOEs, allocation of state-owned capital, features of industries and technologies, market structure, and openness of industrial fields, and then choose appropriate reform measures and reasonable equity structure of mixed enterprises. State-owned capital allocation has different strategic positioning and development goals; therefore, the degree of competition in the fields of state-owned capital allocation is also different. Some industries need to introduce non-state-owned capital for adequate competition to improve resource allocation efficiency. Some major industrial sectors, especially the key fields related to national economic security, can properly introduce non-state-owned capital under the premise of maintaining the dominance of state-owned capital.

In short, classifying different types of measures will help to improve the relevance and efficiency of SOE reform.

6.1.2 *"Classified reform" promotes continuous innovation of enterprise system, aiming to better implement the spirit of the Deepening Reform Decision*

The Guiding Opinions aim at better implementation of the Deeping Reform Decision through the construction of enterprise system, which can be interpreted from the following five aspects:

> First, vigorously develop a mixed economy and make it a "breakthrough" in deepening enterprise reform and further improving the modern corporate system. "Vigorously developing a mixed economy" is the title of Item 6 of the Deepening Reform Decision, showing that we have chosen "mixed ownership" actively. It is a quite important theoretical breakthrough. As we all know, the *Decision on Some Issues Concerning the Establishment of the Socialist Market Economy* adopted at the Third Plenary Session of the 14th CPC Central Committee in 1993 made it clear to "establish a modern corporate system" and regarded it as the target of enterprise reform. The so-called modern corporate system, that is, the modern company system, is also the enterprise system with diversified investment. In real economic scenarios, "diversified investment" does not always mean "mixed ownership", it may be the "diversity" formed by the investments of different corporate legal persons who are state-owned holding or investment companies. This form of "diversity" can introduce a "check-and-balance" mechanism between different legal persons, and bring about changes to the original decision-making model for corporate governance. However, the "ultimate controller" of state-owned holding or investment companies is the assets regulator affiliated to the government, meaning that the "check-and-balance" mechanism cannot be truly put in place. In other words, the "diversified investment" here is only a formal change. In view of this, it is not difficult to understand that it is the diversified capital contributions based on different property rights relationships that can truly constitute "mixed ownership", that is, "joint investment" between public investors and non-public or social investors, which is the basis for developing a "mixed economy" and for forming cooperative and "check-and-balance" mechanisms between investors of different ownership. The main manifestation of check and balance is that, in addition to active participation in corporate governance through voting, investors can also participate in corporate governance in a "negative" manner, that is, "exiting from cooperation". In other words, the capital contributor (investor) has symmetrical rights of

"entry" and "exit". In 1993, we could not directly advocate the development of a "mixed economy"; instead, we could only recognize the "mixed sectors" that were existing in economic life. How to look at the relationship between mixed ownership and the basic economic system with public ownership playing a dominant role? There was no direct answer to this question at that time.[1] By 2013, as result of the continuously deepened reforms and marketization, new investment opportunities had kept sprung up, giving rise to a number of joint ventures co-funded by public and private capitals, and stimulating a large number of SOEs to transform their property rights structure through issuance of stocks and public listing, which had made us learn more about the vitality of mixed ownership. Therefore, we have gained an in-depth understanding of mixed ownership, and got fully prepared to put forward the notion of "vigorously developing a mixed economy", which is an innovation in both theory and practice. After defining "mixed ownership" as the "breakthrough" in the new round of SOE reform, we need to properly deal with the specific tasks for developing a mixed economy through "classified reform", and consciously make efforts in this regard.

Second, the innovation of the state-owned assets management system, that is, to shift focus from "assets management" to "capital manage-ment", will stimulate changes in styles and objectives of management. In contrast to "assets management", "capital management" is a kind of "value-based management" for the goal of preserving and increasing the value of state-owned assets and sustaining the vitality of capital, which will benefit the integration of state-owned capital and market economy. The objects of "assets management" consist of the organizational objects and operating assets of existing enterprises. But such management is restricted by the exclusiveness of assets and the content and structure of enterprise assets accounts, making the management actions hard to be flexible. In the final analysis, along with economic development, industrial-technological progress, and enterprise organizational structure changes, the focus of capital allocation will inevitably change. This change requires the capital value to flow in different industrial fields and sectors, and such flow (entry or exit of capital) is the specific form and objective manifestation of the vitality of capital.

Third, innovate the state-owned capital management system by estab-lishing state-owned capital management or investment companies. Through the authorized operation, the right to operate state-owned capital can be transferred to the market so as to "separate the government from the state-owned assets management", let state-owned capital management or investment companies exercise the rights of "investor", manipulate the allocation of state-owned capital, and realize the market-ized operation of state-owned capital. Specifically, the essence of public ownership is "owned by the whole people" according to classic doctrines, this attribute is manifested as "state ownership" in real life, while "state ownership" is materialized by government departments in performing the state governance functions, thus making "state ownership" directly manifest as government "ownership". But the government functions are performed by competent government departments, so there is an overlapping functional relationship between the right to capital owned by the whole people and the government's daily administration, making the powers and functions of ownership ultimately manifests themselves as the functions and rights of "government departments", no wonder there is the notion of "departmental ownership". Apparently, this notion is not groundless, and it is what people think of the state-owned assets management on specific occasions. What is even more worthy of questioning is that the specific government functions in managing economic activities, which include examination and approval, permitting, license issuance, filing or release, are exercised by government departments. But these matters are in fact handled by individual government staff performing certain job duties within government departments. This has resulted in a phenomenon of "department-oriented government functions and individual-oriented post functions". This is the endogenous mechanism and reason why some government departments are known as "difficult accessibility and difficult dealing", it is also the reason that some people possessing specific approval powers may be involved in "manipulating power for personal ends" and "rent setting". This reveals a simple truth that we must act upon the principles of openness and transparency and exercise supervision and check and balance based on the principles of openness and transparency. Otherwise, there will be breeding grounds for corruption, just like the major corruption cases committed by a director of a Beidaihe-based water supplies company and a deputy director of the Coal Department of the National Energy Administration.[2] The reason is that the public power of the government is in the hands of individuals, and the acts of exercising this "power" are non-transparent and without check and balance. The authorized operation of operating state-owned assets, through the establishment of state-owned assets management or investment companies, is in a sense to transfer the management right to the market and place it under the more transparent market oversight. In this way, the government will be freed from the monumental affairs in state-owned capital management. The authorized capital management companies, which are subject to market constraints and tests, will benefit from the integration of state-owned capital with market mechanisms.

Fourth, implement the classified and stratified management of the heads of SOEs. It is an innovation of the enterprise operator management system, which is conducive to fostering a marketized assessment mechanism for management professionals (entrepreneurs) and to cultivating a contingent of entrepreneurs.

Fifth, promote the innovation of the incentive mechanism for operators and employees. In the process of developing a mixed economy, it is necessary to establish cooperation between capital contributors of different ownership, make the property rights of state-owned capital subject to market pricing, and form an external marketized and open pricing mechanism. An objective and fair environment for pricing property rights will draw enterprise operators and employees to participate in shareholding so as to form a new type of capital-labor relationship in which workers directly hold shares under the dominance of public ownership. This breakthrough in ownership relations is also a development of the existing public-owned productive relations and an innovation of the ownership theories. While taking the mixed-ownership reform as an opportunity, we can implement operator and employee stock ownership and take it as an important step in deepening the reform of SOEs.

6.2 From the Deepening Reform Decision to the Guiding Opinions: explorations and inspirations for the "restart" of SOE reform

In order to obtain a complete and profound understanding of the Deepening Reform Decision issued in November 2013 and the Guiding Opinions released in August 2015, we must focus on the tasks for comprehensively deepening the reform (the so-called "2.0 version of the reform") as proposed in the Decision, and figure out ways to fulfill the tasks for advancing the SOE reform. Different interpretations of the reform design are bound to affect the choice of reform measures. Now that different theoretical interpretations and in-depth theoretical innovations are of great significance to the deepening of reforms, we must maintain theoretical explorations for guiding the reforms.

6.2.1 Effects produced by implementation of the Deepening Reform Decision

The Deepening Reform Decision set out the goal of comprehensively deepening the reform and the "five-in-one" mission ("economic, political, cultural, social and ecological civilization"), drew a comprehensive outline for system construction, and highlighted the "modernization of national governance system and governance capability". It is a systematic theoretical innovation. After the Decision was made public, a "vibrant" atmosphere for "restarting the reform" was formed to focus on the implementation of various reform tasks. It can be examined from the following two aspects:

On the one hand, theoretical circles have made argumentation and interpretation of the reform tasks set out in the Deepening Reform Decision. Different scholars have their own knowledge structure and research style, we should "let a hundred schools of thought contend", which helps to study problems more thoroughly. It is quite normal to have different interpretations of one proposition. But how can we choose applicable theoretical propositions as references and transform them into specific reform measures? We need to make choices in the end and put theoretical thinking into action.

On the other hand, in order to fulfill the reform tasks specified in the Deepening Reform Decision, the competent government departments began to actively think about countermeasures within the scope of their own empowerment and formulate pilot programs to advance the reform. For example, the Ministry of Human Resources and Social Security (MOHRSS) came up with a reform plan for the remuneration of the heads of central enterprises,[3] containing the standards for setting the upper limit of their salary. It will inevitably stimulate the changes in the income level of the entire management inside enterprises, which in turn influences the team-building of management professions of SOEs. In terms of the NDRC, which performs the functions of managing investment in the whole society, put forward a pilot program on selecting SOEs to bring in investors of social capital. In a special meeting held in May 2014, the NDRC picked 80 SOEs to implement this pilot program.[4] In the end, 25 of them had completed the mixed-ownership transformation. The MOF was working out measures for ensuring the income from state capital operations to be turned in per annum. In July 2014, the SASAC brought forth a work plan for carrying out four pilot reforms involving six central SOEs.[5] In short, to implement the SOE reform, the specific functions of state-owned assets management are performed by different departments of the State Council. This situation reminds us of "five dragons governing water" that depicts the overlapped operation and management of SOEs. The advancement of reforms by multiple authorities cannot achieve any combined effect. In such a context, it was urgent to work out a coordinated reform plan with comprehensive considerations. Through more than a year's practice and repeated drafting, the *Guiding Opinions on Deepening the Reform of State-owned Enterprises* were adopted by the CPC Central Committee and the State Council on August 24, 2015, and officially made public on September 13, 2015.[6] The Guiding Opinions did not come out until 22 months after the public release of the Deepening Reform Decision, showing that it took a long time to transform the reform principles specified in the Decision into concrete action plans. Later, the State Council or the SASAC introduced several supporting documents to further refine the work requirements stated in the Guiding Opinions, thus constituting a "1+N" policy framework, which has played a positive role in steadily advancing the SOE reform in an all-round manner.

6.2.2 New measures for promoting SOE reform require holistic design and supporting programs

For the purpose of deepening SOE reform, the notion of "modern corporate system" was put forward at the Third Plenary Session of the 14th CPC Central Committee in 1993, and then the corporate system was widely adopted as a new form of enterprise reform.

In fact, in the sectors with diversified investment, original state-owned (sole proprietorship) enterprises have been restructured into the ones with diversified investment; especially for the enterprises partly funded by social capital (such as state-owned joint-stock companies that have initiated listing), the original "SOEs" should be renamed "state-funded enterprises" from a legal perspective. However, in our daily lives, the concept of "SOEs" has not changed. Enterprises that are wholly state-owned, state-controlled or shareholding are collectively referred to as "SOEs". As a result, on many occasions, the discussions on the content of SOE reform are inconsistent, making the heated debates merely empty talks. What's more, it has become our mindset to take "SOEs" as those under the traditional system. Strictly speaking, quite a number of SOEs have been restructured into "state-funded enterprises" through continuous reforms; only wholly state-owned enterprises are directly called SOEs. If we keep using the notion of "SOEs" indiscriminately, coupled with our fixed thinking and behavioral inertia and call the enterprises with diversified investment (state-owned capital may occupy a controlling stake or remain shareholding) as SOEs, it means that we've ignored the existence of other capitals or other shareholders, and failed to identify whether the state-owned capital in a particular enterprise is "wholly-owned", "controlling" or "shareholding". The notion of "SOEs" is used arbitrarily. No matter it is government officials, theorists, news media or official documents, they have paid no attention to use this notion correctly. In real economic life, the enterprises wholly funded by state-owned capital or with state-owned capital having a controlling stake or only shareholding are under the management of the SASAC. It shows that the standardization of theoretical work is not in place, and it will directly divert the focus of enterprise reform research and practical work. "SOEs" are not abstract concepts but concrete organizations. With regard to particular enterprises in real economic life, "SOEs" only refer to wholly state-owned enterprises in a strict sense. For the enterprises with state-owned capital having a controlling stake or only shareholding, they cannot be broadly classified as "SOEs" because of the existence of other investors. Otherwise, the objects of discussions will be inaccurate, so the contents of discussions are bound to be incorrect, and the conclusions will have no reference value. Due to the simplified and even inaccurate definition of "SOEs", the quantitative empirical analyses are unable to clarify lots of problems, thus making the actual value of research greatly reduced. In enterprises with diversified investments (including state-owned capital), the investor's behavior is market behavior. According to market norms, investors may hold a different quantity of shares, but they should cooperate with each other on an equal basis and abide by the principle of "shares of the same class must have the same rights and benefits". It is quite meaningful to clarify the connotations of relevant concepts, which is also the duty of our theoretical workers.

It should be pointed out that the notion of "state-owned capital" is neither used correctly in real economic life. On many occasions, people often use a generalized notion of "state-owned assets", even if they mean "state-owned capital". Of course, the two notions are not equivalent. The work priority of the SASAC is no longer "assets management", but "capital management", which is an important move for the deepening of reforms. We are well aware of the difference between assets and capital in the accounting sense. Capital is the owner's equity, which is the actual equity and ability of state-owned capital.

In addition, the notion of "mixed-ownership reform" is sometimes not used correctly, and there is a phenomenon of "reform for the sake of reform". In recent years, each Central Economic Work Conference session would specifically point out that the six industrial sectors should accelerate their mixed-ownership reform. To this end, it has kept selecting SOEs to implement the pilot reform programs. In fact, we need to probe into the fundamental significance of "mixed-ownership reform" and identify the key link in property rights to implement this reform. If an industrial sector has not liberalized access (the opening of industry access is conditional since it may concern national economic security), it means that the pricing system of this industry is not truly liberalized or the market-based pricing is yet realized. Under such circumstances, if a certain part of the businesses in this industry is placed under "mixed-ownership reform", there will be "benefit transfer" accompanied by industry price protection or a disguised monopoly under the entry barriers. In other words, genuine "mixing" is only available for the ultimate property rights, but this requires certain prerequisites for industrial safety management. The "mixing" for the derived property rights must be carefully decided and implemented. In particular, when selecting the capital owners to carry out the "mixed-ownership reform", we must abide by the fair and open market rules, the reasonable equity pricing mechanism, and the working procedures. Improper handling will result in benefit transfer or loss of state-owned capital value. In fact, the successful IPO of state-owned commercial banks and some major central enterprises in Hong Kong is a useful experience.

6.3 "Classified" reform is somewhat restricted and in need of cooperation with "stratified" mechanism

We fully understand and affirm the positive significance of the "classified" reform. In daily discussions on the reform of SOEs, the reforms of "state-owned assets and enterprises" are usually expressed together. It is not wrong to put these two topics together, but we will find that their contents are not on the same level if we could go deeply into these two reforms. The reform of state-owned assets management aims at the value-added ability of capital. The reform of SOEs is to reorganize or restructure the production and operation organizations allocated with state-owned capital; in other words, it deals with the problems of the fields, scale and approaches of state-owned capital allocation. The competent authorities of Shanghai once discussed the specific contents of the reforms of state-owned assets and SOEs. Yu Zhengsheng, then secretary of the Shanghai Municipal Party Committee 8 years ago, distinguished the relationship between the two reforms[7] and made it clear that they are issues at different levels and may not be confused. Promoting the reform of SOEs based on this insight will help to continuously accumulate work experience in advancing reforms.

6.3.1 Implementation of "classified" reform measures brings SOE reform to a new depth

As mentioned earlier, the "classified" reform combines the organizational carrier of state-owned capital allocation with the selection of industrial fields, which will deepen the contents of SOE reform. SOEs are classified into commercial ones and public services based on the condition that if they take profit-making as their primary business objective. This classification is more related to the objects of industrial fields and industrial sectors. Commercial SOEs are subdivided into Class A and Class B enterprises. In terms of Class A SOEs, it is not necessary for state-owned capital contributors to be their controlling or largest shareholder while implementing the "mixed-ownership reform", which is specified in the Guiding Opinions. In this sense, it can open up a lot of room for "mixed-ownership reform", which will further integrate industrial reform with market structural reform and promote the opening up of industrial markets.

Taking the telecommunications industry as an example, the "classified" reform has led this industry to move in the direction of protecting industrial safety and complying with technological laws. The network construction services of telecom magnates, that is, China Unicom, China Mobile and China Telecom, were incorporated into a new company (China Tower), which has effectively solved the waste of redundant configuration in network construction,[8] and re-decomposed their value chains and technology chains based on the technical features of the industry. The communication value-added services of telecom terminals are open to the market, allowing 30 private telecom virtual operators to choose to join up the networks of three telecom companies and take part in competitive number allocation. This conforms to the law of openness of the technical fields and satisfies the fundamental requirements for ensuring information security.[9] In terms of the electric power industry, it has kicked off the reform by separating power generation, grid construction, and power transmission and distribution. Such reform remains at the initial stage, with the division of labor and settlement price in need of further improvement.

The advancement of all these reforms will inevitably lead to the reform of the regulatory means and the assessment system. Thanks to SOE classification, the contents and indicators of assessment have got a definite basis. But on specific occasions of operation, the implementation of "classified" reform is not only related to enterprises themselves (objects of reform), but also some historical problems in their organizational structure and business scope, which will affect the actual effect of the "classified" reform.

Shanghai took the lead in bringing forth an SOE reform program which divides municipal SOE into three types: competitive, functional, and public services.[10] SAIC Motor is classified as a competitive SOE, which is not only conducive to its overall public listing but also the reform of the entire organizational system and business system of this automotive group. As the most powerful SOE in Shanghai, SAIC had undertaken certain tasks assigned by the government in the past. Some of its capital contributions did no aim at being rewarded but gave a helping hand to the government at the time. Although well-financed SAIC was fully capable of accomplishing these "tasks", they were in fact not compatible with the company's main business and business accounting goals, which happens to demonstrate another special function of SOEs in macroeconomic operation.

As for the assessment of competitive SOEs, how can these "historical burdens", that is, the tasks performing special functions, enter the scope of capital management responsibility? It is a specific issue that needs to be identified separately. When the enterprise itself makes "a reasonable claim" to the examiner to decompose the contents and objectives of the assessment, there will appear "bargaining" between the examiner and the examinee. In the end, the two parties have to clear up the "historical burdens" and special tasks. That is to say, even though the main business and overall attributes of these SOEs are "competitive" (commercial Class A), their overall business cannot be included in the overall assessment because of a certain part of the business.

This case inspires us. SOEs under the traditional system are engaged in main business and sideline business or even undertaking social affairs beyond their business operations in a certain economic cycle. As such, we have to isolate these non-operational tasks when classifying the business activities of SOEs and to determine their assessment indicators. That is, we have to "stratify" their business structure. It is precisely because of the established business and financial structure, when we have them classified, it is often difficult to separate their main business from "sideline" business, thus leaving room for these enterprises to "bargain" with the assessment authority. In the end, it will be likely to use objective and strict assessment indicators to evaluate these enterprises. It is for this reason that it may affect the deepening of the "classified" reform, making it difficult to implement the reform measures.

6.3.2 The conflict between "classified" reform and "historical burdens" of SOEs triggers the requirement for "stratified" reform

The above analysis of the "classified" reform shows that the thinking of this reform is restricted by many factors: (1) Although the SOEs in "classified" reform are divided into two categories and three sub-categories, the national conditions of China determine that there are differences in the amount of state-owned capital and fiscal revenue and expenditure capacity possessed by the governments at different levels, and their economic and social development tasks require differentiated labor of division. Given this, it is necessary to differentiate the "classification" by combining different levels of government and the distribution of existing SOEs. Objectively speaking, the five levels of government (national, provincial, city, county, and township) have their own fiscal account system. It is natural for them to have their own assets management system. Their stock assets can be regarded as the accumulation of past finances, and the current fiscal revenue and expenditure surplus accumulation will also provide new increments for the state-owned assets account. Governments at all levels will select specific measures for the "classified" reform based on their own fiscal capacity, goals and tasks. (2) Although the "classified" reform has clearly defined the main basis for classification, the state-owned assets management system centering on capital management still needs to straighten out the relationship between state-owned capital contribution and capital use, as well as the equity relationship between investment and the invested at different levels. Therefore, it is necessary to clarify the "ultimate ownership" of the capital contribution, that is, the identity of the "initial" investor. Then it will be able to clarify the ultimate ownership of capital contribution and the property rights of legal persons receiving investment, it can be understood that the subject of "ultimate ownership" is definite, but the contribution of legal persons (ownership of legal persons) has multiple levels of derivation. In other words, the legal person's investment behavior can be derived and nested. This understanding of the relationship between "ultimate ownership" and "ownership of legal persons" helps strengthen the modern corporate governance structure and provides entrepreneurs with a more standardized and relaxed platform. (3) Although the "classified" reform requires the classification of SOEs according to their functional positioning and development goals, the attributes of the classes are not static and immutable. With the deepening of the market development, the boundaries of "classes" will also move and change. Therefore, the differentiation of "classes" is not accomplished overnight, which is also the difficulty of the "classified" reform. Moreover, the government will adjust the "classification" according to the changes in the national economic structure and the economic development requirements in different stages.

In short, in order to maintain the leading role of the state-owned economy, it is necessary to place focus on the technical features and the changes in the global economic structure, establish a dynamic adjustment mechanism for the various components of the national economy and strengthen the control and influence of state-owned capital over key fields and major sectors.

After specifying the work policy for the "classified" reform, we need to effectively carry out this reform, but "classification" is not enough for doing so. To vigorously develop a mixed economy, it is both urgent and necessary to promote the "stratified" reform based on the work policy for the "classified" reform because the "stratified" reform is sure to implement the principles of the "classified" reform and advance it in different levels. "Stratification" and "classification" can complement each other and go hand in hand. The above analysis stresses the "stratified" management of state-owned capital allocation that involves levels of property rights derived from the investment chain, levels of industrial fields invested by state-owned capital, and levels of government that act as the "ultimate investor".

First, in real economic life, investors have a certain amount of "value capital" (amount of monetary value), which is invested into a corporate organization undertaking specific business activities in a certain industrial field, and registered as a "corporate legal person" according to law. According to their development requirements and governance norms, enterprises may have an external investment in their business activities, which is manifested as the derivation of investment property rights. Through the formation of "subsidiaries" or new companies, well-managing enterprises can attract investment from other social capital owners and amplify their own capability in capital operation. The "initiators" who set up new companies will open up equity participation opportunities, and correspondingly have the "harvest" of mobilizing the use of social capital, thus forming a relationship of "mutual cooperation" and "check and balance" between different investors, which is conducive to retaining an active "channel" for optimizing corporate governance structure. However, the responsibility of the property rights chain will ultimately be traced back to the "initial property rights owner" (ultimate owner). There is a relationship between the so-called "initial property rights" (owner of ultimate property rights) and the "derived property rights" (the subject of property rights that accepts and uses the investment). Because of this, we can find out that the vigorous development of a "mixed economy", in combination with investment opportunities in industrial fields, has something to do with the opening of industrial fields. When the subject of the initial property rights ("ultimate property rights") is defined, the vigorous development of a mixed and the dominance of public ownership, which are at two different levels, can go hand in hand. It is true that the opening of industrial fields also involves factors such as their position in the national economic system, the market stability that may arise from the industrial opening and anti-risk ability. These factors are generalized as "industrial security" issues. This is also the point where the reform of state-owned capital management integrates with the deepening of enterprise reform.[11]

Here, the focus of "stratified" reform is to guarantee the compatibility between public ownership and the market economy while maintaining the dominant position of public ownership. We must preserve the public ownership nature of ultimate property rights. According to this line of thinking, the investment subjects of state-owned capital generally take the form of investment companies or sovereign investment funds to maintain flexibility in value capital management. According to the requirements for clarifying the ultimate controller of state-owned capital, and in combination with the existence of multi-level governments which are carriers of all levels of fiscal capacity, it is proposed that there is a fiscal account system based on "five levels of government" and corresponding to the public ownership, which are manifested as the ownership of the central government, the ownership of the provincial and municipal governments, the ownership of the prefectural and municipal governments, the ownership of the county government, and the ownership of the township government. To emphasize that there are five levels of "ultimate owners" of public capital in real economic life, it is a new breakthrough in the public ownership theory.[12]

Upon clarifying the subject of the ultimate ownership, we can determine the link on the same chain of property rights for carrying out the "mixed-ownership reform" so as to ensure its significance. A mixed enterprise is a "capital user" created by multiple "capital contributors"[13] through cooperation and is also an operational organization that materializes the ownership. Investors (capital owners) speak at the general meeting of shareholders and nominate directors (representatives of property rights) to participate in corporate governance. Related to this, the task of accelerating the establishment of state-owned capital management companies is included in the backlog of supporting reforms. Establish market entities that are authorized to operate state-owned capital and exercise the rights of investors, and in combination with the clarified relationship between "capital contribution" and "capital use", it is not difficult to understand that adherence to public ownership can go hand in hand with the development of a mixed economy. But some people still don't understand the relationship between "capital contribution" and "capital use", and even think that "developing a mixed economy is to deny public ownership". The people holding this view actually do not understand the "ownership realization theory", do not understand the separation of "nominal (monetary) ownership" from "actual right to use" or "corporate ownership", and do not understand that modern property rights may continue to be "derived" due to investment behavior. In the process of mixed-ownership reform, when the management of state-owned capital is to be mainly undertaken by state-owned capital management companies which, aiming at industrial security and preservation and appreciation of the value of state-owned capital, on the one hand, play the role of control, influence and risk resistance based on the market conditions and the phased goals of national economic development, and on the other hand, make decisions and judgments according to the characteristics of the market environment and the dynamic characteristics of economic operation, and utilize the "entry-exit mechanism" to vitalize business activities.

Without a comprehensive understanding of the above-mentioned forms and paths for materializing the ownership, there may be a phenomenon of "mixing for the sake of mixing" in the process of promoting the mixed-ownership reform. Take the "mixed-ownership reform" of the Sinopec Sales Company as an example. It sold 29.99% of the equity to 25 domestic and foreign investors, which are basically the stakeholders of the company.[14] It should be noted that China's petroleum industry is not fully liberalized, making it difficult to accurately determine the oil sales price and the settlement of accounts between production, processing and sales companies. In this sense, I think the promotion of mixed-ownership reform is complicated and systematic engineering work, and it should neither be "too fast" nor "too slow". If it is implemented in a hurry when a fair market environment remains absent, it may lead to an outcome of "pseudo-mixing" or "mixing for the sake of mixing". In the final analysis, advancing mixed-ownership reform is a task that requires long-term efforts to create more stringent external conditions.

The above discussion emphasizes the need to clarify the subject of "ultimate ownership", on this basis, the responsibility chain of investment behavior is stratified, which not only contributes to identifying the subject for management of ultimate ownership and provides a basis for the governance of investment occasions but also contributes to the rationalization and continuous optimization of the corporate governance structure of the capital user. Based on the relationship between "investors" and "capital users", a clearer relationship of property rights and responsibilities is to be formed so as to give the corporate legal persons more autonomy in business decision-making and improve the business vitality of enterprises.

Second, considering the relationship between the allocation of state-owned capital and the industrial system in the national economy, when choosing the key fields to be invested by state-owned capital, we need to take account of the industrial system and technical features, allocate the state-owned capital to the basic industries with upstream technologies, and divert more state-owned capital to R&D and infrastructure with positive external spillover effect, as well as to the cultivation of an industrial ecological environment and pay to attention to let state-owned capital play a leading role in all of these fields. In combination with the thinking of "classification", the ultimate owner of state-owned capital has to, based on its own capital, staged goals of industrial development and the market environment, choose to invest state-owned capital at different levels of the industrial technology chain to drive and influence other social capital to carry out open cooperation and transform the economic growth model to the one driven by innovation.

Finally, due to the different levels of "ultimate owner" in the clarified public ownership relationship, there must be different ways for managing the division of labor. Objectively speaking, the state-owned capital management system of the whole society does not appear in the form of "line management". The SASAC plays a special role in guiding the management of "state-owned assets" throughout society. This is also in line with the basic principles of handling central-local relations. Because of the five-level fiscal account system, we can classify the public assets in the fiscal accounts of the central government, provincial and municipal governments, and prefectural and municipal governments as "state-owned assets"; classify the assets in the fiscal accounts of the county and township governments as local public assets and manage them in reference to the state-owned assets management methods. In view of the administrative levels of counties and townships, the content of their daily work is more related to the production and life of the grassroots, and their public assets will inevitably be more integrated with their administration of local affairs. Therefore, the institutional arrangements for the "hierarchical management" of state-owned assets are further clarified, laying the basis for forming a "new state-owned assets management system".

On the basis of definite "classification", "stratified" management of state-owned assets is introduced to promote the better integration of state-owned assets allocation and operations management with the "activity" of the market economy, in a bid to make the actions of "mixed-ownership" reform more solid, more stable and more powerful. Based on the idea of "classification" and in connection with industrial fields and market characteristics, we shall choose different equity structures for mixed enterprises and implement specific schemes for "classified" reform. To this end, it is necessary to introduce a mechanism of cooperation and checks and balances between capitals of different ownership and ensure that state-owned capital can control and influence the operation of the national economy and resist risks in this regard. In the context where mixed economies have been covering more and more industrial fields, the realization of property rights in economic operations has its own characteristics, this is, the "chain of property rights" that accompanies the investment behavior in the management of corporate assets, from this appears the general stipulation of ownership and the extending (derivative) property rights relationship in the ownership realization process, and thus constituting the relationship between "ownership" and "property rights". From this, we can further propose the definition of initial property rights, and at the present stage, the property rights to state ownership are specifically exercised by government agencies in assets accounts affiliated with government finance. Based on a clear government administrative hierarchy, there should be an issue of "multi-level ownership" among multiple levels of government. Besides this, another issue is that how state-owned (public) capital controlled by government develops competitive and cooperative relationships with other sources of social capital and controls and influences the national economy.

By probing into the "stratified" relationship between various capital owners and capital rights developed in the form of a mixed economy, we can better understand the function of governance structure, optimize corporate governance mechanism and implement the responsibilities for governance, in order to improve the operational quality of the corporate system and even the micro-foundation quality of the national economy; better handle the financial and administrative power relationships between governments at all levels, facilitate governments at all levels to better adapt to the operating environment of the market economy, and strengthen the awareness of financial management and the "holistic financial management" ability to dynamically optimize fiscal revenue brought about by stock assets and social, economic operations; and deepen the reform of the government administrative system. In line with the staged objectives of economic and social development and market development conditions, we must maintain the cooperative and competitive relationships between state-owned capital and social capital in the national economic structure and layout and stabilize economic operations while maintaining the vitality of the national economy. Therefore, it can be said that the transition from "classification" to "stratification" is a new alternative for deepening SOE reform.

In short, in the process of deepening the reform of state-owned assets and SOEs, "classified" reform and "stratified" reform are organically combined to promote the reforms of state-owned assets management, SOEs and economic structure. By adhering to the principle of unifying "classified" reform and "stratified" reform, we need to conduct an in-depth study of the implementation of "stratified" reform amid "classified" reform, define the objective and principle of "classification" amid "stratified" reform, and on this basis build a benign mechanism for benefiting the interaction of "classified and stratified" reform measures. By analyzing the national economic operation and reproduction that feature dynamic development, we can find that state-owned capital maintains its liquidity through the market-based "entry" and "exit" mechanisms so that state-owned capital can preserve and increase its value in the flow. Since state-owned capital may be injected into different fields, and the main functions of SOEs – organizational carrier of state-owned capital – are also different, the objects invested by state-owned capital in the entire social reproduction will have functions in varied nature and manifestation. However, generally speaking, there are no more than two ways: one is a direct investment in competitive fields for making profit, these inputs need to be properly regulated due to market development, institutional factors, and industrial safety considerations; the other is an investment in public beneficial infrastructure mainly for giving play to their support function for the overall structure of the national economy, and to achieve the goal of maintaining and increasing value. It is precisely because of the economic operating environment for the effective operation of social reproduction and competitive fields provided by the infrastructural sector that the targets of capital operation performance in the competitive fields can be achieved more smoothly and contribute to the stable growth of national fiscal revenue. Eventually, the goal of maintaining and increasing the value of state-owned capital invested in specific economic fields and infrastructure industries has also been achieved indirectly. It is true that in the dynamic process of continuous adjustment and optimization of the social and economic structure, the profitability of capital invested in the underlying sector can also be ensured to a certain extent, it is just that these investments are large in scale and long in payback periods have their own characteristics different from the investment turnover of general industrial sectors.

6.3.3 Organic combination of "classified" reform and "stratified" reform helps to better utilize the advantages of state-owned capital

After recognizing all levels of state-owned capital contributors as representatives of state-owned property rights, we shall, on the one hand, maintain value-added ability and liquidity of state-owned capital, and on the other hand, take into account its policy and functionality. Governments at different levels differ significantly in their social public administration (service) functions and capital scale; likewise, state-owned capital at different levels is bound to be invested into different fields based on the classification of national economic sectors.

According to the Guiding Opinions, the investment of state-owned capital must follow the principle of advancing and retreating. More state-owned capital shall be invested into key industries and areas vital to national security and are the lifeblood of the economy, focusing on key infrastructure, important and forward-looking strategic industries, and powerful enterprises with core competitiveness. These directions and key areas of state-owned capital investment are the positionings of state-owned economic functions required by the entire society. Specifically, in terms of the capital capability of the central and local governments at all levels, their investment will certainly have their own focus.

Unlike pure private capital, which simply pursues value-added profit, especially cost-benefit considerations in the short run, state-owned capital at a certain level is also obedient to the functional positioning and main work objectives of the local government at the same level. Regarding the allocation and investment of its state-owned (public) capital, the local government must "refrain from doing some things in order to be able to do other things", to form a reasonable division of labor among the various levels of state-owned capital owners and between various levels of state-owned (public) capital and social capital. After being invested in the areas where they can play a role, what is more important is that all levels of state-owned capital are likely to cooperate and support each other, jointly make contributions to social production and the overall situation of China's economic and social development. In the process of developing a mixed economy, all entities invested with state-owned capital shall maintain communication and collaboration, which will benefit the integration of public ownership and market economy. In China, some local governments have been working together to build joint ventures with diversified investments.

The "stratified" reform based on multi-level government financial rights has played a positive role in deepening the reform of state-owned capital management and in enhancing the awareness of state-owned capital contributors at all levels in market competition and profit and loss.

The main body of state-owned capital operation can not only follow the
basic norms of the market economy but also achieve economic development
goals and realize the maintenance and appreciation of capital.

While making it clear to implement "classification" measures for advancing SOE reform, "stratified" reform shall be introduced at the same time,
which will help to straighten out the relationship between state-owned
(public) assets management of all levels of government and their capital
operation and financial management. It is also helpful for better handling
the assets management relationship between the central and local governments at all levels. We shall respect and understand that central and local
state-owned capital at all levels has the general attributes of capital, such as
value-added ability and liquidity, and improve the efficiency of state-owned
capital allocation and value increase. At the same time, we shall respect and
guarantee the independence of state-owned (public) capital held by governments at all levels, and match the rights and responsibilities of state-
owned capital contributors, which will help mobilize and bring into play the
enthusiasm of all levels of government as state-owned capital contributors,
prevent the occurrence of "equalitarianism and free allocation" in the state-
owned assets management account system, ensure clear rights and cooperation order for the management of state-owned capital at all levels.

Realize the reasonable division of labor between central and local state-
owned (public) capital allocation. According to the "classified" reform
principles, as established in the Guiding Opinions, in important industries
and key areas that involve national security and the lifeline of the national
economy, non-competitive commercial SOEs that are mainly responsible
for major special tasks, and major cross-regional engineering works and
projects, it is central state-owned capital that should occupy a controlling
position. The main function of central state-owned capital is to safeguard
national security and control important industries and key areas that are
vital to the national economy, mainly including industries such as tobacco,
petroleum and petrochemical, electric power, telecommunications, postal
communications, military industry and finance. Due to its large scale, central state-owned capital is mainly operated in the form of super large and
large enterprise groups. In terms of industry, central state-owned capital
should be concentrated in strategic key industries at the upstream, important equipment integration industries, and the fields of R&D of cutting-
edge basic technologies. National strategies shall be implemented, regional
development shall be coordinated as a whole, and central state-owned capital shall lead and support the development of the national economy in
order to let central state-owned capital play its role as a radiator and engine
in economies of scale and network economy.

Local state-owned capital is mainly invested and allocated for fulfilling
local economic development goals. Compared with central state-owned

capital, local state-owned capital is more widely distributed. Provincial state-owned capital is mainly distributed in the industries of energy resources (electricity and coal), raw materials (steel, non-ferrous metals and building materials), transportation equipment and installations, transportation and shipping. The state-owned capital controlled by municipal governments is mainly distributed in industries and fields such as water supply, gas supply, heating, public transportation and public facilities. The industry distribution pattern of local state-owned capital and SOEs is attributed to multiple reasons such as historical evolution, local resource endowment, economic development and fiscal balance of local governments. In terms of the state-owned capital related to the daily life of residents at the grassroots level, its management is significantly different from the higher-level state capital management, meaning that state-owned capital at different levels shall be subject to differentiated management.

In case of inter-provincial engineering projects, such as the construction of railways (including high-speed rail) and roads (including expressways), protection and control of the river, lake, forest and nature reserve, and ecological maintenance and restoration of atmospheric environment, they should be jointly invested by the central and provincial or municipal state-owned capital, which is able to guarantee the efficient implementation of these projects. In the case of intra-provincial cross-regional projects, cooperation and joint investment among provincial, municipal and county-level state-owned capital are available to mobilize the enthusiasm of all parties. This kind of multilateral cooperation is able to incentivize all levels of state-owned capital and local governments, which will not only promote the construction of the projects involving overall interests but also raise the efficiency of state-owned capital utilization and manifest the superiority of socialist public ownership.

To carry out the reform of the state-owned assets management system through "classified" and "stratified" measures and the relevant SOE reform will help straighten out the relationship between state-owned assets value-added income and fiscal budgetary revenue. In order to deepen the "stratified" reform, we need to continuously improve the state-owned capital operating budget system and strengthen the value-based management of state-owned assets, give full play to the adjustment function of state-owned capital investment and its profit on fiscal revenue, make the changes in the stock-flow of state-owned capital adapted to the investment behavior of state-owned capital contributors, comprehensively form the "financial management" awareness and financial behavior of governments at all levels, fully perform the regulatory function of state-owned capital in the operation of the national economy, and promote the sustained, healthy and stable development of the national economy.

To properly handle the relationship between state-owned assets value-added income and fiscal budgetary revenue, it is necessary to give full play to the state-owned assets stock-flow adjustment mechanism, enable state-owned capital to accumulate ROI during the boom in line with the changes in the economic cycle and the international economic environment, and then convert accumulated state-owned capital operating profits into new investment during the recession, so as to make up for the lack of investment amid economic downturns and alleviate the market panic, enhance the positive role of the state-owned sector in national macro-control, display the unique attributes of the public functions of state-owned capital, and improve the anti-risk ability of state-owned capital under market economic conditions.

At the same time, the state-owned economy should play an active role in promoting economic transition and improving people's livelihood and welfare, and the state-owned assets stock-flow adjustment mechanism should be given full play. Along with the continuous development of socialist market economic reform and SOE reform, the national economic structure has also changed, so many former "important industries and key fields" may become competitive industries and fields, while the social security, equalization of basic public services, and shortage of other public products that restrict the development of national economy and the people's desire for a better life have gradually become concrete manifestations of major contradictions. Therefore, in order to adapt to the main contradictions of the new era and the requirements of the transition of the socialist market economy, more income from the value-added profit of the state-owned sector should be invested in supporting social security, poverty alleviation, education and other undertakings concerning people's livelihood and welfare, encourage the expansion of domestic demand and strive for high-quality economic growth, give full play to the supporting role of state-owned capital investment and operating income as a source of fiscal revenue, adjust and optimize the economic structure, and achieve the goal of innovation-driven development.

In order to further advance the stratified reform, functions of SOEs shall be transformed, the state-owned economy shall undergo strategic adjustment, and all sorts of market players shall cooperate with each other actively. As a result of a gradually maturing market, continuous economic development and upgrading economic structure, the functional positioning of the state-owned industrial sectors can no longer remain static. In the past, preservation and appreciation of state-owned capital were highly valued, but nowadays, more and more state-owned capital is to be diverted into programs for the public good to benefit the entire society.

The introduction of the "stratified" reform, which is an option fully based on China's realities, not only deepens our understanding of the "classified" reform and confirms the key directions of the reforms of state-owned assets and SOEs but also coordinates macro-economic and micro-economic activities, coordinates the dual functions of the state-owned economy (public service and economic growth) and coordinates the regional distribution of the state-owned economy.

By unifying the three dimensions of the "stratified" reform with the principles of the "classified" reform, it will help to shape a new state-owned assets system and cultivate self-disciplined market entities that are the fittest of all, as well as promote the construction of the socialist rule of law and accelerate the modernization of the national governance system and governance capacity. Moreover, various types of capital are likely to complement each other's advantages, and multiple market entities will be motivated to pursue deep integration and win-win results, which will pave the way for public ownership and market economy to develop side by side. With combined economic and social functions, state-owned capital allocation will become more efficient, thus playing an ever more important role in developing the national economy and safeguarding the interests of the people. In the end, the broad masses of the people will truly have the sense of gain, happiness and security brought along by the socialist public ownership, and the superiority of the socialist public ownership can be truly manifested and brought into play.

6.4 "Classified" and "stratified" reforms call for new breakthroughs in economic theories

What about the enlightenment of "classification" and "stratification" for us today? In combination with the previous analysis, we shall first understand that SOE reform is not a simple economic issue, since the specific content of the reform has "four characteristics": (1) It is an issue with political sensitivity, that is, if someone promotes mixed-ownership reform, there will be rumors that he is trying to restore private ownership. However, as mentioned earlier, the active development of a mixed economy and the adherence to public ownership are two different levels of work, and they can go hand in hand. Moreover, through the value-based management of state-owned capital and the equity investment of state-owned capital, enterprises that undertake specific market operations can appear as mixed enterprises, which is fully in line with the international practice of the market economy. It is a way to integrate the materialization of public ownership with the market economy. (2) It is an issue of "industry security" that arises from the promotion of mixed-ownership reform and the opening of industrial fields. Undoubtedly, the opening of industries needs to be done cautiously to guarantee industry security. Any rash advance is never encouraged. In this sense, the mixed-ownership reform cannot be hastily promoted. We must fully understand this matter and deal with it with a peaceful mind. That kind of reform, for the sake of reform, is actually formalism and self-deception. The "mixed-ownership reform" without mature conditions will inevitably lead to the problem of "asset loss" in inaccurate asset pricing. (3) Owing to the basic attributes of public ownership, the whole people shared the reform achievements, thereby raising the issue of "people's livelihood concerns". Therefore, it is necessary to further promote supporting reforms, create a fair market environment for competition, and prevent social problems caused by "opportunity" mismatch and "profit transfer". (4) The complexity of supporting measures for the "mixed-ownership reform". The relevant supporting measures and market factors involved in actively advancing the mixed-ownership reform are not a simple issue of diversification of property rights. How to fully reveal and handle the coordination of reform measures, the progressive effects of these measures and the elimination of associated risks are quite complicated. Therefore, the "classified" and "stratified" reforms cannot be arranged simply by fulfilling a "task", and it needs to be done steadily.

Second, when explaining the SOE reform principles specified in the Deepening Reform Decision and translating them into specific reform tasks, we have to deal with the existing theoretical stocks in this regard and the behavioral inertia associated with these theoretical stocks. All of them are intertwined with the "path dependence" that we must resolve through reform. The continuous deepening of SOE reform requires new theoretical breakthroughs, and we can get some inspiration from the previous discussion. For example, in order to make theoretical breakthroughs centering on the operation and management of state-owned capital, we shall transform the traditional way to materialize public ownership from administrative behavior (owned by the whole people – owned by the state – owned by the government – implemented by government departments – implemented by government officials) into the market operational behavior (owned by the whole people – owned by the state – owned by the government – assets management companies exercising the actual operating rights empowered by the owner) constrained by market supervision mechanism. It is on the basis of such theoretical breakthroughs that we can truly shape the main body of state-owned capital contribution, identify who will implement the "mixed-ownership reform" and who will operate and maintain state-owned property rights after the reform. The flexible advance and retreat mechanism, which considers the staged objectives of economic development and opportunities arising from market changes, will give state-owned capital the operational vitality and enable its compatibility with the market economy. In this way, we can clearly answer that adhering to public ownership and the active development of a mixed economy can go hand in hand.

Third, the mixed cooperation between state-owned capital and other social capital allocated in specific industrial fields is an important way to enable "the basic economic system with public ownership playing a dominant role and different economic sectors developing side by side" compatible with the market economy. Regarding the issue of developing a mixed economy in China, we have to learn about its introduction means and paths, rather than simply referring to the growth and development of companies in the West. Emphasizing the particularity of this path of introduction will help us face up to the "path dependence" factors in corporate governance behavior. From the macro perspective of social and economic life, the vigorous development of the mixed economy will lead to the coexistence of multiple economic components. We shall enhance the dynamism, dominance and influence of the state sector of the economy. At the micro-level, the development of a mixed economy solves the problem of mutual incentives and mutual checks and balances between the economic components of different ownership, and we shall properly deal with the relationship between different investors and correctly understand the rights and powers of joint capital operations. For example, if you hold 10% of a company's equity, you cannot say that you are the owner of a certain machine but that you own 10% of that machine, including 10% of all other assets of the company. This deepens the understanding that mixed enterprises are the cooperative integration of value capital of all investors. Corporate governance can only be carried out through the decision-making process of the shareholders' meeting and the board of directors. Shareholders cannot directly issue orders to mixed enterprises. The previous practice of the government directly issuing orders to enterprises must be changed. Corresponding to the transformation of government functions, the government shall learn to indirectly affect enterprises through market mechanisms instead of directly issue instructions to enterprises that have been restructured. This may make government officials have behavioral maladjustment so that they have the challenge of "losing" their rights. This is also the deep-seated reason why the ideas of leadership are hard to be turned around. In the process of economic transition, the regulation and control of the market economic operation of the whole society do not adapt in many respects, and there are institutional shortcomings. In particular, there have been insufficient funds and absent management in social public products, showing that the transformation of government functions requires time and even the accumulation of "trial-and-error" experiences. The rhythm of the above understanding and behavioral transformation directly determines the pace of reform. In particular, the importance of ensuring the relationship between economic security and economic development and stability has become a crucial constraint for the deepening of reform. This forms the dialectical understanding that reform cannot be rushed, waited, and cannot be slowed down.

Finally, the existing theoretical stocks and behavioral inertia in practice can be attributed to the power of ideas. Our theoretical workers shall be committed to developing the cultural heritage of mixed ownership to help accelerate the renewal of ideas. We are responsible for doing more work and enriching people's understanding in combination with the history of economic development. In contrast to the emergence of Western companies, the stages when they introduced "mixed-ownership", the means and inlet of introduction, and its significance in protecting and expanding the overall productivity, the current "mixed-ownership" in China has a different historical background. In short, the emergence of a mixed economy in the West in the past is completely different from the one in China. However, we must truly understand that behind the "mixed-ownership reform" is the opening of property rights and the opening of market access. Therefore, every social participant must have an open mind, a sense of equal cooperation, and a spirit of the rule of law, which is exactly what our core values emphasize, and it also has some substantive meaning for us to return to the occasion of promoting SOE reform.

Notes

1 Jiang, Z. M. (1997). *Hold high the great banner of Deng Xiaoping Theory for an all-round advancement of the cause of building socialism with Chinese characteristics into the 21st century*. Retrieved September 12, 1997, from http://www.people.com.cn/item/sj/sdldr/jzm/A106.html

2 See the reports in http://m.haiwainet.cn/middle/3541086/2015/1022/content_29280319_1.html, http://news.sina.com.cn/c/2014-11-01/025931078071.shtml

3 On August 18, 2014, the 18th Review Meeting of the Leading Group for Deepening Reform Comprehensively reviewed the *Remuneration System Reform Plan for the Principal Persons in Charge of Centrally-controlled Enterprises*, and put forward the salary control standards.

4 On May 18, 2014, the NDRC released the list of the first batch of 80 projects that encourage the participation of social capital. http://news.bjx.com.cn/html/20140521/512505.shtml

5 *The SASAC: Six central SOEs to carry out the state-owned assets pilot reform*. https://business.sohu.com/20140715/n402275925.shtml.

6 *Guiding opinions of the CPC Central Committee and the State Council on deepening the reform of state-owned enterprises*. Retrieved August 24, 2015, from http://www.gov.cn/zhengce/2015-09/13/content_2930440.htm

7 *The urgent task at present is to deepen the reforms of state-owned assets and state-owned enterprises*. Retrieved April 9, 2009, from https://wenku.baidu.com/view/828a0e9a50e2524de5187ed0.html

8 Gao, K., & Wang, X. (2016). *Changes brought by an iron tower: A model for state-owned enterprise reform*. Retrieved November 13, 2016, from http://www.xinhuanet.com/politics/2016-11/13/c_1119902236.htm

9 On December 25, 2014, the Ministry of Industry and Information Technology issued the *Notice on Opening the Broadband Access Market to Private Capital*, and attached the *Pilot Program on Opening the Broadband Access Network Business*. Changsha became one of the first pilot cities. http://www.miit.gov.cn/n1146285/n1146352/n3054355/n3057674/n3057693/n3057694/c3542899/content.html.

10 The Shanghai Municipal Party Committee and Municipal Government kicked off the No. 1 Research Project on the "Overall Plan for State-owned Enterprise Reform" in 2013, the relevant documents were officially released at the City-wide State-owned Assets and State-owned Enterprise Reform Work Conference held on December 17, 2013. This Plan sets out the guidelines for "classified" reform and divides SOEs into competitive, functional, and public services ones. In reference to the SOE classification in the Guiding Opinions, competitive SOEs are equivalent to commercial SOEs of Class A, while functional and public services SOEs respectively correspond to commercial SOEs of Class B and public welfare SOEs.

11 The Central Economic Work Conference held on December 14–16, 2016 put forward clear requirements for promoting the "mixed-ownership reform", emphasizing that "this reform is an important breakthrough in the reform of SOEs", and asked to "take substantial steps in the fields of electricity, oil, natural gas,

railways, civil aviation, telecommunications, and military industry in accordance with the requirements for improving governance, strengthening incentives, highlighting the main business, and improving efficiency; and efforts must be made to speed up the pilot reform of state-owned capital investment and operating companies". Later, the Central Economic Work Conference held on December 18–20, 2017 reiterated the requirements for the work in this regard. It can be seen that deepening the mixed-ownership reform is an important task, and its steady advancement deserves the attention of all sectors.

12 This is also a theoretical issue arising from the discussion on the vigorous development of a mixed economy. In fact, the continuous deepening of SOE reform by introducing the modern corporate system and highlighting the independent status of "corporate property rights" (corporate ownership), naturally leads to the requirements for identifying the "investors" of SOEs so as to strengthen the responsibility relationship between capital contribution and capital use and transform the abstract concept of "public ownership" into concrete claims for assuming responsibilities. In response to this, the DRC of the State Council already put forward the proposal for "hierarchical management of state-owned assets" in a research report in November 2002 (http://finance.sina.com.cn/g/2 0021108/0835276398.html). Through careful analysis, hierarchical ownership does not affect the basic nature of public ownership, and it can strengthen the government's state-owned assets management and integrate it with "government's financial management".

13 Under the conditions of a market economy, the allocation of resources in economic operations is generally manifested in the separation of nominal (monetary) capital ownership from the right to use capital, which is fully discussed in Chapters 30–32 of Capital (Vol. 3) of K. Marx.

14 Refer to the relevant report on "Mixed-ownership Reform of Sinopec" on Baidu Encyclopedia, https://baike.baidu.com/item/%E4%B8%AD%E7%9F %B3%E5%8C%96%E6%B7%B7%E6%94%B9%E9%A1%B9%E7%9B%AE/1 6927595?fr=aladdin

7 The role of entrepreneurs in corporate governance

The 40 years' economic structural reform of China, which is to transform the way in which social reproduction resources are allocated, has stimulated continuously deepening marketization, increasingly refined division of labor, and constantly evolving collaborative relationship between various production factors. In this process, we have become more confirmed that business operators are an independent production factor.

The economic restructuring initiated in 1978 required the Chinese government to "delegate powers and transfer profits" to enterprises, implement an economic responsibility system, and link enterprises' retained profits with their business performance, which has gradually made people realize the importance for enterprises to decide their business operations on their own. On this basis, we started paying attention to the role of the subject in business decision-making and then proposed to implement the "factory director responsibility system".

After deciding to establish the socialist market economy – the objective of China's economic structural reform, we have been trying to push enterprises to the market and build them into the micro-foundation of the market economy. To this end, we need to restructure traditional SOEs into legal organizations that are capable of modern corporate governance, which means that we must pay close attention to the selection, appointment, incentives and constraints of business operators (entrepreneurs) and regard them as independent production factor.

In the process of economic restructuring, which is also the process for China to develop the non-public sectors of the economy, the robust development of private companies steered by outstanding individuals also draws people's attention to the role of entrepreneurs (entrepreneurship), which is highly rated as an extremely scarce resource for modern mass production and has become a hot topic in economic theory research.

7.1 Entrepreneurs are gradually regarded as a special production factor

As mentioned earlier, under the traditional highly centralized planned economic system, enterprises were merely an appendage of government administrative organs; the entire society was subject to administrative operation, and enterprises were no exception. As part of the "Social Factory", enterprises had no need for planning anything by themselves. Although a "factory director" was appointed to take charge of business management, he was no more than an "organizer" of production activities as instructed by competent authorities. It can be said that there were no genuine enterprises in the era of a planned economy, not to speak of entrepreneurs.[1]

The "first step" of China's economic structural reform was to "delegate powers and transfer profits" to enterprises. For the purpose of building up enterprise vitality, the autonomy of enterprises must be guaranteed and their survival ability amid market competition must be cultivated. Consequently, the important role of business decision-makers has been taken more and more seriously, and now this group of people is collectively known as "entrepreneurs" in both the workplace and academic circle.

7.1.1 The reform for shaping independent market entities stimulates the development of entrepreneur market

Since enterprises under the centralized planned economic system were lack of vitality, the "first step" of China's economic structural reform was to "delegate powers and transfer profits" from the government to enterprises. While linking retained profits up with their business performance, enterprises should also be aware of "business accounting": distribute part of their retained profits to employees as a bonus (a supplement to the unified wage system) so as to motivate both managers and first-line workers and improve their management of labor productivity. Besides, enterprises are allowed to discretionarily spend their retained profits on replenishing raw materials to fully release the production capacity of existing equipment and decide how to deal with the output that exceeds the production quota. Enterprises have therefore become more autonomous in business operations. All of these stimulants, mainly for enhancing enterprise "autonomy", have made the role of SOE directors or managers more prominent. From today's perspective, we are in dire need of entrepreneurial spirit; in other words, we are in dire need of the special role or contributions of business decision-makers.

The "delegation of powers and transfer of profits", which involve all aspects of the enterprise operational mechanism, have touched the "nervous centralis" of enterprises as an economic subject and exerted an all-round impact on their business operations. It can be described as a recovery of "economic rationality", indicating that Chinese enterprises started to care about their own interests. An enterprise is not only an accounting body of its business activities but also an organization that integrates all sorts of production factors. So enterprise managers that undertake this kind of integration must play a vital role in "independent management". Because of this, how to mobilize the enthusiasm of enterprise managers has gradually become a hot topic. From today's point of view, the concepts in enterprise theory can be boiled down to the "principal-agent" issue.

While stimulating the production enthusiasm of enterprises by "delegating powers and transferring profits" to them, we need to scientifically and objectively evaluate the role of business operators, and in the meantime, give full play to the incentive and restraint mechanism of enterprises, which is an inevitable requirement for advancing the enterprise reform.

In 1983, the director of Wangxingji Fan Factory, located in Huangzhou City of Zhejiang Province, signed a statement of responsibility for operation contract,[2] specifying the rights, responsibilities and interests of the first person responsible for the factory operation, which set a precedent in China. In 1984, all of Zhejiang-based SOEs began to implement the factory director responsibility system, showing that the incentive and restraint mechanism for business operators had become an important part of the enterprise reform. More than that, the enthusiasm of enterprise employees had become unprecedentedly high, and the reform measures for enhancing enterprise vitality – the core of the entire economic structural reform – had achieved substantial results.

In 1992, the Fourteenth National Congress put forward that China's economic structural reform aimed to establish a socialist market economy. The *Decision on Some Issues Concerning the Establishment of the Socialist Market Economy*, adopted at the Third Plenary Session of the 14th CPC Central Committee in 1993, stated that China should establish a modern corporate system and make it the micro-foundation of the market economy; and restructure traditional SOEs into genuine market entities in the form of modern companies.

The *Company Law of the People's Republic of China* enacted in 1993 provided legal norms for enterprise restructuring. Consequently, the "factory director responsibility system" was incorporated into the modern corporate governance structure, the corporate governance theory was popularized and practiced, and the construction of corporate governance structure and the improvement of governance mechanisms got a new start. The modern companies funded by diverse investors have given rise to a new relationship of division and cooperation pursuant to the laws and the "separation of three rights" (ownership right of investors, property right of corporate legal persons, and daily management right). With the development of the market economy, enterprises increasingly desire "specialized" management, thus triggering the professional manager market to come into being.

After implementing the norms for modern corporate governance, entrepreneurs have become a prominent production factor and got universal recognition. The modern corporate system is, in essence, an organizational platform for "professional managers" to display their ability and grow into "entrepreneurs".

7.1.2 *"Two types" and "three generations" of entrepreneurs growing up in the 40-year enterprise reform*

As mentioned above, many reform measures for increasing enterprise vitality have drawn people's attention to the role of enterprise managers.

Owing to the uncertainties in the market itself, enterprise managers have to make definite business plans in this volatile environment, meaning that they are subject to severe tests while playing a vital role in developing their enterprises. In the economic research circle or on other occasions, these persons are honored as "entrepreneurs" for their socio-economic contributions.

According to the descriptions of entrepreneurs in enterprise theory, there are generally two types of entrepreneurs in modern companies: some entrepreneurs themselves are business owners who are still engaged in business operations, while others are professional managers hired by business owners. In most cases, the "entrepreneurs" we often talk about are business owners, while the second type of entrepreneurs goes by the name of "professional managers". In China's real economic life, founders of private companies are directly referred to as "entrepreneurs", but such title is seldom used for addressing managers of SOEs, perhaps it's because managers of SOEs are not owners of enterprise assets (equity), but "cadres dealing with economic affairs" as appointed by the Party organization.

As the reform and opening up kept pressing ahead, especially China's accession to the World Trade Organization (WTO) in 2001, both Chinese state-owned and private enterprises grabbed the opportunities brought about by "globalization": they began to take massive product orders in need of labor-intense manufacturing by making full use of the vast domestic labor resources and by following the law of industrialization. Entrepreneurial talent of Chinese businessmen was therefore brought into full play. In the meantime, SOEs had been going through the corporate system reform to establish the "corporate governance structure" required by the Company Law to facilitate their chairmen and managers to play their unique role based on the independent corporate property rights. Coupled with a favorable external environment (development of a "professional manager market"), managers of SOEs began to be addressed as "entrepreneurs".

The above division of entrepreneurs into two types is the basis for readers to learn more about their contributions in the 40 years' reform and opening up. In the three development stages of the market economy, Chinese entrepreneurs have been front-line "commanders" for organizing and managing social reproduction activities. And three generations of entrepreneurs had come to the fore in these stages:

> In the first stage (from 1978 when the reform and opening up was launched to 1992 when the "market-oriented" reform was initiated), Chinese SOEs were on the way to be vitalized and the non-public sectors were being fostered. It was against such background that the first generation of Chinese entrepreneurs had grown up. At the time of a "shortage economy", private enterprises emerged as "a supplement to the national economy", while state-owned and collective enterprises started to cater to market demand for adapting to the economic environment, especially those manufacturing light industrial products;

quite a number of charismatic and competent entrepreneurs therefrom stepped out to rise to the challenges from the market economy. Being bold enough to think independently, assume responsibilities and make a difference in corporate governance, these persons soon opened up a new prospect for their enterprises. In 1980, Bu Xinsheng, director of Zhejiang-based Haiyan County Shirt Factory – a kind of "big collective"[3] of public ownership – launched an overhaul of the factory, e.g., abolishing the "egalitarian practice", trying all means to mobilize workers' production enthusiasm and seize market opportunities. Just one year later, this small factory developed itself into the industry leader in Zhejiang Province. At the end of 1984, Zhang Ruimin, head of a subdistrict office, was appointed as director of Shandong-based Qingdao Refrigerator Factory (predecessor of Haier Group). He developed the first development strategy for the factory – a brand strategy. He firmly believed that industrial products were either "qualified or unqualified", rather than grade-1, grade-2 or grade-3 products based on their quality. After obtaining an in-depth under-standing of the business process and efficiency evaluation of the factory, Zhang made a bold decision to have 76 defective refrigerators destroyed in 1985. More than a shock to all workers, this action also triggered the transformation of their business philosophy and the reengineering of business process (that is, to develop new standards for management and control). It was in this way that Zhang brought Haier on the track of rapid development. In December 1988, Haier became the first refrig-erator manufacturer to win the Golden Quality Medal Award in China. In 1990, Haier successively won the national-level Golden Horse Award and National Quality Management Award. In December 1991, Haier Group was established with Zhang Ruimin serving as its president. It was at this time that he developed the second development strategy for Haier – a diversification strategy. Bu Xinsheng and Zhang Ruimin are representatives of the first generation of Chinese entrepreneurs. In this stage, private entrepreneurs were far from mature, and they still needed to build up their operation capability. Moreover, with a small scale of capital, private enterprises were unable to access to market dynamics in the first place since the market economy remained at its infancy, thus forcing private entrepreneurs to concentrate on production or circula-tion that met people's life needs in surrounding areas. The most influential private entrepreneur of this kind was Nian Guangjiu – founder of "Fool's Sunflower Seeds".[4] There is no doubt that the first generation of entrepreneurs, including the heads of public enterprises and those of private sectors, had made painstaking efforts in giving a new life to their businesses under the harsh conditions at that time.

The second generation of entrepreneurs, who appeared between 1992 and 2002, has distinct characteristics. Based on the experiences of the first stage of reform and opening up, business operators had initially accumulated the ability to understand and adapt to the market. Especially after Deng Xiaoping made a famous remark during his south China tour in 1992 and the Fourteenth National Congress made it clear that the "establishment of the socialist market economy" was the objective of China's economic structural reform, the goal of economic system transition became more clarified and entrepreneurs finally had a broader stage for display. They took the initiative to welcome the opening and introduce foreign advanced technologies. In the process of advancing industrialization, they have become highly capable of integrating management elements such as technology application, economies of scale, and market development. Entrepreneurs in this stage generally paid attention to learning knowledge about modern enterprise management and decision-making. Their ability to control the market and manage enterprises has been significantly improved. They support the institutional transformation of traditional SOEs by establishing a modern corporate system. The promulgation of the Company Law provides norms for the transformation of SOEs into modern companies and requires building a modern corporate governance structure to adjust and transform the leadership system of SOEs. In the process of advancing the corporate restructuring of enterprises, some companies choose to issue shares and go public. The public market information of "public companies" has stimulated the whole society's understanding of the organic integration of corporate development and capital market, thus ushering the integration of corporate system innovation and market economy into a new realm. As the scale of enterprises grows, the organizational form of enterprises has been evolving into groups. At this stage, a number of state-owned and private enterprises had rapidly grown and become stronger, including some "new SOEs" formed in the context of reform like Lenovo, which was funded by the Institute of Computing Technology of the Chinese Academy of Sciences. Out of accurate judgments about the rapid popularization of electronic computers, Lenovo rapidly grew into an electronic technology enterprise group with global influence and whose main products are computers. As the founder of the group, Liu Chuanzhi is a typical representative of the second generation of entrepreneurs. His philosophy for being the main decision-maker of business operation, which is briefed as "developing strategies, forming a leading group and steering a talents team", reflects the classic statement of the role that entrepreneurs should play. At this stage, the content of the reform was that land as a special production factor was included in the scope of market-oriented allocation in the form of "rental" flow of use rights. This reform had an overall impact on China's economic development. The dormant land resources became an important means of financing, which starts to provide a new source of funding for China's economy to enter the fast lane of rapid development. It was this important background condition that gave birth to a group of private enterprises and entrepreneurs engaged in real estate development. Under the leadership of Chairman Wang Shi, Shenzhen Vanke has rapidly grown into a national real estate development company by raising funds through public offerings. Liu Chuanzhi and Wang Shi have become representatives of entrepreneurs in this stage, and they are also the second generation of entrepreneurs emerging in the reform and opening up. Although each of them has a unique management style, all of them have made good achievements in corporate strategic management, product technology management, brand and corporate culture management, and staff management. Today they are still active participants in economic activities.

The third generation of entrepreneurs started showing extraordinary talents from 2002 to the present, reflecting the characteristics of China's economic development and changes in the market environment in this stage. As we know, China's official accession to the WTO in 2001 opened up channels for domestic companies to take part in the international market. In 2002, the Sixteenth National Congress proposed that the socialist market economy had been basically established and would enter a stage of perfection and in-depth reform. Chinese enterprises quickly integrated into the global division of labor, undertook global industrial transfer, further promoted the process of industrialization, accumulated and improved their abilities to digest, absorb and renovate foreign advanced technologies in the process of opening up, and gradually formed a social industrial technology chain. The universal application of information technology and Internet technology has formed a new force in the transformation and upgrading of the traditional industrial system and has further triggered the entire society to attach great importance to the application of digital technology and digital resources. All of these pose challenges to business management and create conditions for entrepreneurs to play a unique role. During this period, the corporate reform of SOEs was generally implemented in the whole society, and the cooperation between state-owned capital and other social capital facilitated the introduction of more "privatization" mechanisms in SOE operations, thus forming a check-and-balance mechanism in enterprises and promoting corporate governance to better adapt to the objective requirements of market mechanisms. On the other hand, several private enterprises have been expanding rapidly through new technologies and social financing, Alibaba led by Jack Ma and Tencent led by Pony Ma, as well as Gree Electric Appliances (partly funded by the state-owned capital) led by Dong Mingzhu, are typical examples. Song Zhiping, chairman of China National Building Materials Group Corporation (CNBM), is one of the outstanding entrepreneurs of central SOEs. CNBM has succeeded in using equity instruments, market-oriented mergers and other means to strengthen the transformation of the development model of the building materials industry in the whole society, optimize the corporate organization system in the industrial layout, technology and capacity arrangement and planning, and improve the efficiency of resource allocation and capital return. This generation of entrepreneurs has demonstrated a global vision, sensitive awareness of the development of high-tech applications, and the ability to understand and apply modern market economic mechanisms and modern financial means.

The above discussion tells us that the recognition and emphasis on the status of entrepreneurs in China's economic life are one of the results that the whole society has been going through reform and opening up and marketization. The role of entrepreneurs has become an important "production factor" in corporate governance. In view of this, enterprises can be better understood as "a knot of a set of contractual relationships", while entrepreneurs are a specific production factor that specifically integrates and handles this contractual relationship. As a result, the role of entrepreneurs in corporate governance has become a hot topic in economic theoretical research. We can understand that the role of entrepreneurs is an integral part of the modern corporate governance structure. The growth process of Chinese entrepreneurs is directly related to the stage of economic transition and the environment of economic development. There are many inspirations for how to deal with the principal-agent relationship theory formed under the condition of separation of capital ownership from use rights. This theory should be understood in the context of a sound corporate governance mechanism.

7.1.3 The "parties" of corporate governance and environmental conditions for giving play to governance capacity

In modern corporate governance, the goals of corporate development are usually decomposed into different levels, thereby forming a level-by-level principal-agent relationship and a relatively clear chain of the division of rights and responsibilities. The "parties" of corporate governance are divided into principals (shareholders) and agents (managers) in joint-stock enterprises, that is, all shareholders, board members elected by shareholders, and executive managers authorized by the board of directors. Entrepreneurs in the traditional sense are those who also have the ability of shareholders to take risks, share profits and make business decisions. Among the "parties" of corporate governance, entrepreneurs, as the core subject of corporate governance, assume the role of "agents" and perform management functions completely independent, showing a trend that the entrepreneurs engaged in management are being "professionalized". The independence of management labor and the professionalization of entrepreneurs will undoubtedly contribute to the accumulation of management experience and make management itself a specialized subject to be valued. Although entrepreneurship is difficult to quantify, it has a great effect on corporate governance. The specific governance conditions are prone to be affected by the macro-environment such as culture, system, law, and religion, as well as the micro-environment such as the company's nature, scale, and industry where it is located.

At the macro level, law, religion, culture, etc., all have an impact on corporate governance. Objectively speaking, the establishment of written laws and regulations in practice is, to a certain extent, the result of a summary of the experience and effectiveness of reform practice. The reform measures themselves have been bold enough to break through existing laws, regulations and cultural customs. Since the essential requirement of reform is to break through the status quo, the existing system and rules, this will result in a contradiction between observance of existing laws and regulations and implementation of reform and innovation. This requires a relatively loose public opinion environment and correct theoretical understanding in the whole society under the guidance of the policy of emancipating the mind. There are objective uncertainties in reform actions, creation of new rules and standards, and acceptance of new things, not to mention that there is path dependence in the concepts and behaviors of the parties to economic activities. It is precisely for this reason that we need to be courageous enough to advance reform, transform corporate governance structure, and highlight the role of individual entrepreneurs.

Regarding the corporate governance practice in China, we have also introduced an "independent director" system to establish a reasonable governance structure for restructured SOEs. According to the "Chinese Corporate Governance Index"[5] released by Nankai University, since Chinese enterprises began to introduce the western governance systems such as independent directors in 2002, they have been absorbing people with professional knowledge into their board of directors, which has had a positive effect on corporate governance and significantly improved the corporate governance index, but there are still many problems in the "effectiveness" of governance. At the same time, the governance level of private enterprises has exceeded that of SOEs for seven consecutive years since 2011. This makes us think about the compatibility of the mature corporate governance system that originated abroad with China's domestic corporate culture, that is, the localization of the corporate governance system. We have to refer to in Chapter 3, which analyzes the difference between the Chinese path of introducing the corporate system from the spontaneous evolution of Western companies. Chinese SOEs are restructured into the corporate form of organization, meaning that their governance system is implanted. Although it can accelerate the improvement of China's corporate governance system, it ignores the specific factors of Chinese culture, the development stage of Chinese companies and the capital market.

First, China is a country whose economic system is undergoing a transformation. Under the traditional planned economy system, the operation of enterprises was guided by government plans and mainly for completing the planned tasks assigned by government organs. Under the market economy system, the operation of enterprises is market-oriented and revolving around the improvement of the market and economic efficiency. Therefore, it is worth exploring how corporate governance in the era of a planned economy can be transferred to the corporate governance adapted to the characteristics of the market economy.

Second, the "parties" in corporate governance activities, that is, business operators, are formed spontaneously in the market economy, but in the transitional economy, the original identity of corporate managers are administrative cadres, and they will inevitably face the problem of role conversion, especially the conversion of thinking and behavior. How is this conversion realized and are there any constraints? Also, how to deal with the relationship between the understanding, cultivation and maintenance of entrepreneurship and our institutional environment? These internal and external environments will affect the effectiveness of the corporate governance system.

On the micro-level, quite a number of factors, such as the nature of corporate ownership, equity structure, capital structure, company size, industry nature, and demand for investment and financing, have a great impact on corporate governance. Under certain market conditions, factors such as industry investment opportunities, the intensity of industry competition, characteristics of products, and the leverage ratio also greatly impact corporate governance. In connection with these market factors that determine the influence of a company's development in a given corporate organization, the entrepreneur's comprehensive vision and ability in making decisions are particularly important.

First, the nature of the company's ownership has a more prominent impact on corporate governance. In mixed companies controlled by state-owned capital, the agents of state-owned capital operations still enjoy the status as "cadres" who are appointed, assessed, rewarded or punished by relevant government departments. In this sense, the parties as main managers of enterprises, although relevant government departments will give full consideration to the market economic expertise and comprehensive management capacity of relevant "parties", they are not appointed in a market-oriented manner. Especially because at different times or in different places, such "economic cadres" may "flow" back and forth from government agencies to enterprises. As a result, there is a big difference in the evaluation of the parties and the standards of compensation. Compared with private enterprises, SOEs have insufficient motivation for corporate governance and the problems they face are more complicated.

Second, the ownership structure and capital structure of companies will also have an impact on corporate governance. The allocation of equity structure has a direct impact on the corporate governance mechanism. In the process of "mixed-ownership reform" of SOEs, people may worry that dispersion of equity will deprive shareholders of motivation to supervise and manage companies and even attempt to be "free riders", thus leading to connected transactions or other self-interested behavior. As a result, they are unwilling to delegate powers to lower levels. When the equity is concentrated in the hands of major shareholders, they are more willing to supervise and manage companies and improve corporate governance to prevent national and collective interests from being infringed. However, when the equity is too concentrated, major shareholders will have greater control over property, and the personification of the state capital owner will impel them to seek personal gains. Therefore, there is an opportunistic tendency and moral hazard to use one's dominant position to invade the interests of other members, and their entrepreneurial ability and quality cannot be fully utilized.

Finally, the relationship between the size and industries of companies and their corporate governance is relatively complicated. Generally speaking, the larger the company is, the more difficult it is to be governed, and the weaker the governance effect should be. But from another perspective, companies with better governance are more likely to continue and form larger scales. Compared with the West, Chinese enterprises controlled by or in joint ventures with state-owned capital investors have absolute advantages in terms of scale and quantity. And due to the development and reform of China's economic system, SOEs themselves have an inherent large-scale and complex equity structure, making them extremely difficult to conduct corporate governance. Moreover, in a huge scale system, it is difficult to separate the individual abilities and performance of entrepreneurs for consideration. From an industry perspective, monopolistic industries have barriers to entry, often lack competitors, and pay less attention to corporate governance. In addition, these companies are large in scale, which makes governance more difficult. Governance problems in China have been further aggravated – China's monopoly industries are often controlled by state-owned capital, which makes the governance problems of SOEs and monopoly industries superimposed, which is more difficult than Western corporate governance problems. SOEs can be divided into public welfare enterprises, commercial SOEs with main business in fully competitive industries and fields, and commercial SOEs with main business in important industries and key fields related to national security and the lifeline of the national economy and mainly undertake major special tasks. Different types of SOEs have different regulatory mechanisms for state-owned assets, the requirements for the proportion of state-owned shares in a mixed ownership structure are different, and corporate governance mechanisms are also different. The mixing of the three types of businesses makes most SOEs face the "mission conflict" of profitability and public welfare, which is not conducive to the design of SOE corporate governance structure and entrepreneur evaluation mechanism.

In addition, companies' long-term profits have a strong correlation with their governance, but such correlation does not exist between short-term profitability and corporate governance. Regarding the current personnel appointment and incentive and restraint mechanisms of SOEs, entrepreneurs usually care about short-term profits rather than long-term profits, which has affected the effectiveness of corporate governance. The high financing demand of companies is often accompanied by better corporate governance since sound corporate governance is conducive to their financing, and the financing demand of SOEs is not very urgent, which makes their desire for corporate governance not strong enough.

The above analysis shows that in the process of economic transition in China, under the background of establishing a modern company system through SOE restructuring, how to better play the special role of entrepreneurs in corporate governance is restricted by multiple macro and micro factors in the system transition.

7.2 How to deal with the "principal-agent" relationship in corporate governance

Looking at the history of the development of mass production mode in the world economy, due to technological progress, socialization of production and continuous expansion of market scope, enterprises – micro-organizations of social reproduction activities – have scored substantial development. With the influence of various factors such as enterprise growth, capital concentration, expansion of production scale, and diversified ways of competition (factors), the organizational form of enterprises continues to evolve. In order to accelerate the expansion of scale, enterprises have begun to try to pool the capital with equity tools, giving rise to the separation of "nominal capital" from "real capital" and the capital contribution relationship of enterprises, that is, owners of capital may not directly use or manage the capital operation affairs by themselves. Instead, they may entrust "agents" to handle capital operation and management affairs for them, thus constituting a "principal-agent" relationship. This relationship makes modern joint-stock enterprises the most basic and typical corporate form and also the dominant form of corporate organization in contemporary economic life. It is precisely because the ownership of capital is realized through the "principal-agent" mechanism. To strengthen the incentive and restraint of the agents' behavior, capital owners no longer have all the residual control rights and allow the agents to participate in the "surplus" sharing.

Subsequently, economic theories are constantly updated and perfected in line with the changes in corporate organizational forms. In the sense of traditional economics, an enterprise is regarded as a production function that mainly studies the input-output relationship and pursues profit maximization. It was not until the publication of Coase's classic paper *The Nature of the Firm* in 1937 that the academic community began to study the origin and nature of enterprises from the institutional perspective. After the 1960s, this point of view received widespread attention. Oliver E. Williamson perfected Coase's theoretical system by bringing forth the theories of "Optimal Hierarchical Structure" and "Asset Specificity". In the article Production, Information Costs and Economic Organization published by Alchian and Demsetzin in 1972, it was the earliest to associate the enterprise theory with the residual claim rights of enterprises, emphasizing the principal-agent relationship in enterprises. In modern enterprise theory, which mainly studies the transaction relationship between people and pursuing to maximize the personal utility of each company member, an enterprise is an organic combination of a series of (incomplete) contracts, a way for people to trade property rights.[6] Among them, the transaction cost theory focuses on the relationship between the enterprise and the market, while the agency theory focuses on the analysis of the internal organizational structure of the enterprise and the agency relationship between enterprise members.

With the separation of "ownership" from "operation", the organizational form of joint-stock enterprises has been widely adopted, and the principal-agent relationship has become a key topic of discussion in modern enterprise theory. Enterprise theory interprets enterprises as a combination of contracts, the "owner" and "operator" of an enterprise establish a connection through a contract, with the owner acting as the principal of the contract, while the "operator" as the agent of the contract. Both parties invest in different production factors, and only when these factors are combined in the form of a contract and produced in a team manner can the enterprise generate benefits. According to the rational characteristics of the parties, how to effectively handle the principal-agent relationship so as to improve corporate efficiency is the core issue of modern corporate governance.

Starting from the "ownership" level, corporate governance emphasizes how the owner scientifically authorizes and supervises the owner of the operating rights. In this process, it is necessary to supervise, motivate, control and coordinate the company's business management and performance through a series of institutional arrangements to better realize the effectiveness of resource allocation. In the contractual relationship of joint-stock enterprises, the interests of two parties are often inconsistent, which is manifested in the different ways of obtaining and determining remuneration. The so-called corporate governance is a series of institutional arrangements made to solve the inconsistency of interest goals and suppress opportunistic tendencies so as to minimize the loss of the agent's infringement of the principal's interests caused by the incomplete contract. The compensation given to the "operator" is usually in the form of stocks or bonds in order to align his interests with the "owner". However, this incentive mechanism has various problems: one is that the "operator" may receive different returns from the "owner"; the second is that the "owner" usually distributes his investment portfolios in a wide range of companies and investment firms, and tends to pay more attention to company performance and financial status, while the "operator" is affected by a series of other factors, considerations for the size of his company, his power and prestige, and the authority that can be imposed when allocating resources.

Starting from the level of "operating rights", the owner of an enterprise authorizes the manager of the operating right, and the manager needs to adopt a series of operating methods and management behaviors in order to achieve the business objectives. With the progress of social production, the expansion of production scale and the emergence of new markets, the scale and technical complexity of enterprise production and operation activities continue to increase, which also poses challenges to the effective organizational form of enterprises and challenges their management capability. The role of "managers" in the development of enterprises is becoming more and more important so that it gradually becomes independent of other factors of production and becomes a special factor of human capital – the entrepreneur factor.

From the perspective of reproduction theory, an enterprise is a micro-organization form of social reproduction activities, which organizes, allocates and integrates various production resource allocations in production activities. As for the "management" behavior required in resource integration, the organizer who is specifically responsible for resource integration, that is, the head of the enterprise – the entrepreneur, implements it. Therefore, entrepreneurs are of special importance for the survival, growth, competition and development of enterprises. However, under the background that the professional manager market has not yet been established in China, corporate governance issues are different from those in the West. In particular, SOEs have the problem of "owner absence". That is, the state acts as a shareholder and is responsible for assigning company managers, making entrepreneurial talents difficult to emerge and grow.

The research on principal-agent theory in western economic theory has almost been enriched and perfected with the evolution of the corporate organization. China's economic life has gone out of the traditional planned economy and transformed into a market economy. The system construction and improvement of how to deal with the principal-agent relationship are similar to the "compressed" shaping, not to mention the "path dependence" in the system and conceptual behavior, as well as the inevitable "insufficiency" in the evolution of the institutional content of the reform and transition, which is bound to bring about many unsatisfactory aspects in dealing with the principal-agent relationship of enterprises scientifically.

First, the principal-agent relationship of China's SOEs has a different generation method and specific content from the West. Since the public nature of state-owned assets is manifested as a public mission on the principal side, it is no longer the entrustment of private capital's capital contribution to the daily management of enterprises. Although the agent side appears as the subject of the personal personality of a natural person, its managerial identity is mainly not screened by the market but dispatched by the government's personnel management agency.

Second, different from the business management and development of entrepreneur market in the West, in the period of large-scale planned economy production in China, enterprises had been an appendage of the government's administrative agency, and they had full authority to act on the government's administrative instructions in production activities. In other words, they did not need independent management and business planning by themselves. Naturally, there was no "entrepreneur" factor and the concept of "market economy". After the economic structural reform has gradually deepened and clarified that the socialist market economy is the target of China's economic structural reform, the modern corporate system is used to transform traditional enterprises and establish the corporate property rights of enterprises, which naturally provides a stage and space for entrepreneurs to display their talents. Only when the economic theory research on the development and growth of Chinese enterprises introduces the category of "entrepreneurs" can the entrepreneur theory that reflects the characteristics of China gradually develop. It is precisely in this way that the development of China's entrepreneur market is quite late or it is still "underdeveloped".

In addition, the enterprise itself is an incomplete contract, and the principal-agent relationship is also restricted by macro- and micro-environments. The complexity of the environment, the bounded rationality of the actors, and the uncertainty of the future make it impossible for both parties to use existing information to accurately predict all possible future events and states and specify them in the contract clauses. It tries to clarify the state of all events in the contract, and the expected benefits are not enough to make up for the high contracting costs. Therefore, it is particularly important to suppress opportunism and moral hazard and to maximize the control of the consequences of incomplete contracts.

7.3 Recognition of entrepreneur factor as a special factor of production

As an economic activity organization for allocating social reproduction resources, enterprises have to orderly integrate various factors and maintain dynamic competitiveness in the economic operation. Various issues to be dealt with in business decisions are actually complex and systematic projects depending on the special talents of entrepreneurs to manage and deal with it, which demonstrates the important role of entrepreneurship. As early as the 1960s, some scholars discovered that the entrepreneur factor plays an important role in economic growth. Soltow (1960) pointed out that "economic growth must take into account the decision-makers on which it depends – provide full details for citations entrepreneurs". Later studies by Cipolla (2010), Lazonick (1992) and Brouwer (2002) all provided evidence for this view. However, in the 1980s, Romer (1986) and Lucas (1988) developed the theory of endogenous growth by introducing knowledge into the macro-growth model. In addition, the variable of entrepreneurship is difficult to quantify. Scholars turned to believe that investment into R&D of new knowledge could bring forth output, while entrepreneurial activities were regarded as exogenous variables and ignored. It was not until the emergence of the "European Paradox"[7] in the late 1990s that entrepreneurship was brought into the sight of scholars. Many foreign studies during this period showed that the enhancement of entrepreneurial activities could bring about changes in employment, productivity, output, and industrial structure. For example, Henderson (2006), van Praag and Verslot (2007) argued that entrepreneurs create a positive spillover effect in the economy by creating jobs, increasing productivity, and promoting commercial innovation. Metcalfe (2004) and Dias and Mcdermott (2006) proposed that entrepreneurs are an important tool for structural transformation, and the entry of new enterprises causes structural changes through the introduction of innovation and vocational training for workers. Fisscher et al. (2005) and Mueller (2007) mentioned that entrepreneurial activities discover and develop opportunities, create value for existing and new organizations, and thus become the engine of knowledge transfer and capitalization.

Scholars have also conducted research on the role of entrepreneurship in China. Tan (2001) believes that Chinese private entrepreneurs have played an extremely important role in the turbulent economic transition. Wei Jiang et al. (2004) analyzed the growth process of the low-voltage electrical appliance cluster in Liushi County, Zhejiang Province and found that although the entrepreneurial spirit is only a manifestation of personal character, it will have a positive impact on the outside in the process of entrepreneurial action and form external economics. This positive externality is mainly realized through three effects: geographic proximity, industrial linkage and social identity. Li Xinchun et al. (2006) believe that the corporate governance mechanism contains two mutually opposed factors that stimulate and restrict the entrepreneurial spirit of the agents. They conducted an empirical test using the data of Chinese listed family firms and SOEs and found that for family businesses, the incentive mechanism has a significant positive role in promoting entrepreneurship, while the restraint mechanism is manifested as inaction or failure; for SOEs, the incentive mechanism has no significant effect on entrepreneurship, while the restraint mechanism has a more significant "inverted U-shaped" effect on entrepreneurship. In short, private enterprises should mainly use incentive mechanisms, while SOEs should mainly use restraint mechanisms. Li Hongbin et al. (2009) used China's provincial panel data from 1983 to 2003 to prove that entrepreneurship and entrepreneurial innovation have a significant positive effect on economic growth.

With the changes of the times, people's understanding of entrepreneurs is constantly deepening, from "factor integrator" to "leader", and then to "risk taker, resource allocator, and innovator". The gradual expansion of the connotation and extension of the definition itself means that scholars believe that entrepreneurs play an increasingly important role in enterprises (Zhang Huiming, Zhang Liangliang, 2011). Today's discussion of governance structure in Western business circles has shifted the focus to the definition of two types of capital relations: one type of capital is the capital of the investor, collectively referred to as currency capital; the other type of capital is human capital, which refers to entrepreneurs and technological innovators in business. It can be seen that entrepreneurs have become a key factor of production in the establishment and improvement of the corporate governance structure.

The reason why entrepreneurs have become a special factor of production is that in the dynamic process of enterprise ownership arrangements, entrepreneurs actually maintain control over enterprise capital, which is explained in the following aspects:

1. From the perspective of entrepreneurial characteristics. First, in modern society, entrepreneur human capital is a scarcer resource than physical capital. With the development of society and the continuous expansion of material wealth, companies can use a variety of financing methods to obtain the material capital they need. Entrepreneur human capital is fairly rare, which not only requires huge investment in human capital, but also requires more time and greater risks. Second, the invisibility and difficulty of supervision of the entrepreneur human capital make entrepreneurs inevitably have the ownership right of enterprises. The research of modern property right theory and enterprise theory shows that defining the right of residual claim to the members whose behavior is the most difficult to supervise is beneficial to the improvement of efficiency (Zhang Weiying, 1995). The entrepreneur, whose conduct is the most difficult to monitor, should have residual claims. On the other hand, the residual claim right arrangement must correspond to the residual control right to ensure efficiency (Hart, 1998).

2. From the perspective of the role of entrepreneurs in enterprises. The role of entrepreneurs in business efficiency and vitality has been explained above, so I won't repeat them here. In terms of the status of entrepreneur human capital and material capital in enterprises, entrepreneur human capital is more important. The traditional enterprise theory emphasizes the importance of material capital, believing that material capital is the glue of the enterprise and that the separability of material capital from its owners makes it a mortgage function, so material capital should employ human capital (Hart, 1998). However, with the decline in the scarcity of physical capital, the securitization of physical capital, and the development of the capital market, the mortgage function of physical capital has weakened. On the contrary, the specificity of entrepreneur human capital has been strengthened, making it the real bearer of corporate risks (Fang Zhulan, 1997). Moreover, the status of physical capital in enterprises has gradually given way to entrepreneur human capital, and entrepreneur human capital is becoming the glue for enterprises.

3. From the perspective of the relationship between entrepreneur human capital and general human capital. Since changes in control right affect the incentives of those who do not have control right before and after the change, assets should be in the hands of those who have the most important human capital (Hart, 1998). In enterprises, entrepreneur human capital is more important than general human capital, so entrepreneurs should control corporate assets. In the analysis of the internal mechanism of the corporate governance structure with entrepreneurs as the core, shareholders, creditor owners and workers are only the "potential owners" of the enterprise. Not only are they in abnormal operating conditions, they exercise ownership

functions according to certain rules, and under normal operating conditions, they will also have an impact on business operations.

As mentioned earlier, human capital represented by entrepreneurs is more proactive than monetary capital, and the capital ability of entrepreneurs is lurking in the human body. Therefore, entrepreneurs should be determined as the content of the governance structure. In fact, it is necessary to fully mobilize the enthusiasm of entrepreneurs while restraining their behaviors. To enable entrepreneurs to give full play to their important role in the development of modern enterprises, they must be treated as an important factor of the modern enterprise system and incorporated into the enterprise's control right structure. That is, they must be taken as an important part of the corporate governance structure of modern enterprises to make institutional arrangements and establish a set of corresponding incentive and restraint mechanisms.

7.4 The characteristics of entrepreneur factor in the governance of state-funded enterprises

As a special factor of production, at the micro-level, entrepreneurs' management ability directly determines the promotion and implementation of enterprises' organizational innovation, and to a certain extent, determines the success or failure of enterprises. At the macro level, entrepreneurs promote economic development and social progress through their unique professional abilities and innovative activities. Under the existing joint-stock enterprises, entrepreneurs should be a group and "representatives who bear operating risks, possess operating capabilities and powers, and obtain residual claims".

Entrusting the board of directors with the power to independently select and hire the general manager will not only ensure the independence of the board but will also encourage the board to choose highly capable entrepreneurs. Such entrepreneurs who can maximize the satisfaction of the owner's equity must have two qualities: capable and loyal. This requires, first of all, to be good at identifying entrepreneurial talent in the selection process and then establishing an effective supervision and restraint mechanism. However, among state-funded enterprises, it is first difficult to select outstanding entrepreneurs. Competent entrepreneurs often appear in fierce market competition. Due to the lack of market incentives and constraints, it is difficult for entrepreneurs to fully display their management ability by government administrative evaluation alone. The officials promoted from the original industry bureau and other administrative departments are especially restricted by their thinking style and work style, and they are inexperienced in enterprise assets management and operation. According to data, the average entrepreneurial ability index of Chinese listed companies is only 33.47, of which the average entrepreneurial ability index of state-holding companies is 33.19, and the average entrepreneurial ability index of private companies is 33.65.[8]

Moreover, in reality, the board of directors in state-funded enterprises does not really have the power to independently select and hire the general manager. First of all, the assets in state-funded enterprises are owned by the SASAC. As a matter of principle, the appointment and removal of personnel should be implemented by the SASAC. However, according to the principle of "the Party manages cadres", the selection, appointment, and assessment of managers are still carried out by the central or local party committees. In this way, personnel management right and assets management right cannot be completely consistent, resulting in a situation in which, although the owner's representative is in place, the specific functions of the ownership realization process cannot be fully implemented, and the operation and management of state-owned assets cannot escape the intervention of administrative departments. Secondly, for state-holding companies, the independent personnel selection and appointment led by the board of directors is even more difficult. It is usually the state-owned assets supervision and administration agencies that dominate the personnel selection. According to data, there are only 279 companies with general managers selected from the market among Chinese listed companies, accounting for 12.17% of all 2,293 companies. Among them, 112 are state-owned holding companies, accounting for 12.56% of all state-holding companies.[9]

Due to this reality, the entrepreneurs of state-funded enterprises have a certain degree of particularity compared to those who have grown up from market competition. Although they do not have obvious deficiencies in political thought and general knowledge, they still have certain weaknesses in professional knowledge, management ability, and personality charm. Entrepreneurs must have a variety of qualities, first of all, political and ideological qualities. In particular, entrepreneurs of SOEs should have a high sense of self-discipline, remain honest and selfless, and keep close contact with the people. The second is to have a wealth of knowledge. The knowledge here includes not only professional knowledge but also knowledge in other fields. Furthermore, the core is to have operational management capability and strategic insight to create economic benefits for the company and promote the continuous and rapid development of the company. At the same time, they must have leadership, decision-making and organizational skills and be good at employing suitable people. Finally, there is an indispensable personality charm for entrepreneurs. They shall be innovative, adventurous, dedicated, and professional. While working, they must have a sense of responsibility, truth-seeking and pragmatic spirit, and perseverance; while in daily life, they shall remain easygoing.

A study of the Chinese Entrepreneur Survey System shows at present, most business operators value innovation and are good at seizing market opportunities, but their self-evaluation in terms of risk and challenge awareness is relatively low. With higher self-evaluation of entrepreneurship, higher recognition of the professional role of entrepreneurs, they will be more aware of taking risks and continuing innovation and more willing to proactively capture market opportunities, expand external space, and make a forward-looking judgment of the development trend. At the same time, they are more satisfied with the status quo of their companies, and their companies' integrity and comprehensive performance are relatively good. Therefore, the characteristics of entrepreneurs include innovation and management capabilities and a spirit of taking adventures and challenges. Moreover, the study also shows that the external environment has a greater impact on entrepreneurship, especially rapid technological changes and industry growth, which has the most significant impact on entrepreneurship, especially for the improvement of entrepreneurial awareness of innovation and risk. The associated factors are the transformation of government functions, the protection of intellectual property rights, and the human resource environment, which have a more obvious impact on entrepreneurship.[10] Therefore, compared with the behavioral characteristics of SOE operators restricted by the system, in the growth and development of private enterprises (non-public economy), the changing and competitive market environment is more conducive to the rapid growth of the entrepreneurs with "entrepreneurship".

Of course, it does not rule out that some capable entrepreneurs will emerge from state-funded enterprises. It is worth noting that the entrepreneurs of Baosteel have played an especially outstanding role in enterprise development. It is a typical example of entrepreneurial theory with Chinese characteristics.

At the beginning of reform and opening up, Baosteel was founded, and Li Ming, the former vice minister of the metallurgical department, served as the "commander in chief", and then became the director of Baosteel General Plant and the general manager of Baosteel Group. During his 15 years' service in Baosteel, he not only created a new model for the modernization and development of China's steel industry but also created the "Baosteel Road" of continuous innovation in the reform and development of Chinese SOEs. He was the first to put forward the project management mode' which takes the total project schedule as the core and features "guaranteed time limit, improved quality, and not-exceeding investment", which ensured the timely completion of all projects. The product concept of "customer satisfaction", the innovation system, the supporting talent incentive system, and the modern management system have promoted Baosteel's development in an all-around way. Li Ming also attaches great importance to innovation and has embarked on a high-end technological development road of "introduction-digestion-tracking-innovation". He advocates to positively introduce foreign advanced and appropriate technologies. On the premise of ensuring technological leadership, he has managed to spend as little as possible to maximize the economic benefits of limited funds. In this way, Baosteel finally owns a complete set of technical equipment that is ahead of the domestic technology level for about 20 years and has obtained obvious latecomer advantages.[11]

In 1979, Rong Yiren overcame numerous obstacles to propose the establishment of an "international investment trust company" (processor of CITIC Group) and adopted the methods of financing and development of trade that were common in capitalist countries. He formulated the company's first charter, emphasizing that "the company adheres to the principles of socialism, acts in accordance with economic laws, and implements modern scientific management." He also defined the CITIC work style as "abiding by laws, remaining honest and upright, seeking truth from facts, forging ahead, acting modestly and prudently, sticking to unity and mutual assistance, diligence, and doing everything resolutely", and took the lead in practicing. In 1979, Rong proposed important amendments to the draft law on Sino-foreign joint ventures concerning the proportion of foreign investment and corporate decision-making mechanisms, demonstrating extraordinary vision and political courage. In the years that followed, CITIC shouldered the important task of opening the country to the outside world, breaking through institutional barriers many times and exploring a different path from the past. CITIC became the first Chinese enterprise that has developed itself into a genuine "company".[12]

Looking at it again, Song Zhiping once served as the chairman of both CNBM and Sinopharm Group. Under his leadership, these two originally insolvent central SOEs entered the Fortune global 500 companies in 2011 and 2013. Song was thereby highly rated as China's "Inamori Kazuo". He has been in charge of the two central SOEs with Eastern Confucianism for more than 10 years, bringing the two "grassroots SOEs" out of the difficulties. In just a few years in charge of CNBM, he integrated nearly 1,000 companies and had CNBM listed on the Hong Kong Stock Exchange. He also received the nickname "Ultimate Integrator" and created a textbook-like "Song Zhiping Model" – "Integration and optimization". In the past year, he has led the merger of two "giant" central SOEs – CNBM and Sinoma. After reorganization, the total assets of the new group exceed 500 billion yuan, and its listed companies are as many as 15. The practice has proved that the "Integration and optimization" model has not only become the trump card for CNBM to successfully respond to the new normal but also promoted the structural adjustment, transformation and upgrading of the entire building materials industry.[13]

It is not difficult to see that these individual SOE entrepreneurs have been intensively working in their companies and industries for years and have outstanding personal abilities. They are good at innovation, daring to take risks, and diligent in management. However, in most state-funded enterprises today, there is no benign and long-term guarantee mechanism for talent selection, appointment, evaluation and promotion. Due to the incentive and restraint mechanism of the administrative system, it is difficult to find and cultivate individual entrepreneurs with personal charm and ability. The business managers selected from the administrative organs or transferred from other SOEs only take an interest in short-term returns.

They tend to use business operations as a springboard for political advancement instead of caring about the long-term operation of their companies or industries or the cultivation of innovative ability. Those who have been enterprise operators for years or who have transferred from the administrative organs to SOEs often have the psychological state of "free riding", that is, if the profit of the enterprise is too prominent, they will become the focus of attention, thus likely to be promoted. The resulting short-sighted behaviors and "free-riding" phenomena of state-funded enterprise entrepreneurs have become common occurrences. Therefore, it is particularly important to establish a good entrepreneur evaluation system and incentive and restraint mechanism.

7.5 The independence of human capital: how to deal with the relationship between market evaluation and administrative evaluation

In the division of labor in enterprise management, entrepreneurs are subdivided as a special factor and become "leaders" who assume the responsibility of enterprise management. On the basis of affirming the objective existence of the entrepreneur factor, only by explaining the independent meaning of this factor can we have a deeper understanding of it and solve the subsequent evaluation problems.

The corporate governance structure of the modern corporate system ensures the independent status of entrepreneurs, and also protects their unique status and gives full play to their management ability. In the modern corporate system, investors have the rational economic requirement for preserving and increasing the value of their capital investment, thus enabling enterprises with independent legal person property rights to obtain the "legal person will" to guide their own behaviors. It is under this "legal person will" that the duties of managers engaged in the operation of enterprises (including capital management and production management) are further affirmed. The "corporate governance structure" in the operation of modern enterprises organically combines a group of rights in capital investment and operation, makes the division of labor enter the process of ownership realization, makes the responsibilities of subjects exercising different powers more specialized, and promotes the efficiency of function exercise to be greatly improved, so as to improve the efficiency of assets operation. The first is that shareholders have the ultimate ownership of their capital and the right to corresponding earnings and entrust their right of capital operation to the elected board of directors and board of supervisors. As the highest authority of the enterprise, shareholders' meeting formulates articles of association, approves the financial statements for the operation of the business, review the objectives and plans of the enterprise, and urge the enterprise to make better performance. The second is that the board of directors, by holding the property right of the enterprise, takes charge of capital operation, controls the realization of the enterprise's objectives, hire senior managers in production and operations, and pursue the preservation and appreciation of net assets. The third is that the senior managers directly engaged in the daily operation and management of the enterprise accept the appointment of the board of directors, master the decision-making power of the enterprise, effectively control the realization of the enterprise's annual goals, and achieve maximum profits. It can be seen that the latter roles manage enterprise operations at the level of capital operation and production operation, respectively, and perform the functions of entrepreneurs. In short, in a mature enterprise system, entrepreneurs' behavioral norms and goals are established and stable.

At present, China's enterprise reform is moving toward the goal of a modern corporate system, and various types of pilot projects at all levels are being carried out in an orderly manner. In July 2018, the State Council issued a plan for pilot reform of the state-owned investment and operating companies, reforming the state-owned capital authorized operation system, perfecting the state-owned assets management system, realizing the separation of state-owned capital ownership and enterprise management right, implementing state-owned capital market-oriented operation, and requiring to give play to the platform role of state-owned assets investment and operation companies, to promote the rational flow of state-owned capital and optimize the investment direction of state-owned capital.[14] At the same time, the construction of the team of entrepreneurs has also received great attention. In September 2017, the State Council issued relevant documents on the protection of entrepreneurs. For the first time, the State made it clear to protect the development of entrepreneurs with high standards, expounded entrepreneurship in the most authoritative way, and showed care for the growth of entrepreneurs in an all-around way. It not only sent a clear signal that we should care about entrepreneurs and fully recognize their status and role but also responded to a series of problems that are of common concern and an urgent need to be solved.[15]

As mentioned above, an enterprise is a collection of a set of factor contracts, and the specific design, integration, dynamic optimization and adjustment of such factor contracts rely on the contribution and role of entrepreneurs. After the production factors assembled by the enterprise are subdivided, the management's ability to integrate factor resources becomes a special factor of production. In particular, with the deepening of reforms and the development of the market economy, if the external factors and object factors of enterprise development and growth are stripped away, what remains is the factor of entrepreneurship. Therefore, whether it is the dynamic process toward the modern corporate system or the operation, governance, survival and development of enterprises after the corporate system reform, all of them need to be promoted by people. Entrepreneurs are the key talent force for enterprise development. How to screen, cultivate and form a reasonable evaluation system for entrepreneurs is particularly important. It can even be said that creating a large team of professional entrepreneurs who understand the socialist market economy is the basic work for establishing a modern corporate system.

Of course, whether it is the construction of a modern corporate system or the growth of an entrepreneur team and the development of the entrepreneur market, it requires a long period, especially for SOEs. First, by rationalizing the state-owned assets management system, shaping the main body of state-owned assets investment and operation, timely implement the responsibility of maintaining and increasing the value of state-owned assets to every legal person and specific responsible person, form the organization system of state-owned assets management, cultivate the ideology and behavior of the personnel team, and build a team of entrepreneurs dedicated to preserving and increasing the value of state assets. Second, focus on exploring the establishment of an indicator system for the assessment and evaluation of operators by owners, and through the selection, assessment, reward and punishment of operators, the symmetrical check-and-balance mechanism and incentive-constraint mechanism are formed. Third, gradually form a manager market integrating cultivation, recommendation, assessment and supervision, and promote the entrepreneur team to move toward professionalization and marketization. By accelerating the construction of the entrepreneur market, let the personality subject support the operation of the modern corporate system.

Emphasizing the independence of entrepreneurs as a kind of human capital and establishing a mature evaluation system for the manager market also need to create certain conditions. First, the professionalization and marketization of entrepreneurs shall gain a broad understanding, especially the understanding and acceptance of the chairman and managers of state-funded enterprises, and they shall be self-confident enough to participate in the market. As Party cadres, they were sent to lead the enterprises. Since they had been accustomed to accepting the administrative recognition for a long time, this resulted in "dependence" on the Party and government organs. It became difficult for them to accept the sudden change of roles and "price" themselves again. Second, the corporate personnel management system shall be reformed to be mainly subject to market evaluation, with administrative evaluation serving as a supplement. Those who are entrusted to enter the company's board of directors as representatives of state-owned assets should be treated differently from those who are managers of the daily production and operation of the company. The former is selected through a combination of government selection and market evaluation, mainly assessing the level of assets preservation and appreciation; the latter is mainly through market recruitment, mainly assessing the level of after-tax profit. At the same time, it is necessary to combine assets management with personnel management to prevent overlapping management and unclear responsibilities. When problems such as inconsistent assessment standards occur, we must gradually separate the management of the entrepreneur team from the management of government and civil servants. Of course, market forces can also be used to establish a competitive elimination mechanism for entrepreneurs, to implement recruitment, competitive bidding, and trial contract operations within the enterprise, and to establish an "entrepreneur market" within the enterprise.

7.6 Personnel appointment and incentive and restraint mechanism

Based on the understanding of the entrepreneur factor, how to allocate and encourage it on the basis of market evaluation is of great significance for the cultivation of the entrepreneur market and the development of the entrepreneurial factor. Especially for SOEs, it has important reform significance. How to distinguish entrepreneurial talents from general administrative talents and then apply different scientific treatments to their compensation incentives is worthy of discussion.

At present, the selection and appointment of personnel in state-funded enterprises are mainly carried out by state-owned regulatory agencies and organizational departments. The channels for their selection of general managers are generally from the government, from inside the enterprises (usually taken over by a deputy), or transferred from other SOEs. Since the managers of SOEs have administrative levels and benefits, it is basically impossible for them to be selected from private enterprises. The new pilot program for reform of the state-owned investment and operating companies promulgated in July 2018 stated that state-owned capital investment and operating companies should establish a pool of candidates for directors and supervisors, and the nomination committee under the board of directors will recommend qualified candidates according to the situation of the company, and then report to the board of directors for review and appointment. At the same time, it is necessary to strengthen the business training, management and evaluation of directors and supervisors.[16]

The content of the business mechanism involves all aspects, but its core lies in incentives and constraints. Corporate behavior is actually the economic behavior of corporate parties. In order to maintain its economic behavior in the best state of corporate assets operation and operating efficiency, the most important thing is to provide appropriate incentives and constraints. The central issue of the incentive mechanism is how to take effective measures and means to achieve the goal of incentives. The essence of the incentive mechanism is to solve the problem of corporate motivation. As a counter-incentive, restraint is a negative incentive for corporate parties to perform their functions efficiently and reasonably, coordinate various relationships, and not harm corporate interests under the premise of maximizing personal interests.

The core of the transformation of the SOE mechanism lies in incentives and constraints. The current main obstacles are irregular government behavior as the principal, the unreasonable or imperfect corporate govern-ance structure, and the low comparative benefits of labor mobility.[17]

First, the government's excessive intervention as a principal makes the agent's residual power extremely incomplete. In the past, the operating conditions of SOEs were mainly determined through administrative as-sessment, such as the profit rate of the enterprise, the preservation and appreciation of state-owned capital, the market positioning of products, the value of entrepreneurs and their business performance, and even the man-agement level of the enterprise. It was the comprehensive administrative department or the competent department that organized the assessment. This practice was contrary to the requirements of marketization. Under the banner of strengthening management as an owner, replacing the market with the government, and implementing an administrative intervention in corporate behavior, many problems that should have been solved by legal means or through social intermediary organizations are managed by es-tablishing government agencies instead of being handed over to the market.

At present, the trial of establishing state-owned capital investment and op-erating companies in the beginning to "separate government from the state-owned assets management" and create an independent entity representing the organization of state-owned assets in an attempt to solve the problem of irre-gular government behaviors. The pilot program proposes that state-owned capital investment companies should establish a management and control model based on strategic objectives and financial benefits, and the assessment of holding companies should focus on the implementation of corporate strategies and capital returns. State-owned capital operating companies shall establish a financial management and control model, and the assessment of holding companies shall focus on the flow of state-owned capital and the maintenance and appreciation of capital value. At the same time, improve the supervision system, integrate investor supervision and auditing, disciplinary inspection and supervision, establish a supervision work consultation mechanism, and strengthen the overall supervision over the investment and operation of state-owned capital companies and improve supervision efficiency according to the principle of standardizing the system beforehand, strengthening the monitoring in the event and strengthening the accountability afterward.[18]

Second, the inefficient corporate governance structure has a negative ef-fect on the management of SOEs. As the state shares account for the ma-jority, although the chairman is formally elected by the general meeting of shareholders, he is actually appointed by the government, and the manager is appointed or concurrently appointed by the chairman, making the en-terprise still an adjunct of the government. Under such circumstances, even if the state-owned assets management function is independent of the gov-ernment and a non-administrative state-owned capital investment and op-eration company is established, the enterprise will still face the "administrative" intervention brought about by the monopoly and control of state-owned assets management and operating organizations. Due to the special personnel appointment system and the majority of the shareowners are State and state-owned legal persons, it is difficult for the senior managers of state-funded enterprises to maintain long-term stability and cannot hold individual shares. Therefore, senior managers and government leaders who are both leaders of enterprises and cadres of the State have huge psychological barriers and social pressures.

Therefore, the core of the reform is to establish a system, environment, and cultural values that support the growth and development of entrepreneurs. Through the design of incentives and restraint mechanisms, people with the ability to become entrepreneurs are guaranteed to operate independently and fully display their talents, and at the same time, they are allowed to stay at ease and work in the enterprise for a long time, and in this process to fully realize their personal value, develop potentials and improve their personality. A variety of incentives can be employed in addition to remuneration, including equity, options, reputation, takeover market, manager market, selection and removal system, and independent director system.

Third, employment rigidity and labor immobility have caused a serious burden on SOEs. These enterprises often bear the responsibility of solving the employment and stabilizing the society so that their dismissal of employees and their own mobility remains low, and they are also burdened with huge spending on employees' housing, pension and medical insurance. From the management level up to the ordinary employees, the reason why they don't want to move is that they have higher interests to stay in the existing enterprises. If we want to form a mechanism for voluntary employee mobility, we need to greatly increase their comparative benefits of mobility.

Therefore, whether it is the entrepreneur market or the ordinary employee market, it is necessary to establish a sound social security system to separate this part of the functions assumed by SOEs. One is to establish a vocational training system so that everyone will have a stronger professional quality and to improve the specificity of human capital; the other is to have unemployment protection and related supporting measures for medical, housing and education guarantee to solve their worries when choosing new occupations.

Notes

1 Ryutaro, K. (1993). *The contemporary Chinese economy: A Sino-Japanese comparative study* (p. 76). Beijing: The Commercial Press.
2 *Employees have become more enthusiastic after implementing the factory director responsibility system.* http://mini.eastday.com/a/180507080432022.html?qid=02263&vqid=qid02650.
3 "Big collectives" are economic organizations at the village and township levels and owned by county governments. With more capital and more powerful owners, these enterprises are relative to "small collective economic organizations". Considering the economic system at that time, even the enterprises invested by prefectural and municipal governments were categorized as "big collectives".

4 In December 1978, the Third Plenary Session of the 11th CPC Central Committee was convened, sounding the trumpet for the reform and opening up. Just one year later, an ambitious businessman Nian Guangjiu from Wuhu City of Anhui Province, registered the trademark "Fool's Sunflower Seeds", and opened a store selling roasted seeds and nuts. This small workshop developed so rapidly that it even hired more than 100 people, becoming a smash hit at that time. However, at the end of 1983, Nian's labor hiring was reported to the Party Central Committee and drew the attention of Deng Xiaoping. On October 22, 1984, Deng aired his opinions that "let's wait and see for a couple of years ... Just let it keep running, why should we feel afraid, how can it hurt socialism?" (*Selected works of Deng Xiaoping*, Vol. 3, p. 91). In 1992, in his remarks made during the south China tour, Deng once again mentioned "Fool's Sunflower Seeds", saying that "if you take some action, the masses may say the policies are not reliable and feel uneasy. If you put the man who makes 'Fool's Sunflower Seeds' out of business, it will make many people anxious, and that won't do anybody any good. There are still many similar cases, if they are not handled properly, it is easy to shake our policy and affect the overall reform. The basic policy of urban and rural reform must be stable for a long time". (*Selected works of Deng Xiaoping*, Vol. 3, p. 371).

5 The "Chinese Corporate Governance Index" was released by the Research Institute of Corporate Governance of China of Nankai University. It has been released for 15 consecutive years since 2003, and a total of 27,391 sample companies have been evaluated. As the first corporate governance index released in China, the index has a wide range of influences at home and abroad, fully affirmed by the SASAC, CSRC and other relevant departments, and widely used in academia and business circles.

6 Zhang, W. Y. (2015). *Enterprise theory and China's enterprise reform* (pp. 53–54). Shanghai: Shanghai People's Publishing House.

7 The "European Paradox" was first proposed in the EU Green Paper on Innovation (European Commission, 1995). Europe's scientific achievements and high-skilled human capital play a leading role in the world, but it has failed to turn these knowledge investment results into economic growth. Many subsequent scholars confirmed this view, including Robert et al. (1999) and Auditsch et al. (2008).

8 Corporate Governance and Enterprise Development Research Center of Beijing Normal University. *China corporate governance classification index database, Entrepreneur ability index database 2014.*

9 Corporate Governance and Enterprise Development Research Center of Beijing Normal University. *China corporate governance classification index database, Entrepreneur ability index database 2014.*

10 Chinese Entrepreneur Survey System. (2009). Business operators' understanding and evaluation of entrepreneurship – special survey report on the growth and development of Chinese business operators in 2009. *Management World*, Issue 6.

11 China Baosteel Group. (2017). *Li Ming and the road of Baosteel.* Beijing: China CITIC Press.

12 Chen W. Y. (2006). Rong Yiren and CITIC. *Century*, Issue 2.

13 *Integration and optimization: the recipe for CNBM's success.* Retrieved September 7, 2015, from . http://finance.china.com.cn/industry/20150907/3328805.shtml

14 State Council. (2018). *Implementation opinions on promoting the pilot reform of state-owned capital investment and operating companies.*

15 State Council. (2017). *Opinions on creating an environment for the healthy growth of entrepreneurs, promoting outstanding entrepreneurship and better utilizing entrepreneurs' role.*

16 State Council. (2018). *Implementation opinions on promoting the pilot reform of state-owned capital investment and operating companies.*
17 Gao, M. H. (2017). *Corporate governance and state-owned enterprise reform.* Shanghai: Orient Publishing Center.
18 State Council. (2018). *Implementation opinions on promoting the pilot reform of state-owned capital investment and operating companies.*

8 Governance structure optimization of state-funded enterprises

Chapter 7 interprets the role of entrepreneurs in corporate governance, which deepens our understanding of the principal-agent mechanism in modern corporate governance, and enlightens us to fully display the entrepreneurial talents in building and improving corporate governance. It can be said that a scientific, corporate governance structure is a talent showcase for entrepreneurs. Because of this, corporate governance structure needs to be continuously improved and optimized, which is of great importance for further advancing enterprise reform.

The 20 years' reform practices from 1993 to 2013 have proved that diversified investment can directly help shape corporate governance. These practical experiences during this period have made us more determined to keep deepening the SOE reform. In November 2013, the Third Plenary Session of the 18th CPC Central Committee adopted the *Decision on Some Major Issues Concerning Comprehensively Deepening the Reform*, which explicitly stated to transit from "assets management" to "capital management", make the "vigorous development of a mixed economy" as the new direction and goal of reform, and take mixed ownership as a new "breakthrough" for advancing the SOE reform (that is, non-state-owned capital can be introduced to cooperate with state-owned capital), so as to make the "mixed economy" as an important way for materializing public ownership under the market economy, and also an important way for realizing organic integration of public capital allocation with the market economy.

The policy of "vigorous development of a mixed economy" has promoted economic theory innovation: on the basis of diversified capital contribution (multiple investors) of company system enterprises, the ultimate ownership must be established to improve the cooperative and check-and-balance relationships between investors. It also deepens our understanding of the relationships between multiple investors. In real life, the company system enterprises with diversified capital contributions have investors of different types of ownership, but in fact, these enterprises only have one ultimate owner, that is, the government. As a result, on the occasion of corporate governance, it is difficult to form a genuine check-and-balance mechanism between multiple investors; on the contrary, it is easy to slip back to the operational track of traditional SOEs, which features non-separation of government functions from enterprise management and non-separation of the government from the state-owned assets management.

Here, we stress renaming the existing "SOEs" as "state-funded enterprises" to show respect for other capital owners in mixed enterprises. When discussing the issue of corporate governance mechanism in SOE reform, it is particularly necessary to denote that it is to reform and optimize the governance structure and mechanism of "state-funded enterprises". To this end, we need to answer the following questions: How to implement the mixed-ownership reform in traditional SOEs? Which kind of environmental conditions will restrain the optimization of corporate governance structure? What is the "path dependence" in corporate governance behaviors? What are the underlying cultural deposits of "path dependence"?

8.1 "Breakthrough point": how can mixed ownership transform traditional SOEs?

In a seminar with Zhejiang NPC deputies in March 2012, Zhang Dejiang, a former member of the Political Bureau of the CPC Central Committee and Vice Premier of the State Council, drew an analogy that "Private capital is water, while the real economy is a well. We'd better pump water from the well to benefit the people than let it flow quietly underground",[1] which vividly tells that private capital needs an outlet to be brought back to life. More than that, as China's economy keeps developing, SOEs also need to be rejuvenated. After we have scored some results in restructuring traditional SOEs into companies of the modern corporate system, we gained a full understanding of the necessity for transforming the corporate governance structure with "diversified investment". But how could we ensure the check and balance between different investors? It was in this context where the mixed-ownership reform was proposed, marking new progress in the economic theoretical research for "innovating the ways for materializing public ownership". This new round of reform, declared by the *Decision on Some Major Issues Concerning Comprehensively Deepening the Reform* adopted at the Third Plenary Session of the 18th CPC Central Committee, clearly made "vigorous development of a mixed economy" as its new "breakthrough point".

The important foundation of China's economic and social development is made up of the basic economic system "with public ownership playing a dominant role and different economic sectors developing side by side", and SOEs and other forms of enterprises (including collectively-owned, foreign-funded and private enterprises). They are also the main forces for China's economic construction. They are neither separable nor simply opposite. In practice, SOEs cannot sustain without private enterprises, which undertake most of their outsourcing services; private enterprises are also inseparable from SOEs since they need public services (such as power supply) provided by SOEs. These two types of enterprises are not mutually exclusive or in an either-or relationship. Instead, they can be integrated with each other through cross-shareholding and mixed-ownership reform, just like a white fish and a black fish connected end to end depicted in the Chinese classic Tai ji Diagram, which symbolizes the wisdom and power of the Chinese people.[2] In a word, the development of a mixed economy has injected new vitality into China's economic construction.

8.1.1 Development process of China's mixed economy

To pursue the goal of building the socialist market economy, the Third Plenary Session of the 14th CPC Central Committee held in 1993 decided to transform the traditional enterprises owned by the whole people into the enterprises of the modern corporate system and develop them into a solid micro-foundation of the socialist market economy. Guided by the provisions of the Company Law, the following 20 years witnessed SOEs transform the form of corporate registration, restructure themselves into the legal organizations of the corporate system, define the relationship between "investors" and "investees", vigorously attract "diversified investment entities", and concretize the property rights relationships based on specific subjects, which has progressively brought about changes in the corporate governance structure, introduced "investors" (shareholders) and the board of directors (shareholders' representatives), executives in charge of daily management, and a working mechanism that integrates with the operations of predecessor SOEs. A small number of SOEs chose to absorb social capital (especially individual investors) through IPO and implement the mixed-ownership system with diversified sources of investment. These enterprises are subject to the supervision of the open market and public opinion as "public companies", indicating that they have to satisfy higher requirements for corporate governance structure. Given the specific conditions at that time, most SOEs that were going through the corporate system reform preferred seeking diversified capital contribution from other SOEs in a bid to make their legal organization status conform to the basic requirements of the corporate system and then establish a modern corporate governance structure on this basis. Apparently, the SOEs, after going through the corporate system reform, have introduced the interest constraints of multiple legal persons into the government decision-making process to form a check-and-balance mechanism between multiple interest subjects, which has not only improved the governance efficiency but also inspired the state-owned capital "agents" to be familiar with the operating functions of the modern corporate system by playing different roles in corporate governance.

Most of the SOEs with multiple investors were, in fact, dominated by the local government at the same level. Their diverse investments came from the state-owned holding (or investing) companies founded by the government through cross-shareholding. That's why the government was their ultimate owner. Despite pro forma diversified investment, all major issues of these enterprises were determined by the government, showing that the checks and balances between multiple investors were hard to form any powerful restraint, which triggered people to think about how to make the check-and-balance mechanism occur endogenously in corporate governance.

In the context where the public and non-public sectors are equally protected and entitled to all factors of production, the market economy has kept developing and given rise to new business opportunities and corporate system organizations jointly funded by state-owned and social capitals (including private capital). But there are significant and objective differences between the restraint mechanisms for decision making based on private capital and state-owned capital. In order to introduce a check-and-balance mechanism between different market-oriented capitals into the modern corporate governance structure, we must bring non-public capital into the diversified capital contribution to form a genuine "mixed ownership".

Since mixed enterprises are funded by investors of different ownership, they are derivatives from the ownership right of investors, and they are enterprises with independent "legal person property rights" that will realize the ownership right. In this sense, "mixed ownership" is not a primitive, fundamental and ultimate property ownership. Such knowledge will help us correctly understand the actual economic implications of "legal person ownership right" (legal person ownership).

It can be seen that the proposition of "vigorous development of a mixed economy" is a major innovation in the theory of socialist market economy with Chinese characteristics.

From traditional enterprises "owned by the whole people" to modern companies of the "corporate system", from enterprises with "diversified investment" of the same ownership to enterprises with "diversified investment" of mixed ownership, from the situation where the government was the ultimate owner of multiple investors to the situation where investors themselves serving as capital owners, Chinese enterprises have finally built their own endogenous check-and-balance mechanism for investors, which is of great significance for improving the effectiveness of corporate governance.

The development of a mixed economy was mentioned as early as in the report to the Fifteenth National Congress in 1997. At that time, it was only regarded as a new form of enterprise while highlighting the adherence to the principle of public ownership. That is, we must maintain the state-owned and collective part of the mixed-economy. In the process of developing modern companies, we have acquired an in-depth understanding of "mixed ownership". The report to the Sixteenth National Congress in 2002 made it clear that "the shareholding system is a major form for materializing public ownership". Major innovations were made in the state-owned assets management system. Some enterprises directly administered by the government were made as the objects of reform; they established a state-owned assets investor system that features "three separations" (separation of the government from enterprise management, separation of the government from the state-owned assets management, and separation of ownership right from management right), "three unifications" (unification of rights, obligations and responsibilities), and "three combinations" (a combination of administration of assets, personnel and other affairs). The Third Plenary Session of the 18th CPC Central Committee held in 2013 officially set forth the reform principle of "vigorously developing a mixed economy". Through restructuring traditional SOEs into modern companies and constructing corporate governance structure and mechanism, as well as giving full play to the functions of check-and-balance mechanism between multiple investors, we have accumulated rich experiences in "vigorously developing a mixed economy", and created conditions for ushering the enterprise reform into a new stage.

8.1.2 Vigorously develop a mixed economy and open up new prospects in the SOE reform

The *Decision on Some Major Issues Concerning Comprehensively Deepening the Reform* (hereinafter referred to as the "Decision"), adopted at the Third Plenary Session of the 18th CPC Central Committee in 2013, made it clear to vigorously develop a mixed-ownership economy. "A mixed economy with cross-holding by and mutual fusion between state-owned capital, collective capital and non-public capital is an important way to materialize the basic economic system of China. It is conducive to improving the amplification function of state-owned capital, ensuring the appreciation of its value and raising its competitiveness, and it is conducive to enabling capital with all kinds of ownership to draw on one another's strong points to offset weaknesses, stimulate one another and develop together". "We will allow more state-owned enterprises and enterprises of other types of ownership to develop into mixed enterprises". "We will allow non-state-owned capital to hold shares in projects invested by state-owned capital".

Mixed ownership in real economic life can be understood from two different perspectives: mixed-ownership at the macro level and mixed ownership at the micro-level. The former emphasizes the non-uniformity of the ownership structure of a country or region, including public and non-public-owned economies, while the latter is related to the equity structure of enterprises since equity structure is the basis for determining the corporate governance structure.[3]

Mixed ownership at the macro level is a manifestation of China's basic economic system. It is known that in the 40 years' reform and opening up, China's rapid economic growth had been driven by the development of state-owned and non-state-owned enterprises, both of which are indispensable. The basic pattern with public ownership playing a dominant role and diverse forms of ownership developing side by side is the cornerstone for maintaining China's steady economic growth and an important foundation for keeping the entire society safe and stable. There is every reason to predict that whether it is to implement large-scale privatization or promote large-scale public ownership will inevitably lead to drastic fluctuations in the Chinese economy and society. This is also an important reason why the Central Government has repeatedly reiterated and emphasized the "two unswervingly" principle.[4]

All countries have all along been seeking a perfect economic system. In the preface to his book *Capital in the 21st Century*, Thomas Piketty described China as a special case because the public capital in the traditional form of state-owned ownership accounts for about half of its national capital; if all the wealth created by capital could be equally distributed, it is possible for China to avoid the detours taken by other countries and eventually strike a balance between public capital and private capital.[5] This is enough to show the significance of mixed ownership for the SOE reform.

Mixed ownership at the micro-level emphasizes the integration of capitals of different ownership. As mentioned earlier, it is the capitals of different ownership that are "mixed". This form of capital cooperation is based on mutual respect, and different investors make a joint capital contribution to form an integrated legal person and a market entity with several investors compatible with each other and taking risks together.

The vigorous development of a mixed economy can reduce the government intervention in the micro-affairs of enterprises, which is conducive to correctly handle the relationship between the government and the market. Since the government sometimes intervenes in the microeconomic activities of SOEs, the mixed-ownership reform can regulate the relationship between the two sides: the government will be concentrated on the administration and regulation of macroeconomic affairs, leaving all microeconomic activities to be regulated by the market and enterprises will be free from government influence to organize production and operation activities in response to market demand and maximize their profits. As a result, the concept of ownership is to be downplayed on the business occasions of enterprises, and their legal person status will be strengthened, thus enabling enterprises to focus on resolving practical problems and avoid falling into unnecessary disputes over the forms of ownership. The government shall guarantee system-based guidance and regulation, avoid "vacuum and vacancy" of system, and "overthrow certain systems and establish new ones".[6] Besides, it is necessary to emphasize the complementarity between capitals of different ownership or economic forms of different ownership. Mixed ownership involves the economic components of two different types of ownership, which are not in an either-or contradictory relationship, but intermingled and allied seeking for common development and a win-win situation.[7]

8.1.3 Clarify misunderstandings on vigorous development of a mixed economy

First, some people worry that the development of a mixed economy will become a Chinese version of "privatization" and start a wave of SOE restructuring. The people thinking in this way fail to understand the relationship between capital contribution and capital use based on the characteristics of the legal organizational form of enterprises; and from the perspective of basic economic theory, they fail to understand that capital ownership and use should be separated in real economic life. Because of this, we must emphasize that the development of a mixed economy and adherence to public ownership are two issues at different levels. It is fundamentally different from the meaning of "privatization" which denies public ownership in the usual sense. "Privatization" means to divide or discard the value of existing state-owned capital. The development of a mixed economy involves a two-way flow of property rights. It is possible to introduce private capital into enterprises with purely state-owned economic components or to introduce state-owned capital into enterprises with purely private economic components. This two-way flow is actually the diversification of the corporate property rights structure.[8] The implementation of mixed-ownership reform in existing SOEs may relatively lower the share of state-owned capital rather than privatize state-owned capital. The change in the shareholding structure aims to optimize the allocation of capital.

Second, there are disagreements in the applicable scope of mixed ownership in practice. Some people advise that mixed ownership should be applied only in monopolistic fields, others hold that mixed ownership should be applied in competitive fields, and there are even arguments that mixed ownership has no "forbidden zones" in its application. In view of this, we have to investigate the supporting conditions for advancing the mixed-ownership reform, because it is related to the equal rights of multiple social subjects – economic stability and opening of property rights may be restricted by industrial characteristics and market development level, it is not just an issue of the applicable scope of a mixed economy. But this issue will not be repeated here. Please consult with the part about "classified" reform in Chapter 6.

Third, is there an optimal shareholding structure for mixed enterprises? What is an ideal proportion respectively for state-owned capital and non-state-owned capital? When the enterprises wholly funded with state-owned capital implement the mixed-ownership reform, the proportion of introduced non-state-owned or private capital should not be too low, otherwise, it will result in an unreasonable shareholding structure with a single large shareholder; such situation is adverse to the checks and balances between shareholders and harmful to the enthusiasm of investors, and it will be difficult to form a healthy governance structure and operating mechanism for the sustainable development of corporate legal persons, and eventually affect the long-term economic growth of these enterprises.[9] Some scholars investigated the competitive companies listed on the Shanghai Stock Exchange from 2001 to 2013, probed into the relationship between their mixed-ownership structure and corporate performance, and found that simple equity mixing could not improve their performance; it was only when the external environment was relatively perfect that the advantage of diversified investors would become apparent.[10]

In light of the *Guiding Opinions of the CPC Central Committee and the State Council on Deepening the Reform of State-owned Enterprises*, and by following the "classification" principle, the mixed-ownership structure needs to be continuously optimized in practice. When the government implements the mixed-ownership reform on SOEs, it must take specific approaches according to different situations, industries and regions, instead of simply adopting any "one size fits all" approach or "treating them equally without discrimination". For example, for SOEs with a small social burden and strong industry homogeneity, they can introduce a higher proportion of private capital; for SOEs with a slightly heavy social burden and strong industry monopoly, they can introduce a moderate proportion of private capital; but for SOEs with a heavy social burden and strong industry externality, they will have a low proportion of private capital and with state-owned capital always in a controlling position, since private capital owners are less motivated to hold shares in them.

We should fully understand the objective meaning of mixed ownership and make the vigorous development of a mixed economy a breakthrough point in deepening the SOE reform. Only in this way can we do a good job in ushering the SOE reform into a new stage. One of the fundamental purposes for developing a mixed economy is to break the monopoly of SOEs on certain industries, better handle the relationship between government and state-owned assets management and also between government administration and enterprise management, make mixed economy an important way to materialize public ownership under market economy conditions, and make public ownership and the market economy more compatible. On the macro level, by opening industry access, lowering the barriers to entry, allowing private economic components to enter monopoly industries, and enabling state-owned and private economic components to compete at the same time, we can eliminate the monopolistic situation in certain industries within the society as a whole. On the micro-level, by introducing private capital into the original wholly state-owned enterprises, we can form joint venture enterprises where the modern corporate governance structure will cure the chronic illness such as non-separation of government from state-owned assets management and non-separation of government administration from enterprise management.

Making mixed ownership as a breakthrough point in the SOE reform is of great significance. The mixture of public and non-public sectors of the economy is fascinating. Mixed ownership is not the privatization of state-owned capital, and it is also not any "panacea" for revitalizing SOEs. While implementing the mixed-ownership reform, which seems like walking on the ice that we need to remain cautious and sober and adjust every step to forge ahead more steadily, we must actively create supporting conditions in economic, social and political spheres to win the final victory.

8.2 Localization practice of corporate governance

The typical characteristics of corporate system enterprises can be summarized into three aspects: an independent legal person status, investors holding shares and bearing limited liability, and a specific corporate governance structure.[11] The first two characteristics are already discussed in the previous chapters of this book. This section will focus on the third characteristic, namely, the corporate governance structure. It should be noted that the two concepts of "corporate governance" and "corporate governance structure" are not clearly distinguished in some literature. Understandably, the relationships between stakeholders must be properly coordinated during corporate operations. The core content of "corporate governance" is to design and establish a specific and effective corporate governance structure. Regarding the Chinese SOEs that have gone through the corporate system reform,[12] they are registered as enterprises with a new legal status and a new organizational form. But they are still known as "SOEs" in a general way. It is easy to change an enterprise's organizational form and legal status, but it is hard to change its corporate governance structure. An enterprise is not a closed organization. Although the corporate governance structure is a set of internal rules, it is largely affected by the external environment and directly determines the operating effects of the governance structure.

8.2.1 How to handle the multiple relationships in the corporate governance structure of state-funded enterprises

"Corporate governance" is a foreign term that denotes the interest relationship and power structure between the company's managers and owners. It is specifically expressed as an organizational structure formed by the company's owners (shareholders), directors and senior managers, as well as the division and coupling of their powers, responsibilities and interests. It is also an institutional arrangement for owners to supervise and control the business management and performance of their enterprises.

Corporate governance in a narrow sense refers to the arrangement of the functions and structure of the company's board of directors and the powers of shareholders, while the corporate governance broad sense refers to a set of legal, cultural and institutional arrangements concerning the distribution of the company's control right and residual claimant right. How to concretize these abstract provisions into the specific process of enterprise operation and the standards for evaluating the work performance requires continuous trial and error and accumulation of experiences.

After China decided to establish the socialist market economy and made it the goal of the economic structural reform, efforts have been made to build SOEs into genuinely independent market entities according to the general principles of the market economy and reshape the legal status of enterprises through the corporate system reform. The corporate system in China's economic life is not a phenomenon that spontaneously evolves and grows. It can be said that people lack a deep understanding of the cultural deposits for the corporate system to emerge and accommodate the development of productive forces.

Therefore, before discussing the governance structure of corporate system enterprises, we have to brief on the development of enterprise theory. In traditional neoclassical economics, an enterprise is just a unit that pursues profit maximization or cost minimization, and it accepts factor input and determines output. At that time, the enterprise in economic theory remained as a black box. As for why enterprises exist and how about their internal operating mechanism, economists had made no further elaboration. In other words, economic theory itself gave no direct answer to why enterprises exist and why they exist in a certain scale and a certain organizational form. The pioneer of this field, Mr. Ronald Coase, in his classic paper *The Nature of the Firm* (R. Coase, 1937), for the first time, analyzed the question of "why does the enterprise exist" that has been ignored for a long time. By categorizing the communication and cooperation in economic and social life, he highlighted that the maintenance of various "relationships" (which he generalized by the category of "transactions") has "costs" (or "expenses"), thereby obtaining the "transaction cost" – the tool for analyzing "relational efficiency". He has proved that the enterprise is an economic phenomenon that replaces market means with administrative means. Since then, enterprise theory has entered a stage of vigorous development, becoming one of the fastest-developing realms in economic theory in the past few decades, which has greatly deepened people's understanding of corporate organization and operating mechanism.

Modern enterprise theory believes that the enterprise is a knot of a set of contracts. Economic theory research has shifted its focus from the relationship between enterprises and the market to the impact of "specificity of capital" and related "opportunism" on the development of enterprise operations, and then pays attention to the cooperative relationship between various production factors within an enterprise. As a teamwork organization, an enterprise shall make institutional arrangements that are compatible with the incentives and constraints of manager's behaviors so as to maximize the interests of investors (shareholders). Despite the noises from market information, capital owners (shareholders) shall effectively supervise their enterprises. In addition to handling the relationship between capital and labor, efforts shall be made to integrate all sorts of production factors and coordinate with multiple "stakeholders". Apparently, these theories have certain enlightening significance for China's SOE reform.

But Western scholars' research on enterprise theory is based on the evolution of corporate organization in western economic life. After we clarified the reform task in China – restructure traditional SOEs into modern companies and make them the micro-foundation of the socialist market economy, the construction of corporate governance structure, governance mechanism, and governance performance has become the key task of modern corporate system construction. The seminars, research projects and a large number of monographs in this regard have directly promoted the reform and the construction of a modern corporate system.

The achievements of the reform are directly manifested in the successive promulgation of laws and regulations (such as the Company Law) for the construction of a modern corporate system. For example, the "corporate governance guidelines" guide the generation of the rules of procedure for corporate governance; the principle of "the minority is subordinate to the majority" respects the voting rights of shareholders in making decisions; the "independent director system" gives full play to the professionals that take part in corporate governance; the "withdrawal from voting" system regulates the behaviors of related shareholders in voting; and the "cumulative voting system" is applicable for voting for director candidates. All of them have exerted a positive effect on standardizing and consolidating the results achieved in reform.

As for the corporate governance in practice, the specific work arrangements and the handling of the interest relationship of participating governors generally involve the following eight economic relationships: (1) The relationship between investors based on the arrangement for their stock holding quantity. (2) The relationship between major shareholders and minority shareholders. (3) The relationship between shareholders and directors. (4) The relationship between shareholders and managers. (5) The relationship between managers and employees. (6) The relationship between borrowing and raising debts, own capital capacity and debt management. (7) The relationship between company operations and customers. (8) The relationship between company operations and public supervision.

In accordance with relevant laws and regulations, the above relationships are to be handled by forming a structure of rights and responsibilities among investors (shareholders), the board of directors, the board of supervisors and managers, and this structure shall have a relatively clear hierarchy, division of work and cooperation. This structural design needs to be organically unified and functionally coupled in dynamic business operations, which requires continuous improvement, adjustment and optimization in practice.

As mentioned earlier, after China's SOEs are restructured into corporate system enterprises, people keep referring to state-funded enterprises (including wholly-owned, holding or participating) as "SOEs" out of habit. Despite wholly-owned enterprises, holding or participating enterprises have already absorbed capital contributions from other social shareholders. When we adjust the relationship between government and state-owned assets management and between government administration and enterprise management, if we are still confined to the traditional concept of "SOEs", it will be hard to generate a new corporate governance mechanism. This requires a new understanding of what "SOEs" refers to, perhaps only wholly state-owned enterprises can continue to be labeled as "SOEs". After the traditional SOEs owned by the whole people are restructured into the corporate system enterprises, the wholly state-owned enterprises, as a special market entity, will have a new meaning that differs from traditional SOEs.

The organizational form of a mixed enterprise funded by multiple investors is actually an economic phenomenon arising from the separation of capital ownership right and capital use right, and it also reflects the division of labor between ownership right and management right. It shows that the refinement of the social division of labor has penetrated into the "realization process" of capital ownership right. The evolution of this economic phenomenon has already been analyzed by Marx in his book *Das Kapital* (Vol. 3). He confirmed the organizational form of joint-stock enterprise emerged based on the capitalist mode of production and remarked that it was a "sublation" of private ownership in the social sphere: such organizational form of enterprises boasts "centralized capital raising" within a society. It accommodates a larger scale of capital demand and a higher technological level of productivity.

Because of the changes in the "division of labor", economic relationships have undergone so many changes in the aspects of capital allocation, corporate organizational forms, and the process of business activities. The multiple sets of economic relationships we've listed above need to be integrated and coordinated so as to maintain harmony, but what is more important is the integration and coupling of these relationships in enterprise operation, thereby sustaining the cooperative relationship between stakeholders during enterprise operation.

8.2.2 Improvement of corporate governance structure of state-funded enterprises

The so-called corporate governance is a series of institutional arrangements made to solve the inconsistent goals of members and suppress opportunistic tendencies. In the multi-relational combination of corporate governance, while revolving around the central goal of realizing capital appreciation, the key issue is how to minimize the loss of interests of the principal (shareholder) inflicted by the agent due to the incompleteness of the contract. Generally speaking, under the mature manager system in the West, corporate governance mainly deals with the principal-agent issues between managers and shareholders. However, in China, where the professional manager market has not fully developed, the problems to be solved by corporate governance are different from those in the West. For example, the State not only acts as a shareholder but also appoints the managers of SOEs; in private enterprises, large shareholders and managers are often unified, and corporate governance is mainly to prevent large shareholders from infringing on the rights and interests of small and medium shareholders. Since the objects of corporate governance in China and the West are different, it is worth discussing whether the directly introduced corporate governance system from the West is effective.

In the previous chapter, we have also said that the Western corporate system has undergone a century of development and has a spontaneous formation process. That is, the system itself is endogenous. But in China, its corporate system was introduced from the West after learning from the Western corporate governance experiences. Although it can rapidly improve China's corporate governance system, the different internal and external factors (such as the institutional environment, the development stage of corporate organization and the capital market) will affect the normal operation of corporate governance and the effectiveness of the goals of institutional design.

Specifically, factors such as companies' industry, equity structure, scale, and entrepreneurial spirit all greatly impact corporate governance.

Generally speaking, monopolistic industries often lack competitors, so they pay less attention to corporate governance as compared with their counterparts in competitive industries. Companies' equity structure also has an impact on corporate governance: if there is equity concentration, major shareholders that hold large shares tend to promote the improvement of corporate governance to prevent their own interests from being infringed; if there is equity separation and no shareholder holds a high proportion of shares, then related transactions or other self-interested behaviors are more likely to take place, and corporate governance is more prone to be chaotic. The relationship between the size of a company and its corporate governance is relatively complicated. On the one hand, the larger the company, the more difficult it is to govern, and the weaker corporate governance should be. On the other hand, better governance will make the company easier to continue and expand. In addition, the nature of ownership of a company also has an impact on corporate governance. The problems faced by SOEs in corporate governance are often more complex, while private enterprises often have greater motivation to improve corporate governance.

On the macro level, in terms of corporate organizational forms across the entire society, the state-owned economy in Western countries accounts for a relatively low proportion of only about 5%. In contrast, Chinese enterprises in which state-owned capital participates and controls have an absolute advantage in both size and quantity; about 67% of companies are funded by state-owned capital. In addition, companies in monopoly industries often suffer from weak governance due to entry barriers, and these companies are relatively large in scale, which makes their governance even more difficult. In China, governance problems are further aggravated – Chinese monopoly industries are often controlled by state-owned capital, which makes the governance problems of SOEs and monopoly industries superimposed. Thus the corporate governance in China is more difficult than that in the West.

According to a series of research made by the Corporate Governance Research Center of Nankai University,[13] the development of the external capital market and the awareness of shareholders to participate in corporate governance also have a great impact on corporate governance. Objectively speaking, China's corporate governance should match its financing model and shareholder situation.

The current national conditions of China are as follows: (1) Small and medium shareholders have weak awareness of rights protection, which is reflected in the fact that the dividend rate is much lower than that of Western countries. (2) The financing of enterprises is still mainly through banks, and the four major banks remain the major providers of funds (the funds from these banks accounts for about 50%). (3) The equity structure is relatively concentrated. Among Chinese companies, family businesses and state-owned holding companies account for a high proportion, and the equity structures of both are relatively concentrated. Among A-share listed companies, more than half of the companies' largest shareholders own more than 30% of the shares. With reference to the formation path of mature corporate governance models in the West, China should focus on internal governance, that is, setting a board of supervisors within the company to supervise operators, improve the disclosure rules of the capital market, and gradually improve the level of external supervision. However, the model adopted in China is to introduce external independent directors into the board of directors and to establish a supervisory board in the company. It seems that the advantages of various systems are concentrated, but it has caused the dilemma of unclear responsibilities.

The design of China's current corporate governance model integrates the characteristics of the British-American model and the German-Japanese model. It seems that China has borrowed from other countries' existing governance experience models, but in fact, there exist certain problems in structural design, cultural integration and practical operation. In terms of structural design, the model of adding independent directors to the board of directors and setting a board of supervisors is likely to result in an unclear division of labor and false office duties, and it also increases the company's supervision costs. Drawing lessons from the British and American practices, the establishment of an independent director system also has certain positioning deviations. Theoretically speaking, the functions of independent directors and the board of supervisors are to supervise the board of directors. The United States and Germany have selected supervisory agencies based on their own equity structure. In the United States, because shareholders are relatively dispersed, the general meeting of shareholders is usually idle, resulting in excessively large functions of the board of directors. In order to prevent collusion between the board and management, the United States chose to set up independent directors on the board for supervision. In Germany, due to the relatively concentrated equity structure and the governance goal of "maximizing the interests of stakeholders", the board of supervisors is a more effective supervisory agency.

Practice has proved that a single supervisory agency often has clear responsibilities and there is no circumvention of responsibilities. However, the establishment of two supervisory agencies in China at the same time will result in an unclear division of labor. Originally, the board of supervisors was mainly responsible for supervising the board of directors. In 2001, China Securities Regulatory Commission (CSRC) issued the *Guiding Opinions on Establishing an Independent Director System in Listed Companies*. The British-American corporate governance mechanism of independent directors was subsequently introduced into China's Company Law. However, the old practices were not discarded or replaced with the new ones; namely, the independent director system was introduced while retaining the board of supervisors. Independent directors have the obligation of integrity and diligence to the company and all shareholders, safeguard the overall interests of the company and pay particular attention to the protection of the legitimate rights and interests of small and medium shareholders. If the board of supervisor system and the independent director system exist at the same time, how to coordinate their relationship? How is the theoretical division of labor implemented in practice? Since there is a certain degree of separation and disconnection, it is easy to cause buck-passing and free-riding problems between the two.

Other relevant research[14] has found that many listed companies ignore the board of supervisors and treat it only as a decoration. According to a survey of private companies listed on the SME board of the Shenzhen Stock Exchange, most companies do not have a board of supervisors, and half of the companies believe that the board of supervisors is not a permanent agency but only a temporary one. In Germany, one of the purposes of establishing the supervisory board system is that its corporate governance goal is not to "maximize the interests of shareholders" but to "maximize the interests of stakeholders"; therefore, they require a certain proportion of employees in the board of supervisors. When China introduced this system, it also referred to Germany's practice and required one-third of the supervisory board members to be employees. But it is worth noting that Chinese culture is different from that of the West. The West has always emphasized equality and contract, but in Chinese culture, the "hierarchical system" is rooted in people's minds, which makes the participation of employees in the board of supervisors of no avail. This can be seen in the difference between "union" in Chinese and Western companies.

In specific operations, the powers of the board of supervisors and the incentive system of independent directors are different from those in the West. In China, the board of supervisors conducts "lateral" supervision of the board of directors, there is no hierarchical distinction between the two, and all the personnel are elected by the shareholders' meeting. The board of supervisors does not have the right to appoint or remove directors, which makes the supervision in practice less effective and difficult to be carried out.

For the independent director system, there are also problems in the incentive system. The current salary of independent directors in the United States is linked to the stock price, but in China, independent directors still earn a "fixed salary". This type of salary has a weak incentive effect and may reduce independent directors' enthusiasm for work and cause other problems.

Faced with the above-mentioned practical problems in corporate governance, China has made adjustments accordingly. The Decision adopted at the Third Plenary Session of the 18th CPC Central Committee made it clear that "We will improve the state-owned assets management system, strengthen state-owned assets oversight with capital management at the core, reform the authorized operation mechanism for state-owned capital, establish a number of state-owned capital operating companies, support qualified SOEs to reorganize themselves into state-owned capital investment companies". The most important step from managing assets to managing capital is the establishment of a "professional manager market". The Decision also stated the need to accelerate the pace of establishing the professional manager market. The rapid development of the entrepreneur market involves the identifications, selection, reward and punishment of corporate governance and management talents, and it is related to the reform and follow-up measures of the personnel management system. Since personnel appointment is objectively different from other production factors and relevant to administrative management and political system, special research and specially designed measures are required.

In connection with the basic "facility conditions" in the external environment where the enterprise operates, the more urgent supporting requirement lies in constructing and improving legislation. At present, the failure of Western corporate governance models in China is related to the lack of a legal mechanism that causes companies or investors to "take advantage of loopholes". For example, the distinction between the targets of supervision and the objects of supervision plays a key role in the action scope of the board of supervisors. The targets of supervision refer to the companies and individuals supervised by the board of supervisors of listed companies, while the objects of supervision refer to the operation and management activities of the targets of supervision. The accurate determination of the targets of supervision by the board of supervisors of listed companies is an important prerequisite for the reform of the object system of the board of supervisors of listed companies. First, for the consideration of management trust, company managers and other executives should be supervised by the board of directors with independent management leadership of the company, and the targets of the board of supervisors of listed companies only refer to the company's board of directors. Second, the objects of the board of supervisors of listed companies should be the operation and management activities of the board of directors, not the directors' acts of duty, because the board's operation and management behaviors can cover the directors' acts of duty. On the contrary, the directors' acts of duty cannot cover the board's operation and management activities. At the same time, the supervision of the board of supervisors of listed companies should include both legal and appropriate supervision. Therefore, the legislative reform centering on the improvement of corporate governance must make corresponding adjustments to the supervisory targets and objects and specify the proper supervision power and the requirements for the exercise of the board of supervisors of listed companies. In the future, the improvement of legal provisions such as this will be of great significance to the improvement of the overall level of corporate governance in China.

In short, the introduction of the western corporate governance model into China has the phenomenon of non-acclimatization, which is mainly related to the "path dependence" in the conceptual understanding and behavioral inertia accompanying institutional changes and the differences between Chinese and Western cultures and legal systems. It is worth noting that China has been on the way to solve some of the stubborn problems faced in corporate governance, such as the absence of owners and professional managers. In addition, in the top-level design, some other factors that affect corporate governance are also being addressed, such as the nature of ownership structure and external environment. These changes will make China's corporate governance move in an optimistic direction. With the gradual improvement of these problems, the level of corporate governance in China is sure to reach a new level.

8.3 Understand the influence of cultural factors in corporate governance practices through comparative analysis

The above analysis shows that in their study on modern corporate governance theories, scholars have been trying to explain the diversity of governance systems from their different structures and contents: there are differences in several elements such as financing structures, requirements for economic effectiveness, constraints on financial institutions, and essence of legislation system. These elements are important for shaping the worldwide corporate governance model, but all of them are reproduced in certain social scenarios.

In some corporate governance literature, scholars specifically mentioned the concept of "path dependence", pointing out that owing to the old systems and the existing thinking and behavioral inertia, the system innovation and the new institutional arrangements cannot be given full play. Here, we will classify this issue into "cultural factors" for discussion. Lots of scholars have been thinking about this issue: the corporate governance structure introduced into China is similar to that of Japan and continental Europe, but its function display is not always consistent with the expected goal of reform or not "in place". The previous chapters have discussed the impact from the different "path" and "entrance" for introducing the corporate system, while the analysis in this section is mainly from the "cultural" perspective.

The vitality of mixed enterprises will largely depend on the role of government shareholders. This point of view has been elucidated in much literature discussing the significance of mixed-ownership reform. In real life, the government and enterprises are dependent on each other, and such a relationship was traced back to the era of the planned economy. For a long time, the government has been operating the entire country like running a giant enterprise, and enterprises have been serving as a tool to carry out the will of the government with the type, quantity and prices of products, as well as personnel and financial matters decided by government officials. In the process of transition to a market economy, redefining the government's administrative power will be a long-term endeavor. In fact, there exists a layer-by-layer agency inside the government since its administrative power is exercised by specific department officials who are deeply attached to power. But successive Chinese governments are aware of the need to streamline administration and delegate powers to lower levels to make the government work more effectively. Essentially speaking, streamlining administration and delegating powers is to redefine the respective power boundary of the government and enterprises. But it will be a hard process that is likened to cutting one's arm to save one's body. These difficulties are fully manifested in the behavior of government officials, especially in their way of thinking. More than that, in practice, the pre-supervision of enterprises is taken seriously, but laws and rules are not effectively used for cultivating the self-discipline of enterprises, and the government is more involved in the supervision at present and the management after the event.

Another typical manifestation is that when an enterprise becomes an independent legal person, it will have relatively focused and simplistic goals. That is, it will be dedicated to making profits within the scope of the law. But the government has multiple goals. When it finds some goals are hard to be achieved or necessary resources are in shortage, it tends to employ enterprises as a tool to accomplish some social goals on its behalf. Now that the government is a shareholder of enterprises, government officials have been all along taking it for granted to employ enterprises as a tool and give orders to them. However, the intervention in enterprises will make the government never able to clarify its relationship with enterprises, which will give rise to the problem of "soft budget constraints". Economist János Kornai has made a profound analysis in this regard.

We can include "path dependence" into the broad cultural category. There has been no consensus on the definition of culture. From an abstract perspective, culture is a complex of basic assumptions, values and social norms that people have acquired in a given society. That is, culture is a summation of people's social lifestyles. Owing to different living environments and spiritual beliefs, each country and nation has its own unique cultural tradition. Although a cultural tradition keeps changing due to the evolution of survival modes and exchanges with foreign cultures, its main ideas and connotations can be inherited and remain relatively stable. That's why people sharing the same cultural tradition have common behavioral characteristics. It can be said that culture determines the norms of common behavior. From a concrete perspective, in corporate operation and economic activities, the cultural recognition of the management rules of the corporate system and the social acceptance of these rules are manifested in the spirit of the rule of law, executive culture and behavioral habits. Culture has a far-reaching impact on corporate governance, from the initial main body selection to the overall effect.

8.3.1 Influence of culture on choosing corporate governance body

In a broad sense, corporate governance refers to a set of institutional arrangements for organization mode, control mechanism and benefit distribution between a company and its stakeholders (including managers, creditors and employees) in the legal, organizational, contractual and cultural aspects. From the perspective of enterprise contracts, the corporate governance body consists of individuals and groups that live or die together with the company, and their interests are closely related to the overall corporate interests. Through institutional and contractual arrangements, the relationship between these individuals or groups and the company is established; in other words, their status in the corporate governance structure is determined. Different cultural traditions have different requirements for choosing the corporate governance body, and this difference is mainly attributed to varied equity structures under different cultural backgrounds. We can refer to the corporate governance of the US, German and Japanese companies; their logic of "culture → equity structure → governance body" is clear and distinct.

In the United States, a large number of companies with decentralized public ownership hold a dominant position. Managerial behavior is closely linked to the interests of shareholders, which is the central content of corporate governance in the United States. But for the companies in other developed countries, typically Japan and Germany, their equity is not scattered but concentrated. Why is there such a difference? American scholars usually adopt the paradigm of Burley and Means to answer this question. This paradigm believes that technology requires companies to have such a large scale that they can only meet their huge capital needs by selling stocks to massive investors. The decentralization of shareholders makes the powers in an enterprise transfer from shareholders to managers and separates ownership right from control right, thus creating an unmanageable organizational structure. This paradigm obviously treats the decentralization of American corporate equity as a pure economic fact and a natural result of economic development. However, recent studies have shown that equity diversification is not simply a set of economic facts; it should be explained from the cultural perspective.

The United States is a rising capitalist country. It has introduced and copied the British institutional model, highlighting individualism, private property, heroism, and elite thinking in culture, and emphasizes risk awareness and participation awareness. As a result, in the United States, there are a large number of individuals holding shares of corporate legal persons. In the process of economic development, in order to prevent banks from investing in companies and entering their board of directors, the laws of the United States inhibit financial intermediaries from forming financial alliances, promotes financial decentralization, and are committed to breaking up their investment portfolios. Modern American companies are forced to adapt to these conventions. This also directly formed the decentralized shareholding structure in American companies. Finally, in the United States, a society full of the concept of "capital employing labor", if employees do not own shares in their companies, it is almost impossible for them to gain the same rights as German employees in corporate governance. Faced with the fact that human capital is becoming more important and the trend of valuing human capital owners and allowing them to participate in corporate governance, American companies hold a negative or even resistant attitude and still follow the governance philosophy centering on "investor sovereignty" and "shareholder supremacy".

Japan and the countries in continental Europe place more emphasis on teamwork, social justice, collectivism, and harmonious interpersonal relationships. This is especially the case in Japan, which is influenced by Confucianism. The social-democratic culture in Europe requires managers to take the responsibility of stabilizing employment when necessary and give up some profitable but risky opportunities. When the market can no longer accommodate the production capacity of enterprises, it is still necessary to use up funds instead of downsizing their scale. Because of this, the pressure of social democracy makes managers feel confused in the pursuit of profit maximization and go further and further away from the interests of shareholders. Moreover, some advanced measures used in the United States to closely link the interests of managers and shareholders – incentive compensation, transparent accounts, takeover policies, and the principle of maximizing shareholder returns – are fragile under the European democratic political system, and sometimes they were even reprimanded because pure shareholder interest is not the policy goal of democratic politics in these countries. In such a political and cultural environment, the relationship between managers and "distant" shareholders is difficult to maintain. Companies have higher agency costs. To better control this cost, large-scale shareholding institutions or individuals are adopted to be the best way to retain shareholders. Therefore, in Germany and Japan, the legislation also supports bank equity participation in enterprises. In modern large enterprises, financial institutions can rely on their strong economic strength to become major shareholders of companies and further promote the concentration of company equity. Banks have played a leading role in corporate governance since at least the times of Bismarck. The current main banking system has finally been formed after long-term development.

On the other hand, Germany is the origin of utopian socialism. Coupled with the special role of employees in business operations and management during World War II, many factors prompted the ruler to clarify the status of employees in corporate governance. In fact, the role of employees in corporate management has been clarified in law in Germany for a long time. The extent to which German company employees participate in corporate management is probably unmatched by any capitalist country. Either in the executive agency or organ of power in a company, there are employee representatives; and the share of employees in these agencies is almost equal to that of investors. This is the so-called "employee participation system". In addition, the German government actively participates in the operation and management of some companies and sends representatives to participate in corporate governance. This is inseparable from Germany's adherence to the "social market economic system".

It can be seen from the above discussion that the unitary corporate governance model of "shareholder first" adopted by the United States is compatible with the decentralized equity structure, and the dual corporate governance structure model of "co-determination type" represented by Germany and Japan is compatible with the centralized equity structure. The status of the equity structure is not a purely economic fact, and it is deeply affected by political and cultural factors in different countries. Therefore, the choice of appropriate governance subjects is also a cultural phenomenon, and different cultural backgrounds have different effects on the choice of corporate governance subjects.

8.3.2 A comparative analysis of the influence of culture on governance measures and mechanisms

For the corporate governance structure, in order to achieve a reasonable distribution of residual claim right and control right, certain procedures and mechanisms must be in place. Culture restricts corporate governance mechanisms and measures mainly from two ways: the first is an indirect effect. Namely, culture indirectly determines the main direction of governance through the choice of equity structure and governance subjects.

The US corporate governance structure of "shareholder first" is also known as market control-oriented corporate governance structure from the perspective of governance mechanisms and measures. Its characteristics are reflected in market supervision and control. Because of a high degree of decentralization of equity, the ability of shareholders to directly manage and control companies is very limited. All relevant subjects are unable or unwilling to pay for monitoring costs alone. It is difficult for small shareholders to exercise the supervision right granted by the law, and the only way to express their dissatisfaction with the company is to sell the stocks held in their hands. This "voting with feet" mechanism promotes the development of the securities market. Therefore, shareholders have to transition from direct to indirect management and control of companies, that is, to manage and control companies and their executives through the securities market and indirectly implement control through non-executive directors, takeover, bankruptcy, and operator incentive.

The German and Japanese corporate governance structure of "co-determination" is also known as the governance structure of internal organization control model. Its characteristics are reflected in the supervision and control of the equity structure and internal organization. The equity is relatively concentrated, especially mutual shareholding between shareholders and bank control of companies. Therefore, there is a realistic possibility for shareholders to directly control and manage companies, and its distinctive feature, which is different from the equity structure in British and American corporate governance, is that banks and other financial institutions hold shares, and they are often the largest shareholders. Banks and enterprises are closely related and even integrated.

The second way that culture influences corporate governance mechanisms and measures are a direct effect. This point is relatively subtle and complicated, which is mainly reflected in some specific processes of companies.

Individualism is the core of American values. This cultural feature makes the leadership system of companies often implement greater separation of powers. The coordination in companies is through formal systems, and the relationship between employees is based on job arrangements, unlike Chinese companies, which value human connection and informal relationships. The pragmatic characteristics make effective manager incentives based on material incentives. In business innovation activities, Americans prefer some short-term or incremental innovation projects and emphasize the rate of return on capital (Hua Jinyang, He Yaping, 2001). The typical characteristic of Japanese culture is consistency between collectivism and decision-making. Emphasis on the common interests of different parties and loyalty and trust in business relations have formed a corporate governance culture that values long-term interests. Inside companies, the systems such as cross-shareholding, life-long employment and seniority-based promotion are all manifestations of this culture. Employees and their companies have formed a community of destiny, and there is no mature labor market, manager market, and director market.

The above two types of corporate governance structures are institutional arrangements formed to adapt to the national culture, and each has its own advantages. As a market-controlled corporate governance structure in the United States and Britain, it is the rise and fall of stock price that guides the behavior of companies. Shareholders hold shares mainly for profit and take an interest in companies' short-term development, thus resulting in a high rate of stock turnover. The corporate governance structure in Germany and Japan is based on the direct management and control of internal organizations. The mutual shareholding between shareholders, banks and enterprises are less speculative and more profitable in the short-term. They maintain business partnerships through shareholding; even at lower stock prices, they do not sell shares to the detriment of suppliers, customers or lending banks with whom they do long-term business. They care about the long-term and stable development of their companies.

Culture generally consists of two parts: one is the core culture shared by all members of society, and the other is a subculture composed of different values, customs and aesthetics. The cultural concepts discussed above basically belong to the first type, that is, national culture. Whether in Britain, the United States, Japan, Germany or China, in addition to the culture of the entire nation, companies also have their own culture. As a form of subculture, corporate culture refers to a spirit that has its own characteristics of an enterprise and a certain materialized spirit which is gradually formed inside an enterprise under a certain socio-economic and cultural background through the long-term production and operation practice, and recognized and followed by all employees of the enterprise. It is embodied in the corporate system, code of conduct, corporate image and products. It contains values, business philosophy, corporate spirit, corporate governance structure, various management systems, codes of conduct and corporate image. Corporate culture is an organizational culture that is gradually established through long-term management practices of the organization on the basis of national culture and reacts to organizational management activities. Although the laws of all countries try to cultivate a certain degree of unified corporate governance, the corporate culture formed through the internal evolution of each company has made the governance structure of each company more diversified.

The foundation or core of the corporate governance structure is the principal-agent relationship, and this relationship is established through a certain contract. The purpose of the contract is to regulate the behavior of both parties to improve the agency effect. Therefore, the ultimate goal of the corporate governance structure is to "govern" the behavior of both the principal and the agent, especially the agent that is the governing subject, in order to maximize the agency effect. After the governance subject is determined, whether it is an individual or a group, whether it is a shareholder or an operator, as long as it lives or exists in a cultural atmosphere, its actions will be affected and restricted by this cultural model.

When the various measures and mechanisms of governance are in play, cultural traditions are also used as informal institutional arrangements to constrain people's behavioral norms and directly affect the expectations of institutional players. In this way, corporate governance is embodied in the establishment of a common cultural value model so that people will form a value identity with the functions, responsibilities and rights of related subjects and generate behavior expectations. The behaviors of the relevant subjects of corporate governance are always under the inherent constraints of the value model. It is through the recognition of this cultural value model that corporate governance as a system gains authority in the enterprise.

If we compare an enterprise to a machine in operation, then the enterprise system stipulates the meshing relationship between the parts of the machine. Without the enterprise system, the enterprise machine will not function normally. The corporate culture is equivalent to the lubricating oil of the machine. Without lubricating oil, the machine can also operate, but this kind of operation must be inefficient and cannot last long. But if this lubricant is added, the enterprise machine can run efficiently and continuously. This also helps explain why there is a huge difference in business performance and business life between enterprises of the same system.

The corporate governance mechanism undoubtedly falls into the category of systems, so the governance efficiency depends not only on the formal system but also on the informal corporate culture, that is, the specific behavior and work attitude of each participant. Most of the world's top 500 companies have a special culture that their employees cherish and pursue together, and they also have a common culture that the entire society can use. These cultures are reflected in the corporate system and governance structure of these companies, especially in the personal qualities of employees.

The company realizes the self-adjustment of each governance subject through a corporate culture that condenses ethics and moral rules and guides and restricts corporate governance behaviors and employee behavior values. This forms an important part of corporate culture – corporate governance culture. To put it simply, it refers to the "software" of the corporate governance structure.

A positive, united, cooperative, and strictly self-disciplined corporate culture can guide company behavior, leadership behavior and employee behavior, ensuring that their activities can be within a range that is recognized and accepted by the company. Good corporate culture helps reduce the cost of supervision within the company, weaken the personal preference, reduce the uncertain behaviors of business activities, ease the conflict of interests and power disputes between the principal and the agent; it has spawned a large number of coordinated activities, to enable the company to improve performance and enhance competitiveness through self-management, self-control, self-supervision and self-motivation (Feng Genfu, 2001).

In an enterprise, corporate governance structure and corporate culture often influence each other, sometimes reinforce each other or contradict each other. The potential tension and conflict between corporate culture and corporate governance structure are also remarkable.

Companies can introduce excellent governance structures and policies, but their development is still difficult to measure if they do not change their traditional corporate governance culture.

With the gradual deregulation of governments and the evolution of economic globalization, the national differences in corporate governance culture have gradually narrowed, and market forces have played an increasingly important role in the selection of corporate governance structure. Only when companies win in the fierce market competition can they truly maximize the interests of their shareholders, operators and other stakeholders. Therefore, companies must establish a governance concept that adapts to market competition and aims to enhance market competitiveness. Different companies must take account of their own governance environment, and at the same time adapt to the development trend that corporate governance factors transform from being singular (such as capital) into being complex (such as human capital), employees become more important in governance structure, risk control is highlighted, and operational crises are prevented, for the purpose of building a corporate governance culture that suits their specific situations.

8.3.3   An empirical study on the effect of cultural factors in corporate governance practice

The corporate governance reform in China has been gradually going deeper with the proposition of modern corporate system construction and the deepening of theoretical research on corporate governance. Many companies have empathized with improving the tangible system of governance structure and being in line with international standards. However, the governance structure formed after the corporate system reform is always unsatisfactory. Companies of the same system have produced heterogeneous results. The reason is that various subjects (parties) participating in governance are affected by path dependence or cultural factors in the way of thinking and behavior and in the work process and work style.

As an institutional arrangement, the choice of corporate governance model always depends on the specific cultural background and institutional environment. The ability to adapt and execute the corporate governance model is determined to a large extent by the nature and characteristics of its national culture and corporate culture, which are internally correlated.

For a country like China, with a civilization of five thousand years, the influence of culture is even more prominent. For example, "hierarchical culture" allows us to simply rank different roles in corporate governance based on their positions, and then keep following the principle of "the lower level is subordinate to the higher level" without equal discussion on the content of governance work (the "proposals" for related work). In specific discussions about governance decision-making, the assessment of innovation risks, disputes over different opinions, and attitudes toward decision-making goals and one's own position and interests may all be influenced by people's habits and traditional culture.

In SOEs that have gone through the corporate system reform, state-owned capital still maintains a controlling position in the board of directors, and the shareholder representatives of state-owned capital retain a majority of seats on the board of directors. Generally speaking, the heads of an investment company (usually a state-owned capital investment company or an authorized state-owned capital operating company), together with the HR director and department heads from the same company, will jointly enter the board of directors of the invested mixed company. In actual work, when there is disagreement over a proposal, it is difficult for directors to fully express their independent judgments or opinions due to the level of their positions. This phenomenon is inconsistent with the voting system of "one vote per person for the board of directors" and "one vote per share for the shareholders' meeting" in corporate governance. This shows the existence of cultural factors.

To make further analysis, the planned economic model has also distorted corporate culture. The traditional centralized planned economy has strengthened the consciousness of "being an official is better" in traditional Chinese culture. The inheritance of this old concept has made the awareness and quality of managers unable to satisfy the requirements of the corporate system, and there are serious cultural perplexities in the environment for cultivating entrepreneurs and for fostering their consciousness of right.

The identity of business operators is always intermingled with the identity of administrative officials. The relationship between "capital contribution" and "capital use" is regarded as the administrative relationship between superior and subordinate, which is a concrete manifestation of "political culture", and also a habitual influencing factor that makes "separation of government from enterprise" hard to be effectively solved.

Objectively speaking, although the government is separated from the state-owned assets management through the mixed-ownership reform and the corporate system reform, the traditional factory-style governance and the integration of government and enterprise still have strong institutional inertia, which is mainly manifested in the behavioral inertia of enterprise managers and government officials. And this behavioral inertia is the result of "political culture" under the traditional planning system. In fact, when the legal organization form of the corporate system is established, the relationship between capital contribution and capital use should be transformed into a market-based relationship, namely, an equal relationship between capital contributors and capital users under market economy conditions.

It is also worth mentioning that the employment and distribution systems under the planned economic system "created" the "employment culture" of individuals participating in the social division of labor. The years' reforms have completely broken and abandoned the "egalitarian" thinking and stimulated people's awareness of development, competition and crisis. However, the dependence between enterprises and the government under the traditional system has not been completely eliminated. In addition, the reform of the social security system is relatively lagging, and enterprise employees have relatively insufficient understanding and adaptability to the modern corporate system.

In short, shaping the SOEs born under the traditional planned economy into standardized companies is a profound change. On the surface, this is a change in the organizational form of enterprises, but in essence, it is the adjustment of production relations. More importantly, it is to straighten out the economic property rights relationship and the principal-agent relationship in management, separate decision-making and supervision from operation and management, and make enterprises loyal to the ultimate interests of investors and stakeholders; under a certain external environment, enterprises can rely on established operating mechanisms and characteristic culture to achieve long-term and continuous self-development. In this sense, the ultimate solution of deep-seated problems in corporate governance reform will inevitably touch on human issues and cultural traditions. Humans are not only the subject of reform practice but also the carrier of cultural traditions. The practices in 40 years' reform and opening up have proved that the reform of corporate governance structure must have a humanistic spirit as the pillar and driving force, and this humanistic spirit can regulate and promote the development of corporate governance.

At the same time, by strengthening the construction of the legal system, cultivating the rule-of-law spirit and legal awareness, it has become an important task for social and cultural construction and for citizens to improve their survivability. Here, the key is not whether the rules are enacted or not, but to make people understand and recognize these rules. Under these conditions, enterprises can get rid of the interference of other social factors and become more proactive. Various capital investment entities can merge with each other, give play to their respective strength, continuously improve their own ability to participate in market competition, and support and consolidate national competitive ability with enterprise competitive ability.

Notes

1 *Zhang Dejiang and Zhejiang delegation talk about private capital: It's better to give it an outlet.* Retrieved March 7, 2012, from http://jingji.cntv.cn/20120307/1081 86.shtml
2 *CNBM Chairman Song Zhiping, Such argument as "the state sector advances, the private sector retreats" is groundless.* Retrieved January 9, 2018, from http://www.chinanews.com/cj/2018/01-09/8419468.shtml
3 Qin, D. D. (2014). Mixed ownership is an effective way to improve corporate governance. *China Market*, Issue 3.
4 Qiu, H. P. (March, 2014). On several matters of principle about mixed ownership. *Academic Frontier*, Part 2.
5 Piketty, T. (2014). *Capital in the 21st century*. Beijing: China CITIC Press.
6 Li, Y. P. (2015). Return to the nature of enterprises: The path choice of state-owned enterprise mixed-ownership reform. *Economic Theory and Business Management*, Issue 1.
7 Xiao, G. Q., & Qiao, H. B. (2015). Mixed economy and state-owned enterprise reform. *Socialism Studies*, Issue 3.
8 Wang, S. G. (2016). Mixed economy and deepening of state-owned enterprise reform. *Expanding Horizons*, Issue 3.
9 Yin, J. (2016). Study on the internal mechanism and optimal proportion of mixed ownership of state-owned enterprises. *Nankai Economic Studies*, Issue 1.

10 Ma, L. F., et al. (2015). *The priority choice of mixed ownership: The logic of the market*. China Industrial Economics, Issue 7.

11 Wu, J. L., Zhou, X. C., et al. (1999). *Corporate governance structure, debt restructuring and bankruptcy procedures* (p. 2). Beijing: Central Compilation & Translation Press.

12 The "SOEs" here are in the general sense that includes wholly state-owned enterprises, state-controlled enterprises and state-participated enterprises.

13 The Corporate Governance Research Center of Nankai University has published relevant research reports in the Management World magazine sponsored by the DRC of the State Council for many years since 2004.

14 Guo, L. (2016). Chinese-style board of supervisors: Where to go and where to settle? – re-examination from an international comparative perspective. *Journal of Comparative Law*, Issue 2, 74–87.

9 The significance of SOE reform on the modernization of national governance

SOE reform is directly related to the specific allocation methods and realization mechanisms of public-owned production relations and the corresponding changes in the state-owned capital management system and management methods. It is an important work content for the self-improvement of the socialist (market) economic system with Chinese characteristics.

How can state-owned capital be managed and operated under the conditions of a market economy to achieve an organic combination of capital and social functions? How to deal with the relationship between the account management of state-owned capital and the fiscal account of the government and incorporate them into the "government financial management" system? How can state-owned capital carried in the form of enterprise and other forms of state-owned capital in society form a complete assets account system? How can state-owned capital allocation, operation and management dynamically optimize the macro structure? How can the dynamic optimization on the macro level, through the changes of capital form manifested by capital advance and retreat in micro situations, act on the macroeconomic regulation to ensure the stable growth of the macroeconomy and prevent structural crises with serious imbalances? Regarding specific industrial fields and in the context of innovating the ways for materializing public ownership and clarifying the identity of investors, how to transform and innovate the relationship between labor rights and capital rights? We will discuss the related theoretical issues in these aspects from the perspective of the modernization of national governance.

9.1 The social attributes of state-owned capital and the maintenance of public interests

Through the transformation of corporate organizational form, the reform of SOEs is to build a compatible relationship between state-owned capital and market economy in the form of a mixed economy. It is an innovation of the ways to realize public ownership and will ultimately improve the vitality of state-owned capital allocation and management. For the existing state-owned capital layout and organizational system, by combining the characteristics of market competition and the technical characteristics of capital allocation, "classified" reform is implemented to optimize the capital allocation structure in specific enterprise organizations in different ways. The thoughts in this aspect are already analyzed in the previous chapter when we talk about the significance of "classified" reform on promoting the innovation of enterprise system and propose the organic combination of "stratification" and "classification" to further deepen the reform. This section is mainly about dealing with the relationship between the capital attribute and public attribute of state-owned capital.

9.1.1 The dual attributes and functions of state-owned capital

As its name implies, state-owned capital is capital owned by the state, and its name reveals its natural multiple attributes. "State-owned" means that state-owned capital has the social attribute to safeguard public interests, and "capital" means that state-owned capital demands value preservation and appreciation, which has the same economic attributes as the capital owned by general social (other) subjects. Starting from the attributes of state-owned capital, the functions of state-owned capital can be summarized as social functions, including meeting public and administrative goals and economic functions with meeting commercial goals as the core content. Among them, the public goal mainly refers to the provision of public goods to the society, while the administrative goal mainly refers to the development goals of the State such as maintaining social stability or guaranteeing employment, maintaining social security and promoting social equity.

The reform of state-owned capital in the new era needs to effectively define, distinguish and balance the social and economic functions of state-owned capital. The allocation of state-owned capital must take full account of the dual attributes and functions for concrete development. First of all, it is necessary to consider the requirements for realizing the development goals of the society in a certain period of time. At the same time, it is also necessary to consider the division of labor and cooperation between state-owned capital and other social capital in terms of quantity and capacity. A certain cooperative pattern based on different capital functions is formed in terms of allocation structure, industry and technology. In a certain sense, corresponding to the demand structure of specific industries and public utilities, the market structure of social reproduction (a relationship of monopolistic competition) needs to be designed and regulated by the government. The allocation of state-owned capital needs to meet the requirements of the staged goals of social development. This is an objective and pure theoretical analysis. The specific allocation in real life must be in the process of constantly adjusting and optimizing capital flows and continuously selecting new combinations. The state-owned capital allocation chooses the form of enterprise organization or other forms of social legal person organization. An enterprise organization must build its ability to "assume sole responsibility for its profits or losses", because the boundaries of "classification" may change along with market development.

According to the principle of "classification", for the enterprises in fully competitive industries of the commercial category, their main assessment indicator is profit; for the enterprises with profitability but constrained by market environment, technical features and industrial division of labor and dedicated to realizing public goals, there should be no direct contradiction between their pursuit of public goals and profits. However, it is difficult to find objective and standard prices for products or services owing to un-available conditions for opening up the competition. Just because of this, the key to the contribution and operation of this type of capital is to find objective and reasonable pricing for it. In the case of the capital injected into public welfare industries, the achievement of public welfare goals is taken as its assessment indicator. It does not mean that these kinds of enterprises do not need business accounting or do not care about profits and losses, what they need is reasonable "pricing" and special supervision. If conditions permit, the means of "franchising" and "business right auction" can be introduced indirectly to enhance the transparency of price discovery.

While the reform promotes the development of the market, the way to price various social affairs and the operation of various affairs themselves, the pricing characteristics of various business operations (not "running"), or the social impact of the pricing level, plus the factor of "path dependence" on system transition, all of which determines that "self-financing" at a certain price level is not a purely economic issue.

According to different capital owners' characteristics, the "division of labor" between state-owned capital and other social capital must give full play to the former's own strengths, let it undertake more basic and public services, and create conditions for the smooth operation of social re-production. The ability to maintain and increase the value of state-owned capital shall be dealt with scientifically on the basis of its public attribute. Under normal circumstances, the main attribute of other social capital and non-state-owned capital is to maintain and increase their value. They will not be willing to undertake social projects that are difficult to be self-financing. In this case, state-owned capital shall come out to undertake the construction and improvement of the environmental conditions required for social and economic operations. The operations and maintenance of the businesses that are objectively difficult to be self-financing are undertaken by state-owned capital. In this way, government subsidies are used to make up for the ability to balance accounting because the government has the taxation right. This may lead to a discussion about why state-owned capital should suffer losses, but this is a necessary condition for ensuring the healthy operation of social reproduction based on a reasonable economic and social structure and a favorable environment. It also reflects the aforementioned division of labor and cooperation between state-owned capital and other social capital. This can lead to a discussion about the true meaning of the statement that state-owned capital "does not compete with the people for profit". In other words, ordinary business projects can be opened to private capital, while the government has the capital capacity to undertake more affairs related to the social environment and structural rationality.

To clarify the dual attributes of state-owned capital helps to deal with it scientifically and objectively by combining with the staged goals of social development and the strength of other social capital, and by means of a reasonable division of labor between different capital owners. Some scholars have made negative comments on the operation and performance of state-owned capital based on two implicit premises: the dual functions of state-owned capital are inseparable; therefore, with the dual functions, the positioning of state-owned capital will be disordered and always at the expense of economic goals. But in fact, the inseparability of the dual functions of state-owned capital is not an iron law, and there is not necessarily a disorder between public goals, administrative goals, and economic goals.

When the functions of specific allocation occasions can be clearly defined and divided, the relationship between state-owned capital and economic performance will change non-monotonously. This is the fundamental reason for drawing different conclusions when discussing the relationship between the functions of state-owned capital and economic performance or even using the empirical method to analyze the same problem. As a successful case, the "Temasek" wholly-owned by the Ministry of Finance of Singapore has created huge wealth for its shareholders for more than 40 years. Although the background of Temasek's success is somewhat different from that of China, for example, Singapore boasts the boundedness of public and administrative goals, relatively high price affordability of residents and a mature market-based system. This model has a significant impact on China's state-owned capital management and SOE reform. When the social and economic functions of state capital can be accurately divided and are respectively allocated to operate independently under two different quasi-pricing systems, the presupposition of the discussion on the functions of state capital will be broken. Under the commercial operation model, state-owned capital, especially capital that meets commercial goals, exhibits the same efficiency as non-state-owned capital.

Here are some introductions to Singapore's Temasek Holdings. Through the clear definition of the functions of state-owned capital and the precise positioning of the goals, Temasek successfully achieved a balance between government public goals and commercial interests. According to the nature and functions of its business, Temasek labels its invested companies as "government-linked companies" (GLCs).[1] According to the operation of their invested capital, these companies are divided into two categories: One is related to Singapore's important strategic resources and public policy goals, such as energy, water resources, airports and ports, housing, education and medical companies. Such companies are positioned for pursuing public goals and administrative goals rather than for profits. The other one is competitive companies that are able to participate in local or foreign market activities.

The division of these two types of companies represents the two different functions of SOEs, and the management of companies with different functions is achieved through Temasek's differential control of shares. The overall operations of Temasek still follow market rules. It holds 100% or a majority of shares in the first type of companies that are responsible for public functions. For the second type of companies that participate in competitive industries, Temasek adopts market-oriented methods such as acquisition, sale or reduction of shares to promote the effective operation of these companies.

9.1.2 Better understand the functions of state-owned capital while deepening the reform

State-owned capital naturally has dual functions, namely, social and economic functions. And they need to be distinguished to avoid confusion, otherwise, it may lower the efficiency in capital operation. The SOE reform has helped us better understand the distinction and relationship between the dual functions of state-owned capital. In the era of the planned economy when China's industrial strength remained weak, especially military and heavy industries, national security was a matter of primary importance. That's why most of the state-owned capital was poured into the heavy industry at that time to create heavy industrial products out of nothing.

SOEs had to take care of all the life needs of their employees as if they were performing the government functions and serving administrative goals without any commercial pursuit. This practice of replacing enterprises' economic functions with social functions indeed played a good role in the catch-up stage, enabling China to establish a relatively complete military and industrial system in the short term and laying the foundation for national security. After that, China started to expedite its economic development, but the overwhelming social responsibilities of enterprises had lowered their production efficiency, which had restricted the economic growth, brought down people's living standards, and worsened the situation of shortage. No wonder Chinese people were longing for the day of reform and opening up. In short, although the dual functions of state-owned capital are natural and cannot be eliminated, they may be substituted for each other in a given period.

In the early stage of SOE reform, the most immediate need was to solve the shortage of daily necessities. A slew of measures with low risks and quick effects (e.g., delegation of powers and transfer of profits) were adopted to support SOEs to perform more economic functions. Because of a low starting point and a strong demand for products, SOEs remarkably increased their profits and avoided apparent contradiction between their dual functions. However, by the end of the 1990s, when the external environment changed significantly and multiple industries were caught in oversupply, a large number of SOEs sank into a serious survival crisis, forcing the government to "strategically adjust the layout of the state-owned economy by combining with the upgrading of the industrial structure and the improvement of the ownership structure, insist on advancing and retreating, and do something more important by leaving the others undone".

In real economic life, the state-owned sector was in excessively wide distribution, the overall quality was not high, and the resource allocation was unreasonable; all of these drawbacks must be resolved. "The industries and fields that the state-owned economy needs to control mainly include: industries involving national security, industries that are naturally monopolized, industries that provide important public products and services, and important backbone enterprises in pillar industries and high-tech industries. In other industries and fields, through assets reorganization and structural adjustment, we can make concerted efforts, strengthen key points and improve the overall quality of the state-owned economy".[2] From such statements as "do something more important by leaving the others undone" and "excessively wide distribution" and the industries and fields that are identified to be controlled by the state-owned economy, it can be seen that the reform is to gradually define the functions of state-owned capital, which is the inevitable result from the dual functions of state-owned capital and the efficiency-oriented enterprise management. During this period, through "invigorating large enterprises and relaxing control over small ones", "reducing staff to increase efficiency", and shrinking the frontline of SOEs, state-owned capital was concentrated in a few key industries, and SOEs gradually got out of the predicament.

Until November 2013, the Third Plenary Session of the 18th CPC Central Committee of the Communist Party of China proposed to actively develop mixed ownership and pointed out that "A mixed economy with cross-holding by and mutual fusion between state-owned capital, collective capital and non-public capital is an important way to materialize the basic economic system of China. It is conducive to improving the amplification function of state-owned capital, ensuring the appreciation of its value and raising its competitiveness, and it is conducive to enabling capital with all kinds of ownership to draw on one another's strong points to offset weaknesses, stimulate one another and develop together. We will allow more state-owned enterprises (SOEs) and enterprises of other types of ownership to develop into mixed enterprises". Under the guidance of thought, the Central Committee of the Communist Party of China and the State Council jointly promulgated the *Guiding Opinions on Deepening the Reform of State-owned Enterprises* in August 2015, proposing the idea of classified reform of SOEs and raising the definition of state-owned capital to a whole new level. It also guided the deepening of new breakthroughs in reform.

9.2 Management of state-owned assets account and "government financial management" from the perspective of capital management

The discussion on the rights and interests of the investors of SOEs can be extended to the accounting evaluation of state-owned capital management itself, so that it is natural to conclude that state-owned capital (assets) needs to have a budget and final accounting system, thereby giving rise to the issue of state-owned capital account management. It is not difficult to understand that the study of the state-owned assets account system is of great significance to China. On the one hand, from the perspective of fiscal policy, China is a country dominated by socialist public ownership, the government holds or controls a large amount of stock assets. Compared with many other countries, the financial basis for China's fiscal policy is mainly reflected in government assets. With a different financial base, the implementation and operation of fiscal policy will naturally be very different. On the other hand, the establishment of a state-owned assets accounts system is helpful to strengthen the management of various state-owned assets, better sort out the relationship between the functions of government departments, distinguish the responsibilities of government administration and management, enhance the functional coupling between government departments, and eliminate departmental barriers to profit, thereby helping to improve the efficiency of government operations, enhance the government's prestige and ability to govern, and realize the modernization of the national governance system and governance capability.

9.2.1 Strengthening the management of state-owned assets requires the establishment of a sound state-owned assets account system

On January 14, 2018, the *Opinions of the CPC Central Committee on Establishing a System for the State Council to Report State-owned Assets Management to the Standing Committee of the National People's Congress* was officially released, requiring the State Council to report the management of state-owned assets to the Standing Committee of the NPC annually, establish and improve the national reporting system for the management of all types of state-owned assets, and speed up the preparation of government comprehensive financial reports and natural resource balance sheets.[3]

From the *Decision on Some Major Issues Concerning Comprehensively Deepening the Reform* adopted in November 2013 to the requirement for preparing the "national and local balance sheets" and today's establishment of a sound "state-owned assets management" reporting system, marks that China's state-owned assets account has become mature from the experimental stage and the state-owned assets account management has been increasingly perfect. However, in both theoretical and practical work, how can multi-form and multi-level accounts of state-owned assets be connected? How can the government fiscal account of the original payment realization system match the state-owned assets account based on the accrual system? What is the relationship between the government fiscal account and the state-owned assets account? How can the daily management be organically unified to reflect the integrity of the government's assets management capability?

To discuss the establishment of a sound state-owned assets account system, we need to start with the connotation and extension of state-owned assets and government assets.

First, from the literal meaning, state-owned assets are owned by the state, including properties and property rights; while the government controls government assets. In terms of the nature of assets, "state-owned assets in a broad sense refer to the various forms of government investment and its income, appropriations, acceptance of donations, acquisitions in accordance with national rights or various types of properties or property rights recognized by law, including operating assets, non-operating (administrative) assets, and resource assets; in a narrow sense, state-owned assets refer to operating state-owned assets, which are capital and rights owned by the government based on its own investment, including state-owned assets of enterprises, and the assets occupied by administrative institutions but converted to business use for profits, state-owned resource assets that have been put into production and operation".[4] From the perspective of the department of assets, state-owned assets are government assets in a broad sense, including government (central and local), state-owned or state-controlled financial institutions (including the central bank) and non-financial SOEs. In a narrow sense, government assets are only assets owned and controlled by government departments and administrative institutions and do not include the assets of state-owned financial enterprises.

Second, state-owned assets are biased toward economic concepts, while government assets are biased toward defining public resources owned by the government from an accounting perspective. Government assets are economic resources owned or controlled by the government as a subject. The opposite of state-owned is private. The meaning of state-owned assets is slightly wider than that of government assets. However, if the government accepts taxpayers' entrustment to manage state assets as a public fiduciary responsibility, the scope of state-owned assets should be basically the same as that of general government assets. Government assets refer to the assets in government accounting, including assets in government accounting statements (meeting the recognition conditions of government assets) and assets disclosed in the notes to the accounting statements (not meeting the recognition conditions, but meeting the disclosure conditions of assets).

The *Opinions of the CPC Central Committee on Establishing a System for the State Council to Report State-owned Assets Management to the Standing Committee of the National People's Congress* have clearly defined state-owned assets as state-owned assets of enterprises (excluding financial enterprises), state-owned assets of financial enterprises, state-owned assets of administrative institutions, and state-owned natural resources. The first two categories belong to the state-owned assets with operational characteristics that are allocated in enterprises. Here we can classify state-owned assets into three major categories: operating state-owned assets, administrative (non-operating) state-owned assets, and resource state-owned assets.

First, operating state-owned assets refer to the investment in SOEs and mixed enterprises owned by the State or the government. These assets are financial assets of the government and fundamentally different from the assets (such as the assets of administrative institutions) that the government directly provides public goods. The government is the investor or one of the investors of companies. These assets are only one of the owners' equity (total net assets) in its statements for the company. These assets are not the same as the assets of SOEs and should be distinguished from them. They are equal to the subtraction of the liabilities of SOEs from their total amount of state-owned assets, coupled with the deduction of the equity of other owners. They are actually state-owned equity. What we are discussing here are competitive SOEs that are not affiliated with the government. As independent legal persons, they have independent legal person property rights, operate independently, and assume responsibility for their own profits and losses. The government is only one of their investors and does not directly interfere with their daily business activities. The relationship between the government and SOEs is an investment relationship. State-owned capital is the owner's equity in the balance sheet for enterprises and equity investment for the government as the investor, which can bring capital gains to the government. Therefore, state-owned capital is included in the scope of government assets.

Second, administrative state-owned assets are mainly owned by administrative units and public institutions. They are various assets occupied and used by budgetary units that are legally owned by the State and can be measured in currency to ensure the normal performance of their functions. State-owned assets of administrative institutions include appropriations from the state budget, acceptance of gifts in accordance with regulations, and the use of state-owned assets to organize income. The assets of administrative units are generally non-operating, while the assets of public institutions are usually based on whether they are fiscal budget units due to partial reforms. If so, the assets of public institutions will be government assets. This part of assets supports the government to perform the functions of public administration. It has a certain scale, with fixed assets accounting for a considerable proportion. Some people think that this type of asset has specificity, which to a certain extent determines its insufficient liquidity and limited realizability. Even if these administrative assets cannot be circulated, they can be reasonably valued. The buildings of some administrative institutions are usually located in the center of the city, and the assets they occupy are quite high-quality in terms of scale and quality. Although some administrative institutions do not do business accounting, they actually have strong market management capability. In the socialist market economy, the assets of some administrative institutions have been quietly transformed from non-operating to operating. This phenomenon should be acknowledged and treated reasonably, while tracking and monitoring should be done to prevent the loss of state-owned assets. Since operating assets are characterized by accounting and profit and loss, and the input-output (cost-benefit) in the sense of economic value serves as the main line of operation, the state-owned assets in the administrative and institutional fields are not based on economic value pricing as the main work evaluation. However, as a type of legal person, under the premise of budget constraint, administrative institutions need to have the awareness of cost and accounting.

Third, resource-based state-owned assets refer to the economic resources that can bring certain economic value to the development of a certain resource under the current knowledge and technology level, and they are regulated by law, such as state-owned land, mineral deposits, forests, rivers and ocean. According to the Constitution of China, "Land in the cities is owned by the state. Land in the rural and suburban areas is owned by collectives except for those portions that belong to the state according to the law; house sites and privately farmed plots of cropland and hilly land are also owned by collectives". The collectively-owned land does not belong to state-owned assets, but it can enter the category of state-owned assets by changing the legal procedures of expropriation or requisition. In China, this part of resource assets cannot be sold for ownership and can only be realized through the transfer of development and use rights, and the income is mainly in the form of the earnings from the transfer of use right. The data on the balance sheet of natural resources shall be collected, accounted and reported once a year. Learning the changes in the value of natural resource assets is helpful to accurately grasp the situation of economic entities' possession, use, consumption, restoration and value-added activities of natural resource assets, reflecting the resource environmental costs and ecological effects of economic development, and providing an important basis for the comprehensive decision of environment and development, government performance evaluation, an audit of outgoing leaders' work on natural resource assets. It should be noted that natural resources occupy a large proportion of state-owned assets, but in practice, the reasonable and standardized natural resource detection, mining approval mechanism, and pricing mechanism are quite lagging, leading to serious corruption in this field. The valuation and pricing of natural resources are very important. Although the resource itself does not cost much, the compensation for environmental damage and non-renewable resources should be considered within the scope of pricing evaluation. At the same time, market operational factors should be considered, and the approval mechanism should be reasonably evaluated and standardized to prevent the loss of resource state-owned assets.

Finally, in the Chinese sovereign balance sheet produced by the team of Li Yang from the Chinese Academy of Social Sciences, there are three state-owned assets: external sovereignty state-owned assets, state-owned assets of the National Social Security Fund (NSSF), and government deposits in the central bank. The external sovereign assets are reserved assets held by the authorities in the International Investment Position. The state-owned assets of the NSSF are a national strategic reserve fund concentrated by the Central Government; they are composed of the funds allocated by the Central Government, funds obtained from the reduction or transfer of state-owned shares, and equity assets (There may be double counting between this part of assets and the previous state-owned assets of non-financial/financial enterprises. It is actually transferred to the social security fund in the process of reducing or transferring state-owned shares. And the department that performs the functions of investors is the NSSF Council instead of the SASAC or the MOF). The government deposits in the central bank refer to the fiscal state treasury funds opened in the single account of the People's Bank of China by the treasury at all levels: the budget fund deposits of the treasury, including central state treasury funds and local state treasury funds. It is a financial asset that the financial departments at all levels take charge of and control on behalf of the government at the same level.[5]

9.2.2 Discussion on the management method of state-owned assets account

The report to the Nineteenth National Congress pointed out that "We will improve the systems for managing different types of state assets, and reform the system of authorized operation of state capital. In the state-owned sector, we will step up improved distribution, structural adjustment, and strategic reorganization. We will work to see that state assets maintain and increase their value; we will support state capital in becoming stronger, doing better, and growing bigger, and take effective measures to prevent the loss of state assets".[6] Regarding the above-mentioned three different types of state-owned assets (operating state-owned assets, administrative and in-stitutional state-owned assets, and resource state-owned assets), there shall be three different management methods for regulating these assets.

First, operating state-owned assets, administrative and institutional state-owned assets or resource state-owned assets that have been converted into operating assets should be managed in a business manner. For SOEs (in-cluding state-controlled and non-state-controlled enterprises), the assets management shall be replaced by capital management. We should learn from the Temasek model in Singapore to manage capital through state-owned assets management and investment companies, and take SOEs as truly independent legal persons through the full authorization of operations, enable them to have independent legal person property rights, independent decision-making, and self-financing, and push them into the socialist market. The government no longer manages people and affairs related to specific assets but only ensures the preservation and appreciation of state-owned capital (state-owned rights and interests). It can choose to withdraw and invest in a certain field or a certain enterprise in a timely manner, en-courage the development of emerging industries through investment, and stop loss of state-owned assets in time by way of withdrawal. In a business manner, the other meaning management is to adopt a market-oriented operating accounting method, use the accounting method on the accrual basis of business for the legally compliant administrative and institutional state-owned assets and resource state-owned, as well as strengthen the supervision and tracking of transitional assets.

Second, the administrative management method is adopted for the administrative and institutional and resource state-owned assets, that is, daily administrative order management. We should standardize the administrative management procedures. For land expropriation and requisition, land use rights allocation and auction, and exploration and mining of natural resources such as mineral deposits, the administrative examination and approval procedures should be strictly followed, especially when the laws and regulations for transitional supervision are not complete, it is also necessary to observe procedures and order in the daily administrative process, and do a good job in guarding and managing state-owned assets.

Finally, we should manage various state-owned assets according to laws and regulations. In the era of the rule of law, the law should be the most powerful code, but the current laws and regulations on state-owned assets in China are relatively lagging and there are many imperfections. Up to now, there is no special state-owned assets law for unified regulation. At present, the *Law of the People's Republic of China on State-owned Assets in Enterprises* specifically regulates the management of state-owned assets of enterprises. There are relevant provisions in the *Law of the People's Republic of China on Supervision of the Standing Committees of the National People's Congress at All Levels* and the *Budget Law of the People's Republic of China*. The Ministry of Finance, which is responsible for the reform of the capital management system, took the lead in formulating the *Guiding Opinions on the Reform of State-owned Capital Investment and Operation*. Among them, the *Law of the People's Republic of China on State-owned Assets in Enterprises* stipulates that the "state-owned assets of enterprises (hereinafter referred to as state-owned assets) refer to the rights and interests formed by the state's various forms of investment in enterprises". "State-owned assets are owned by the State, that is, owned by the whole people. The State Council exercises state-owned assets ownership right". "The State Council and local people's governments shall perform the duties of investors in accordance with the principles of separation of government from enterprises, separation of social public management functions from the functions of state-owned asset investors, and non-interference in the independent operation of enterprises in accordance with the law". It is said that the basis for operational management can be found in the legal provisions, but in practice, it has been slow to allow SOEs to operate independently. In reality, there are even phenomena of non-compliance with the law. The binding force of the law should be strengthened, and the formulation of the state-owned assets laws should continue to be advanced.

9.3 Construction of state-owned assets account system and creation and improvement of national balance sheet

Establishing and improving the state-owned assets account system is of special value to creating and improving the national balance sheet. Creating and improving the national balance sheet and evaluating the national economic strength based on the strict standards of accounting will help to better generate the concept of macroeconomic management of "government finance" and promote the expansion of macroeconomic management functions and the improvement of management capability. In particular, in response to the market economy's requirements for the performance evaluation of resource value and allocation, it helps to deepen the understanding of the functions of the market in terms of resource valuation tools, give better play to the decisive role of market resource allocation and the role of the government in macro-control.

9.3.1 The necessity of creating and improving the national balance sheet

Western scholars have done a lot of research on the national balance sheet in the state-owned assets account. Their research and practice have lasted for nearly half a century. The United States, Australia, the United Kingdom, Canada, and Japan are able to regularly compile and publish their national balance sheets. From 1945 to 1990 in the United States,[7] the net assets of the government sector (including non-financial assets) had remained negative, and the net financial assets from 1980 to 2011 were also negative. The general net assets of the British government sector were positive but showing a significant deteriorating trend. If the pension gap was added, the government's net assets would remain negative and continue to deteriorate. Japan's general net assets had shown a clear trend of shrinking. Canada's general net assets of the government sector had been changing: from 1990 to 1996, the sector's net assets were negative and continued to decline, while from 1996 to 2011, the net assets began to increase and gradually turned positive. This reflects that the government functions in developed countries have shifted from a production and construction type to a service type, the resources they control tend to decrease, and the social responsibilities they bear continue to expand. Therefore, the government net assets in developed countries are often small or even negative.

In the economic life of China, the research on the national balance sheet started relatively late. The NBS only published the national and local balance sheets before 2004 in 2007 and then stopped doing so. In 2012, Li Yang, Cao Yuanzheng, and Ma Jun respectively took the lead in researching and compiling the national balance sheet. After that, the Central People's Bank and the DRC under the State Council also tried to compile the government balance sheet. The Third Plenary Session of the 18th CPC Central

Committee held in 2013 clearly proposed the construction of central and local balance sheets. Since then, the National Balance Sheet Research Center of the Chinese Academy of Social Sciences has continued to compile and publish the national balance sheet.

Here our analysis is mainly based on the theoretical research results produced by Li Yang's team on the national balance sheet. They believe that the preparation and improvement of the national balance sheet are to learn from the corporate balance sheet preparation technology, take a country as a specific economic entity, and classify assets and debts of the country at a given time point in a sheet. It can comprehensively reflect the country's total assets, assets structure, total debts, debt structure, and the relationship between assets and debts. Besides, it can separately reflect the assets and debts of major domestic economic entities (non-financial enterprises, financial institutions, governments, residents, etc.) Therefore, the national balance sheet can provide an important basis for comprehensively understanding the total amount and structure of China's assets and debts, the distribution and changes of assets and debts, and find out the true situation of its properties. It is also one of the main tools for studying national debt risks and very important for macro-control. The national balance sheet is the sum of all sectors of the national economy, while the state-owned balance sheet (called "sovereign balance sheet" by Li Yang) is the sum of the assets and debts of the government or sovereign sector. Studying the latter can find out the status of sovereign assets, sovereign debt risks and provide a basis for government financial management.

With reference to the accounting entities of the national balance sheet in SNA 2008, Li Yang's team divided them into non-financial enterprises, financial institutions, government organs, households, non-profit organizations for residents, and foreign departments, and used accounting tools to compile the 2007–2011 national balance sheet of China, thus exhibiting the theoretical methods of the sovereign balance sheet (the state-owned balance sheet in this section), the current characteristics of sovereign assets and sovereign debts.[8]

The sovereign assets listed by them (general government assets) include state treasury, reserve assets, land and resource assets, state-owned assets of administrative institutions, total state-owned assets of non-financial enterprises, total state-owned assets of financial institutions, and assets of social security funds; sovereign debts (general government debts) include central fiscal domestic debt, foreign debt, non-financing platform local government debt, financing-platform local government debt, non-financial SOE debt, policy bank financial debt, bank non-performing assets, debt arising from the disposal of bank non-performing assets, and implicit pension debt.

Based on the account index system formed by the classification of the specific content of government assets, Li Yang's team used the analysis method of the balance sheet to conclude that the Chinese government has sufficient sovereign assets to cover its sovereign debts. "With a positive net asset value of the sovereign sector, it is highly unlikely that a sovereign debt crisis will occur in China over a long period of time". In general, Li Yang's report has depicted a clear and complete structure of the government balance sheet, measured the government balance sheet from 2000 to 2010, thought about the debt problem from the perspective of the balance sheet, put forward the "risk transfer between sectors", and used state-owned operating assets to make up for the pension debt.

Regarding China's national balance sheet, there has yet any consensus on the scope and classification of accounting items (assets and debts), such as large amounts of natural resources and foreign exchange reserves. If a certain asset owned by the country and that can bring benefits to the government is converted into the current value of the asset, the corresponding debt should also be converted into the current value of the debt to match it so that assets and debts are of the consistent basis. Regarding government debt, not only must the ratio of government debt to GDP should be considered, but also the realizability of assets and the ability to offset debts. The local debt and pension debt are issues that the government needs to consider.

9.3.2 Research on the relationship between state-owned assets account and government fiscal account

In Chapter 4 , we've discussed that the enterprise system innovation requires the state-owned assets management to shift from the existing "assets management" to "capital management," that is, to adapt to the characteristics of the market economy and realize management flexibility through the flow of capital value, and improve the efficiency of state-owned capital allocation. For example, we regard the stock of state-owned assets as the value of capital accumulated by the previous fiscal in the government assets account. Therefore, this stock will inevitably be matched with the government's fiscal revenue flow under the dynamic allocation and flow of the government's asset account. Therefore, we need to deal with the organic and unified relationship between the accounts of the two types of assets.

From the perspective of national governance, we will further discuss the organic unity of the two types of assets account and examine the meaning of their organic unity around "construction of government governance system" and "improvement of government governance capability". As the name implies, the government fiscal account is a system for the government as the main body to calculate the current value distribution. In June 1974, the International Monetary Fund organized the compilation of the *Government Finance Statistics Manual: Draft*, which was updated in 2001. At present, GFS 2014 is the latest version. The government fiscal statistical accounting system includes balance sheet, government operation statement, cash source and use statement, and other economic flow statements, which have a checking relationship; and the flow and stock are linked through this relationship.[9]

The state-owned assets account refers to the balance sheet, government operation statement, cash source and use statement, and other economic flow statements of the government or related sovereign departments, while the government fiscal account refers to the current government fiscal budget and final accounts, including general public budget revenue and expenditure final accounts, government fund revenue and expenditure final accounts, state-owned capital operation revenue and expenditure final accounts, social insurance fund revenue and expenditure final accounts, and the final statement of social insurance fund revenue and expenditure, and how to establish a comprehensive fiscal account that uses government financial management as the utility in the future.

The MOF is responsible for the fiscal account system of the Chinese government. Local government departments at all levels are responsible for compiling the fiscal statements of local governments at the same level. The statistical scope includes administrative units, some public institutions, and some SOEs. China's fiscal account system is based on budget final accounts, combined with statistical accounting and financial accounting (financial accounting – financial income and expenditure statement – annual final report – next year's budget report); the core is the flow of financial funds, the basis of accounting is the realization system of receipt and payment, and the main statistics are cash transactions. China's government fiscal account system, with the center of four accounts (public budget revenue and expenditure budget and final accounts, government fund revenue and expenditure budget and final accounts, state-owned capital operating revenue and expenditure budget and final accounts, social insurance fund revenue and expenditure budget and final accounts), draw conclusions about fiscal deficit or surplus.

In addition, the fiscal system adopted by China is a tax-sharing system, that is, the division of income and expenditure authority between the central and local governments. The core budget management system is divided into five levels budget of five levels of governments of the central, provinces (autonomous regions and municipalities), cities divided into districts (autonomous prefectures), counties (autonomous counties, cities without districts, municipal districts), townships (ethnic townships and towns). At present, China's government fiscal account system only has fiscal revenue and expenditure budget and final accounts, which reflect the source and use of cash, and can only reflect the flow. The international standard GFS can reflect not only the flow but also the stock. The government fiscal account system of China has no account for the stock, the establishment of a balance sheet only announces the total amount of stocks, so there is no relationship between flows and stocks. The fiscal status can only be summarized by deficits or balances without understanding and analyzing the structure of assets and debts.

The *Opinions of the CPC Central Committee on Establishing a System for the State Council to Report State-owned Assets Management to the Standing*

Committee of the National People's Congress, issued on January 14, 2018, clearly stated that "the Standing Committee of the National People's Congress shall strengthen state-owned assets supervision and listen to and review the reporting of the State Council's management of state-owned assets, closely link with budgets and final accounts review and supervision, especially with the review and supervision of state-owned capital operating budgets and final accounts, departmental budgets and final accounts, and when conditions are available, combined with the government's comprehensive financial report supervision to establish a multi-tiered and multi-angle mechanism for reporting and supervising the state-owned assets of the NPC from different perspectives.

From the perspective of the account system, China's future government fiscal account should establish a state-owned balance sheet in addition to the final budget statement and add the stock statement to the government fiscal account to open up the cross-check relationship between flow and stock. The government accounting model that should be adopted is the "dual track system" in which budget accounting and government financial accounting coexist. Budget accounting is the entire process of government budget revenue and expenditure, reflecting the implementation of the budget, mainly the financial accounting of budget revenue and expenditure in the fiscal year, but not physical assets; government financial accounting accounts for government economic business activities, existing budget revenue and expenditure activities, there are also assets and debts, as well as information on net assets, which can be used for analyzing financial risk status, assets allocation structure, and distribution of indebted sectors.

Based on the above analysis, we can think that the connotation and extension of state-owned assets are similar to the scope of government assets, and there is no qualitative barrier between the two. The state balance sheet should be placed in the government fiscal account system to open up the cross-check relationship between flow and stock. On the basis of the national financial strength, we can better realize government financial management and government performance assessment.

We've mentioned that the assets in the state assets account can be regarded as the accumulation of the government's past fiscal accounts. On this basis, if the entire social resources are respectively owned by enterprises, natural persons, and state (government), the first two parts will be the private sector, while the last part is the public sector. The public resources owned by the state include stock resources and flow resources. The scale of state-owned stock resources is huge, and many resources have certain difficulties in value evaluation. The acquisition of flow resources is closely related to the overall economic operation of the society, such as tax revenue and debt revenue. Fiscal budget revenue and expenditure are flows, and state-owned assets and debts are stocks, which are manifested in incorporating past resources, economic activities or results into the current accounting scope, and on this basis, the government can make expectations and judgments on future economic development.

With this understanding, it is possible to build an integrated account system for the stock and flow of state-owned assets. According to the *Reform Plan for the Government Comprehensive Financial Reporting System on Accrual Basis* approved by the State Council on December 31, 2014, "a comprehensive government financial reporting system based on accrual basis that comprehensively reflects financial information such as government assets and debts, revenue and expenses, operating costs and cash flow shall be established". It also further clarified that the stock and flow sheets should be included in a unified financial report. From the perspective of dynamic national economic operation, connecting stock and flow has a positive meaning for improving government financial management.

First, the capital flows that occur in the conversion of different forms of state-owned assets will be reflected in the flow statement as income, but in the state balance sheet of the stock statement, it is only an adjustment between different forms of assets, which may not be changed in terms of net assets. For example, the transfer of land leases to the accounts is not the appreciation of resource state-owned assets, but a way of value utilization of the land assets themselves, so to some extent, it cannot be counted as the government's work performance. This is also one of the important meanings of connecting flow and stock, which is to really examine the government's financial management ability. In this way, we can precisely regard the capital stock in the state-owned assets account as the government's past fiscal accumulation. The annual fiscal revenue flow is the value-added income of government assets. In fact, the source of value collected in the form of taxation into the government financial account is the main component of the state-owned operating income.

Second, in the general fiscal budget accounting, the "general budget expenditure" account is used to account for the government's foreign investment, but it does not reflect the state-owned property rights formed by foreign investment; the "general budget revenue" account is used to account for the proceeds from the sale and transfer of state-owned assets, it does not reflect the reduction in government foreign investment assets; as for the operation of state-owned property rights formed by the government's foreign investment, there is no account in the general fiscal budget accounting. This is not conducive to the preservation and appreciation of state-owned assets.[10] Therefore, a state-owned assets account is needed to monitor the maintenance and appreciation of state-owned assets. Especially for the macroeconomic operation that will be more deeply integrated into the track of the market economy, the allocation of value-based global resources allocation will inevitably be impacted or disturbed by the external market on the stability of China's economic operation, which highlights the positive significance of integrating the stock and flow of state-owned assets to fight against the impact of external uncertainties.

We can further examine the management and balance ability of the Chinese government's fiscal account. China's current budgeting is based on the realization of receipt and payment systems, and the basis of budget accounting is also the realization of receipt and payment systems. Budget accounting mainly serves the needs of budget management but cannot provide information on the true financial status of the government. What is released to the public is only a budget report reflecting the flow of budget revenue and expenditure. The budget report only explains the budget revenue and expenditure in the budget year and cannot be used to measure the government's financial status. The state balance sheet (government balance sheet) is used to measure the government's financial status. China's current budget accounting system has yet to provide a state balance sheet. Objectively, it is because the state balance sheet is based on the accrual basis as the accounting standard, and there is no direct link between the sheets of different accounting standards.

Only on the basis of accrual accounting can the information on assets and liabilities provided by government accounting be true and reliable. However, the introduction of this accounting system will increase costs. It should be introduced gradually, first in the local government debt and asset accounting, and then introduced at the central level of sovereign assets and liabilities accounting. At this stage, there is still a need for a revenue-and-payment implementation budget. First, it is introduced into the government accounting system and then into the government budget. A dual-track system can be implemented for a certain period of time, and an accrual-based, inclusive and concurrent system can be gradually established. The government's comprehensive fiscal account is linked to the state balance sheet.

9.4 Allocation liquidity of state-owned assets as a "tool for macroeconomic control"

State-owned capital and SOEs are an important economic foundation for achieving economic growth, ensuring employment, creating tax revenue, and maintaining stability. Japanese-American economist Masahiko Aoki pointed out in his book The Role of the Government in East Asian Economic Development that "The function of government policy is to promote or supplement the coordination function of the private sector, rather than treating the government and the market as merely mutually exclusive ... The government should be regarded as an internal participant interacting with the economic system. It represents a set of coherent and coordinated mechanisms, not an external, neutral and omnipotent body attached to the economic system and responsible for resolving (coordination failures.)".[11]

There is no country that does not have a state-owned economy or state-owned assets capacity in modern economic life. It is only reflected in the specific amount or its proportion in the total social assets, and of course, in what way are state-owned assets allocated and to which sectors and enterprises they are allocated.

9.4.1 The allocation of the state-owned economy can be organically combined with macroeconomic control

By observing China's growth process, we can find interesting phenomena. On the one hand, China's economic miracle is inseparable from the release of incentives brought about by market-oriented mechanisms after the reform and opening up, such as the "household contract responsibility system" implemented in the agricultural sector, and the emergence of migrant workers, deregulation of prices and rationing in the process of urbanization, and other regulations and the "federal-like" decentralization system of local governments, which have released the impetus for local governments to develop the economy. Of course, openness allows the development of a non-public economy, which shows that carrying out thorough public ownership and planned economy in the current stage of economic development was not conducive to economic growth. But on the other hand, the growth miracle is rooted in the leadership and promotion of the state-owned economy. The decentralized authoritarian political system has brought about a "tournament" for officials to pursue political achievements, which makes local governments exhaust all available resources to promote economic growth. In the practice of macro-control management in China's state-owned economy, there are both advantages and problems that are being thrown into doubt. From the practical perspective, China's state-owned economy has the characteristics of strong control, counter-cyclicality, guaranteeing employment, bearing tax burden, promoting industrial development and innovation.

The state-owned economy needs to take into account both short-term and long-term development. Short-term regulation is to prevent economic fluctuations from harming economic growth, and the main forms are counter-cyclical regulation, employment protection and financial support. Long-term regulation is to fully allocate resources to achieve sustainable innovation, growth and development, and the main forms are to implement industrial policies and launch innovative plans. Counter-economic regulation is mainly to ensure that the economic system will not experience destructive blows under the impact of the economic crisis, thereby shortening the recovery time; ensuring the fairness of social welfare. The foundation of the macro-control capability is the government's ability to control the state-owned economy. Such capability depends on the government's overall economic operation and management framework, ideas, and theories, and ability to face the economic uncertainty that may occur in the market economy and the external market against the background of globalization. The government can use the economic power of state-owned capital to adopt acquisition, transfer or withdrawal to adjust the economic operation situation and maintain the stability of economic growth.

The scientificization of the national macro-control system is conducive to improving the scientific nature of the state-owned economy's macro-control capability. In the short term, macroeconomic control can help avoid irreversible damage to the economic system under severe economic fluctuations. In case of any economic downturn, SOEs can play a counter-cyclical stabilizing role. In response to the imbalance between effective demand and supply in the short-term, the state-owned economy can alleviate the short-term economic volatility by increasing social capital investment (especially in infrastructure construction), averaging cost pricing and other means to control inflation, absorb employment, and rescue downstream companies. Especially in the case of a certain impact from an external economic crisis, the state-owned economy can help the state avoid high rates of unemployment.

In the field of industrial policy, appropriate government intervention is to promote the upgrading of industrial structure, improve the international competitiveness of the economy, and promote sustained growth. In this context, the allocation of state-owned capital can be an extension of government functions. The government enters enterprises as a shareholder, participates in corporate governance, and has micro-specific channels for corporate management and production activities. The institutional form of the state-owned economy (state-funded enterprises) has strengthened the implementation of industrial policies.

First, in the process of industrialization, the State can solve the problem of insufficient industrial investment motivation in natural monopoly sectors by nationalizing key public sectors, such as railways and communications, and use upstream industries to drive the development of downstream industries. The construction of China's high-speed rail network is a typical case, which plays a key role in supporting economic interaction between various regions.

Second, as a developing country, the factor market is underdeveloped and imperfect. Through state-owned capital investment, the role of coordinating various industrial sectors to jointly promote economic development can be achieved. This was particularly evident in the early industrialization process of China.

Third, state-funded enterprises generally have a considerable scale and have stronger economic strength in technological innovation and play a leading role in the entire social-economic system through the value chain in technology, division of labor and cooperation. Since the process of technological innovation has spillovers, initial innovators need to bear the risks that may result from project failure. After successful innovation, it will have a spillover effect of knowledge on the whole society. Successful Chinese companies, such as Baosteel, Lenovo and Gree, can also be seen as examples of state-owned capital allocation to promote innovation and successfully gain international competitiveness.

9.4.2 Enlightenment from the regulation and control of state-owned economy under the background of financial crisis

After the baptism of the global financial crisis in 2008, the academic circles began to reflect on how to play the role of state-owned capital in the allocation of equity in dealing with market failures. When the subprime mortgage crisis swept the world in 2008, China's financial system remained stable, but a debt crisis broke out in Europe. After the financial crisis broke out, the U.S. federal government quickly took the lead to rescue large banks and large companies, buying equity in these companies or injecting capital into them, which is actually a hidden nationalization process. Nationalization has taken over and injected capital into large financial institutions such as banks, effectively preventing them from running on during the crisis and ensuring that the financial system would not collapse. There was no doubt about the role and performance of China's economy in this specific process. It is in this sense that nationalization has become an important means of the government's macroeconomic regulation and control, and such a state-owned economy may not directly show the essential characteristics of socialism. The security of large banks (special enterprises) is important for the stability of the financial system as a whole.

In the context of China's deepening reform of the economic system, the state-owned economy still retains its key economic intervention capabilities. The result of the gradual reform is that the principle of "crossing the river by feeling the stones" is followed, and the top-level design is combined with pilot tests, instead of adopting the "shock therapy" that failed in Eastern Europe and Latin America. An important theoretical conclusion can be drawn from this: the issue of the state-owned economy is not "should exist or not" but "how does it exist". The system innovation in the Deepening Reform Opinions guarantees the influence and scientific implementation of the macro-control of state ownership at multiple levels. In particular, it is emphasized that the direct goal of SOE reform is to continuously improve the vitality, control, influence and risk resistance of the state-owned economy. It echoes how to consciously use the allocation and flow of state-owned capital to enhance the government's ability to control the macro-economy to ensure the stability of macroeconomic operations and effectively resist market uncertainties and external market crises that may impact the Chinese economy. In a more general sense, the understanding and application of the macro-control and management functions of the state-owned economy have enriched the depth and breadth of the political economy theory on the functions of the state-owned economy and the operation and flow of state-owned capital.

9.5 Institutional innovation of labor rights-interests relationships based on state funding

The previous section mainly discusses the positive impact of transformation and innovation brought about by the government's macro-management work method resulting from the transformation of SOEs into "state-funded enterprises". We need to emphasize the concept of "state contribution", in specific corporate situations, the investment behavior of public assets requires a specific "investor", which results in changes to the allocation of the existing public ownership right and the property rights relations of laborers.

For enterprises of the traditional ownership by the whole people, there is a theoretical saying that employees are the "owners" of the means of production for employment placement and use of labor in their business activities. This statement seems to convey that employees are the "owners" of enterprises. This understanding has always been emphasized in corporate management situations. However, what is the meaning of the owner and how to exercise the rights of the owner have not been clearly defined for a long time. Although there are no written laws and regulations, enterprises have formed a relatively stable model in the development process. The "three fixed" are the most closely related to the interests of employees: fixed wages, fixed rights, and fixed positions. At the same time, because enterprises pay their employees lower salaries, and they are obliged to ensure the lives of employees, such as medical care, housing, pensions, and children's education. These factors seem to prove that employees are the "owner" of their enterprises. This may be in line with Marxist criticism of private ownership, pointing out that private ownership brings inequality to workers in participating in social production activities. Therefore, public ownership of the means of production must be established so that workers have fair and common ownership of the means of production. However, in reality, the establishment of the socialist system is the first to succeed in countries with relatively underdeveloped productivity. Restricted by the industrial division of labor, technological application, and regional economic conditions, it is difficult for the whole society to produce completely equal production conditions for all production occasions. Therefore, the proposition that workers on specific occasions are "owners" of the enterprises owned by the whole people are restricted by the differences in the production materials and conditions of different enterprises. In addition, under the old system, the "egalitarian practice" and "one size fits all" of the wage distribution standard have dampened the production enthusiasm of enterprise employees. In the dynamic economic development, negative incentives are gradually formed, which is directly manifested in the lack of enthusiasm of employees and the lack of vitality of enterprises.

In response to the shortcomings of the old system, the economic structural reform started from stimulating the profits of enterprises. After introducing reform measures that link the income of employees to the operating performance of enterprises, it was gradually confirmed that the ownership right of enterprises could be appropriately separated from their management right so as to better mobilize the enthusiasm of enterprises and enable them to independently face the market and make business decisions. The original enterprises owned by the whole people (also known as "state-run enterprises") generally accepted and adopted the "separation of two rights", and thus forming the concept of "state-owned enterprises". Along with the "market-oriented" reform, the goal of establishing the socialist market economy was set, enterprises were pushed to the market, the modern corporate system was proposed to restructure traditional SOEs and establish the status of enterprises as independent market subjects. In particular, the Third Plenary Session of the 18th CPC Central Committee held in November 2013 clearly stated to "vigorously develop a mixed economy" by inviting investors with different ownership of capital. Thereby giving rise to the concept of "state-funded enterprises". The government has established a state-owned assets management agency that specifically assumes the role of investors, and in corporate situations, there are also "property rights representatives" who invest with state-owned assets. In the traditional system, the argument that employees of enterprises are the "masters" (owners) of the means of production has been denied under the new state-owned assets management system. The cooperative relationship between capital and labor in actual production activities needs a new explanation.

Under the conditions of the socialist market economy, various factors of production cooperate within the corporate organizations, and the subjects of factors have equal rights. The rights of labor are the rights enjoyed by enterprise employees to work, get remuneration, labor protection, medical care, and pension insurance premiums. Therefore, a new definition can be given to workers' status in enterprises. Laborers use their labor participation in enterprises to guarantee their personal interests, and their work attitudes and contributions have a direct impact on enterprise performance, and the realization of enterprise performance will also give laborers a certain "sharing" incentive. As a result, employees' personal interests and corporate interests are "united" to become direct "stakeholders".

We can deduce from the relationship between capital rights and labor rights of investors in state-funded enterprises how to bring this relationship into the track of the law so as to promote mutual restraint between all rights. Across society, the profit-chasing behavior of capital may infringe on labor rights. One of the most direct manifestations is to lower laborers' wages and other labor welfare expenditures. This requires several other auxiliary means to deal with it. The laws and regulations on labor rights shall be continuously improved to protect the rights of laborers. On this basis, it is necessary to create better-supporting conditions for the development of the labor market to promote social benchmarks and information release of labor wage (price) levels. At the same time, the government should issue "minimum wage standards" and "relevant regulations on the protection of labor rights" and supervise the implementation of enterprises based on relevant determinations; in addition, the capital in the labor-management partnership is in a "strong" position, it is necessary to form trade unions, strengthen the role of trade unions, form the strength of the organization to protect the rights and interests of workers in the organization, and promote the healthy development of enterprises by building a new and harmonious labor relationship.

This chapter examines the significance of enterprise reform from the perspective of national governance modernization, which helps us deepen our understanding of the modern corporate system as the micro-foundation of the socialist market economy. As the microscopic main body of social reproduction activities under the market economy, it adopts the form of a mixed-ownership corporate system, which opens up a new path for the integration of public ownership and market economy, and puts forward new requirements on the state-owned assets management system and management methods, until it becomes an important content of self-improvement of the socialist economic system with Chinese characteristics.

The management and allocation of state-owned assets by means of "value-based management" helps to maintain the flexibility of capital flow, and the establishment of a sound capital account system is of fundamental significance to the development of management work, providing accounting basis for the construction and consolidation of "government financial management" ability under the market economy, promoting the improvement and consolidation of the national governance system, and at the same time promoting the use of state-owned capital flows to regulate and control the macro-economy, so as to promote the stability of the macroeconomic operation. Simultaneously, the establishment and improvement of the state-owned capital account system will also help strengthen the evaluation of the main economic responsibilities of state-owned capital operations and handle the relationship between the public and operating attributes of state-owned capital. In the specific operation of state-owned capital in the economic activities, the economic relationship with workers must be improved so that the allocation and operation of state-owned capital and the construction of harmonious labor relations will have strong system support and implementation of follow-up work, which reflects the social foundation of national governance capacity building.

Notes

1 The mixed companies funded by Temasek are known as "government-linked companies" (GLCs), meaning that these companies have state-owned capital or government investment, rather than purely "SOEs". They are similar to the "state-funded enterprises" mentioned in this book.
2 *Decision of the CPC Central Committee on several major issues concerning the reform and development of state-owned enterprises.* (1999). Retrieved September 22, 1999, from http://www.gcdr.gov.cn/content.html?id=16800
3 *Opinions of the CCCPC on establishing a system for the State Council to report state-owned assets management to the Standing Committee of the NPC.* (2018). Retrieved January 14, 2018, http://www.gov.cn/zhengce/2018-01/14/content_525 6573.htm
4 Li, S. S. (2004). *Management of state-owned assets.* Beijing: China Financial & Economic Publishing House.
5 Li, Y., Zhang, X. J., et al. (2012). China's sovereign balance sheet and its risk assessment (part 1). *Economic Research Journal*, Issue 6.
6 Xi, J. P. (2017). *Secure a decisive victory in building a moderately prosperous society in all respects and strive for the great success of socialism with Chinese characteristics for a new era – delivered at the 19th National Congress of the*

Communist Party of China. Retrieved October 18, 2017, from http://www.xinhuanet.com/politics/19cpcnc/2017-10/27/c_1121867529.htm

7 Li, Y., Zhang, X. J., et al. (2012). China's sovereign balance sheet and its risk assessment (part 2). *Economic Research Journal*, Issue 7.

8 Li, Y., Zhang, X. J., et al. (2012). China's sovereign balance sheet and its risk assessment (part 1). *Economic Research Journal*, Issue 6.

9 *How can we understand China's fiscal system*. https://baijiahao.baidu.com/s?id=1592613672079894991&wfr=spider&for=pc.

10 Tang, L. M. (2014). Chinese local government balance sheet: framework construction and scale estimation. *Public Finance Research*, Issue 7.

11 Masahiko, A., et al. (1998). *The role of the government in East Asian economic development* (p. 2). Beijing: Economic Press China.

10 SOE reform enriches and perfects the connotation of the basic economic system

The previous chapters have discussed the main content of SOE reform and described the progressive reform track for "enhancing the vitality of enterprises", which is the "central link" of the economic system in the past 40 years, as well as the reform measures to liberate and develop the working mechanism of the productive forces.

In this chapter, we focus on the theoretical and practical significance of SOE reform in improving and optimizing the basic socialist economic system. As mentioned earlier, the enterprise is the main body of social reproduction and market economy. What kind of property rights structure and legal organization form the enterprise adopts constitutes the ontological content of the social-economic system. It is precisely in this way that the continuous deepening of SOE has promoted the scientific handling of production relations in the practice of real socialism, enriched and consolidated the specific content of the basic economic system, and endowed real socialism with vigorous vitality.

While leading the reform of the economic system, our party has always adhered to the ideological line of "seeking truth from facts" and the basic principles of socialism to open up new development space for realistic socialism. Attention is paid to the positive interaction between top-level design and grassroots initiative in the specific working methods for promoting enterprise reform. A path of socialist development with Chinese characteristics is being explored. After entering a new stage of "comprehensively deepening reforms", we are inspired to build up our confidence in reforms, strengthen our resilience to "tackle the hardest tasks" and our determination to "carry the reform to the end".

10.1 "Problem-oriented" "pilot exploration", and gradual promotion of "incremental reform" and system transformation

"Problem-oriented" stimulates a deep review of the performance of actual socialist operations. In a certain sense, compared with the traditional planned economy, the process of reform is to introduce commodity-currency relations and market regulation mechanisms into the resource allocation of economic operations. Practice has proved that this cannot be done simply overnight. The understanding of traditional socialist theories that have been accumulated over a long period of time needs to be "enlightened" by the facts and changes brought about by reform and opening up. The resulting driving force of the "inducible" institutional changes[1] will gradually eliminate the frictional fetters between the old ideological and theoretical concepts and economic system reform measures and get rid of the inertia of the "path dependence" generated by these old concepts so that the cause of reform is always in a gradual and progressive way.

10.1.1 Pilot exploration to open the way for forming a benign interaction between "centralized leadership" and "grassroots innovation", and between theoretical innovation and system performance testing, and ensure the stable system transition

The Third Plenary Session of the 11th CPC Central Committee made a wise decision and established the "reform and opening" policy. In response to the shortcomings of the traditional system, the rejection of commodity-currency relations and market mechanisms, and the disrespect of the "economic rationality" of enterprises as the main body of interest, the reform started by influencing the intensity and scope of plan management, and adopted the specific "incremental reform" and "market orientation". The measures started with "expansion of enterprise autonomy", aroused the return of "economic rationality" of various economic entities, recognized and respected the independent interests of economic entities, and formed a situation in which numerous people were actively concerned about labor performance. The new mechanism dissolves the "inertia" of the old system, stimulates the enhancement of the vitality of the national economy, and drives China's economy into the fast lane of development.

Looking back on the course of the reform, we choose two typical cases here that demonstrate pilot exploration before large-scale implementation. From these, we can see that the reform has been advanced step by step and its benign interaction with the grassroots initiative under the unified leadership of the Party. Each new breakthrough in deepening the reform has promoted the benign interaction between theoretical innovation and performance improvement testing, thus forming a joint force, gradually progressing with "incremental reform", and successfully realizing the goal of economic system transition.

Undoubtedly, reform means "innovation" of systems and mechanisms. However, innovation theory tells us that, compared with the cognitive understanding of the status quo, there is "uncertainty" in innovation and this "uncertainty" may produce "psychological fear" of the subject of innovation. It is worthy of special discussion that in view of the "shortage" in the traditional planned economy, the existing state is not obvious to the "vested interests" generated by various actors in the society or the social subject's response to the existing state is not "attached".

It was against this background that reforms characterized by "market orientation" introduced commodity-currency relations. After the "pilot exploration", the "delegation of powers and transfer of profits" to enterprises quickly broke the pattern of the traditional system, and the Central Government timely issued pilot programs for providing guidance. In July 1979, the State Council promulgated five documents, including the *Regulations on Expanding the Management Autonomy of State-owned Enterprises* and the *Provisions on the Implementation of Profit Retention in State-owned Enterprises*. Six SOEs, including Sichuan Chongqing Iron and Steel Co., Ltd., were selected to try out 14 measures, including "profit retention", the "Factory Director Responsibility System" and arousing the enthusiasm for reform across the whole society.

Shortly afterward, the concept of the "economic responsibility system" was promoted as a corporate management system and quickly spread across society. The exploration and implementation of corporate operating responsibilities are also seen at the grassroots level. In the metallurgical industry, by 1981, 17 provinces, autonomous regions, and municipalities across China had implemented regional industry general contracting, and more than 80% of enterprises implemented profit contracting and loss contracting. Various forms of contracting soon generated benefits. Gradually, a "contracted management responsibility system" represented by "Shougang experience"[2] has been formed. The basic principles of the contractual management responsibility system are "fixing the base, ensuring the payment, keeping the excess output and making up for poor output".

There are five specific forms: two guarantees and one linkage, incremental payment for profits, payment of profits for the base, guarantee the profits or losses of small or loss-making enterprises, and guarantee industry input and output. It can be seen that they adhere to the ideological principle of "seeking truth from facts". Aiming at the specific reality of enterprises in different industries, the implementation of the business responsibility system has shown diversity. As a result, a consensus that "ownership and management rights can be appropriately separated" was formed at the level of economic theory. It was included in the *Decision on Reform of the Economic Structure* adopted by the Third Plenary Session of the 12th CPC Central Committee. This Decision clearly affirmed that the separation of ownership and management rights is the direction of reform for the transformation of enterprise management mechanisms.

The same characteristics are also shown in the specific actions of exploring the establishment of a "modern corporate system" to transform traditional SOEs. After the first stage of the reform with "market orientation", commodity-currency relations were introduced into the economic life, calling for the return of economic rationality of various social subjects and the continuous deepening of market development. In real economic life, grassroots initiatives have also opened the way for the continuous deepening of reforms. With the development of market exchange relations and facing new market business opportunities, there have been economic activities in China's economic life in which multiple economic entities jointly funded new enterprises.

The most representative example was that on November 14, 1984, as approved by the Shanghai Branch of the People's Bank of China, Shanghai Feile Electroacoustic Factory, Feile Electroacoustic Factory Third Branch, Shanghai Electronic Components Industry Corporation, and the Shanghai Jing'an Branch of the Industrial and Commercial Bank initiated the establishment of Shanghai Feilo Acoustics Co., Ltd., and issued shares to the public and employees, becoming the first joint-stock company in Shanghai, and the shares issued by this company (commonly known as "Little Feilo") had no time limit and no withdrawal, but they could be circulated and transferred. It can be said that it was the first real stock in the new era of reform and opening up in China.

This kind of spontaneous "funding" for raising registered capital formed a capital alliance in the form of "equity" (stock accounting) and specified that the investors cannot directly withdraw shares from the funded company but can withdraw from the "secondary market", in order to maintain the stable operation of raised capital. It can be seen that the development of the market itself has given birth to the emergence of a joint-stock enterprise as a typical form of the modern corporate system. It is also an ice-breaking work that uses or relies on the development of the capital market to advance China's property rights reform. Its historical significance is also that it directly affected the early trials and subsequent development of China's stock market and profoundly impacted China's economic system reform. Deng Xiaoping affirmed this model. On November 14, 1986, when he received the then chairman of the New York Stock Exchange, John Van Erlin (John J. Phelan), he gave the "Little Feilo stock" to him as a gift, fully showing the significance of this stock for China's reform and opening up. When Deng Xiaoping made his famous remark in the south China tour during the Spring Festival in 1992, he mentioned that securities and the stock market should be "tested resolutely".[3]

On the basis of conscientiously summarizing the pattern of reform and opening up, that has been opened and the experience gained, we have acquired a clear understanding of the goals of economic system reform. In 1992, the Fourteenth National Congress formally established the establishment of a socialist market economy as the target of reform. In order to adapt to the requirements of building a socialist market economy, enterprises must be pushed to the market to become real market entities. Therefore, traditional SOEs should be registered as the legal organization form of the corporate system, draw multiple sources of capital contribution, marking that the basic legal person organization system has entered a new stage. This required that the identity of investors must be definite.

Let investors first exercise their own ownership right at the investor conference, form a corresponding corporate governance structure, and then a special market relationship is formed between investors and the corporate organization that accepts the capital contribution, and this corporate organization will have complete autonomous management right. The existing theory of "ownership right and management right" and "separation of the two rights" has evolved into the "separation of the three rights" of investor ownership, corporate property rights, and daily management rights. It is precisely in this way that the conscious "active actions" of the grassroots are promptly affirmed by the top-level guidance and are established and consolidated in the form of a series of laws and regulations. A number of laws and regulations have been promulgated around the construction of the modern corporate system and the development of the capital market. The Company Law promulgated in 1993 played a leading role in the top-level design and provided legal systems and relevant implementation regulations for the deepening of practice. While the modern and multi-funded corporate system continues to penetrate into economic life and become well-known to people, the system innovation of "mixed-ownership reform" of SOEs has become natural and easier to understand and accept.

Since the Eighteenth National Congress (2012), the Party Central Committee with General Secretary Xi Jinping as the core has made a comprehensive plan for the comprehensive and deepening reform of the economic system. The Third Plenary Session of the 18th CPC Central Committee held in November 2013 adopted the *Decision on Some Major Issues Concerning Comprehensively Deepening the Reform*, and decided to establish a leading group of the CPC Central Committee to comprehensively deepen reform, responsible for overall reform design, overall coordination, overall promotion, and supervision of implementation. General Secretary Xi Jinping emphasized, "To deepen reform comprehensively, it is necessary to coordinate and promote reforms in various fields, it is necessary to have the general goal of management and to answer the question of what is the ultimate goal of promoting reform in various fields and what overall results are to be achieved". "This project is extremely ambitious. Moderate adjustments and fragmented repairs are to no avail. It must be a comprehensive and systematic reform and improvement, which is the linkage and integration of reforms and improvements in various fields".[4]

It is not difficult to understand that comprehensively deepening reform has the characteristics of "system integration" and requires strengthening the top-level and overall design and coordinated advancement of various reform measures. At the same time, it is necessary to encourage and allow differentiated exploration in different places. The heavier the task of comprehensively deepening reform, the more attention must be paid to grassroots exploration and practice. The working methods of promoting reform accumulated throughout the 40 years of economic structural reform must be applied more consciously. Efforts must be made to strengthen the benign interaction between the Party Central Committee's leadership and the independent innovation of the grassroots. We shall emphasize the application of the law-based thinking and the promotion of reform according to law; emphasize the development of a path with Chinese characteristics is to develop oneself based on Chinese history, Chinese culture, and the environmental conditions and opportunities that China faces today. We should properly handle the corporate positioning in the socialist market economy and the role that SOEs should play. In particular, the dialectical relationship between top-level design and grassroots innovation shall be explored to further advance the reform.

10.1.2 The special status of enterprise reform in economic structural reform and the internal logic of deepening the reform

As mentioned earlier, China's economic structural reform adopts a gradual transition strategy of "incremental reform". A vivid description of this strategy is "crossing the river by feeling the stones". This was originally a folk saying, referring to the fact that in the absence of previous experience and no existing bridges and boats, one has to test the water and fumble forward in order to cross the river. The reason why this folk saying is introduced into the working methods for promoting the reform is that in the case of insufficient practical experience, especially when facing the task of institutional innovation such as reform, we must boldly experiment and actively explore, find out the law and move forward steadily, which is the implications of the so-called "reform is to cross the river by feeling the stones". This statement is quoted in actual workplaces. However, I've found that on some occasions, some people think that this kind of work strategy is related to the lack of overall thinking and clear planning arrangements for the reform, and even think that the reform has entered a deep-water zone and "the stone is found nowhere". This understanding needs to be clarified. In reference to the previous discussions of the relevant reform content, it is inaccurate to say that the reform lacks an understanding of the overall plan.

First, China's economic structural reform was made on the basis of "emancipating the mind" and thoroughly reviewing the shortcomings of the traditional system. The goal and task of reform and opening up are to liberate and develop productive forces and realize socialist modernization. Moreover, the focus of reform is to solve the problem of insufficient enterprise vitality. Therefore, the enterprise reform has been scientifically positioned from the beginning, and the position of enterprise reform in the overall economic structural reform has been corrected. This is to "enhance the vitality of large and medium-sized SOEs as the central link of the overall economic structural reform". From the perspective of the structure of the economic system, the focus of economic structural reform is to address the enterprises that undertake resource allocation and reproduction activities and to drive other aspects of the economic system through corporate reform to reflect the overall compatibility of the reform to promote economic system transformation.

Second, looking back at the deepening and evolution of enterprise reform over the past 40 years, it is not difficult to find a clear, logical clue. This is to focus on enhancing the vitality of enterprises, from "delegating powers and transferring profits" to "retained profits" to activate corporate rationality, promote the development of corporate accounting consciousness, adjust the relationship between the government and enterprises, and form "interest constraints" on enterprises. Since then, due to the enhancement of the corporate self-retention awareness, the game relationship between the government and the enterprise in the way of corporate profit division has changed. The reform has also introduced a two-step reform approach of "profit-to-tax" (income tax plus adjustment tax) because of the difference in the amount of retained profits of different enterprises; the "adjustment tax" after bearing the same income tax has been subject to inconsistent tax rates. This has led to the "whipping the fast bull" and the blind pursuit of more profit by enterprises, leading to insignificant growth in the amount of profits that the government might concentrate. It was against this background that in order to better handle the relationship between the government and enterprises, the contracting contracts were used to define the interest relationships between government and enterprises and to form a government revenue arrangement for "three years" of the contract period, which was also helpful for the government to better use certain financial resources to promote reforms in other areas. These kinds of measures to deal with the interest relationship between the government and enterprises by means of contract tools are known as "contractual constraints." They can nest the interest constraint of the existing government-enterprise interest relationship in the contract, that is, the contract constraint that includes the existing interest constraint. However, due to the direct contradiction between the certainty of the contract and the uncertainty of the business environment due to changes in the reform system, a fixed "three-year" contract may be a mere formality and the enterprises may not be able to fulfill the contracting promise, because the contracting business environment is mainly created and provided by the government. Therefore, there is still no benchmark for such a constraint mechanism. With the further deepening of reforms, they will inevitably concern the issues as to how state ownership rights and business management rights are clearly defined and integrated with the market economic environment and mechanism. There is a necessity for finding the basis for property rights. Because of this, we need to shape the micro-subjects of the market economy in the form of modern companies, transform the traditional state ownership (owned by the whole people) in the form of a corporate legal organization, and form a new relationship between the state capital and corporate capital. Investors should get the equity interest and equity income return of the business operation. As the creator of the market environment and the maintainer of the market order, the State levies taxes on enterprises and obtains tax revenue. Both the relationship between the government and capital and the relationship between the government and enterprises need to be transformed. As a result, a "property rights constraint" for handling the relationship between the government and enterprises is formed. Obviously, this kind of property rights constraint mechanism covers the interest constraints and contract constraints on the existing government-enterprise relationship. In other words, the existing interest constraints and contract constraints are embedded in the property rights constraints. As a result, a fundamental institutional arrangement for the relationship between the government and enterprises is formed. The problem of integrating state ownership with market economic mechanisms shall be properly solved. The above analysis shows that the phased advancement of reform has its own internal logic. Based on the adjustment of the quasi-government and the main contradictory relationship between enterprises, it must be able to deepen its own system evolution.

Finally, the continuous deepening of enterprise reform will inevitably impose requirements on reforms in other aspects of the economic system, which will lead to multiple reforms. On the other hand, reforms in other aspects also provide a supportive environment for the in-depth advancement of enterprise reform to form a positive interaction that promotes each other. There will be market mechanism reform, price system reform, financial system reform, employment and social security system reform, and foreign trade system reform. The previous chapters have pointed out the changes in the legal person status of enterprises – micro-foundation of the market economy – will impact the overall economic structural reform and the development of system quality. This has also contributed to our understanding of the theory of system structure and has also enriched our understanding of how the content of the economic restructuring itself adjusts the relationships between various economic subjects, the specific content of different levels of institutions and mechanisms, and their relationships.

From the analysis of the above three aspects, we can clarify the argument that improperly deduces the "crossing the river by feeling the stones", which is a working method of promoting and deepening the reform. Of course, today's reform has entered the "five-in-one" (economic, political, cultural, social and ecological civilization) stage of comprehensive deepening. We have more consciously emphasized the importance of top-level design. The *Communiqué of the Third Plenary Session of the 18th CPC Central Committee* and the *Decision on Some Major Issues Concerning Comprehensively Deepening the Reform* emphasize that "the combination of strengthening the top-level design and crossing the river by feeling the stones" is necessary. Because the reform coverage and the areas involved need "system integration", the five-dimensional synergic relationship needs to be integrated, and different dimensions have different ways of evolution and they are nested and entangled with each other.

10.2 SOE reform has led to the continuous improvement of production relations, enriching and consolidating the connotation of the basic economic system

The advancement of SOE reform cannot circumvent the understanding of the regulations and specific contents of ownership relations and the basic economic system. Objectively speaking, as an organizational carrier for the allocation of social reproduction resources, an enterprise is an active subject that integrates various production factors to form realistic productivity. The institutional environment of its business activities changes from a "planned economy" to a socialist market economy. The legal system of the enterprise organization adopts the "modern corporate system" jointly funded by multiple "investors". Starting from the general principles of the market economy, the multiple entities that jointly contribute have the willingness to contribute funds on "equal cooperation". State-owned capital is one of the most important forms of capital.

"The state protects the property rights and legitimate interests of all economic sectors, ensures that they have equal access to the factors of production according to the law, participate in a market competition on an open, fair and just footing, and are accorded with equal protection and oversight according to the law".[5] Therefore, traditional SOEs have transformed into "state-funded" enterprises, and enterprises have become market entities with independent legal person property rights in market economic activities. To deepen reforms in an all-around way, we must adhere to the direction of socialism, which is reflected in the persistence and improvement of public-owned production relations in the reform of the economic system. Productivity decides the relations of production, and the ownership of the means of production is an important part of the relations of production. Therefore, the relationship between development and the level of ownership that is compatible with the level of productivity is a basic proposition for social progress and healthy and orderly economic growth. The basic economic system expresses the structure of social ownership in a more standardized way and reflects the essential characteristics of the economy. In particular, understanding and establishing the basic economic system from the dynamic operation of the national economy must be continuously improved and optimized through specific practices.

10.2.1 *The rapid growth of the non-public economy provides external reference for SOEs and enriches the content of the basic economic system*

In order to better understand the specific provisions of the "basic economic system", or to discuss how to define the content of the basic economic system, we can briefly review how the constitution has changed since the founding of New China. A better understanding of how the basic economic system can fully characterize the most important institutional features of real socialism and better handle the allocation of social reproduction resources and liberate and develop productive forces.[6]

From the *Common Program of the Chinese People's Political Consultative Conference,* which was first adopted in September 1949 to paint a preliminary "image" of how the socialist system can be practiced to the Constitution (draft) of 1954 and then to the Constitution of 1975, all of these stress to uphold public ownership of the means of production – the specific content of China's basic socialist economic system, including "all-people ownership" and "collective ownership"; but completely exclude the existence of non-public economy in the basic economic system. In reaching economic life, the serious deviation from the level of productivity and large-scale equalization and collectivization has substantially severely restricted productivity development.

China's current constitution is the 1982 Constitution. This Constitution was born in the early period of reform and opening up and has undergone five major revisions in the following 30 years. The 1982 Constitution clarified the legal status of the individual economy as part of the non-public sector of the economy. Until 1988, the constitutional amendment added that "The state allows the private economy to exist and develop within the scope prescribed by law. The private economy is a supplement to the socialist public economy. The state protects the legal rights and interests of the private economy, and guides, supervise and manage the private economy." This amendment confirmed the constitutional status of the private economy and guaranteed the development of the non-public economy. The second amendment to the Constitution took place in 1993, affirming the legal status of the socialist market economy. The third constitutional amendment in 1999 confirmed that "we will continue to follow the basic economic system to keep public ownership in a dominant position and have diverse forms of ownership develop side by side" and clearly mentioned that "the non-public sector of self-employed, private and other forms of ownership is an important component part of the socialist market economy", further affirming the status of the non-public economy. The fourth amendment to the constitution took place in 2004, adding that "the public economy shall be consolidated and developed by the state, and the development of the non-public economy shall be encouraged, supported and guided".

Practice has proved that starting from the reality of China's economic development, developing the non-public economy is not an expedient measure but an important way to protect and develop productivity. Therefore, the non-public economy is recognized as an important part of China's socialist basic economic system and ought to develop side by side with the public sector. With the continuous deepening of reforms, the resource allocation methods in China have gone through a transformation, and the private economy (non-public economy) has gained a "constitutional status", that is, it is defined as an important part of the socialist economy in the Constitution. On the one hand, the reform practice inspired us to realize how to fully mobilize the enthusiasm of various social subjects to carry out production activities and the direct practical significance of the development of the non-public economy in accelerating the development of productivity. On the other hand, the development of a non-public economy also needs to be protected by the constitution and laws. The continuous revision and improvement of the content of China's Constitution precisely reflect that the principle of how to better protect and develop productivity has kept deepening based on the ownership of the means of production. When we discuss the SOE reform, we cannot talk about SOEs for their own sake; neither should we only discuss the changes in the corporate system and governance mechanism of the reform of SOEs themselves. We need to see the influence of the environment of market operation and competition mechanism of the non-public economy on the survival, growth and development of SOEs. As a form of enterprise organization with a different allocation of ownership relations, the characteristics of enterprise property rights system and operating mechanism form an external reference and inspiration for the reform of SOEs.

Returning to the discussion on the prescriptive nature of China's basic economic system, the statutory expressions of the basic economic system in both the Constitution and Party documents are inspired by the continuous deepening of practice and are important content of the socialist market economy theory with Chinese characteristics. It shows that the development of mixed ownership and the adherence to public ownership as the main body can go hand in hand. It helps to sort out the relationship between the basic economic system and the structure for economic operation, especially how to play the leading role of public ownership in the dynamic economic operation; it also helps to deal with the vitality of the basic economic system.

10.2.2 The occurrence path and development of a mixed economy in China and the innovation of the ownership realization theory

In Chapter 3 we have discussed the "introduction" method and specific path of "mixed ownership" (namely, "modern corporate system") in real life, mainly based on the historical evolution of socialized mass production, showing its characteristics of "spontaneous evolution", so that the development of the corporate system itself and the mechanism of action can easily let nature take its course. That's why Marx fully affirmed in his book *Capital*. Here mixed ownership is mentioned again to better understand China's reform and opening up practice has advanced to the new theoretical realm of "vigorously developing mixed ownership economy", and also understand why there are big differences in theory and practice.

Objectively speaking, with the development of economic activities, and considering the random diversity in technology, market and other aspects, for the acquisition and evaluation of business opportunities, newly-found enterprises choose to attract joint investment of different ownership to form mixed corporate organizations. These "new economic organizations" are easy to understand and accept and free from being elaborated too much here. However, for the existing organizational form of SOEs, the transformation from a single investor to a mixed-ownership system with multiple investments is to transform the "public" ownership system into multiple investments and to attract private capital, which will inevitably produce a cooperative relationship between "investors". Therefore, the original SOEs need to be redefined. It is precisely in this way that the concept of "state-funded enterprises" is confirmed.

Through further analysis, in the case of the operations of the assets of a mixed enterprise, the relationship between "capital contribution" and "capital use" is formed accordingly, and investors of different ownership have an "equal" status with each other in cooperation. Owners just send their property rights representatives to participate in corporate governance, and capital ownership and operation (legal person property rights and daily management rights) are separated, forming a cooperative relationship between the "property rights" subjects of different production factors and these property rights subjects at the business site. The subjects of business activities that appear at the "front-end" of enterprise decision-making are the subjects of governance activities that maintain independent "legal person property rights" and the management subjects who manage the daily business affairs of the enterprise. The derivation of the traditional ownership relationship is manifested as the property relationship of subjects. The traditional owners hide in the "backstage" of the corporate legal person ("returns" to the position of shareholders) and manage the separated capital use rights like other owners who jointly contribute capital. Here we can have a clearer understanding of the theory of ownership realization and a more objective understanding of the relationship between the two concepts of "ownership right" and "property right".

Therefore, the vigorous development of mixed ownership, as an important form of realization of the basic economic system, is conducive to various types of ownership capital to complement each other and develop together; it is definitely not to deny public ownership but to help integrate public ownership and market economy. The "worries" that the development of a mixed economy might deny public ownership is actually because some people do not understand the realization forms of ownership from the behavioral characteristics of economic activities. Similarly, the objective and scientific nature of the proposition that different investors have equal status should no longer be a problem. In other words, there should not be any privileged shareholders or super shareholders in market economic activities. The number of shares is equal, and the status of shareholders is equal. Based on this understanding, it will also help to better deal with issues related to corporate governance mechanisms.

Based on the above analysis, we can propose that the evolution from ownership right theory to property right theory is the specific manifestation and requirements of the progress of social production methods, as well as the specific manifestation of social system innovation. The development and evolution of the property rights system are in line with the level of productivity development. Since the independent existence of property rights is manifested as the contribution ability of certain production factors, such ability may be direct labor ability or it may appear in the form of material and non-material (intellectual) assets such as technology and information. They all reflect a certain property right relationship and are allocated through a certain property right system. It is in this way that the concept of property rights can be universalized. Thus, the property rights system has become the cornerstone of modern economic organization. The above analysis also inspires us to come out of the traditional ownership theory, separate the ownership right from the use right of capital, integrate with the actual economic operation, and understand the innovative significance of the "division of labor" in the ownership realization. In particular, it is necessary to use the property right theory to discuss the efficiency of capital allocation and corporate governance mechanisms.

10.2.3 How to view the nature of economic system of "mixed enterprises" (mixed economy)?

Mixed-economy refers to an economic form in which property rights belong to different owners. At the macro level, mixed economy refers to the non-uniformity of the ownership structure of a country or region. That is, in the ownership structure, there are state-owned, collective and other public-owned economies, as well as individual, private, and foreign-owned non-public economies, as well as joint-venture and cooperative economies with state-owned and collective components. At the micro-level, it refers to the enterprises jointly funded by investors of different ownership.

As mentioned earlier, the vigorous development of a mixed economy and adherence to public ownership are two issues at different levels. However, the long-standing thinking inertia on ownership relations has caused us to probe into the nature of specific mixed enterprises and classify them in the binary division of public and private enterprises. Such thinking really bothers us because "public or private" is linked to the bottom line of choosing "socialism or capitalism". Therefore, there issues of how to view the nature of an economic system of specific "mixed" enterprises and whether it is necessary to determine their nature.

There are lots of different theories on the determination of the nature of the mixed economy in Chinese academic circles. They can be roughly divided into "controlling" theory, non-"public" non-"private" theory and "public ownership" theory. Those who hold the "controlling" theory believe that the mixed economy is a kind of "controlling" economy. The shareholding system, an important form of property rights organization in the modern market economy, is the most typical. Its nature is defined as "neither the traditional public economy nor is it a typical capitalist economy with private ownership". A mixed economy is actually a form of asset organization, and its nature is determined by the nature of the ownership of the assets that hold the controlling position in its components.[7] Those who hold the non-"public" non-"private" theory believe that the mixed economy itself is an independent economic form that is not "public" or "private". It coexists with various forms of ownership; it has independent property rights. And its own laws of evolution and development, along with private ownership, were produced in the process of transition from primitive public ownership to private ownership; and emphasize that the mixed economy is neither a public economy nor a private economy, but a non-"public" non-"private", and a new property ownership structure formed by the amalgamation of public property right and non-public property right inside an enterprise.[8] Scholars who hold the view of "public ownership" believe that the economic nature of ownership depends on the nature of the basic economic system in the final analysis. Therefore, the dominant position of the public economy in the mixed economy determines the nature of public ownership.[9]

Since the mixed economy is a complex organic system from both the macro and the micro-level, to define the nature of the mixed p economy, it is necessary to analyze its complicated internal structure and grasp its principal contradiction and its principal aspects. As a form of capital of modern enterprises, a mixed economy is not the ultimate ownership itself, nor the specific form of ownership, but the realization form of ownership in terms of capital combination. Therefore, considering it at a secondary level compared to the classification of public and private ownership, the mixing of different economic components does not in itself stipulate the nature of mixed ownership, and there is no need to determine the nature of mixed enterprises. Moreover, at the micro-level, the dynamics of the property rights structure determine the complexity and dynamics of the economic nature of mixed ownership.

Mixed ownership is the ownership relationship manifested in capital use occasions. According to the theory of legal person property rights in modern companies, the assets of companies are owned by shareholder investors. Still, under the arrangement of the modern property rights system, investors cannot arbitrarily withdraw their assets from companies according to the capital contribution contract, unless all shareholders agree to close the business and wind up the companies. The companies (capital users) can only cancel their legal person status and no longer exist. However, when an individual investor (shareholder) wants to withdraw from the position of investor (shareholder), he can only go to the secondary market to find a new investor (shareholder) who is willing to take over his investor. The original investor (shareholder) can redeem the capital contribution only when they are traded and settled at an agreed asset price (equity selling value). The transaction price of equity trading is affected by market fluctuations, and there is a certain degree of uncertainty. Due to the existence of the secondary market for investor rights, stock trading has become an investment behavior in real economic life. With the influence of market, technology and other factors, the price of equity will fluctuate so that the number of investors holding shares of specific mixed enterprises changes, and the identity of shareholders who actually hold equity also changes. Therefore, the determination on the nature of specific mixed enterprises is difficult to be stable, which makes proceeding determination on nature lose its necessary and significance. Taking into account the equality of investors in the business environment of enterprises, it is meaningless to discuss the nature of specific mixed enterprises alone.

10.3 Fair capital pricing in the process of mixed-ownership reform to prevent the loss of state-owned assets

Actively developing a mixed economy, to a large extent, is to allow existing SOEs to draw investment of social capital, which is in essence correlated to the openness of industry access. This gives rise to two issues: how to maintain stable and fair industry access and how to maintain objective and fair equity valuation and consideration. Owing to long-standing administrative barriers, there are bound to be unreasonable gains from monopolistic pricing of products and services provided by an industry, which requires that the way to widen industry access must be open and public rather than closed and directed. Then a prominent problem comes to the surface: when we absorb social capital through public bidding and call auction, we must guard against the loss of state-owned assets caused by unreasonable pricing. If the assets are priced too high, it will be too difficult to find suitable buyers in the market. But if the assets are priced too low, which is likened to "fire-sale prices", it may lead to loss of state-owned assets. In a word, a reasonable pricing mechanism is the key that ensures the mixed-ownership reform of SOEs to form a virtuous and orderly investment cycle.

With the inevitable cyclical characteristics of economic operation, enterprises need to manage and coordinate the flow and reorganization of resources. Therefore, the entry and exit of state-owned assets should be the norm in the operation of the market economy. Such a mobile reorganization of the property rights market is actually a production factor property rights market. Such a market is relatively underdeveloped in China. The insufficient development of this market has restricted the implementation of mixed-ownership reform in the use of "reduction of the proportion of state-owned stock, incremental stock offering" to attract new entrants, and any improper handling will lead to "assets loss" or "profits transfer". It can be seen that the promotion of mixed-ownership reform is subject to various supporting conditions. Regardless of the relevant conditions, the pursuit of formal "mixing" can easily lead to the loss of state-owned assets, such as inaccurate pricing and "profits transfer".

The mixed-ownership reform of SOEs is not only a mixture of state-owned capital and private capital in companies' property rights structure but also a mixture of state-owned capital and private capital at the industrial level, especially to improve the level of market competition in monopolistic fields, some formerly monopolistic industries controlled by state capital began to absorb social capital. This kind of industry mix has increased the difficulty of state-owned assets pricing. Although asset pricing mechanisms and pricing theories in competitive industries have been relatively mature, scientific and reliable pricing methods have not yet been formed in monopolistic industries. In actual work, due to the constraints of supporting conditions, the work in promoting the mixed-ownership has generally opened up, but there are still many unsatisfactory places. On May 21, 2014, the NDRC unveiled 80 investment projects of mixed ownership system. As a result of the first round of implementation, only 28 projects have achieved the objective of mixed-ownership reform.

Here we try to discuss the mixed reform of the oil product sales business of Sinopec, which is a demonstration of the mixed-ownership reform of central SOEs. The mixed reform of the Sinopec Sales Company introduced a total of 29.99% of social and private capital. The specific work has gone through three stages:

In the first stage, Sinopec completed its business restructuring and started asset evaluation. In February 2014, Sinopec announced that it would take the lead in introducing social and private capital into its oil product sales business to achieve mixed operations. In addition, the chairman of the board of directors had the right to determine the final investors, terms of participation, implementation procedures and other related matters if the social and private capital held no more than 30% of the equity. In April 2014, Sinopec merged the entire sales business into Sinopec Sales Company and completed the business reorganization. At the same time, four large domestic and foreign investment banks, including China International Capital Corporation (CICC), Deutsche Bank Group, CITIC Securities, and Bank of America Group, were appointed as financial advisors.

In the second stage, the assets auditing and evaluation work was completed and the work of attracting investment was started. The work of attracting investment was carried out through multiple rounds of screening and competitive negotiations. First of all, investor qualification certification for those showing investment intention was carried out. Subsequently, investors were organized to conduct two rounds of binding and non-binding quotations. Sinopec formed an independent review committee composed of experts from the company and the industry and comprehensively considered the investors' quotation, investment scale, and investors' industry background, and the shortlist of investors was finalized in August 2014.

The third stage was the stage for negotiation and settlement. The two parties negotiated the Sinopec Sales Company's future equity transfer, capital increase and share expansion agreement, company articles of association, and listing arrangements. On September 12, 2014, 25 domestic and foreign investors subscribed to Sinopec for the purchase of 29.99% of its shares for 107.094 billion yuan (including equivalent US dollars), clarifying the rights and obligations of state-owned and private capital owners. So far, the registered capital of Sinopec Sales Company has increased from 20 billion yuan to 28.567 billion yuan, completing the mixed-ownership transformation of wholly SOEs.

In terms of the characteristics of the reform advancement and the actual results, it has shown relatively good results in achieving the objective of the mixed-ownership reform. According to relevant data,[10] the author believes that two aspects are worthy of further discussion. On the one hand, China implements a special management mechanism for oil prices. Under this premise, how to open access to the sales link and allow other social capital to enter investment operations does not have complete opening conditions in a sense. On the other hand, in terms of actually getting investment opportunities and becoming shareholders of this round of mixed reform, the 25 shareholders are mainly business-related companies of Sinopec. The superposition of these two factors makes "outsiders" feel that the company was reforming for only the reform's sake.

Objectively speaking, the pricing of state-owned assets is not as simple as to be completely left to the market for decision. This is mainly because SOEs not only involve the issue of fairness for the whole society but also involve the interests of the central and local governments. and at the same time, they must consider the industry factors in which they are located. After two rounds of reforms by delegating powers and transferring profits, and invigorating large enterprises and relaxing control over small ones, several large-scale central enterprise groups with strong market positions have been formed in basic industries (energy and communications) and service industries. In theory, such a strong market position must be priced with a corresponding premium. The following table lists the distribution of state-owned assets in various industries. Among them, industrial sectors, social services, and transportation are the industries with the most state-owned capital coverage, and the petrochemical industry is the most important industrial sector (Table 10.1).

From the perspective of game theory, there are two games in the process of mixed-ownership reform. One is the game between governments at all levels, and the other is the game between the government and private investors. Out of "self-rationality," local governments mainly aim to improve officials' performance and raise local taxes when attracting investment. Although the Central Government can play a role in policy guidance, its interests are not the goal of local governments to maximize. Especially when attracting foreign investment, the competition among local governments for

Table 10.1 Distribution of state-owned assets by industry (unit: billion yuan)

Year	Industrial	Construction	Real estate	Transportation	Posts and telecommunications	Social service	Others
2002	3,166.4	196.8	146.5	886.9	738.2	618.4	616.9
2003	3,350	178.2	150.7	981.6	791.3	737.9	660.6
2004	3,463.8	193.7	206.1	1,047.2	841.2	833.8	732.4
2005	3,996.1	224	251.4	1,211.6	902.7	1,103.2	833.6
2006	4,445.3	287.3	359.5	1,351.9	1,048.9	1,161.3	1,002.5
2007	5,643.7	399.4	414.2	1,559	1,082.8	1,429.1	881.5
2008	6,455.8	559.8	638.8	1,816.8	1,074.3	1,496.3	929.3
2009	7,341.0	766.6	756.9	2,231.8	1,117.3	2,164.9	1,112
2010	14,248.8	1,414.4	2,043.0	6,267.9	3,341.3	5,901.2	3,276.7
2011	18,583.2	2,052	2,515.5	7,391.3	3,916.3	7,422.5	4,547
2012	21,067	2,753.9	3,214.8	9,024.5	4,152.1	9,404.2	5,506.7
2013	23,419.2	3,331	4,450.3	10,198	4,279.2	11,009.1	6,507.2
2014	23,237.9	3,284.2	3,975.9	5,166.8	4,230.7	10,540.4	5,431.2
2015	23,481.1	4,027.2	4,935.2	6,239.3	4,320.7	14,122.8	6,753.4

Note: All the data are excerpted from the statistical yearbooks from 2002 to 2015.

projects has become more intense. The game between the government and private investors is not only reflected in the different quotations of assets by the two parties but also in the agreement of many terms such as the company's articles of association and the rights and obligations of the parties in the future.

In terms of the production line and industrial chain layout, there are two ways for private capital to participate in SOEs: horizontal and vertical. Horizontal equity participation refers to holding shares in companies that produce the same goods or provide the same services. This method is relatively common among financial service industries (such as banks, insurance, and trust companies). Vertical equity participation refers to equity investment in companies upstream and downstream of the industrial chain to reduce transaction costs when purchasing raw materials and selling commodities, thereby achieving vertical integration. The direct result of the cross-holding of multiple companies is equity diversification, which creates synergies in company management and finance. If the private investor manages the enterprise more efficiently than the state-owned investor, then the management level of the SOE will be improved after receiving the private investment. Of course, this is based on the fact that both parties have equal rights to operate in accordance with the shares they hold, which is the basis of the modern corporate system.

It should be said that the relevant factors involved in advancing the mixed-ownership reform are relatively complicated, subject to market conditions and industry characteristics, as well as differences in the work methods of collaborators, which may directly affect the cooperative consideration, resulting in inconsistent pricing of state-owned assets and unreasonable "loss" of state-owned assets, which is something that we must attach great importance to in our work. This is also the proper meaning of maintaining the basic characteristics of state-owned assets. In the final analysis, the direction of advancing mixed-ownership reform as a new "breakthrough point" for SOE reform has been fully understood and recognized and based on the experience gained in pilot projects, and it is necessary to coordinate reform measures to accelerate market growth so as to obtain the comprehensive results of mixed-ownership reform.

Notes

1 American economist Douglas C. North incorporated institutional factors into the explanation of economic growth in the study of economic history and distinguished institutional changes into two types: "inducible" and "compulsive". His theory of new economic history and institutional change made him one of the representatives of new institutional economics, and he won the Nobel Prize in Economics in 1993 for this reason.

2 *Pioneer experiment of state-owned enterprise reform – Shougang's contracting system.* http://www.sino-ma.org/djgds.asp?id=323.

3 Deng, X. P. (1993). Excerpts from talks given in Wuchang, Shenzhen, Zhuhai and Shanghai. *Selected works of Deng Xiaoping* (Vol. 3, p. 373). Beijing: People's Publishing House.

4 Xi, J. P. (2014). *Speech at a study session on implementing the decisions of the Third Plenary Session of the 18th CPC Central Committee on comprehensively deepening the reform, attended by officials at the provincial/ministerial level.* Retrieved February 17, 2014, from https://www.ccps.gov.cn/xxsxk/xldxgz/201908/t20190829_133857.shtml

5 *Decision of the CPC Central Committee on some major issues concerning comprehensively deepening the reform.* (2013). Retrieved November 15, 2013, from http://www.scio.gov.cn/zxbd/nd/2013/document/1374228/1374228_1.htm

6 Li, T. Q. (2018). *What changes has the Constitution of New China gone through since the founding of the People's Republic of China.* Retrieved May 4, 2018, from http://www.mzyfz.com/cms/benwangzhuanfang/xinwenzhongxin/zuixinbaodao/html/1040/2018-05-04/content-1332935.html

7 Sun, Z. W. (2014). Accurately understand "making mixed economy an important realization form of basic economic system". *Leading Journal of Ideological & Theoretical Education*, Issue 8.

8 Ding, X. L. (1998). On mixed ownership. *Academic Monthly*, Issue 6.

9 He, Z. L. (2014). Mixed economy: Nature, purpose and fundamental direction. *Frontiers*, Issue 9.

10 *Sinopec's mixed-ownership reform.* https://baike.baidu.com/item/%E4%B8%AD%E7%9F%B3%E5%8C%96%E6%B7%B7%E6%94%B9%E9%A1%B9%E7%9B%AE/16927595?fr=aladdin

Epilogue

From the perspective of political economics, this book takes enterprises as the microscopic subject of resource allocation in the operation of social reproduction economy, or as a micro-organization carrier ("platform") for resource allocation, which fits the positioning enterprise system as the "central link" or "central position" of the entire economic system structure, and facilitates a panoramic review of China's SOE reform in the past 40 years. We use time as a clue to examine the work content of the different stages of SOE reform in order to discover how the continuous deepening of reform advancement is carried out, how the measures at different stages are put in place, and how the purpose of these measures is realized, thus we will have a deeper understanding of the reform actions and the achieved results. The relevant discussions centered on the adjustment of the relationship between the government and enterprises, based on the "reform and opening up" policy set by the Third Plenary Session of the 11th CPC Central Committee, especially the *Decision on Reform of the Economic Structure* adopted by the Third Plenary Session of the 12th CPC Central Committee makes "enhancing the vitality of enterprises" as the "central link" of the entire economic structural reform, so as to resolve the crux of lacking enterprise vitality, get rid of the highly-centralized and "uniform revenue and unified expenditure" economic management model prevailing in the planned economic era, "delegate powers and transfer profits" to enterprises to simulate their enthusiasm, form the lever mechanism that stimulates the vitality of the enterprise's operation by changing interest relations, form the "inductive" force for the reform of the enterprise leadership management system, enterprise organization system and enterprise economic system, promote the continuous deepening of reforms, and continuously improve the corporate system in line with China's reality.

While examining the process of SOE reform, it is not difficult to find that, on the one hand, the government delegates powers to enterprises so that they can use certain autonomous management rights to generate "unplanned" "market behavior"; on the other hand, by combining the practice of adjusting the price of agricultural and sideline products and non-staple food subsidy for urban workers in the initial stage of reform, the commodity-currency relationship of urban-rural exchange behavior was introduced, so as to determine the "market orientation" of economic restructuring. The economic rationality of the subjects of social economy and the concept of economic accounting were recognized and highlighted, giving birth to the business environment that market grows, forming the "endogenous" force that drives the mutual promotion of enterprise reform and market development, transforming the "state-owned" model of enterprises, and forming the theoretical innovation of "state ownership and independent operation of enterprises". With the enhancement of enterprises' own consciousness of independent interests, while centering on how to scientifically handle the interest relationship between the government and enterprises, the SOE reform has successively gone through two steps of "profits to tax" and "contract system". The entire economic structural reform was specified to pursue the goal of "establishing a socialist market economy". On this basis, it is further proposed to shape the enterprise into a completely independent market entity of the modern corporate system, standardize and consolidate the results of enterprise reform in legal forms, and transform the traditional "state-owned" enterprises into "state-funded" enterprises and completely independent market entities.

From this, we can clearly see the internal logic between the reform advancement phases. Through this logic, we can better understand how enterprise reform can promote changes in various aspects of the entire economic structural reform and the resources of the whole society. The changes in the methods of resource allocation include the development of the market for factors of production (including labor, capital, land, and technology), changes in product pricing methods, adjustments in the relationship between government and enterprises, changes in tax collection and administration; changes in tax collection and management and tax structure, the relationships between government and capital management and between government and enterprises, industrial access and investment approval management methods. In particular, it is necessary to point out that international business rules have been introduced for opening up and attracting foreign capital investment, forming an external reference to the traditional economic system and incremental reform.

All these aspects converge to form a strong force for reform to drive the Chinese economy forward. In this process, the deeper impact on China's economy and society is also manifested in the changes in the employment methods and employment concepts of residents. At the same time, it is also manifested in adapting to the practical requirements of economic system reform to produce new economic theories and theoretical innovations. It can also better guide and lead to the continuous deepening of reforms.

The efforts of SOE reform in institutional innovation have laid a micro foundation for the overall transformation of the economic system. Objectively speaking, as the subjects of concrete undertaking and execution of social reproduction activities, their organizational form and institutional arrangements must be compatible with the specific characteristics of the socialist market economic system. Taking the modern corporate system as the specific organizational form has become the micro foundation for building the socialist market economy system. With the institutional positioning of such microeconomic entities, other aspects of the economic system also have specific service targets and supporting benchmarks for their own system functions. It also reflects the scientific positioning of the corporate system reform as the "central link" of the entire economic system reform and reflects the organic connection between the corporate system and other aspects of the economic system's institutional arrangements and the development of coordinated supporting functions.

As for traditional SOEs, they should get rid of the administrative status of "appendant" of government and the "state-owned" state in production activities under the planned economic system. The government should separate from enterprises by "delegating powers and transferring profits" to them, which will give SOEs a new way of survival to adapt to the requirements of the market economy. By building SOEs into modern companies, their relationship with the government will be further adjusted and regulated, forming a market-oriented relationship between "investment" and "invested", shaping a new division of labor between "nominal capital" and "real capital", and enabling the investment capital to be in the form of equity (shares) of companies. Therefore, the traditional ownership relationship of the means of production of SOEs in dynamic business activities is manifested in the "property rights" relationship between the specific allocation of capital and other factors of production, that is, "transform" the concept and meaning of property rights from ownership (as a general theoretical understanding of economic nature and legal definition) to the factors property rights for resource allocation in social reproduction and dynamic economic operation, which helps to better deal with the relationship between public ownership and the market economy. It is precisely in this way that we have a clearer and more effective institutional arrangement for the innovation of public ownership. It helps to better allocate state-owned capital according to the needs of economic and social development, combine with the characteristics of industrial technology, consciously manage the allocation of public capital in specific social reproduction activities and different links of the industrial system, maintain the ability of public capital to regulate and guide social reproduction, and form a main working mechanism of capital management operation in the dynamic process of national economic operation. Furthermore, in specific situations of capital allocation, a brand-new cooperative relationship is formed between public-owned capital and other social capital, that is, a mixed economy, which in turn generates a modern corporate governance structure.

We can better understand the relationship between investors' "market-oriented" capital investment behavior and the mixed economic entities that receive investment (that is, the subject of capital use), and clearly obtain "adherence to public ownership" and "vigorous development of a mixed economy" can go hand in hand. The capital contributor and capital user are on two different levels of business behavior. Based on this theoretical analysis, understanding the legal person "ownership" undertaken by the mixed enterprise subject can be clearly distinguished from the state "ownership". They are two "ownership (rights)" with different levels and different meanings. It is precisely because of the existence of such differences that the "ownership" of "property rights" expressed by the mixed enterprise subjects (objectively speaking, in market operations, corporate enterprises will also have "capital ownership" of foreign investment behaviors) are known as "legal person property rights". In other words, a mixed enterprise is a legal person enterprise formed by the joint cooperation of different types of capital contributors. The assets and rights of the legal person enterprise are ultimately the "investors". The "investors" exercise the right to contribute capital in accordance with the rules of the market economy and cooperate with the corporate legal person, thus forming a certain market-based contract relationship between them and a relationship between two market subjects.

Based on the above discussion, we will inevitably raise the question of who will be the investor of state-owned capital. As everyone knows, the SASAC, as a special agency of the State Council, assumes the role of state-owned asset owners on behalf of the State Council. However, since the "investment" in the operation of state-owned assets is a market behavior, the SASAC's direct action obviously exists as the contradiction between the supervision and management of the whole society's state-owned capital and the investment behavior, confusing the roles of "referees" and "athletes". Therefore, it is necessary to sort out the functions of the SASAC, separate its operational capital contributions, and authorize state-owned capital investment or operating companies to enter the market as a state-owned capital investment and operation entity to perform the function of "investor". It can be seen that the deepening of SOE reform has put forward requirements for supporting reforms of the state-owned assets management system, and the establishment of state-owned capital management companies (or investment and operation companies) has become an important task for the deepening of reforms.

According to the *Decision on Some Major Issues Concerning Comprehensively Deepening the Reform*,[1] "We will improve the state-owned assets management system, strengthen state-owned assets oversight with capital management at the core, reform the authorized operation mechanism for state-owned capital, establish a number of state-owned capital operating companies, support qualified SOEs to reorganize themselves into state-owned capital investment companies". The state-owned capital operating companies function as pure holding companies specialized in state-owned capital investment operations, similar to Singapore's Temasek, to isolate the relationship between the government and ordinary enterprises. They are SOEs with special functions, and we can regard them as a "sovereign investment fund". As a result, a three-level and new state-owned capital management system (the SASAC – state-owned capital operating companies – state-funded companies) has been constructed, which will also help state-owned capital management to successfully shift from "assets management" to "capital management". The concepts of "assets" and "capital" are different in terms of category and carrier: "assets" have the carrier of corporate organization and are subject to the specific persons, properties and affairs of the specific enterprise that undertakes production and business activities; "capital" is the value object, according to the requirements of value preservation and appreciation goals, capital can flow more flexibly, which helps to improve the efficiency of capital operation. Furthermore, as a capital investment behavior, the complete rights of investors should also include the right to "exit", forming complete investor rights for investment entry, transfer and exit. This is also the proper meaning of solving the problem of improving the vitality of state-owned capital operation, and it is also an important content of the theory and practice of focusing on improving the influence and anti-risk ability of state-owned capital. It also helps to better realize the change in the management of state-owned assets from "assets management" to "capital management".

To establish state-owned capital operating companies that specifically exercise the rights of state-owned capital "investors", it is necessary to establish the final investor accounts of state-owned capital so as to clarify the multi-level investment relationship that may be continuously derived in market operations. The concept of "ultimate owner" naturally comes down to the multi-level governments' authorization of the establishment of state-owned capital operating companies and the multiple levels of ownership of state capital. Compared with the multi-level state-owned capital account represented by this vertical administrative hierarchy, there may be a chain of corporate investment behavior horizontally. Looking at the state-owned capital operating companies authorized by the government as the initial (first) investor of state-owned capital and other mixed enterprises jointly funded by social capital, such mixed enterprises may face new investment opportunities, which may lead to the emergence of an investment chain of corporate investment. Such investment behavior has practical significance for us to follow up and discuss the understanding of corporate governance theory and practice. According to the characteristics of corporate governance of "clear property rights and clear rights and responsibilities", the rights and responsibilities of corporate governance in practice must be manifested between the investment and the "party" being invested. The content of corporate governance guidelines and governance behaviors (rights) are divided among the shareholders (investor) meetings, a board of directors, and day-to-day operators in accordance with the written governance guidelines that have clearly defined the investment scale and the number of rights, forming a responsibility chain between "parties" without the intervention or participation of indirect parties who cross the investment chain.

To emphasize the identity of the "party" of corporate governance, it is necessary to further discuss the representatives of state-owned capital property rights: how to select, delegate, and assess the management of "agents" in the new state-owned capital management system. It is necessary to train and cultivate a group of specialized talents who are specifically responsible for the management of state-owned capital, and together with the daily operation and management talents of corporate enterprises, constitute an important work content for the development and construction of an entrepreneur market for modern company operation and management. With the help of the talent market, we can discover the value of talents and gradually form an incentive and restraint mechanism for the daily management talents of state-owned capital management and mixed enterprises. By opening to the outside world, we have learned the business rules of a mature market economy in our investment and trade exchanges and improved our adaptability; at the same time, as the subject of competition, the private capital gradually grew up in the domestic open market and competed with SOEs, which has improved the governance structure and efficiency of modern corporate operation. As the "party" of corporate governance, entrepreneurs play a crucial role in this regard, which highlights the special status and role of entrepreneurs as a special factor of production. The role of entrepreneurs as a special and scarce factor of production requires a deeper understanding. The above discussion shows that the reform of SOEs and the reform of the state-owned capital management system, as two different objects, have a related linkage relationship with each other. Through the organizational form of mixed enterprises, capitals of different ownership jointly invest so that public capital and non-public capital can complement each other, promote each other, and develop side by side. It can better exert the influence and control of state-owned capital and improve the operational vitality and anti-risk ability of state-owned capital. It also helps to better handle the organic integration of state-owned capital with the market economy, better realize the market-oriented allocation and operation of state-owned capital, and become an important way for materializing the basic socialist economic system.

Based on the scientific and accurate positioning of SOE reform, the continuous deepening of reform has its own internal logic. Studies have found that this logic has special theoretical and practical significance for our confidence and determination to carry out the reform to the end. Following this logic, it is necessary to further strengthen the construction and improvement of the modern corporate system in practice, focus on the work principles of adhering to and improving the basic economic system, and work hard on corporate system specifications, functions and operational quality, and finally have it implemented to protect enterprises to achieve more stable development, and foster world-class enterprises with global competitiveness with the support of systems. The internal logic of SOE reform and the accumulated experience of reform practice have been incorporated into the results of enterprise theory with Chinese characteristics, which is an important part of the socialist economic theory with Chinese characteristics. This theoretical wealth, together with multiple dimensions of characteristics and contents of the basic economic system and the resource allocation organizations for social reproduction, will constitute organic and dynamic system optimization and co-integration capabilities, thereby guiding the economic behavior of enterprises to have sufficient vitality and then endows realistic socialism with fresh vitality.

Note

1 *Decision of the Central Committee of the Communist Party of China on some major issues concerning comprehensively deepening the reform* (p. 9). (2013). Beijing: People's Publishing House.

Afterword

In recent years, I've been thinking about writing a book to commemorate the 40th anniversary of China's reform and opening up. After a period of concentration on writing in combination with my teaching and research practices, I've finally accomplished this "top priority".

I shall first thank Deng Xiaoping, who strongly advocated to resume the national college entrance examination. His insistence enabled millions of young people to access higher education, and I was lucky enough to be admitted by Fudan University with a major in economics after spending 5 years doing manual work in the countryside. My thanks also go to all my mentors in the university who imparted knowledge of economics to me without reservation. At that time, the specialized courses in the Department of Economics were taught by a cluster of masters, including Jiang Xuemo, Wu Feidan, Song Chengxian, Xia Yande, Chen Guanlie, Hong Wenda, Chen Shaowen, Jiang Jiajun, Zhang Xunhua, Wu Bailin, Hong Yuanpeng and Ye Shichang. I even attended the lectures given by senior economists such as Qi Qisheng and Zhu Bokang. The college students of my generation were blessed to learn from so many "masters". Their international vision, professional knowledge, Chinese traditional cultural attainments, meticulous logical thinking, and strong capability in language organization and expression are lifelong benefits of ours. They closely combined with China's national conditions when teaching knowledge of economics, and they were open-minded to introduce western microeconomics and macroeconomic when interpreting the Sinicization of Marxist economic theory. They could always bring us the dynamics of world economic theories, thus making us remain at the frontiers of economic theories and practices and helping us build a body of professional knowledge in economics.

I'm grateful to the great era of reform and opening up in which I came to realize the power of theories from social practices and communication with the real world in addition to the knowledge in books, and gradually cultivated the feelings of nation and country and the sense of social responsibility. I'm grateful to the CPC, which has been adhering to the policy of reform and opening up and leading the people across the country to continuously forge ahead, thus giving me an opportunity to join in theoretical research and policy design related to the great reforms after I became a teacher. I'm grateful to my parents, who have not only brought me up but also taught me to be loyal to the Party and the government and maintain a pure heart all the time.

The 40 years' reform and opening up is a magnificent process where there are numerous remarkable cases in all aspects of reform worthy of intensive study. We shall inherit and carry forward the academic tradition and work style of predecessor economists, integrate with the realistic conditions of China, and "stick to our original intention, absorb foreign ideas, and look into the future". Every contemporary Chinese economist, including our Fudan people, must assume our responsibility to call collective wisdom into full pay to further advance the reforms.

In addition to organizing the composition of a series of books to commemorate the 40th anniversary of reform and opening up, I am also the author of one of these books on China's SOE reform. While preparing for this book, I consulted relevant literature to draw on important judgments and conclusions. For example, I referred to my book *The Logic of China's State-owned Enterprise Reform*, which was published by Shanxi Economic Publishing House in 1998 to commemorate the 20th anniversary of reform and opening up. This book combs the internal logic of China's enterprise reform and argues that the adjustment of the relationship between the government and enterprises is a "principal line" of China's economic restructuring. Through adjustment of the government-enterprise relationship, we can activate the rationality of enterprises with "interest constraint", then gradually replace it with standardized "contract constraint" and identify enterprises as independent legal entities, and eventually look for legal norms that constitute "institutional constraint" of the government-enterprise relationship. In the "Outlook" of this book, there are suggestions for deepening the reforms by "diverting more state-owned assets into powerful industries" and "outstanding entrepreneurs". Moreover, based on the knowledge that "invigorating enterprises" and "invigorating the state-owned economy" is, in essence, to "invigorate state-owned capital", this book discusses the underlying problem of how to "integrate state-owned capital with the market economy", and stresses that the enterprise vitality should be boiled down to "capital vitality". In another book of mine *Study on the Structural Adjustment of State-owned Stock Capital*, which was co-authored with Prof. Deng Ting and published by Fudan University Press in 1999, I have distinguished "state-owned assets" from "state-owned capital", and proposed that we should pay great attention to the concept of "capital" and to the construction of a capital management system. In this book, there is a conceived state-owned capital management model which features "value-based management, equity allocation, privatization governance, and market-based flow" and gives flow flexibility to state-owned capital. Since the owner's equity and responsibility relationship in business operation activities are manifested in the concrete "property rights and responsibility relationship", it is related to the connection between the property rights relationship and the "ownership of means of production" that is valued by traditional political-economic theories. This issue seems to be back on track with political economics research. In my book *Jumping out of the Restricted Zone of Ownership: An Analysis of Modern Enterprise Property Rights Theory*, published by Shanghai Translation Publishing House in 1994, I have also discussed and distinguished "ownership" and "property rights". It can be seen that there is a broad space for making theoretical explanations and innovations from the political-economic perspective. It seems to me that political economics is always a fascinating discipline.

In 2008, the global financial crisis broke out, which posed severe challenges to existing economic theories and aroused my interest in the comparison of different economic theories. Combining with the 30 years' reform and opening-up experiences, I've realized how to raise the successful experience of reform and opening up to the theoretical level to become an important component of China's "cultural soft power". To this end, it is necessary to "sum up experience from successful cases and learn from experiences, make summarization and generate new conceptual categories, and discover the logical connections between the accumulation of conceptual categories and form a category system, thus contributing wisdom to the innovation of the theory of socialism with Chinese characteristics.

I have successively published related papers on the "Economic Effects of Soft Power" and the interpretation of China's rise and construction of "Chinese Economics". In 2015, I was assigned to take over the work of the political economy teaching and research and given the opportunity to design and plan the development of Fudan political economy disciplines. It was at the time when General Secretary Xi Jinping proposed to innovate and develop a socialist political economy with Chinese characteristics and "open up a new realm of Marxism". I joined Fudan's political economy teaching and research team, organized discussions and exchanges, published relevant results and planned to come out with a series of books on the theme of commemorating the 40th anniversary of reform and opening up.

The theme of SOE reform discussed in this book has always been a hot topic in China's economic theory circles. How to understand the public relations of production, how to position it, and what significance does its prescription have for the nature of the national economic system? How to allocate public production relations and make them efficient or "more efficient"? How to integrate public production relations with the market economy? How to deal with the relationship between the government and enterprises in terms of industrial access, employment, taxation, accounting, and market competition in business activities? What impact will different treatment methods have on economic and social construction and social order? The content of these topics can be described as "high-end"; however, "high-end" ultimately needs to be expressed and reflected in the actual resource allocation and economic operation; that is to say, it must be "down to earth".

In the discussion in this book, although I always want to explain things thoroughly, there are always limitations in personal understanding, and there are inaccuracies and incompleteness. I would be grateful if readers may point them out. Please contact me via my email: hmzhang@fudan.edu.cn.

It should be noted that while I was writing this book, some graduate students of mine held rounds of discussions with me on all issues about China's SOE reform. In addition to introducing them to read relevant literature, I also hope that I could write down all my knowledge in this regard to prompt them to understand the actual process of enterprise reform and the positive effects and facilitate them to gain theoretical training and academic ability in participating in problem research. I must thank them for collecting materials for me and they have even written down their own thinking to be a supplement of my writing. Liu Rujia and Wan Jianjun, Chen Xin, Zhang Jun, Jing Wenjuan, Cheng Xi, Ding Yuanxuan, thank you very much. Some of them have combined the research content with the topic selection of their dissertation and have embarked on in-depth studies. Being able to do research work together with my students, we can learn from each other, which is also the unique achievement of being a teacher.

Deputy editor-in-chief Xu Huiping and Editor Qi Yasi of Fudan University Press, I really appreciate their professionalism and meticulous work attitude. They put forward suggestions for polishing the expressions and language style of my book, thus making it more brilliant. I would like to express my heartfelt thanks to them.

Zhang Huiming
Fudan University,
December 1, 2018

Bibliography

Black, B. S., Jang, H., & Kim, W. (2006). Predicting firms' corporate governance choices: Evidence from Korea. *Journal of Corporate Finance, 12*(3), 660–691.

Bo, Y. B. (1991). *Review of some major decisions and events* (Vol. 1). Beijing: CPC Central Party School Press.

Brouwer, M. T. (2002). Weber, Schumpeter and Knight on entrepreneurship and economic development. *Journal of Evolutionary Economics, 12*(1–2), 83–105.

Cai, F. (2010). *Economic essays of Cai Fang*. Beijing: China Times Economic Publishing House.

CCTV. (2010). *The power of corporations*. Taiyuan: Shanxi Education Press.

Chang, X. Z. (2017). An outline of China's mixed-ownership economy. *Academics, 10*, 16–35.

Chen, B. L., Zhang, H. M., & Li, Y. J. (2004). *The process and thinking of taking the lead in exploring: Review and outlook of Shanghai's state-owned assets management system reform*. Shanghai: Shanghai People's Publishing House.

Chen, J. G. (2001). *Incentives and constraints of state-owned enterprise managers: Theory, demonstration and policy*. Beijing: Economic Management Press.

Chen, L. (2018). Natural monopoly and mixed-ownership reform – Based on natural experiments and cost function analysis. *Economic Research Journal, 1*, 81–96.

Chen, Q. T. (2005). Thoughts for reform of state-owned enterprises and reform of state-owned assets management system. *Review of Economic Research, 50*, 2–5.

Chen, Q. T. (2008). *Reshaping the enterprise system: 30 years' changes on China's enterprise system*. Beijing: China Development Press.

Chen, Q. T. (2014). Eight points on "re-reform" of state-owned enterprises. *State-owned Enterprises, 6*, 74–75.

Chen, Q. T. (2016). Capitalization is a breakthrough in state-owned enterprise reform. *China Finance, 4*, 17–20.

Chen, X. (1999). Development of the non-public sectors and state-owned enterprise reform. *Capital Shanghai, 11*, 22–24.

Chen, Y. (1986). New issues after the basic completion of socialist transformation. *Selected works of Chen Yun* (Vol. 3). Beijing: People's Publishing House.

Cheng, Z. P. (2006). *Thirty years of price reform (1997–2006)* (p. 648). Beijing: China Market Press.

Chi, F. L. (2013). *A full record of China's reform and opening up (1978–2012)* (p. 402). Beijing: Wuzhou Communication Press.

Chinese Entrepreneur Survey System. (2009). Business operators' understanding and evaluation of entrepreneurship – Special survey report on the growth and development of Chinese business operators in 2009. *Management World*, 6, 91–101.

Chu, M. (2017). *Government paradox, state-owned enterprise behavior and harmonious growth of China's economy*. Beijing: China Social Sciences Publishing House.

Cipolla, C. M. (2010). *Before the industrial revolution: European society and economy*. New York: Norton.

Coase, R. H. (1937). The nature of the firm. *Economica*, 4, 386–405.

Coffee, J. (1999). The future as history: The prospects for global convergence in corporate governance and its implications. *Social Science Electronic Publishing*, *93*(3), 641–707.

Commentator. (2014). *Everyone should be a qualified constructor to build the China dream*. Retrieved November 26, 2014, from http://opinion.people.com.cn/n/2014/1202/c49217-26132992.html

Communiqué of the 2016 Central Economic Work Conference. (2016). Retrieved from https://wenku.baidu.com/view/819fb0aa0342a8956bec0975f46527d3250ca657.html

Communiqué of the 2017 Central Economic Work Conference. (2017). Retrieved from https://wenku.baidu.com/view/767d6938814d2b160b4e767f5acfa1c7aa0082ec.html

Communiqué of the Third Plenary Session of the 11th CPC Central Committee. (1978). Retrieved December 22, 1978, from http://cpc.people.com.cn/GB/64162/64168/64563/65371/4441902.html

Company law of the People's Republic of China. (2014). Beijing: China Legal Publishing House.

Completing mixed-ownership reform and settlement, Sinopec Sales saw 105 billion yuan on its account. (2015). Retrieved March 7, 2015, from https://www.guancha.cn/economy/2015_03_07_311392.shtml

Constitution of the People's Republic of China. (2018). Beijing: China Legal Publishing House.

Decision of the CPC Central Committee on several major issues concerning the reform and development of state-owned enterprises. (1999). Retrieved September 22, 1999, from http://www.gcdr.gov.cn/content.html?id=16800

Decision of the CPC Central Committee on some major issues concerning comprehensively deepening the reform. (2013). Retrieved November 15, 2013, from http://www.scio.gov.cn/zxbd/nd/2013/document/1374228/1374228_1.htm

Decision on some issues concerning the establishment of the socialist market economy. (1993). Retrieved November 14, 1993, from http://www.people.com.cn/item/20years/newfiles/b1080.html

Decision on some issues concerning the improvement of the socialist market economy. (2003). Retrieved October 14, 2003, from http://jingji.cntv.cn/2012/11/05/ARTI1352087360703188.shtml

Decision the CPC Central Committee on reform of the economic structure. (1984). Retrieved October, 1984, from http://www.gov.cn/test/2008-06/26/content_1028140.htm

Department of National Accounts of National Bureau of statistics. (2004). *China national economic accounting*. Beijing: China Statistics Press.

Department of National Accounts of National Bureau of statistics. (2007). *China's balance sheet preparation method*. Beijing: China Statistics Press.

Dias, J., & Mcdermott J. (2006). Institutions, education, and development: The role of Entrepreneurs. *Journal of Development Economics*, *80*(2), 299–328.

Ding, J. T. (1982). How does Shougang Group implement the economic responsibility system? *Economic Management Journal*, 3, 15–20.

Doidge, C., Karolyi, G. A., & Stulz, R. (2004). Why do countries matter so much for corporate governance? *Journal of Financial Economics*, *86*(1), 1–39.

Dong, F. F. (1999). *The economic history of the People's Republic of China*. Beijing: Economic Science Press.

Dong, F. R. (1987). Ownership reform and economic operating mechanism reform. *Journal of Graduate School of Chinese Academy of Social Sciences*, 1, 12–21.

Durnev, A., & Kim, E. H. (2005). To steal or not to steal: Firm attributes, legal environment and valuation. *Journal of Finance*, *60*(3), 1461–1493.

Fan, L. M., Li, Q. Y., et al. (2001). *Analysis of China's local fiscal operation*. Beijing: Economic Science Press.

Fang, Y. (2017). *New road to reform of state-owned enterprises*. Beijing: China Financial & Economic Publishing House.

Fang, Z. L. (1997). It's a trend for human capital owners to have business ownership. *Economic Research Journal*, 6, 36–40.

Feng, G.F.(2001). Thinking some key problems to perfect corporate governance in china.*Modern Economic Science*, *23*(6), 23–28.

Feng, J. S., & Xu, H. Z. (2005). Analysis of the combined construction model of independent directors and supervisory boards of Chinese listed companies. *Journal of North China Electric Power University (social sciences)*, 1, 36–39.

Fisscher, O., Frenkel, D., Lurie, Y, et al. (2005). Stretching the frontiers: Exploring the relationships between entrepreneurship and ethics. *Journal of Business Ethics*, *60*(3), 207–209.

Gao, K., & Wang, X. (2016). *Changes brought by an iron tower: A model for state-owned enterprise reform*. Retrieved November 13, 2016, from http://www.xinhuanet.com/politics/2016-11/13/c_1119902236.htm

Gao, M. H., Du, W., et al. (2014). Several issues regarding the development of a mixed economy. *China Review of Political Economy*, *5*(4), 122–139.

Gao, M. H. (2017). *Corporate governance and state-owned enterprise reform*. Shanghai: Orient Publishing Center.

Geng, M. Z., & Li, Y. (2003). *Survival boundary and management model of state-owned capital*. Beijing: Economic Press China.

Gillan, S. L., Hartzell, J. C., & Starks, L. T. (2003). Explaining corporate governance: Boards, bylaws and charter provisions. *Weinberg Center for Corporate Governance Working Paper*, No. 03.

Guan, Y. Q. (2017). *Exploration of state-owned enterprise reform and development*. Nanning: Guangxi People's Publishing House.

Guiding opinions of the CPC Central Committee and the State Council on deepening the reform of state-owned enterprises. (2015). Retrieved August 24, 2015, from http://www.gov.cn/zhengce/2015-09/13/content_2930440.htm

Guo, L. (2016). Chinese-style board of supervisors: Where to go and where to settle? – Re-examination from an international comparative perspective. *Journal of Comparative Law*, 2, 74–87.

Hao, Y. H., & Wang, Q. (2015). Research on the equity check-and-balance mechanism of mixed enterprises – Based on the case of "fighting for control power of Wuhan Department Store Group". *China Industrial Economics*, 3, 148–160.

Hart, O. (1998). *Firms, contracts, and financial structure*. Shanghai: Shanghai People's Publishing House, Shanghai Sanlian Bookstore.

He, Y. M. (2003). Expanding powers and transferring profits: A breakthrough in state-owned enterprise reform – Interview with Comrade Yuan Baohua. *Journal of Hundred Year Tide*, 8, 4–11.

He, Z. L. (2014). Developing a mixed economy is an important way to maintain the dominant position of public ownership under the new situation. *Journal of Qiushi*, Issue 18.

Henderson, J. (2006). Building the rural economy with high-growth entrepreneurs. *Economic Review*, 87(3), 45–70.

Hong, H. (1997). Thoughts on the property rights of corporate legal persons. *China Industrial Economics*, 1, 5–9.

Hu, J. Y. (2016). *The innovative development of ownership theory in the new era*. Retrieved August 1, 2016, from http://theory.people.com.cn/n1/2016/0801/c4 0531-28599328.html

Hu, Z. C. (2017). Promote price reform, improve price supervision, and kick off the 19th National Congress of the CPC with excellent performance in price work. *Price: Theory & Practice*, 1, 5–11.

Hua, J. Y., & He, Y. P. (2001). An analysis on the cultural factor for corporate governance and its policy meaning for reforming the state - owned enterprises. *Studies in Dialectics of Nature*, 17(4), 53–57.

Huang, Q. H. (2000). *Incentives and constraints of entrepreneurs and state-owned enterprise reform*. Beijing: China Renmin University Press.

Huang, Q. H. (2002). *Analysis of the status quo of state-owned enterprise management*. Beijing: Economic Management Press.

Huang, Q. H. (2017). Clarifying the eight misunderstandings of mixed-ownership reform. *Modern Enterprise*, 9, 4–5.

Huang, Q. H., & Yu, J. (2013). New thinking in the new era: Classified reform and governance of state-owned enterprises. *China Industrial Economics*, 11, 5–17.

Huang, Y. (2007). On the definition and confirmation of government assets. *Budget Management & Accounting*, 9, 36–38.

Jensen, M. (1993). The modern industrial revolution, exit, and the failure of internal control system. *Journal of Finance*, 48(3), 831–880.

Jiang, Q. G. (1995). Construct a state-owned assets management, supervision and operation system with clarified powers and responsibilities. *China Economic & Trade Herald*, 15, 12–14.

Jiang, Z. M. (1977). *Hold high the great banner of Deng Xiaoping Theory for an all-round advancement of the cause of building socialism with Chinese characteristics into the 21st century*. Retrieved September 12, 1997, from http://www.people.com.cn/item/sj/sdldr/jzm/A106.html

Jiang, Z. M. (2002). *Build a well-off society in an all-round way and create a new situation in building socialism with Chinese characteristics*. Retrieved November 17, 2002, from http://www.china.com.cn/zhuanti2005/txt/2002-11/17/content_5233867.htm

Joint Research Group of the Institute of Industrial Economics of CASS and the State-owned Investment Company Professional Committee of IAC. (2017). *Optimizing the layout of state-owned economy and industrial integration of state-owned investment companies*. Beijing: Economic Management Press.

Kong, X. J. (1996). Study on the property rights of corporate legal persons – The inevitable trend from management rights, legal person's property rights to legal person's ownership. *Journal of Renmin University of China*, 3, 52–60.

Law of the People's Republic of China of industrial enterprises owned by the whole people. (1997). Beijing: China Legal Publishing House.

Lazonick, W. (1992). Business organization and the myth of the market economy. *Business History Review*, 67(3), 372–503.

Lenin. (1995). *Lenin collected works* (Vol. 3). Beijing: People's Publishing House.

Li, H. B., Li, X., Yao, X. G., et al. (2009). The impact of entrepreneurs' entrepreneurship and innovation on China's economic growth. *Economic Research Journal*, 10, 99–108.

Li, J. (2015). *Analysis of the top-level design of state-owned enterprise reform.* Beijing: China Yanshi Press.

Li, J. G., et al. (2006). *Study on government financial report.* Xiamen: Xiamen University Press.

Li, S. S. (2004). *Management of state-owned assets.* Beijing: China Financial & Economic Publishing House.

Li, T. (2005). State-owned equity, operational risk, soft budget constraints and corporate performance: Empirical findings of Chinese listed companies. *Economic Research Journal*, 7, 77–89.

Li, W. A. (2001). *Chinese corporate governance principles and international comparisons.* Beijing: China Financial & Economic Publishing House.

Li, X. C., Su, Q., & Dong, W. Z. (2006). Corporate governance and entrepreneurship. *Economic Research Journal*, 2, 57–68.

Li, Y. (2015). *China's national balance sheet.* Beijing: China Social Sciences Press.

Li, Y., Zhang, X. J., et al. (2012). China's sovereign balance sheet and its risk assessment (part 1). *Economic Research Journal*, 6, 4–19.

Li, Y., Zhang, X. J., et al. (2012). China's sovereign balance sheet and its risk assessment (part 2). *Economic Research Journal*, 7, 4–21.

Li, Y. N. (1987). Explorations into the socialist ownership system. *Hebei Academic Journal*, 1, 78–86.

Li, Y. N. (2014). Four benefits of mixed ownership. *West China Development*, 3, 36–37.

Li, Y. P. (2015). Return to the nature of enterprises: The path choice of state-owned enterprise mixed-ownership reform. *Economic Theory and Business Management*, 1, 22–25.

Liang, Q., & Yu, F. Y. (2014). Financial crisis, state-owned equity and capital investment. *Journal of Financial Research*, 4, 47–61.

Lin, Y. F. (2012). *Interpreting Chinese economy* (pp. 175–176). Beijing: Peking University Press.

Lin, Y. F., & Li, Z. Y. (2004). Policy burden, moral hazard and soft budget constraints. *Economic Research Journal*, 2, 17–27.

Lin, Y. F., et al. (2014). *Sufficient information and state-owned enterprise reform.* Shanghai: Truth & Wisdom Press.

Liu, X. X., & Li, S. X. (2007). The relative efficiency of mixed enterprise in the transitional period: An analysis of the empirical data of China's electronic and electrical manufacturing industry from 2000 to 2004. *World Economic Papers*, 1, 58–71.

Lou, J. W. (2016). Reform and improve the state-owned assets management system focusing on "capital management". *Current Affairs Report (Party Committee Central Group of Study)*, 1, 44–59.

Lu, J. R. (2014). *Analysis of industrial economics of state-owned enterprises.* Shanghai: Shanghai People's Publishing House.

Lucas, R. E. (1988). On the mechanics of economic development. *Journal of Monetary Economics, 22*(1), 3–42.

Ludwig, V. M. (2008). *Socialism: An economic and sociological analysis.* Beijing: China Social Sciences Press.

Lv, Z., & Huang, S. J. (2008). *A study of China's state-owned enterprise reform in 30 years.* Beijing: Economic Management Press.

Ma, J., & Zhang, W. K. (2015). *Research on the reform of state-owned capital management system.* Beijing: China Development Press.

Ma, L. F., et al. (2015). The priority choice of mixed ownership: The logic of the market. *China Industrial Economics, 7,* 5–20.

Marx. (2014). *Capital* (Vols. 1–3). Beijing: People's Publishing House.

Masahiko, A., et al. (1998). *The role of the government in East Asian economic development* (p. 2). Beijing: Economic Press China.

Metcalfe, J. S. (2004). The entrepreneur and the style of modern economics. *Journal of Evolutionary Economics, 14*(2), 157–175.

Min, L. (2017). *Research on the reform of China's state-owned assets management system – Based on nature and characteristics of state-owned capital.* Beijing: Economic Science Press.

Ministry of Finance. (2015). *Government accounting standards – Basic standards (decree No. 78 of the Ministry of Finance of the People's Republic of China).*

Mueller, P. (2007). Exploiting entrepreneurial opportunities: The impact of entrepreneurship on growth. *Small Business Economics, 28*(4), 355–362.

National Bureau of Statistic. (2003). *China national economic accounting system.* Beijing: China Statistics Press.

Opinions of the State Council on the development of mixed economy by state-owned enterprises. (2015). Retrieved September 24, 2015, from http://www.gov.cn/zhengce/content/2015-09/24/content_10177.htm

Pei, C. H. (2014). Quantitative estimation of the dominating position of public ownership in China and its development trend. *Social Sciences in China, 1,* 4–29.

Porta, R. L., Shleifer, A., & Vishny, R. W. (1997). Legal determinants of external finance. *Crsp Working Papers, 52*(3), 1131–1150.

Porta, R. L., Lopez-De-Silanes, F., Shleifer, A., et al. (1998). Law and finance. *Journal of Political Economy, 106*(6), 1113–1155.

Porta, R. L., Lopez-De-Silanes, F., Shleifer, A., et al. (2000). Investor protection and corporate governance. *Journal of Political Economy, 58*(1–2), 3–27.

Porta, R. L., Lopez-De-Silanes, F., Shleifer, A., et al. (2002). Investor protection and corporate governance. *Journal of Finance, 57*(3), 1147–1170.

Qi, Y. X. (2015). Analysis of the characteristics of Chinese government's comprehensive financial reporting system and suggestions for improvement. *Finance and Accounting Monthly, 13,* 16–18.

Qiu, H. P. (2014). On several matters of principle about mixed ownership. *Academic Frontier, 3*(Part 2), 42–48.

René, M. S., & Rohan, W. (2003). Culture, openness and finance. *Journal of Financial Economics, 70*(3), 313–349.

Research Group of the Institute of Industrial Economics of CASS. (2014). On the important task of comprehensively deepening the reform of state-owned economy in the new period. *China Industrial Economics*, 9, 5–24.

Romer, P. M. (1986). Increasing returns and economic growth. *American Economic Review*, 94, 1002–1037.

SAIC. (2017). *Analysis of national enterprise development since the 18th CPC National Congress.* Retrieved October 27, 2017, from http://www.gov.cn/zhuanti/2 017-10/27/content_5234848.htm

SASAC of the State Council. (2017). *State-owned enterprise reform has achieved important phased results.* Retrieved June 2, 2017, from http://finance.sina.com.cn/ wm/2017-06-02/doc-ifyfuzym7756726.shtml

SASAC Research Office. (2007). *Exploration and research: Research report on state-owned assets supervision & management and state-owned enterprise reform (2006).* Beijing: Economic Press China.

School of Economics and Resource Management of Beijing Normal University. (2008). *Report on China's market economy development in 2008* (p. 80). Beijing: Beijing Normal University Publishing Group.

Selected works of Deng Xiaoping (Vols. 1–3). (1994). Beijing: People's Publishing House.

Shen H. H., Yu P., et al. (2012). State-owned equity, environmental uncertainty and investment efficiency. *Economic Research Journal*, 7, 113–126.

Shen P. L., & Fan H. (2012). Research on China's government debt risk based on liquidity balance sheet. *Economic Research Journal*, 2, 93–105.

Shi J. C. (2015). *Enterprise and company law* (4th ed., pp. 226–230). Beijing: China Renmin University Press.

Soltow, James H. (1960). Economics of the business firm: economics of decision making in the business enterprise. *The Journal of Economic History*, 20, 112–113.

State Council's new 36 opinions on promoting the healthy development of non-public economy. (2008). Retrieved from http://www.gov.cn/zhengce/content/2008-03/28/ content_1647.htm

Study book of the "guiding opinions on deepening the reform of state-owned enterprises". (2016). Beijing: Economic Press China.

Sun, L. (2011). Traditional culture and corporate governance: A comparative analysis of business models in China. Japan and South Korea. *Comparative Management*, 3, 80–90.

Tang, L. M. (2014a). Chinese government balance sheet: Construction and estimation. *Review of Economic Research*, 22, 71–103.

Tang,L. M. (2014b). Chinese government balance sheet: Theoretical framework and realistic choices. *Chinese Review of Financial Studies*, 1, 94–109.

Tang, L. M. (2014c). Chinese local government balance sheet: Framework construction and scale estimation. *Public Finance Research*, 7, 18–22.

Tang, L. M. (2017). Chinese government balance sheet 2017. *Financial Minds*, 5, 103–138.

The DRC recommends the implementation of a "hierarchical ownership system" for state-owned assets management. (2002). Retrieved from http://finance.sina.com.cn/ g/20021108/0835276398.html

The DRC's Research Group on the "prominent challenges and countermeasures in deepening SOE reform". (2016). Suggestions for promoting the adjustment of China's state-owned capital distribution.*Development Research*, 10, 4–8.

The Research Group on Corporate Governance Evaluation of the Corporate Governance Research Center of Nankai University. (2004). An empirical analysis of the governance index and governance performance of Chinese listed companies. *Management World*, 2, 63–74.

The Research Group on Corporate Governance Evaluation of the Corporate Governance Research Center of Nankai University. (2006). An empirical analysis of the governance index and governance performance of Chinese listed companies – Based on the research of 1,149 Chinese listed companies. *Management World*, 1, 104–113.

The Research Group on Corporate Governance Evaluation of the Corporate Governance Research Center of Nankai University. (2007). An empirical analysis of the governance index and governance performance of Chinese listed companies – Based on the research of 1,249 Chinese listed companies. *Management World*, 5, 104–114.

The Research Group on Corporate Governance Evaluation of the Corporate Governance Research Center of Nankai University. (2008). Report on Chinese companies' corporate governance evaluation and index – Based on the research of 1,162 Chinese listed companies. *Management World*, 1, 145–151.

The Research Group on Corporate Governance Evaluation of the Corporate Governance Research Center of Nankai University. (2010). Research on corporate governance evaluation of Chinese companies – Based on the research of 1,127 Chinese listed companies in 2008. *Management World*, 1, 142–151.

The Shanghai Municipal Committee of the CPC, & the Shanghai Municipal People's Government. (2013). *Opinions on further deepening Shanghai's state-owned assets reform and promoting enterprise development.* Retrieved from http://finance.people.com.cn/n/2013/1217/c70846-23862381.html

The 16th Central Committee of the Communist Party of China. (2003). *Communiqué of the Third Plenary Session of the 16th Central Committee of the Communist Party of China.* Retrieved from http://cpc.people.com.cn/GB/64162/64168/64569/65411/4429167.html

van Praag, C. M., & Versloot, P. H. (2007). What is the value of entrepreneurship? A review of recent research. *Small Business Economics*, 29, 351–382.

Wang, D. H. (2007). Chinese culture and corporate governance. *Journal of Dalian Nationalities University*, 2, 28–32.

Wang, H. B. (2010). *History of China's modern industrial economy (Oct 1949-2009)* (pp. 473–474). Taiyuan: Shanxi Economic Publishing House.

Wang, S. G. (2016). Mixed economy and deepening of state-owned enterprise reform. *Expanding Horizons*, 3, 17–23.

Wang, Y. (2012). *Report of the State Council on the work in the reform and development of state-owned enterprises – At the 29th Meeting of the Standing Committee of the Eleventh National People's Congress.* Retrieved from http://www.npc.gov.cn/wxzl/gongbao/2013-02/25/content_1790879.htm

Wang, Z. (2012). Empirical analysis of the governance and performance of small and medium board listed companies based on different ownership types. *On Economic Problems*, 1, 95–99.

Wei, J., Chen, Z. H., & Zhang, B. (2004). A survey of the external economics of entrepreneurship in enterprise clusters. *Science Research Management*, 2, 20–25.

Wu, J. L. (1991). On planning and market as a method for resource allocation. *Social Sciences in China*, 6, 125–144.

Wu, J. L. (2016). *Tutorial of economic reform of contemporary China.* Shanghai: Shanghai Far East Publishers.

Wu, J. L., Zhou, X. C., et al. (1999). *Corporate governance structure, debt restructuring and bankruptcy procedures* (p. 2). Beijing: Central Compilation & Translation Press.

Wu, L. S. (2009). State-owned equity, tax preference and corporate tax burden. *Economic Research Journal*, 10, 109–120.

Xi Jinping inspects Xuzhou Construction Machinery Group. (2018). Retrieved January 2, 2018, from http://jjckb.xinhuanet.com/2018-01/02/c_136865459.htm

Xi, J. P. (2014). *Speech at a study session on implementing the decisions of the Third Plenary Session of the 18th CPC Central Committee on comprehensively deepening the reform, attended by officials at the provincial/ministerial level.* Retrieved February 17, 2014, from https://www.ccps.gov.cn/xxsxk/xldxgz/201908/t20190829_13385 7.shtml

Xi, J. P. (August 26, 2015). *Speech at the Fourth Work Conference of the National Security Commission of the Communist Party of China.*

Xi, J. P. (2017). *Secure a decisive victory in building a moderately prosperous society in all respects and strive for the great success of socialism with Chinese characteristics for a new era – Delivered at the 19th National Congress of the Communist Party of China.* Retrieved October 18, 2017, from http://www.xinhuanet.com/politics/1 9cpcnc/2017-10/27/c_1121867529.htm

Xiao, G. Q., & Qiao, H. B. (2015). Mixed economy and state-owned enterprise reform. *Socialism Studies*, 3, 50–56.

Xiao, Q. W. *Quantity, type and industry distribution of mixed enterprises.* Retrieved from https://cdrf.org.cn/xqw/3973.jhtml

Yin, J. (2016). Study on the internal mechanism and optimal proportion of mixed ownership of state-owned enterprises. *Nankai Economic Studies*, 1, 18–32.

Yu, J., & Huang, Q. H. (2017). Progress, problems and suggestions for comprehensively deepening state-owned enterprise reform in the new era, *Journal of the Party School of the Central Committee of the C.T.C*, 5, 113–121.

Yuan, D. M. (2006). A new probe into the adjustment of state-owned assets distribution. *China Policy Review*, 9, 38–41.

Zhang, C. L. (2003). Commercialization of state owners: Imitation of institutional owners. *International Economic Review*, 5, 40–43.

Zhang, D. C. (2006). *The chronicle of China's state-owned enterprise reform (1978–2005).* Beijing: China Worker Publishing House.

Zhang, H. M. (1998). *The logic of China's state-owned enterprise reform.* Taiyuan: Shanxi Economic Publishing House.

Zhang, H. M. (1999). Deepening the understanding and practice of modern corporate system. *Journal of International Trade*, 4, 4–5.

Zhang, H. M. (2004). *Cultivation of enterprise core competitiveness and the role of entrepreneurs, proceedings of the second annual conference of the Shanghai Federation of Social Science Associations (2004).* Shanghai: Shanghai People's Publishing House.

Zhang, H. M., & Chen, Z. G. (2002). Incentives for senior manages and corporate performance: An empirical study on Shanghai-listed companies. *World Economic Papers*, 4, 29–37.

Zhang, H. M., & Deng, T. (1999). *Study on the structural adjustment of state-owned stock capital*. Shanghai: Fudan University Press.

Zhang, H. M., & Lu, J. F. (2015). A new inquiry into the attributes and introduction features of mixed economy. *Research on the Theories of Mao Zedong and Deng Xiaoping*, 2, 23–28.

Zhang, H. M., & Zhang, L. L. (2010). Reconsideration of the functions and positioning of state-owned capital – Starting from the name of Temasek Holdings Private Limited. *Dongyue Tribune*, 4, 28–34.

Zhang, H. M., & Zhang, L. L. (2011). Entrepreneur capital and economic growth: A literature review. *Shanghai Journal of Economics*, 9, 40–54.

Zhang, H. M., et al. (1998). Marketization of state-owned enterprises and reform of government institutions. *Fudan Journal (Social Sciences Edition)*, 6, 34–39.

Zhang, L. S., & Liu, X. W. (2015). Continuously enhance the vitality, control and influence of the state-owned economy. *China Economic & Trade Herald*, 11, 23–26.

Zhang, W. Y. (1995). *Entrepreneurs of enterprises: Contract theory*. Shanghai: Shanghai People's Publishing House.

Zhang, W. Y. (2013). *Understanding companies: Property rights, incentives and governance*. Shanghai: Shanghai People's Publishing House.

Zhang, W. Y. (2015). *Enterprise theory and China's enterprise reform*. Shanghai: Shanghai People's Publishing House.

Zhang, Z. Y., Fang, H. T., et al. (2017). *Historical breakthroughs decided by the market: 40 years of China's market development and modern market system construction*. Guangzhou: Guangdong Economy Publishing House.

Zhong, X. (2015). *Government promotion, public participation, and legal protection – Enlightenment from the building of common values in Singapore*. Retrieved June 19, 2015, from http://china.chinadaily.com.cn/2015-06/19/content_21051741.htm

Index